Mac OS® X and iLife™: Using iTunes®, iPhoto™, iMovie™, and iDVD™

Brad Miser

© 2003 by Premier Press, a division of Course Technology. All rights reserved. No part of this book may be reproduced or transmitted in any form or by any means, electronic or mechanical, including photocopying, recording, or by any information storage or retrieval system without written permission from Premier Press, except for the inclusion of brief quotations in a review.

The Premier Press logo and related trade dress are trademarks of Premier Press and may not be used without written permission.

Mac OS X, iLife, iPhoto, iTunes, iMovie, iDVD, and QuickTime are either registered trademarks or trademarks of Apple Computer, Inc., in the United States and/or other countries.

All other trademarks are the property of their respective owners.

Important: Premier Press cannot provide software support. Please contact the appropriate software manufacturer's technical support line or Web site for assistance.

Premier Press and the author have attempted throughout this book to distinguish proprietary trademarks from descriptive terms by following the capitalization style used by the manufacturer.

Information contained in this book has been obtained by Premier Press from sources believed to be reliable. However, because of the possibility of human or mechanical error by our sources, Premier Press, or others, the Publisher does not guarantee the accuracy, adequacy, or completeness of any information and is not responsible for any errors or omissions or the results obtained from use of such information. Readers should be particularly aware of the fact that the Internet is an ever-changing entity. Some facts may have changed since this book went to press.

ISBN: 1-59200-101-7

Library of Congress Catalog Card Number: 2003105369

Printed in the United States of America

03 04 05 06 07 BH 10 9 8 7 6 5 4 3 2 1

Premier Press, a division of Course Technology

25 Thomson Place

Boston, MA 02210

SVP, Retail and Strategic Market Group:
Andy Shafran

Publisher:
Stacy L. Hiquet

Senior Marketing Manager:
Sarah O'Donnell

Marketing Manager:
Heather Hurley

Manager of Editorial Services:
Heather Talbot

Senior Acquisitions Editor:
Kevin Harreld

Associate Marketing Manager:
Kristin Eisenzopf

Project Editor:
Justak Literary Services

Technical Reviewer:
Brown Partington

Retail Market Coordinator:
Sarah Dubois

Copy Editor:
Marta Justak

Interior Layout:
Jay Hilgenberg

Cover Designer:
Mike Tanamachi

Indexer:
Sharon Hilgenberg

Proofreader:
Melba Hopper

Acknowledgments

A book like this one is definitely a team effort. The following people were a critical part of this book's team:

Stacy Hiquet, Publisher at Premier Press, for supporting this project and providing overall management from the publisher's perspective.

Kevin Harreld, my acquisitions editor at Premier Press. Kevin made this project possible and allowed me to write it. Kevin also made sure that the resources needed to complete the project were available. Kevin, thanks for making this book happen!

Marta Justak, the owner of Justak Literary Services. Marta is my agent and was responsible for making the business arrangements needed to turn the project into a reality. As if that wasn't enough, Marta also was the book's packager and managed the production process that transformed a bunch of raw Word and TIFF files into the book you are holding in your hands. Marta, I really appreciate your great work (as usual!) on this project. Thanks!

Don Mayer, CEO and Founder of Small Dog Electronics; Hapy Mayer, CFO and co-owner; and especially, Dawn D'Angelillo, VP of Marketing Small Dog provided much of the hardware and software that I needed to write this book. Small Dog is a great Mac-friendly retailer; check them out at www.smalldog.com or call them at 802-496-7171. Also check out the ad at the back of this book. Many thanks to Small Dog for being such an important part of this project!

Brown Partington, an up-and-coming iLife guru. Brown did a user review of this book to make sure that the information I provided is actually useful. Brown, you made this book much better, and I appreciate your work.

Jay Hilgenberg, who did the production of this book. Jay made this book something that is pleasing to read, and I am amazed at how quickly and accurately he was able to make a book from the files I provided. Thanks, Jay!

Sharon Hilgenberg, who did the critical task of creating the index for this book. After all, a computer book is only as good as its index. Sharon, thanks for creating such a good index—I hope the book is worthy of it!

Melba Hopper, who proofread this book. Melba helped catch many of my goofs and made this book much better because of it. Thanks, I really appreciate your work on this project!

Mike Tanamachi, who designed the cover of this book. Mike created a cover that draws the eye to the book and entices people to pick it up—just what a cover is supposed to do! Thanks!

Premier Press's printing and sales team, who are responsible for getting this book into your hands. Without their work, this project would have remained a pile of electrons that never did anyone any good. I really appreciate the support of Premier on this book!

Living with an author during a book project like this one is not an easy challenge, so some thanks to important people in my life are also in order:

To Amy, thanks for putting up with the stress and busyness that this book brought to our lives.

To Jill, Emily, and Grace who help me focus on what is really important—and who make great subjects for iLife projects!

About the Author

Brad Miser has written extensively about all things Macintosh, with his favorite topics being the amazing "i" applications that empower Mac OS X users to unleash their digital creativity. In addition to *Mac OS X and iLife*, Brad has written many other books, including *Final Cut Express Fast & Easy, iDVD 3 Fast & Easy, Special Edition Using Mac OS X v10.2, Mac OS X and the Digital Lifestyle, Special Edition Using Mac OS X, The iMac Way, The Complete Idiot's Guide to iMovie 2, The Complete Idiot's Guide to the iMac,* and *Using Mac OS 8.5*. He has also been a contributing author, development editor, or technical editor on more than 50 other titles. He has been a featured speaker on various Macintosh-related topics at Macworld Expo, user group meetings, and in other venues.

Brad is the senior technical communicator for an Indianapolis-based software development company. Here, Brad is responsible for all product documentation, training materials, online help, and other communication materials. He also manages the customer support operations for the company and provides training to its customers. Previously, he was the lead engineering proposal specialist for an aircraft engine manufacturer, a development editor for a computer book publisher, and a civilian aviation test officer/engineer for the U.S. Army. Brad holds a bachelor of science degree in mechanical engineering from California Polytechnic State University at San Luis Obispo (1986) and has received advanced education in maintainability engineering and other topics.

Contents at a Glance

	Introduction................................... xxi
Part I	**iTunes: Burning Down the House............ 1**
1	Touring Your iTunes Music Studio 3
2	Making Music with iTunes 43
3	Putting Your iTunes Music on the Move 83
Part II	**iPhoto: Not Your Father's Photo Album 99**
4	Touring Your iPhoto Digital Darkroom.............. 101
5	Building Your iPhoto Photo Library 119
6	Editing the Images in Your iPhoto Photo Library...... 147
7	Making the Most of Your Images 167
Part III	**iMovie: The Swiss Army Knife of Digital Video Software................... 203**
8	Touring Your iMovie Movie Studio................. 205
9	Building a Movie in iMovie 239
10	Building a Better Video Track in iMovie............. 269
11	Building a Soundtrack That Rocks 299
12	Producing Your Movies 329
Part IV	**iDVD: The Power of a Movie Production Studio in Your Mac..................... 343**
13	Touring Your iDVD Production Powerhouse 345
14	Building a DVD............................... 363
15	Designing a DVD 407
16	Previewing, Fixing, and Burning a DVD 455

Part V   iLife: The Only Way to Live............ 479

    17   Adding Video and Sound from Movies or TV Shows to iLife Projects 481

    18   Creating Cool Soundtracks for iLife Projects 499

Index **515**

Contents

Introduction xxi

    Living the iLife xxi
    The iLife Tools xxi
        iTunes Rocks xxi
        iPhoto Makes the Most of Your Photos xxii
        iMovie Unleashes the Director within You xxii
        iDVD Puts It All on Disc xxii
    The iLife Apps: So Happy Together xxii
    Mac OS X and iLife: Using iTunes, iPhoto, iMovie,
    and iDVD xxiii
        Part I: iTunes: Burning Down the House xxiii
        Part II: iPhoto: Not Your Father's Photo Album xxiv
        Part III: iMovie: The Swiss Army Knife of Digital
        Video Software xxiv
        Part IV: iDVD: The Power of a Movie Production
        Studio in Your Mac xxiv
        Part V: iLife: The Only Way to Live xxv
        Special Features of This Book xxv

Part I   **iTunes: Burning Down the House** 1

Chapter 1   **Touring Your iTunes Music Studio** 3

    Understanding the Audio Formats of the iLife 5
        Listening to CD Audio 5
        Rocking with MP3 5
        Moving Ahead with AAC 6

Making the Most of AIFF 7
Catching the WAV 7
iTuning Your Music Experience 8
iTunes Modes 9
iTunes Controls 10
The iTunes Source Pane 14
The iTunes Browse Pane 15
The iTunes Contents Pane 16
The iTunes Equalizer 19
Making Your iTunes Preferences Known 21
Setting iTunes General Preferences 22
Setting iTunes Effects Preferences 23
Setting iTunes Import Preferences 24
Understanding MP3 Encoding 25
Configuring Standard Levels of MP3 Encoding ... 26
Configuring Custom Levels of MP3 Encoding 27
Configuring AAC Encoding 28
Configuring AIFF and WAV Encoding 28
Setting iTunes Burning Preferences 29
Setting Sharing Preferences 30
Setting Store Preferences 32
Setting iTunes Advanced Preferences 34
Using iTunes in Your iLife Projects 36

Chapter 2 Making Music with iTunes 43

Making Sweet Music with iTunes 44
Listening to Audio CDs 44
Listening to Internet Audio 49
Building, Listening to, and Managing Your Music Library 50
Building Your iTunes MP3 Library 51
Adding Audio CDs to Your iTunes Library 52
Adding Audio from the Internet to Your iTunes
Library 54

Contents

        Adding Music from the Apple Music Store to Your
        iTunes Library 56
        Browsing and Listening to Your Library 63
        Searching for Music 65
        Removing Songs from the Library 67
        Classifying and Configuring the Music in Your Library . . 67
Playing with Playlists 72
        Making Playlists 73
        Making Your Music Smarter with Smart Playlists 76
Sharing Music 80
        Sharing Your Music on a Network 80
        Listening to Music Being Shared with You 81

Chapter 3   **Putting Your iTunes Music on the Move. 83**

Burning Your Own CDs 84
        Prepping Your Burner 85
        Choosing a Burn Format 87
        Creating a Playlist to Burn 87
        Burning a CD 88
Taking Your Digital Music on the Road with MP3 Players 90
        Choosing an MP3 Player 90
        Moving Your Music to an MP3 Player 91
Mastering Your Mobile Music with the iPod 93
        Moving Your Music Collection to an iPod 95
        Managing Your iPod Music Collection 95

Part II   **iPhoto: Not Your Father's Photo Album . . . 99**

Chapter 4   **Touring Your iPhoto Digital Darkroom 101**

Working in the iPhoto Window 102
        The iPhoto Source Pane 103

The iPhoto Contents Pane 104
iPhoto Controls 104
Using iPhoto Modes and Tools 106
　The iPhoto Import Mode 106
　The iPhoto Organize Mode 108
　The iPhoto Edit Mode 109
　The iPhoto Book Mode 111
Making Your iPhoto Preferences Known 113
Using iPhoto in Your iLife Projects 115

Chapter 5 Building Your iPhoto Photo Library 119

Importing Images into the Photo Library 120
　Importing Images from a Digital Camera 120
　Importing Images from Other Sources 123
Labeling Your Images 126
　Adding Titles and Comments to Your Images 127
　Associating Keywords with Your Images 129
　　Defining Your Own Keywords 129
　　Assigning Keywords to Images in Your
　　Photo Library 132
Configuring the Information You See in the Organize Mode ...134
Viewing Detailed Information for Your Images 137
Finding Images in the Photo Library 138
Building Photo Albums 141

Chapter 6 Editing the Images in Your iPhoto Photo Library 147

Rotating Images 148
Preparing to Edit Images 149
　Deciding to Edit a Copy or the Original 150
　Choosing How You Want to Edit Images in iPhoto ...150
　Selecting Parts of an Image You Want to Edit 154
　Zooming on Images for Editing 156

Contents

Cropping Images 158
Enhancing Images 159
Removing Red-Eye from Images 160
Retouching Images 162
Making Images Black-and-White 163
Adjusting Brightness and Contrast of Images 164
Restoring an Image to Original Condition 165

Chapter 7 Making the Most of Your Images 167

Printing Images 168
Viewing Slideshows 171
Emailing Your Images 175
Ordering Prints 177
Creating, Printing, and Ordering Photo Books 179
    Creating a Photo Book 180
    Previewing a Photo Book 184
    Printing a Photo Book 185
    Ordering a Photo Book 186
Building a Photo HomePage 188
Creating .Mac Slides 191
Adding Images to the Desktop and as a Screen Saver 192
Putting Images on DVD 194
Putting Images on CD 195
Exporting Images Outside of iPhoto 197
    Exporting Photos as Separate Files 197
    Exporting Images as a Web Site 199
    Exporting Images as a QuickTime Movie 202

Part III iMovie: The Swiss Army Knife of Digital Video Software 203

Chapter 8 Touring Your iMovie Movie Studio 205

Working in the iMovie Window 207
    The iMovie Window 207
    iMovie Modes 207
    The Monitor 209
        The Monitor in Edit Mode 209
        The Monitor in Camera Mode 212
    The Tools Palette 214
        The Clips Pane (aka the Shelf) 214
        The Photos Palette 215
        The Audio Palette 216
        The Titles Palette 217
        The Transitions Palette 220
        The Effects Palette 222
        The iDVD Palette 224
    The Clip Viewer 225
    The Timeline Viewer 226
    The Disk Gauge 229
    The iMovie Trash 230
Making Your iMovie Preferences Known 230
Using iMovie in Your iLife Projects 233

Chapter 9 Building a Movie in iMovie............... 239

Planning a Movie 240
    Deciding What Your Movie Will Be 241
    Preparing the iMovie Project 242
    Building a Basic Video Track 244
Stocking the Shelf (aka the Clips Pane) with Clips and Images .. 244
    Stocking the Shelf with Video Clips from a DV Camera 245
    Stocking the Shelf with QuickTime Clips 247
    Stocking the Shelf with Still Images 248
Hacking (aka Editing) Your Clips 250
    Previewing Clips 251
    Deleting Clips 253

Viewing and Changing a Clip's Information 253
Splitting Clips 255
Editing Clips 255
Building the Basic Video Track 259
Adding Video Clips and QuickTime Movies to the
Video Track 259
Adding Images from the Shelf to the Video Track 263
Adding iPhoto Images to the Video Track 263
Arranging the Clips in a Movie 268

Chapter 10 Building a Better Video Track in iMovie 269

Explaining Yourself with Titles 270
Adding Opening Credits 273
Adding a Caption to a Clip 277
Changing a Title Clip That Had Been Placed in a
Movie 279
Smoothing the Digital Flow with Transitions 280
Adding a Fade Out Transition 281
Adding a Push Transition 283
Changing a Transition That Has Been Placed in a
Movie 284
Making Your Movie Special with Special Effects 286
Making New Clips Look Old 289
Improving a Clip's Brightness and Contrast 291
Changing a Special Effect 292
Restoring a Clip 292
Using Cool iMovie Tricks to Liven Things Up 293
Speeding Clips Up or Slowing Them Down 293
Changing the Direction Clips Play 295
Adding Instant Replay 296

Creating a Freeze Frame 296
Pasting Over a Clip 298

Chapter 11 Building a Soundtrack That Rocks 299

Going Native (Native Sound That Is) 301
    Muting Native Sound 301
    Changing the Relative Volumes of Native Sound Clips . 302
    Fading Native Sound 304
    Extracting Native Sound 308
Livening Up Your Movie with Sound Effects 310
    Adding iMovie's Built-In Sound Effects 310
    Adding Your Own Sound Effects 313
Making Your Movie Sing with Music 314
    Adding Music from Your iTunes Library 315
    Adding Music from an Audio CD 317
Recording Your Own Sounds 318
Bringing All That Sound Together 320
    Changing the Location of Sound Within a Soundtrack . 321
    Cropping Sound 321
    Fading Sound 322
    Adjusting Relative Volume Levels of Audio Clips 323
    Adjusting Relative Volume Levels Within Audio Clips . 323
    Locking Sound in Place 325

Chapter 12 Producing Your Movies 329

Polishing a Movie Until It Shines 330
Exporting a Movie to Videotape 330
    Recording an iMovie Project on a DV Camera 331
    Recording from a DV Camera to VHS 333
Exporting a Movie to DVD 333
    Adding Chapter Markers 334
    Moving a Movie to iDVD 336

Exporting a Movie to QuickTime 336
    Exporting a Movie Using a Standard Format 337
    Exporting a Movie Using Expert Settings 339

Part IV   iDVD: The Power of a Movie Production Studio in Your Mac 343

Chapter 13   Touring Your iDVD Production Powerhouse . . 345

Working in the iDVD Window 346
    The iDVD Window 347
        iDVD Controls 348
        The iDVD Drawer (aka the Customize Panel) . . . 349
    iDVD Modes 351
        Design Mode 351
        Slideshow Mode 353
        Preview Mode 354
        Burn Mode 355
    iDVD Projects 355
Making Your iDVD Preferences Known 356
Making DVDs with iDVD 360
Using iDVD for Your iLife Projects 361

Chapter 14   Building a DVD 363

Planning a DVD 364
    Understanding a DVD's Structure 364
    Planning an iDVD Project 365
    Organizing and Outlining a DVD's Content 366
    Creating an iDVD Project 369
    Creating the Menus on a DVD 371
Building a Slideshow on DVD 376
    Adding a Slideshow Button to a Menu 377
    Adding Images to a Slideshow 378

Adding Images to a Slideshow from iPhoto 378
Adding Images from the Finder 380
Changing the Appearance of the Slideshow Window . . 382
Changing the Order of Images in an iDVD Slideshow . 382
Removing Images from an iDVD Slideshow 384
Previewing an iDVD Slideshow 384
Setting the Playback of a Slideshow 385
Adding a Soundtrack to a Slideshow 387
Using iTunes Music as a Soundtrack for an iDVD
Slideshow 387
Adding Audio Files from the Finder as a Soundtrack
for an iDVD Slideshow 389
Naming a Slideshow Button 390
Placing High-Resolution Images from a Slideshow on
a DVD 391
Adding iMovie Movies to a DVD 393
Adding iMovie Projects to the iMedia Browser 394
Using the iMedia Browser to Add Movies to a DVD . . . 396
Importing Movies to a DVD 399
Adding iMovies to a DVD from within iMovie 399
Adding QuickTime Movies to a DVD 401
Adding a QuickTime Movie on the iMedia Browser to
a DVD 402
Importing a QuickTime Movie to DVD 402
Removing Movies from a DVD 403
Understanding Encoding 403
Adding Other Files to the DVD-ROM Portion of a DVD 405

Chapter 15 Designing a DVD. 407

Understanding the Art of Designing a DVD 408
Working with Themes 408
Working with Drop Zones 409

   Working with Motion Effects 410
   Using the TV Safe Area 411
 Designing Menus 413
   Naming Menus 413
   Using Built-In Themes to Design Menus 415
     Applying a Built-In Theme to a Menu 415
     Adding Content to Drop Zones 417
     Applying a Standard Theme to Every Menu on
     a DVD 421
   Using Custom Themes to Design Menus 421
     Applying a Background Image to a Menu 423
     Applying a Background Movie to a Menu 427
     Applying Background Sound to a Menu 430
     Setting a Menu's Motion Duration 433
     Formatting Menu Titles 434
 Designing Buttons 437
   Naming Buttons 438
   Designing Buttons by Applying Themes 439
   Customizing the Buttons on a Menu 439
   Setting Button Previews 443
     Setting a Button Preview for Folder Buttons 444
     Setting a Button Preview for Slideshow Buttons . . 444
     Setting a Button Preview for Movie Buttons 446
     Using an Image or a Movie as a Preview for
     Any Button 447
 Saving and Applying Custom Themes 449
   Saving Custom Themes 450
   Applying Custom Themes to Other Menus 451

Chapter 16 Previewing, Fixing, and Burning a DVD 455

 Previewing a DVD 456
   Logging Problems 456
   Previewing an iDVD Project 457

　　　　　Previewing Menus 460
　　　　　Previewing Buttons 461
　　　　　Previewing Movies 462
　　　　　Previewing Slideshows 463
　　　　　Fixing Problems 464
　　　Assessing a DVD Project's Status 465
　　　　　Assessing a Project 465
　　　　　Finding Missing Files 468
　　　Burning an iDVD Project on DVD 469
　　　　　Understanding the Burning Process 470
　　　　　Maximizing Burn Performance 471
　　　　　Burning a DVD 474

Part V　　　**iLife: The Only Way to Live 479**

Chapter 17　**Adding Video and Sound from Movies or**
　　　　　　　TV Shows to iLife Projects. 481

　　　Mining Sources of Content 483
　　　Capturing Content from VHS 484
　　　　　Obtaining VHS Content 485
　　　　　Connecting a DV Camera to a VCR 485
　　　　　Recording VHS Content on a DV Camera 486
　　　　　Importing VHS Content into iMovie 487
　　　Capturing Content from DVD 488
　　　　　Recording Content from DVD 489
　　　　　Ripping Content from DVD 489
　　　Downloading and Using QuickTime Movie Trailers from
　　　　　the Web 491
　　　Downloading and Using Movie and TV Sound Clips from
　　　　　the Web 495
　　　Using Captured Content in Your iLife Projects 498

Chapter 18 Creating Cool Soundtracks for iLife Projects 499

Designing a Soundtrack 501
    Selecting the Music for a Soundtrack 501
    Selecting Sound Effects for the Soundtrack 502
Using iTunes to Prepare Music and Sound Clips for the Soundtrack 503
Using iMovie to Create the Soundtrack 504
    Creating the iMovie Soundtrack Project 504
    Creating the Music Track 506
    Adding Sound Effects 507
    Adding Recorded Sounds 508
    Mixing the Soundtrack 508
Exporting the Soundtrack as an AIFF File 508
Creating Your Own Soundtrack CDs 510

Index 515

Introduction

Living the iLife

From the moment its smiling face first appeared on a screen as it started up, the Macintosh has been all about empowerment. The Mac was the first computer to provide powerful tools that work the way you expect them to. It was the first computer to provide the power to create documents and have them look like they do on the screen when you print them. The Mac was the first, and is still the best, to provide the power to publish from the desktop. The Mac was the first, and is still the best, to provide the power for regular people to surf the Internet and make their own presence on the Internet felt. Apple's Macintosh was created to make the power of the personal computer available to the rest of us.

And now Apple has done it again.

With its iLife suite, Apple has made the Macintosh the premier computer platform to empower you to create, view, and manage digital media. From digital images and music to digital movies to your own DVDs, the Mac gives you the power to transform your life from the analog to the digital.

The iLife Tools

The iLife suite includes a superb set of four "i" applications that are amazingly powerful, and just like the Mac, they work in a way that the rest of us can understand.

iTunes Rocks

iTunes is the Mac's way-cool digital music application. Of course, iTunes enables you to do the basics such as listening to CDs, MP3 music, and so on, but it does so much more. You can create your own custom audio CDs, create and manage your own playlists, interface with mobile music players, and more. With its innovative Music Store, you can even buy individual tracks or entire albums with a few clicks of the mouse. With iTunes, you can master the music in your life.

iPhoto Makes the Most of Your Photos

If any application matches the cliché "last but not least," iPhoto is it. While it is the youngest "i" application, iPhoto more than matches its older siblings in power, flexibility, and ease of use. iPhoto enables you to do many amazing things with your photos, from the creative, such as making Web sites and slideshows, to the practical, such as providing prints for the important people in your life. From downloading images from a digital camera to publishing your own picture books, iPhoto gives you the tools to take your photos to the limit of your imagination.

iMovie Unleashes the Director within You

If I had to pick only one iLife tool to take with me on a deserted island, iMovie would be it. That's because iMovie enables you to work with all types of digital media, from still images to digital video to music and sound effects. You can use iMovie's incredible tools to build fantastic movies with which you will amaze even yourself. And I'm not talking about boring home movies here—I'm talking about movies that jump off the screen with titles, transitions, special effects, custom music soundtracks, sound effects, and much more.

iDVD Puts It All on Disc

While iMovie is the one application I would take to a deserted island, iDVD is the one that makes me say "Wow!" the loudest. There is something totally cool about putting your own movies and slideshows on a DVD and then playing that DVD on the same player you use to watch your favorite DVD movies. And, just like those movies you rent from your local video store, your DVDs can have cool menus that have motion and sound effects.

The iLife Apps: So Happy Together

Each of the "i" applications is totally cool and amazing in its own right, but the true power of iLife comes when you realize that these tools work together just as well as they work individually. Want to use some music from your iTunes Library on your latest DVD creation? No sweat. Want to add that great picture you just took to the iMovie you created last week? That will take you all of one minute to do (if that long). Want to build a movie that really captures the great time you had on the last vacation you took? Get into iMovie, add the video, import some iPhoto photos, and match it with the perfect iTunes music. Care to put that movie on a DVD to send to a friend? No problemo, a few clicks of the mouse, and your wish is the iLife's command. And on it goes; there are no limits to what you can accomplish when you understand how to use each digital lifestyle application individually and, to an even greater extent, how to make them work together.

That is where this book comes in.

Mac OS X and iLife: Using iTunes, iPhoto, iMovie, and iDVD

The genesis of this book came when I realized that, while there is some information available on the various "i" applications, there isn't much to help someone put all the pieces together in a meaningful, practical, and fun way. When it comes to iLife, the whole is definitely greater than the sum of the parts. This book will help you understand each part and how to use these parts together in your own digital projects.

To facilitate the stages of your own digital lifestyle, this book is organized into five distinct parts.

Part I: iTunes: Burning Down the House

This part will teach you everything you need to know about the amazing iTunes. Some of what you will learn here is how to do the following:

- Understand the various types of music files you can use.
- Listen to audio CDs, MP3, and other kinds of music.
- Build your iTunes Library by adding music from many sources, including your audio CDs, the Internet, and the Apple Music Store.
- Create custom playlists to listen to and to put playlists on your own CDs.
- Take your music on the road with the iPod.

Part II: iPhoto: Not Your Father's Photo Album

iPhoto is more than a match for today's way-cool digital cameras. It gives you the tools to do whatever you want to with the images that you capture, including the following iTricks:

- Import images from a camera and other sources.
- Build photo albums and use iPhoto tools to label your images so you can find them easily and at will.
- Use its editing tools to make poor photos into good ones and good ones into great ones.
- Build custom photo books to display the results of your creativity.
- Display your images in prints, on Web pages, on DVD, and in many more ways.

Part III: iMovie: The Swiss Army Knife of Digital Video Software

iMovie is perhaps the most powerful of all the iLife applications. That's because in iMovie, you can bring the output of iTunes and iPhoto together with digital video you capture with a camcorder, QuickTime movies, and more to create your own digital movie masterpieces. In this part of the book, you will take iMovie through its paces.

- Import video clips from a camcorder, from QuickTime movies, and so on.
- Edit those clips and build a movie from them.
- Add titles, transitions, and special effects, oh my!
- Create soundtracks that include music, sound effects, and audio that you record.
- Move your movies to DVD, videotape, and the Web.

Part IV: iDVD: The Power of a Movie Production Studio in Your Mac

There is something incredibly cool about viewing and hearing your content via a DVD. It gets even cooler when you see the neat things you can create on those

DVDs, such as motion menus, scene selection indexes, and more. In this part of the book, you get the skinny on iDVD.

- Plan an iDVD project.
- Add your content to a project, including photos, movies, and so on.
- Use built-in designs to format a project in seconds.
- Create a DVD interface as unique as you are.
- Burn a disc.

Part V: iLife: The Only Way to Live

In this part, you will take the last step, go the extra mile, bring it home, (insert your own cliché here). While the previous parts explain how to use each application and how to take advantage of the built-in integration of each tool in the others, this part teaches you some iLife tricks that aren't part of its standard bag. These tricks will help you expand your understanding of how the iLife applications can really be used together to accomplish more than you thought possible.

Special Features of This Book

To make this book more effective in helping you make the most of iLife, it contains several special features.

Because this book is more about *doing* rather than just *reading*, it contains many step-by-step instructions that you can follow to learn how to accomplish specific tasks. To help you find these step-by-steps easily, I offset them from the "regular" text, as in the following example.

Live the iLife

1. Buy *Mac OS X and iLife: Using iTunes, iPhoto, iMovie, and iDVD* at your favorite bookstore.
2. Put the book next to your Mac and open the book to page 1.
3. Start living the iLife—it is the good life after all.

Sometimes, I like to tell you about something that isn't exactly required for you to do—whatever it is you happen to be reading about at the time. In these situations, you'll see a note that looks like the following one.

> **NOTE**
>
> I hope you read the book's notes because I think you'll find them meaningful. However, if you don't read them, you won't hurt my feelings—much.

I want you to be the best you can be, so I have included a number of tips throughout the book that provide information to help you work faster, smarter, or simply in another way. The tips in this book look like this:

> **TIP**
>
> Your author is conducting a test of this book's tip broadcasting system. This is only a test. Had this been a real tip, you would have been told something cool to help you be even more powerful with your Mac. This concludes this test of this book's tip broadcasting system.

Finally, there are times when you might want to know about something that is related to a chapter's topic, but that goes beyond it. In these situations, you will see a sidebar, like the one that concludes this introduction.

> **It's Time to Get on with It**
>
> As introductions go, this one's been fun, but it's time that you get on with your own iLife. I hope that you find the information contained in this book to be as empowering to you as your Mac and its wonderful "i" tools are. It's all here, just waiting for you. So, get "igoing."

PART I

iTunes: Burning Down the House

1   Touring Your iTunes Music Studio
2   Making Music with iTunes
3   Putting Your iTunes Music on the Move

Chapter 1

Touring Your iTunes Music Studio

Music is one of the most important parts of the digital life. From listening to your favorite tunes while you surf the Web to creating soundtracks for your iLife projects to taking your music collection with you when you are on the move, music makes every aspect of your own digital lifestyle better.

With iTunes, you can take complete control over the music in your life. iTunes is a powerful digital music application that enables you to do just about anything with your music, including the following tasks:

- Manage your entire music collection
- Listen to audio CDs, Internet audio, and MP3
- Convert music to and from various audio formats (the most important of which is MP3)
- Build your own music library from your audio CD collection, the online Apple Music Store, and the Internet
- Create and manage custom playlists
- Burn audio and MP3 CDs
- Download music to a portable MP3 player (the best of which is the iPod)
- Convert music into formats you need for your iLife projects

In this part of this book, you will learn everything you need to know to get the most out of iTunes.

> **NOTE**
>
> Just so you know, this part of the book is based on version 4.0.1 of iTunes.

Understanding the Audio Formats of the iLife

When you are working with music and sound in iTunes, there are five primary audio file formats with which you will work. Before you jump into iTunes, take a few moments to become familiar with each of these formats.

Listening to CD Audio

CD Audio is the "native" file format for audio that is recorded on standard audio CDs. You probably won't work with this format much directly because you will convert it to other formats when you add this type of audio to your iTunes Library.

The CD Audio format offers very high quality sound, but the file size that comes along with that quality is quite large. For example, a 3-minute song is about 32MB.

CD Audio files have the file extension .cdda.

Rocking with MP3

MP3 is the abbreviation for an audio compression scheme whose full name is *Motion Picture Experts Group (MPEG)* audio layer 3. The amazing thing about the MP3 encoding scheme, and the reason that MP3 has become such a dominant file format for audio, is that audio data can be stored in files that are only about $1/12^{th}$ the size of unencoded digital music without a noticeable degradation in the quality of the music. A typical music CD consumes about 650MB of storage space. The same music encoded in the MP3 format shrinks down to about 55MB. Put another way, a single 3-minute song shrinks from its 32MB on audio CD down to a paltry 3MB or less.

MP3's ability to deliver high-quality sound with small file sizes has opened up a world of possibilities. For the first time, music files can be transferred practically over the Internet, even for people who use a dial-up connection. This format enables artists to distribute their music to anyone, no matter where they live (as long as they can get online, of course).

Because it is quite easy to convert Audio CD files into the MP3 format (this is a one-step operation with iTunes), you can create MP3 files for all of your music and store them on your hard drive. This innovation means that your entire music collection is always available to you, and you never need to bother with individual CDs. You also get other nifty features, such as playlists, which you will learn about in the next chapter.

The small file sizes of MP3 music also lead to a new type of hardware device, the MP3 player. Because MP3 files can be stored in small amounts of memory, it is possible to store a large amount of music in a small physical device. Some MP3 players don't have any moving parts, thus eliminating any chance for skipping, even under the most rigorous environments. Other devices, such as the Apple iPod, contain their own hard drives so that you can take your entire music collection with you wherever you go.

Because MP3 is such a popular and useful format, you will use it in many of your iLife projects. You can play MP3 files with a number of applications, including iTunes, QuickTime Player, and so on. You can also use these applications to convert other file formats into MP3 and to convert MP3 files into other formats.

MP3 files have the file extension .mp3.

Moving Ahead with AAC

With the release of iTunes version 4, Apple introduced a new audio format. The AAC format (which stands for Advanced Audio Coding) is part of the larger MPEG-4 specification. The basic purpose of the AAC format is the same as the MP3 format: to deliver excellent sound quality while keeping file size small. However, the AAC format produces files that have better quality than MP3 at even smaller file sizes.

Also like MP3, you can easily convert audio CD files into the AAC format.

One of the most important aspects of the AAC format is that all the music in the Apple Music Store is stored in this format; when you purchase music from the store, it will be downloaded in this format.

AAC files have the m4p file name extension.

> **NOTE**
>
> Functionally, you aren't likely to notice any difference between AAC music files and MP3 files except in one area, which is that most MP3 players don't support AAC formatted music. The Apple iPod is a notable exception, so any music you purchase from the Apple Music Store can be placed on an iPod for playing on the move. You can also convert music in the AAC format into the MP3 format to put that music on regular MP3 players. (You'll learn how to do this later in this book.)

Making the Most of AIFF

The Audio Interchange File Format (AIFF) also provides high-quality sound, but its file sizes are larger than MP3. As you can probably guess from its name, this format was originally used to exchange audio among various platforms. However, along with that important function, it is now also a useful format in its own right.

The AIFF is supported by the iLife applications, including iTunes, iMovie, and so on. It is also the file format in which Mac OS X's system alerts are stored.

You will frequently use the AIFF format for music, sound effects, and other audio.

AIFF files have the file extension .aif.

Catching the WAV

The Windows Waveform (WAV) audio format is a standard on Windows computers. It is widely used for various kinds of audio, but because it does not offer the quality versus file size benefits of MP3, it is mostly used for sound effects or clips that people have recorded from various sources. There are millions of WAV files on the Internet that you can download and use in your projects because the iLife applications can play WAV files and also convert them into other formats.

WAV files have the file extension .wav.

> **iTunes for the First, but Definitely Not the Last, Time**
>
> The first time that you launch iTunes, you move into the iTunes Setup Assistant that does some basic configuration for you. For example, you determine if iTunes should connect automatically to the Internet when you insert a CD to download information about that CD. If you have already used the Assistant, you can skip the remaining material in this sidebar (you'll learn how to configure iTunes manually a little later in this chapter). If not, launch iTunes (for example, by clicking its icon on the Dock) and choose the following Setup Assistant options:
>
> - **Internet Playback**. You should choose to have iTunes used when you play MP3 music on the Internet.
>
> - **Internet Access**. When you insert an audio CD into your Mac, iTunes can connect to the Internet and look up information about that CD for you. This information includes album title, artist, and so on. You should allow this if your Mac can connect to the Net.
>
> - **Find MP3 Files**. iTunes can search your Mac for any MP3 music that is already stored there. You should allow this so that any MP3 music you already have on your Mac will be brought into iTunes (you can delete it later if you no longer want it).

iTuning Your Music Experience

The iTunes window might look a bit complicated initially, but as you work with the application, you will get comfortable with it quite quickly. The iTunes window has four major areas: the Controls area, the Source pane, the Browse pane, and the Contents pane (see Figure 1.1).

Touring Your iTunes Music Studio   Chapter 1   9

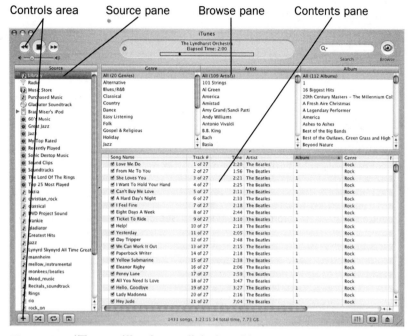

Figure 1.1 *iTunes will rock your digital world.*

iTunes Modes

Before you dig into the iTunes interface, you need to understand that iTunes has different modes. In each mode, you will be performing different tasks. iTunes adapts its interface to the task that you are doing, so you will see different controls when you are in the various modes. For example, the Contents pane will look different to reflect the mode that you are in, and the Browse pane appears only in certain modes. The iTunes modes are listed below:

- ◆ **Audio CD**. As you can probably guess, you use this mode to listen to audio CDs. You also use it to create MP3 or AAC files from those CDs.
- ◆ **Library**. When you create MP3 or other versions of your music, you store them in your Library. In this mode, you can work with all of the music that you have stored there.
- ◆ **Radio**. In this mode, you can use iTunes to listen to a variety of content that comes from the Internet.

◆ **Playlists.** Playlists are custom music collections that you can create and listen to. You can also burn CDs that contain the music in your playlists.

◆ **Portable Music Player.** In this mode, you can transfer music to a portable music player, such as an MP3 player or an Apple iPod.

iTunes Controls

At the top and bottom of the iTunes window, you will see iTunes' major controls. The specific controls that you see depend on the mode you are in, but Figure 1.2 and Table 1.1 explain the controls you will use most often.

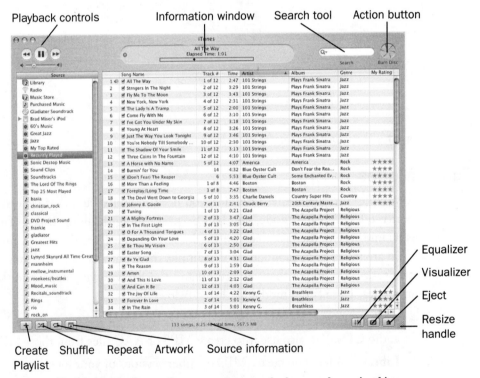

Figure 1.2 *In the Playlist mode, you see the controls that are shown in this figure; in other modes you might see some slightly different controls.*

Table 1.1 iTunes Controls

Control	What It Does
Playback controls	The buttons and slider in this area control the playback of the selected source. These buttons work just like they do on CD players. From top to bottom and left to right, they are the following: Scan Backwards, which moves you backward through the source at high speed; Play/Pause, which starts or stops the selected source; Scan Forward, which moves you forward through the selected source at high speed; and the Volume slider, which enables you to control the volume level of the selected source.
Information window	This window provides information and controls that are relevant to the mode in which you are operating. (See the text following this table for more information.)
Search box	When you type text in this box, the items listed in the Contents pane are reduced so that only those songs whose information (such as track name or artist) has the text that you type are found. This enables you to quickly find specific music with which you want to work. If you click on the small triangle next to the magnifying glass icon, you can choose the field you want to search from a pop-up menu.
Action button	This button changes depending on the mode in which you are working. In the Audio CD mode, this button will be Import, which enables you to create MP3, AAC, or other files from the tracks on a CD. In the Library mode, this is the Browse button, which opens or closes the Browse pane. In the Internet Radio mode, this is the Refresh button, which updates the list of available radio stations. In the Playlist mode, this is the Burn CD button, which enables you to burn a CD from the selected playlist.
Create playlist	You use this button to create playlists or smart playlists. You'll learn all about playlists in the next chapter.
Shuffle	This button causes the songs in the selected source to play in random order.
Repeat	Click this button once to cause the current song to play through and then repeat one time. Click this twice to repeat every song in the selected source.

Table 1.1 iTunes Controls (continued)

Control	What It Does
Equalizer	This button opens the Equalizer window (you'll learn about this in the section called "The iTunes Equalizer" a bit later in this chapter).
Visualizer	The iTunes window can play visual effects on the screen while the selected music plays. You click the Visualizer button to turn on the effects and click it again to turn them off. You can use the commands on the Visualizer menu to control the size of the Visualizer, including making it large enough so it fills the screen (you click the mouse button to return to the iTunes window). You can also add more visuals to those that come with iTunes (but since that won't help you with your iLife projects, this is beyond the scope of this chapter).
Eject	This button ejects a selected CD, portable music player, or other mounted source.
Resize handle	Drag this handle to resize the iTunes window.

> **NOTE**
>
> Some controls that you see are specific to a mode and don't appear in all modes. For example, when you choose an MP3 player as a source, you will see buttons that are related to specific commands for MP3 players. You'll learn about these commands in Chapter 3.

The Information window offers information (as if you couldn't guess that) along with controls that you can use. What you see in this window also depends on the mode in which you are operating. For example, Figure 1.3 shows iTunes while it is creating MP3 versions of the songs on an audio CD.

In other modes, the Information window shows the song currently being played, including both album name and elapsed or remaining time. If you click the Mode Change button, the information shown in the window will change. For example, when you are playing a song and click the button once, the information will be replaced by a graph that displays the relative volume levels of sounds at various

Figure 1.3 *In this mode, the Information window provides information about and control over the import process.*

frequencies for the left and right channels. When you are importing music or when you are burning a CD, you can use the Stop button to stop the process.

TIP

To see all of the information available in the Information window, click the information that you see, such as the Elapsed Time. The information will change (for example, when you click the Elapsed Time, it changes to Remaining Time).

Naturally, you can also address iTunes' commands via the application's menus and keyboard shortcuts. Table 1.4 at the end of this chapter provides a summary of the iTunes menu commands and their keyboard shortcuts (if available). Of course, you can use iTunes' standard Mac OS X commands, such as Hide and Quit.

> **TIP**
>
> You can also use the Apple Pro Keyboard's media keys (located above the numeric keypad) to decrease the volume, increase the volume, mute the sound, or eject a CD. Note that when you use the keyboard to change the volume, you are changing your Mac's system volume, not the volume of iTunes relative to the system volume, which is what you change when you use iTunes Volume slider, menu commands, or keyboard shortcuts to change the volume.

The iTunes Source Pane

The iTunes Source pane, located along the left side of the window, enables you to choose a source with which you want to work (see Figure 1.4). When you select a source by clicking it, you see its contents in the Contents pane. Selecting the source is always the first step in any iTunes activity.

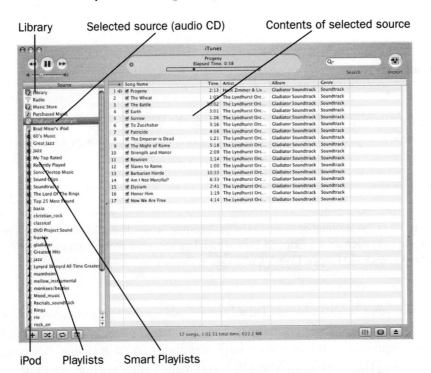

Figure 1.4 *When you choose a source (in this figure, the selected source is an audio CD), you see its contents in the Contents pane.*

Table 1.2 lists some of the more common sources with which you will work.

Table 1.2 iTunes Sources

Source	What It Is
Library	Contains all of the songs and other sounds that you have imported or have added via the Add to Library command. The Library contains all of the music and sounds that you manage with iTunes.
Radio	Lists Internet radio stations that you can listen to using iTunes.
Music Store	Enables you to access the Apple Music Store from which you can purchase and download music. The music you download is added to the Library.
CD	Enables you to view, listen to, or import the contents of an audio CD.
Mobile Music Player	Enables you to view and manage the contents of a mobile music player, such as an MP3 player or an iPod.
Shared Music	Provides access to iTunes music that is shared on your local network.
Smart Playlist	Enables you to select and listen to a smart playlist.
Playlist	Enables you to listen to or change the contents of a playlist.

The iTunes Browse Pane

When you are working with your iTunes Library, you can use the Browse pane to browse the contents of your Library (see Figure 1.5). Because you are likely to have hundreds or thousands of songs stored there, it isn't practical to view them all in the list that appears in the Contents pane. The Browse pane enables you to browse this content by Genre, Artist, or Album. This helps you get to specific content with just a few mouse clicks. If shown (you can choose to hide or display it), when you click on the Genre, the artists associated with that genre appear in the Artist column. Then you can click on an artist. That artist's albums will then appear in the Album column. When you click on an album, that album's songs appear in the Contents pane. Selecting All in any of these columns displays all items in that category.

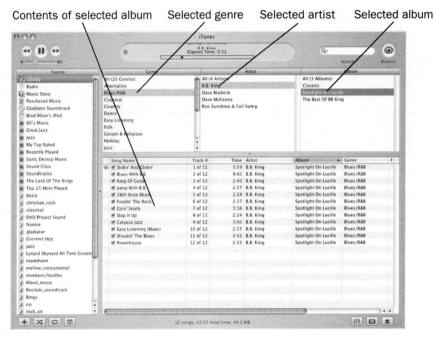

Figure 1.5 *The Browse pane helps you browse your music collection with a few mouse clicks.*

The iTunes Contents Pane

When you select a source in the Source pane, you see its contents in the Contents pane, which is located on the right side of the iTunes window (see Figure 1.6). You use the Contents pane to browse a source, as well as to work with it. For example, when you select an audio CD as a source, you will see its songs in the source pane. You can choose songs to import, play songs, and so on. You will learn how to work with the Contents pane in its various modes as you read through the rest of this part of the book.

The columns that you see in the Content pane work similarly to columns in Mac OS X Finder windows. You can do the following tasks:

- ◆ **Sort the Contents pane.** To sort the Contents pane by a column, click its column heading. The list of contents will be sorted by that column; the column heading is highlighted to show you which column is currently being used to sort the pane. You also will see the sort direction indicator

Touring Your iTunes Music Studio   Chapter 1   **17**

Figure 1.6 *Here, I have selected a playlist called "Frankie," and its contents are displayed in the Contents pane.*

TIP

To make the size of the Source pane larger or smaller relative to the Contents pane, drag the Resizing handle (it is a small dot) located in the middle of the border between the Source and Contents pane. Drag it to the left to make the Source pane narrower or to the right to make it wider.

---

that points up or down. To change the order in which the column is sorted, click the column heading again. The pane will be sorted in the opposite direction.

◆ **Change the order of the columns.** You can change the order in which the columns appear by dragging the columns by their column headings. You can move the columns so they appear in any order you'd like.

◆ **Change the width of the columns.** To change the width of a column, point to the right edge of its column heading. The pointer will become a vertical line with an arrow coming out of each side. When you see this, drag to the left to make the column narrower or to the right to make it wider.

◆ **Set the columns that appear in the window.** If you select a source and choose Edit, View Options (or press ⌘+J), you can choose the columns that you want to be displayed by checking or unchecking their check boxes in the View Options dialog box (see Figure 1.7). Each source type has its own set of view options (for example, you can select a different set of columns when you select an audio CD than are available when you select a playlist). If you add columns, you can resize the columns to show more of them in the iTunes window.

Figure 1.7 *The View Options dialog box enables you to set which columns appear in the Contents pane for various sources, such as a playlist as shown in this figure.*

> **NOTE**
>
> Changes you make to the Contents pane apply only for the selected source. You can have a different set of viewing options for each source (for example, you can have a custom set of view options for each playlist).

In several modes, such as when you are working with the Library, a CD, or a playlist, you will see a check box next to each song in the source. By default, this check box is checked. If you uncheck a song's check box, it will be skipped when that source is played or imported. When you check the box again, the song will be played or imported.

The iTunes Equalizer

iTunes includes a graphic equalizer that you can use to fine-tune the music to which you listen. Like hardware graphic equalizers, you can adjust the relative volume levels of various audio frequencies to suit your preferences. Unlike hardware graphic equalizers, you can select different preset configurations, and you can create your own configurations. You can apply an equalizer configuration to your music even down to individual songs so that each tune can have its own equalization settings.

To see the iTunes equalizer, click the Equalizer button, choose Window, Equalizer, or press ⌘+2. The Equalizer window will appear (see Figure 1.8).

Figure 1.8 *With the Jazz equalizer configuration, both bass and treble frequencies are emphasized.*

Because the Equalizer doesn't really impact your iLife lifestyle projects, you won't learn everything about it in this book. However, the following list will get you started with it:

- ◆ To activate the Equalizer, open its window, check the On check box, and choose the Equalizer preset configuration you want from the pop-up menu. All iTunes music that you play will be adjusted according to the preset level that you selected.
- ◆ Use the Preamp slider to change the relative volume level, which is useful when a piece of music is recorded at a particularly high or low volume level.

- You can create your own Equalizer settings by first choosing Manual from the pop-up menu (or just dragging a slider and the Equalizer will move into manual mode automatically). Then drag the slider for each frequency to the relative volume level at which you want that frequency to be played.
- You can add your custom Equalizer preset to the pop-up menu by configuring the Equalizer and choosing Make Preset from the pop-up menu. In the Make Preset dialog box, name your preset and click OK. Your preset will be added to the list, and you can choose it just as you can one of the iTunes default presets.
- You can edit the list of presets by choosing Edit List from the pop-up menu. The Edit Presets dialog box will appear. You can use this to rename or delete any of the presets, including the default presets.

You can also associate Equalizer presets with specific songs.

Associate a Specific Equalizer Preset with an Individual Song

1. In the Contents pane, select the song to which you want to apply a preset.
2. Choose File, Get Info (or press ⌘+I). The Song Information window will appear.
3. Click the Options tab.
4. On the Equalizer Preset pop-up menu, choose the preset that you want to be used for that song (see Figure 1.9).
5. Click OK. When that song plays, the selected preset will be used.

> **TIP**
>
> Using the View Options dialog box, you can have the Equalizer column displayed in the Content pane (refer to Figure 1.7). This column includes an Equalizer preset pop-up menu from which you can choose a preset for a song.

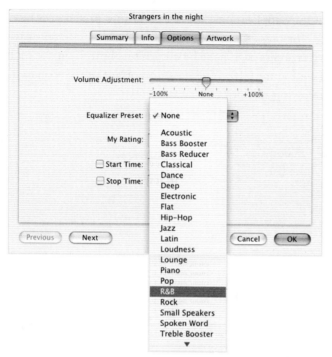

Figure 1.9 *You can apply an Equalizer preset to individual songs; when you play those songs, their Equalizer settings will be used.*

Making Your iTunes Preferences Known

With this quick iTunes tour under your belt, you know everything you need to know in order to start using iTunes to master your music and to use the application for your iLife projects. However, it will be beneficial if you take a few moments to configure iTunes to suit your preferences. If you don't want to do this now, but prefer to get started using the application, skip to the section called "Using iTunes in Your iLife Projects." You can always come back here when you are ready to fine-tune iTunes.

> **NOTE**
>
> This book contains lots of step-by-step instructions to help you accomplish specific tasks. These steps are based on the preferences settings described in this section. You will have the best experience with the steps if you choose the same settings that I did. After you have worked through the steps, you can always change the preferences to match your personal preferences.

Similar to other Mac OS X applications, you access iTunes preferences by choosing iTunes, Preferences (or press ⌘+,). The resulting iTunes Preferences window contains seven panes; you access each pane by clicking its button on the toolbar at the top of the screen (see Figure 1.10). The most important settings on each pane are explained in the following sections.

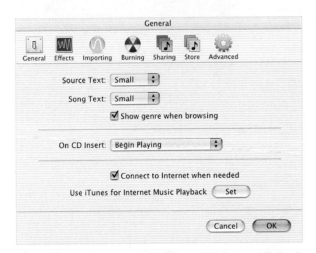

Figure 1.10 *You can use the iTunes Preferences dialog box to configure iTunes to your liking (or if you follow the advice in the previous note, set them to my liking until you have completed all the steps in this part of the book).*

Setting iTunes General Preferences

On the General pane, you can set the following preferences (see Figure 1.10):

- ◆ Use the Display pop-up menus to control the size of the font used in the Source (the Source Text pop-up menu) and Contents (the Song Text pop-up menu) panes. Check the "Show genre when browsing" check box to add the Genre column when you are browsing the Library (you will learn more about this later).

- ◆ Use the On CD Insert pop-up menu to control what happens when you insert an audio CD into your Mac. The options are to Show Songs, Begin Playing, Import Songs, or Import Songs and Eject. When you start using iTunes, the Import Songs and Eject setting is very useful because it helps you import all of your CDs quickly. After you have imported all of your CDs into the iTunes Library, the Begin Playing option is a good choice.

◆ In the Internet section, check the "Connect to Internet when needed" check box to turn on the automatic lookup feature; this causes iTunes to attempt to identify audio CDs when you insert them into your Mac. If it finds the CD's information (such as title, artist, songs, and so on), which it will for almost all commercially produced CDs, the information will be added to the CD. Each time you insert that CD, the information will be shown again. It is also attached to that music when you add it to your Library. If you don't want this lookup to be done (perhaps you are listening to CDs from a Mac that can't connect to the Net), uncheck this check box. Use the Set button to set iTunes as the default application for playing all music on the Internet. Most of the time, both of these options should be on (check the check box and click the Set button).

Setting iTunes Effects Preferences

Click on the Effects button to open the Effects pane that has the following preference settings (see Figure 1.11):

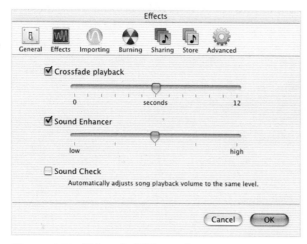

Figure 1.11 *Using the Effect preferences, you can further customize your music playback.*

◆ Use the Crossfade playback slider to control the amount of silent time between songs in your playlists. To use this effect, check the Crossfade playback check box and then drag the slider. If the slider is set to 0, there will be no silence; one song will fade directly into the next. Set the slider to a value greater than 0 up to 12 seconds to have that specific amount of silence between tracks.

- ◆ Use the Sound Enhancer to enable iTunes to apply digital effects to your music to improve its quality (that is a matter of opinion, of course). To use the effect, check the Sound Enhancer check box and then drag the slider to set the relative amount of "enhancing" that iTunes does. Drag the slider to the right to increase the enhancement or to the right to lessen it.
- ◆ Check the Sound Check check box to have iTunes play all of your music at the same volume level, regardless of the relative volume settings of individual songs (which you can set using the Information window as you will learn later).

Setting iTunes Import Preferences

Click on the Importing button to open the Importing pane. This is one of the more useful panes because you use it to configure how iTunes will import (convert) your music and sound files into the MP3, AAC, or other format (see Figure 1.12).

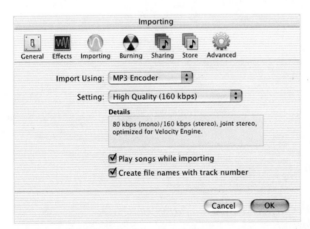

Figure 1.12 *The Importing tab is quite important because you use it to determine how iTunes will encode audio files when you add them to your Library.*

First, you choose the encoder that you want to configure by using the Import Using pop-up menu. You have four options, which are AAC Encoder, MP3 Encoder, AIFF Encoder, and WAV Encoder. Then you use the controls for each encoder to configure it.

> **TIP**
>
> You can have only one encoder active at a time. For example, if you choose the MP3 encoder, all music and sound that you import to your Library will be encoded in MP3. If you choose the WAV encoder, all music will be converted into WAV until you choose a different encoder.

After you have configured one encoder, configuring the others is similar. Since you are most likely to use iTunes to convert files into MP3, some detail on configuring this encoder will be helpful.

Although the default MP3 encoding settings are probably fine, you might want to experiment with the MP3 encoding settings to get the smallest file sizes possible while retaining an acceptable quality of playback.

Understanding MP3 Encoding

The quality of encoded music is determined by the amount of data that is stored in the MP3 file per second of music playback. This is measured in KiloBits Per Second or kbps. The higher the number of kbps, the better the music will sound. Of course, this means that the file size is larger as well. The goal of MP3 encoding is to obtain an acceptable quality of playback while minimizing the size of the resulting MP3 files.

The encoding level that you should use depends on several factors, which include the following:

- **Your sensitivity to imperfections.** If you dislike even minor imperfections in music playback, you should use higher quality encoding settings. If you don't mind the occasional "bump" in the flow of the music, you can probably get away with lower quality settings.
- **The music to which you listen.** Some music hides "flaws" better than others. For example, you are less likely to notice subtle problems in the music while listening to grinding heavy metal music than when listening to classical music.

- **How you listen to music.** If you use a low-quality sound system with poor speakers, you probably won't notice any difference between high-quality and low-quality encoding. If your Mac is connected to high-fidelity speakers, the differences in music quality will be more noticeable.
- **How important file size is.** If you are going to be listening to music on an MP3 player, you might be willing to trade off some quality to be able to fit more music on the player. If you are mostly storing music on a hard drive, you can choose higher quality because file size won't be as important.

There are three standard levels of MP3 encoding that iTunes provides: Good Quality, High Quality, and Higher Quality. As an experiment, I encoded the same four-minute song using each of these levels; the results are shown in Table 1.3. These results might or might not match the particular encoding that you do, but they should give you some idea of the effect of quality level settings on file sizes. In this experiment, I couldn't detect much difference between the quality levels on the sound of the music, so I could save almost 0.5MB per minute of music by sticking with the Good Quality level.

Table 1.3 Default Encoding Quality Settings versus File Size

Quality Level	Data Rate (kbps)	File Size (MB)
Good Quality	128	3.8
High Quality	160	4.8
Higher Quality	192	5.7

If none of the three standard levels of MP3 coding is acceptable, you can also create custom encoding levels.

Configuring Standard Levels of MP3 Encoding

To configure iTunes to use one of the standard levels of MP3 encoding, use the following steps.

Choose an MP3 Encoding Quality Level

1. Open the iTunes Preferences dialog box and click the Importing button.

2. On the Import Using pop-up menu, choose MP3 Encoder.
3. Use the Setting pop-up menu to choose the quality level of the encoding; your options are Good Quality, High Quality, Higher Quality, or Custom (you'll learn about the Custom option in the next steps). When you make your choice, the Settings area of the dialog box will provide information about the encoding level that you have selected.
4. If the "Play songs while importing" check box is checked, the music that you encode will play while you are encoding it.
5. Check the "Create files names with track numbers" check box to have iTunes use the track name as part of the file name of the encoded file. This is a good option to use because it helps you easily identify song files you might need when working outside of iTunes.
6. Click OK to close the dialog box. When you import sound or music to your Library, the encoding settings you selected will be used.

> **TIP**
>
> You can vary the encoding quality level that you use from album to album or even from song to song. For example, if you want to play certain songs on a portable MP3 player, you might want to use a lower quality level for those songs so that you can download more of them to the player. Or you might want to create one version of the tracks at lower quality levels and another version at higher quality levels. You could then create a low-quality playlist to import to an MP3 player.

Configuring Custom Levels of MP3 Encoding

In almost all cases, you can stick with one of the three standard quality levels. However, you can also customize the MP3 encoder to squeeze the most quality out of the smallest file sizes for the specific kind of music you are dealing with.

To create custom encoding settings, repeat the previous steps up to Step 3. Instead of choosing one of the standard quality levels, choose Custom. You will see the MP3 Encoder dialog box (see Figure 1.13).

Going into the details of each of these settings is beyond the scope of this book (besides which, you aren't likely to ever use them). However, if you have the interest and time, you can experiment with these settings to see how they impact file size and playback quality.

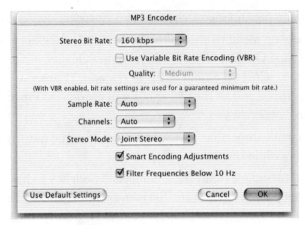

Figure 1.13 *When it comes to MP3 encoding, iTunes enables you to get into the details.*

Configuring AAC Encoding

The AAC format provides even better music quality with smaller files sizes than does the MP3 format. And this is the format in which music you purchase from the Apple Music Store is encoded. Unless you prefer that your music be in the MP3 format because you use an MP3 player that can't handle the AAC format, this format might become your format of choice.

Configuring the AAC encoder is simpler than the MP3 encoder. There is only one default setting for this encoder, which is High Quality (128 kbps). This setting is likely the only one you will ever use.

Like the MP3 encoder, you can choose Custom that enables you to customize the encoder. When you choose the Custom setting, you can select a bit rate, sample rate, and channel configuration.

Configuring AIFF and WAV Encoding

It's also easier to configure the AIFF and WAV encoders than the MP3 encoder because you have fewer options. For these encoders, your configuration choices are Automatic or Custom. In almost all cases, the Automatic setting is fine. If you want to explore the Custom settings, choose Custom and then set the channels and sample size that you want to use.

Setting iTunes Burning Preferences

You can make a few adjustments to how iTunes creates CDs when you burn them by using the Burning pane (see Figure 1.14). At the top of the pane, you will see the CD burner that is recognized by your Mac.

Figure 1.14 *The drive that you use to burn CDs is shown on the Burning pane, and you can use the controls to determine how burning works on your Mac.*

This pane has the following controls:

- ◆ Use the Preferred Speed pop-up menu to select the speed at which you want to burn your CDs. Most of the time, Maximum is the right choice. However, if you have problems burning CDs (especially if you use an external burner), you can set a low burn speed (such as 2x) to see if that solves your problem.

- ◆ Use the Disc Format radio buttons to choose the type of CDs you will burn. Audio CDs are those that can be played in any CD player, while MP3 CDs require a player capable of playing MP3 files. The benefit of choosing the MP3 CD format is that many more songs will fit on a single CD because MP3 files are much smaller than audio CD files. The disadvantage of MP3 CDs is that many CD players will not be able to play them.

    If you choose the Audio CD format, set the amount of silence between tracks on the Gap Between Songs pop-up menu. The default is 2 seconds, which means that there will be 2 seconds of silence between songs.

This setting can be anywhere from None, which causes one song to end and the next to begin immediately, to 5 seconds, which is the longest gap you can have. If you check the Sound Check check box, iTunes will level out the volume of the songs when it burns a disc.

You can also choose the Data CD or DVD format that causes the disc to be burned onto a data CD or DVD. You should only choose this format when you will be using the resulting disc in a computer.

> **TIP**
>
> Using the Data CD or DVD option is a good way to back up your music, especially for music that you have purchased from the Apple Music Store. Select this format, and you can burn music onto a DVD, which will enable you to store about 4.2GB of music on a single disc.

Setting Sharing Preferences

With iTunes, you can share your music with other iTunes-equipped Macs on your local network. When you share your iTunes music, your machine appears as a source on the Source pane of the other Macs on your network. You configure sharing by using the Sharing pane of the iTunes Preferences dialog box (see Figure 1.15).

The controls in the Sharing pane are explained in the following list:

- **"Look for shared music" check box.** If you check this check box, iTunes will look for music that is being shared on the local network by other Macs. If it finds shared music, that music will appear in the Source pane. Shared music sources have a blue icon so you can distinguish them from other sources. You can select and listen to shared sources just like audio CDs or your own playlists (see Figure 1.16). If you click the Expansion triangle next to the shared source, you will see the playlists that source contains.

> **NOTE**
>
> You can't copy music from a shared source into your Library, nor can you burn music from a shared source onto a CD.

Touring Your iTunes Music Studio — Chapter 1 — 31

Figure 1.15 *If you want to access music that is being shared with you or if you want to share your music on a local network, you use the Sharing preferences.*

Figure 1.16 *The source "PowerBook" is being shared from a PowerBook via an AirPort network.*

- **"Share my music" check box and radio buttons.** If you check this check box, your iTunes music will be shared with others on your local network. When you share your music, you choose the specific music you want to share by using the radio buttons. If you select the "Share entire library" radio button, your entire iTunes Library will be available to others on your network. If you want to share only specific playlists, select the "Share selected playlists" radio button and check the check box next to each playlist you want to share; only the playlists you select will be available to other people on your local network.
- **"Shared name" text box.** If you share your iTunes music, give your machine a name in the "Shared name" text box. This will be the name that appears in the Source pane when others access your shared music.
- **"Require password" check box and text box.** If you want to require that anyone who accesses your shared music input a password to do so, check the "Require password" check box and enter the password in the text box. When a user attempts to access your music, that person will have to enter the password you input (don't forget to provide the password to those whom you want to share music with!).

At the bottom of the pane, you will see the current status of sharing for your machine (whether sharing is on or off) and how many users are connected to your iTunes music (if sharing is on of course).

Setting Store Preferences

The Apple Music Store enables you to sample and purchase music from a huge collection that is available to you online. And you can access this music from within iTunes so that adding more music to your Library requires only a few mouse clicks. You will learn how to work with the iTunes Music Store in the next chapter, but for now, take a look at the store preferences that are accessible on the Store pane of the iTunes Preferences dialog box (see Figure 1.17).

The Store preferences that are available to you are the following:

- **"Show iTunes Music Store" check box.** If this check box is checked, the Music Store source will appear in the Source pane. You select the Music Source to access it. You'll learn how to work with the Music Store in Chapter 2.

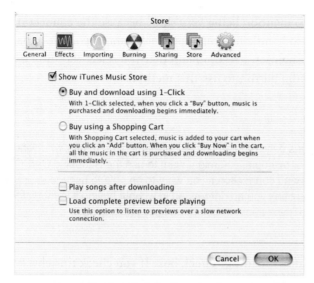

Figure 1.17 *Configuring the Store preferences enables you to fine-tune your Music Store shopping experience.*

◆ **"Buy" radio buttons**. The iTunes Store experience depends on how you connect to the Internet. If you use a broadband connection to the Net, working with the Music Store will be about as fast as working with music stored on your Mac. If you use a slow connection, such as a dialup connection, working with the Music Store won't be as satisfying—still it can be very useful even if it will be a bit slow.

There are two basic ways you can buy music from the Apple Store.

The 1-Click method causes music to be purchased and downloaded with a single mouse click. This method is most applicable if you use a broadband connection because you can be doing other things while music is being downloaded to your Mac. If you use a broadband connection, I recommend that you select the "Buy and download using 1-Click" radio button to make this option active.

The Shopping Cart method causes music you want to buy to be placed in a shopping cart while you do other things in the Music Store. When you are ready to buy, you check out from the store at which point the music in your shopping cart is downloaded to your Mac. This option is primarily designed for people who use a slow connection to the Internet because attempting to do other tasks while downloading music will be problematic (not to mention being very slow) because the connection might not be able to handle moving that much data. If you use a dialup connection to the Internet, I recommend that you select the "Buy using a Shopping Cart" radio button to use this method.

> **NOTE**
>
> These are recommendations only. You can use either method, no matter what kind of Net connection you use. For example, you might want to use the Shopping Cart method even with a broadband connection if you want to be able to use the shopping cart to store music that you think you are interested in without buying it immediately. This gives you a chance to "think about it" before actually purchasing it.

- **"Play songs after downloading" check box.** If you check this check box, any music you purchase from the iTunes Store is played immediately after it is downloaded.
- **"Load complete preview before playing" check box.** You can listen to a 30-second preview of the songs available in the iTunes Store. This enables you to check out music before you decide to buy it. If you check this check box, that preview is downloaded to your Mac before it begins to play. This option is useful when you use a slow Internet connection because the preview will play smoothly if it has been downloaded to your Mac, while it might not play smoothly if you listen to it while it is being downloaded.

Setting iTunes Advanced Preferences

The Advanced pane contains a few, specialized settings (see Figure 1.18).

This pane has the following settings:

- **iTunes Music folder Location.** By default, iTunes stores all the music and audio files that you import in the following location: *shortusername*/Music/iTunes/iTunes Music/, where *shortusername* is the short name for the current user account. If you open the iTunes folder within your Music folder, you will see the iTunes Music Library file and the iTunes Music folder. Within the iTunes Music folder, the music files are contained

Figure 1.18 *You probably won't need to change the settings on the Advanced pane, but you should be aware of them just in case you need them at some point.*

within folders that are named with the artist's name. Within each artist's folder, each album has its own folder. If you prefer to have imported music stored in a different location, use the Change button to set a different location for the files that you import into iTunes.

TIP

If you want to share the same Library among several user accounts on your Mac, you need to store the iTunes Music folder in a location that all user accounts can access. In these cases, you can use the Change button to have the iTunes Music folder stored in the Public folder on the machine. Each user would need to use the Advanced pane to select the Public folder; then all user accounts can share the same music.

◆ **Streaming Buffer Size.** When you use iTunes to listen to content from a streaming source, such as the Internet, a certain amount of that data is stored in a buffer before it begins to play. This ensures that you have a constant flow of sound even if the flow of data to your Mac isn't smooth. Use the Streaming Buffer Size pop-up menu to change the size of the buffer you want. For example, if you find Internet content starting and stopping frequently, choose Large to increase the size of your buffer.

- **Shuffle by**. When you use the Shuffle feature, the Shuffle by radio buttons determine how music is randomly played. If you select the Song radio button, songs are randomly selected, regardless of the albums from which those songs came. If you choose the Album radio button, albums are randomly selected; all the songs on each album are played before the next album is selected.
- **Folder organization**. Check the "Keep iTunes Music folder organized" check box to have iTunes use its standard organization scheme for the music you add to the Library, such as by artist and album. As you add songs to the Library, iTunes will continue to use this scheme no matter how you add the music. If you don't want to keep your music organized in this way, uncheck the check box.
- **Copying files**. If you check the "Copy files to iTunes Music folder when adding to library" check box, iTunes will place a copy of any music files that you add to the Library to the iTunes Music folder and will keep that music in a central location. If you uncheck this check box, iTunes will include a reference to the file instead of a copy of the file itself. Unless you are extremely low on disk space and don't want to delete the original files for music stored outside of iTunes, you should leave this check box checked.

Using iTunes in Your iLife Projects

When it comes to listening to and working with music, iTunes is the cat's meow (why being a cat's meow means something is good, I will never know). And iTunes is also very useful for your iLife projects. See some examples of how cool iTunes is in the following list:

- Creating and using custom playlists
- Managing music on portable MP3 players
- Burning your own CDs
- Adding music to your collection by buying it from the iTunes Music Store
- Using iTunes music in iMovie projects
- Using iTunes music as soundtracks for slideshows in iPhoto

- Using iTunes music as soundtracks for menus and slideshows in iDVD
- Putting soundtracks from your iMovie projects on a CD
- Storing and organizing sound effects and other sounds that you will use in your projects

iTunes Menu Commands and Keyboard Shortcuts

While some of the commands listed in the following table might not be familiar to you the first time you read through this book, they will make perfect sense later. You can use this table as a handy reference whenever you need a quick refresher on a specific command or to learn the keyboard shortcut for commands you use frequently.

Table 1.4 Useful iTunes Menu Commands and Keyboard Shortcuts

Menu	Command	Keyboard Shortcut	What It Does
iTunes	Preferences	⌘+,	Enables you to set iTunes preferences.
File	New Playlist	⌘+N	Creates a new playlist.
File	New Playlist From Selection	Shift+⌘+N	Creates a new playlist containing the songs that are currently selected.
File	New Smart Playlist	Option+⌘+N	Creates a new smart playlist.
File	Add to Library	⌘+O	Enables you to add MP3 files that were created outside of iTunes, such as those you download from the Internet, to your iTunes Library.
File	Import	Shift+⌘+O	Enables you to import various audio files into your Library.
File	Export Song List	None	Exports a selected playlist.
File	Export Library	None	Exports all of the playlists.

Table 1.5 Useful iTunes Menu Commands and Keyboard Shortcuts (continued)

Menu	Command	Keyboard Shortcut	What It Does
File	Get Info	⌘+I	Opens the Information window for the selected item or items.
File	Show Song File	⌘+R	Finds the encoded file located on your Mac for the selected song.
File	Show Current Song	⌘+L	Shows the song currently playing in the Contents pane.
File	Burn Playlist to CD	None	Burns a selected playlist onto a CD.
File	Update Songs on iPod	None	Enables you to synchronize the contents of your Library with an Apple iPod MP3 player.
Edit	Hide/Show Browser	⌘+B	Closes or opens the Browser pane.
Edit	Show/Hide Artwork	⌘+G	Opens the Artwork pane, which shows the album art associated with the current song.
Edit	View Options	⌘+J	Enables you to determine which columns are shown in the Contents pane.
Controls	Play/Stop	Spacebar	Plays or stops playing the selected song or source.
Controls	Next Song	⌘+Right arrow	Jumps to the next song in the selected source.
Controls	Previous Song	⌘+Left arrow	Jumps to the previous song in the selected source.

Table 1.5 Useful iTunes Menu Commands and Keyboard Shortcuts (continued)

Menu	Command	Keyboard Shortcut	What It Does
Controls	Shuffle	None	Plays the songs in the selected source in random order.
Controls	Repeat Off	None	Plays the selected source one time.
Controls	Repeat All	None	Plays the selected source twice.
Controls	Repeat One	None	Plays the current song and then repeats it once.
Controls	Volume Up	⌘+Up arrow	Increases the volume.
Controls	Volume Down	⌘+Down arrow	Decreases the volume.
Controls	Mute/Unmute	Option+⌘+Down arrow	Mutes or unmutes the volume.
Controls	Eject/Disconnect Source	⌘+E	Ejects the selected source, such as a CD or an iPod. Disconnects a shared source.
Visualizer	Turn Visualizer On/Turn Visualizer Off	⌘+T	Shows/hides the visual display.
Visualizer	Small	None	Displays the Visualizer at the smallest size.
Visualizer	Medium	None	Displays the Visualizer at the medium size.
Visualizer	Large	None	Displays the Visualizer at the largest size.
Visualizer	Full Screen	⌘+F	Makes the Visualizer fill the screen.

Table 1.5 Useful iTunes Menu Commands and Keyboard Shortcuts (continued)

Menu	Command	Keyboard Shortcut	What It Does
Advanced	Open Stream	⌘+U	Enables you to enter a URL for an Internet audio stream to play in iTunes.
Advanced	Convert Selection to *Format*	None	Enables you to convert selected files to the format indicated by the word *Format*, such as WAV to covert the selected files to the WAV format. Format is determined by the Importing preference settings.
Advanced	Consolidate Library	None	Places copies of any songs located outside of your iTunes Music folder, which is where the music you import into iTunes is stored by default, into that folder so that all of your music files are in one place.
Advanced	Get CD Track Names	None	Connects to the Internet to download information about the audio CD shown in the Source pane. (If you configure iTunes to do this automatically, you'll never need to use this command.)
Advanced	Submit CD Track Names	None	Enables you to upload information about a CD in the event you have a CD that can't be located in the online databases.

Table 1.5 Useful iTunes Menu Commands and Keyboard Shortcuts (continued)

Menu	Command	Keyboard Shortcut	What It Does
Advanced	Join CD Tracks	None	Removes the "gap" between songs so that one song plays right into the next one.
Advanced	Deauthorize Computer	None	When you purchase music from the Apple Music Store, you can play that music on up to three computers. When you choose this command, the current machine becomes unauthorized, which means the music will no longer be able to be played on the machine until it is reauthorized again.
Advanced	Check for Purchased Music	None	Causes iTunes to check the Apple Music Store for music you have purchased, but haven't downloaded yet.
Window	iTunes	⌘+1	Shows the iTunes window.
Window	Equalizer	⌘+2	Shows the Equalizer window.

Chapter 2

Making Music with iTunes

Now that you understand audio file formats, the iTunes application, and how to configure iTunes for the various tasks for which you will use it, it is time to start making music. In this chapter, you'll learn how to master your music by doing the following tasks:

- Listen to audio CDs and audio from the Internet
- Build your own iTunes Library from several different sources
- Listen to and manage your iTunes Library
- Create and work with playlists
- Create and work with smart playlists

> **NOTE**
>
> For the remainder of this chapter, I have assumed that you have configured iTunes as recommended in Chapter 1. If you haven't, you might have a slightly different experience. For example, if you don't have iTunes connected to the Internet automatically, you won't see a message telling you that iTunes is looking up a CD's information when you insert it into your Mac because iTunes won't look up the CD's information for you.

Making Sweet Music with iTunes

At its most basic level, iTunes exists to enable you to listen to music. There are two "original" sources of music that you can listen to with iTunes: audio CDs and music from the Internet. (There are actually many other sources of music that you can configure and listen to; you'll learn about these later in this chapter.)

Listening to Audio CDs

Playing audio CDs using iTunes is similar to listening to CDs using any other CD player.

Listen to an Audio CD

1. Insert an audio CD into your Mac. By default, Mac OS X will open iTunes if it isn't already running or will move the application to the front if it is open and hidden or minimized.

> **TIP**
>
> If your Mac doesn't automatically launch iTunes when you insert an audio CD, you can make it do so. Open System Preferences and click on the CDs & DVDs icon. When the CDs & DVDs pane appears, choose Open iTunes on the "When you insert a music CD" pop-up menu.

   If this is the first time you have listened to the CD, when iTunes is the active application, you'll see a message telling you that iTunes is looking up the CD's information. Depending on how you connect to the Internet, this process can take a few moments, or you might not even notice it if you are using a broadband connection. If the CD's information is found, you will return to the iTunes window, and the CD will be shown in the Source pane.

   If you have previously listened to the CD in iTunes, you won't see this message because iTunes remembers a CD after it has looked it up once.

   If multiple matches are found for the CD, you will be prompted to choose the correct one. Do so, and then click OK.

2. Select the CD's icon in the Source pane. You will see a listing of its contents in the Contents pane (see Figure 2.1). Information about the CD, including number of songs, total time, and total file size, will be shown in the bottom center of the iTunes window.

3. Click the Play button and use the other playback controls to control the music. These controls work just like the controls on just about any other CD player you have ever used; you aren't likely to need help using them.

Figure 2.1 *The audio CD Gladiator Soundtrack is selected as the source so its contents appear in the Contents pane.*

Here are some additional notes related to playing audio CDs (many of these notes apply to other sources of music to which you will listen as well):

- If you have configured iTunes to play CDs when you insert them, you won't need to click the play button. (Remember from Chapter 1 that you control what iTunes does with audio CDs by using the General pane of the iTunes Preferences dialog box.)

- If you have iTunes set to automatically import music from an audio CD into your Library, that process will start, and the music will begin playing.

- As a song plays, information about that song appears in the Information window. This information includes the album name and song title, which scrolls so you see one piece of information at a time. You also see time data and a progress bar to show how far along in the song you are. If you click on the time being displayed, such as Elapsed Time, it will change to Remaining Time. If you click on it again, it will show Total Time. Click again to return to Elapsed Time.

- You can change the display by clicking the Mode Change button. The information will be replaced by an audiometer that shows the relative volume levels at various frequencies.

Making Music with iTunes   Chapter 2   **47**

- You can play a track by double-clicking it.
- The track that is currently playing is marked with a speaker icon in the Contents pane. You can jump to the current song by choosing File, Show Current Song (⌘+L).
- If you uncheck the checkbox next to a track's title, it will be skipped.
- You can change the order in which the columns in the Contents pane appear by dragging them. Just like the other panes, you can also sort the contents (by default, CDs are sorted by track number) and choose the information that is displayed.
- You can change the order in which tracks will play by dragging them up and down in the window; iTunes remembers this order, and the next time you insert the CD, the same order will be used.

> **NOTE**
>
> When iTunes obtains song information for a CD that you are playing, that information isn't limited to iTunes itself. If you view the audio CD in a Finder window, the track names that iTunes looked up will appear.

If you click the Maximize button (the green one), the iTunes window will shrink down so that only the playback controls and information window are shown (see Figure 2.2). You can use the Resize handle to reduce the size of the window even further until only the playback and volume controls are shown (see Figure 2.3). Click the Maximize button again to restore the iTunes window to its full size.

Figure 2.2 *When you want to conserve screen space, you can shrink the iTunes window.*

Figure 2.3 *You can make the iTunes window even smaller by dragging its Resize handle.*

In the full-size mode, you can manually resize the window by dragging its Resize handle. Making it larger will display more information. Making it smaller will display less; the window has a minimum size that is still quite a bit larger than the reduced size you get with the Maximize button.

Controlling iTunes from the Dock

Another cool thing about iTunes is that you can control it from its icon on the Dock so that you don't have to display the iTunes window at all. You can open the application and then hide it so that it doesn't take up any desktop real estate (choose iTunes, Hide or press ⌘+H). Most of the common tasks you will do can be done from the iTunes icon on the Dock. To do so, point to the iTunes icon on the Dock and hold the mouse button down. After a moment, a menu will pop up (see Figure 2.4). On this menu, you can see the song that is currently playing, pause or play the music, choose the next or previous song, and choose the repeat setting.

Figure 2.4 *The iTunes icon on the Dock is more than just cool looking; you can use its pop-up menu to control iTunes even when you don't see the application.*

Listening to Internet Audio

You can also use iTunes to listen to various Internet radio broadcasts. To do so, use the following steps.

Listen to Internet Radio

1. Select Radio as the source. A list of content genres will appear in the Contents pane.
2. Click the Expansion triangle next to a genre to view the content available in that genre (see Figure 2.5). The content is presented in "channels" that represent different audio streams that are available on the Internet.

Figure 2.5 *Here, you can see that the Jazz genre currently has several channels (streams) for your listening pleasure.*

3. Select the channel that you want to play and click the Play button (or press the spacebar). The selected channel will begin to stream to your Mac; when the prebuffer is full, it will begin to play. You can control the music using the same controls that you use for other sources, such as an audio CD.

Here are some notes about listening to Internet audio:

- When you first select the Radio source, iTunes downloads the list of available genres and channels. You can refresh this list at any time by clicking the Action button, which is called Refresh when the Radio Tuner source is selected.
- Each channel has a bit rate associated with it, such as 56 kbps or 128 kbps. The higher the rate, the better the sound quality will be and the more data that have to be downloaded to your Mac. If you use a broadband connection, such as a cable modem, this is not a concern for you because all the sources will play smoothly no matter what bit rate they are. If you use a slow connection, such as a dial-up modem, this can be important because your connection might not be able to handle a high bit rate stream so that it plays smoothly.
- Hear something you like and want to know what it is? Check out the Information window, which displays the artist and song title just like when you listen to an audio CD. The Web site from which the channel originates is also shown.
- You can also listen to an Internet stream by choosing Advanced, Open Stream and pasting the stream's URL in the resulting dialog box.
- Some of the channels are live, while some are just large playlists (you'll learn more about playlists later in this chapter). When you listen to one that is a playlist, it will be repeated until you stop playing it.

> **NOTE**
>
> You can also use iTunes to download and listen to audio books from audible.com. Explaining this process is beyond the scope of this book—you can learn more about it by visiting www.audible.com or by opening iTunes Help and searching for audible.

Building, Listening to, and Managing Your Music Library

Listening to audio CDs and Internet radio with iTunes is fine, but it's nothing to get too excited about because you can do these tasks just as easily with other tools. Where iTunes separates itself from all the rest of the pack is that it enables you to create, listen to, and manage an entire music library. This library can include as much music as you like—including all of your audio CDs, songs that you buy from the online Apple Music store, MP3s that you download from the Internet, and so on.

By adding all of your favorite music to iTunes, you never need to fuss with a CD again; all of your music is right at the tip of your mouse all the time. Plus, you can do all sorts of cool things with your Library's music, such as creating custom albums (called playlists), as you will learn later in this chapter.

Building Your iTunes MP3 Library

There are three basic ways to get music into your Library: importing files from audio CDs, adding files to your Library from the Internet or other locations, or buying music from the online Apple Music Store.

> **NOTE**
>
> iTunes uses the term "import" for the act of encoding your music in various formats, because when you encode music, it is imported into your Library. In more hip lingo, this process is called *ripping* a CD.

There's More to Sound than MP3

In the following sections, I focus on MP3 because that is the format that you are most likely to use with music. However, you can import audio files as AAC, AIFF, or WAV just as easily. When you add music to your Library from the Music Store, you don't have an option; AAC is used for all music from this source.

In Chapter 1, you learned how to configure encoding for these formats—simply choose the encoding format and settings that you want to use on the Importing pane of the iTunes preferences dialog box. Whenever you import music, the encoding format that is currently selected on the Import Using pop-up menu will be used.

Adding Audio CDs to Your iTunes Library

Hate dealing with a CD when you want to listen to music? Add a CD to your Library, and you never have to touch it again.

Add an Audio CD to Your iTunes Library

1. Insert the CD containing the music you want to add to your iTunes Library. iTunes will connect to the Internet and identify the CD (assuming that you haven't disabled this feature or that iTunes hasn't already identified the CD).
2. Select the CD in the Source pane.
3. Check the check box next to the title of each song that you want to import—by default, every track is selected.
4. Click the Import button (the Action button becomes Import after you insert an audio CD). iTunes will begin to encode the songs that you selected. Depending on how fast your Mac is and the number of songs that you selected, this process can take just a few minutes to a half hour or so. You can see the progress of the encoding process in the iTunes display window (see Figure 2.6). When the encoding process is completed, the song is marked with a green circle containing a check mark. The resulting files (MP3 if you use that format) are added to your Library, and you can listen to them from there, add them to playlists, and so on. When all of the selected songs have been imported, a chime will play.
5. When the selected songs have been added to your Library, eject the CD and repeat the process with other CDs.

Here are some notes on importing your CDs:

◆ When you first start building your Library, set iTunes to Import Songs and Eject a CD when you insert it (use the General pane of the iTunes Preferences dialog box). When you insert an audio CD, iTunes will import it automatically. After iTunes finishes importing a CD, it will eject it. Then you can insert another and add it to the Library. After you have built your Library, choose a different CD insert option, or you might end up with multiple versions of the same song in your Library (iTunes enables you to create multiple versions of the same songs in case you want to have songs encoded with different quality levels or in different formats).

Making Music with iTunes — Chapter 2

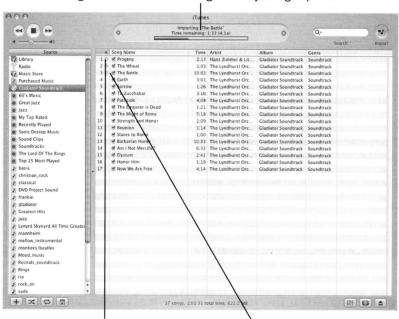

Figure 2.6 *The Gladiator Soundtrack CD is being added to my Library.*

- You can cancel the encoding process by clicking the small "x" at the right end of the encoding progress bar in the Information window.
- You can listen to the music that you are encoding while you are encoding it. Because the encoding process moves faster than real-time, the import process will be done before the selected songs stop playing. This can be confusing because it seems natural that both should stop at the same time. If you set CDs to eject after they are imported, the end of the importing process will be quite clear (because the CD will be ejected).
- You can also listen to other songs in your Library or playlists at the same time that you are importing songs from a CD.
- You can find the location of the encoded file for any song in your Library by selecting it and choosing File, Show Song File (⌘+R). A Finder window containing the file that you imported will be opened, and the file will be highlighted.

> **NOTE**
>
> If you purchased a new Mac with iTunes installed on it, your Library might contain quite a few songs already, courtesy of Apple.

Adding Audio from the Internet to Your iTunes Library

You can also add music and sound files directly to your Library without encoding them first. For example, you can add MP3 files that you download from the Internet to your Library. After you add such files to your Library, they behave just like files that you added by encoding them.

> **TIP**
>
> A good source of MP3 files that you can download is www.mp3.com.

Add Audio Files from the Internet to Your iTunes Library

1. Download the files from the Internet that you want to add to your Library.
2. Choose File, Add to Library (or press ⌘+O). You will see the Add To Library dialog box.
3. Move to the files that you want to add to your Library, select them, and click Choose (see Figure 2.7). The files will be added to your Library and you can listen to them from there, add them to playlists, and so on.

> **NOTE**
>
> Files that you add to the Library probably won't be labeled with artist, album, and genre information like songs you import from a CD are. You should use the Info window to label such music so you can identify it easily. You learn how to do this in the section called "Classifying and Configuring the Music in Your Library," later in this chapter.

To keep all of your music files neatly organized, you should have iTunes place files that you add to your Library in the iTunes Music folder, just like songs that you import from a CD. This area is controlled by the "Copy files to iTunes Music folder when adding to library" preference on the Advanced pane of the

Making Music with iTunes — Chapter 2

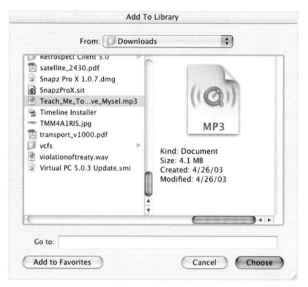

Figure 2.7 *You can add files you download to your Library; you can then use them just like files you import from an audio CD.*

Preferences dialog box. By checking this preference, you place a copy of the file in that folder so your music remains in a central location. After you have added a file to your Library, you can delete the file that you downloaded because you won't need it anymore.

If you don't have this preference enabled, iTunes will store a reference to the file in your Library instead. If you ever move or delete the file, iTunes won't be able to find it, and you will have to find it manually when you are prompted to do so.

Downloading MP3 from the Net versus Listening to MP3 on the Net

If you have configured iTunes to be used for Internet Music Playback (by clicking the Set button on the General pane of the Preferences dialog box), when you click on an MP3 file to play it from the Net, it will be played in iTunes from the Internet similar to Internet radio. Playing music from the Internet doesn't add the song to your Library like songs that you import from a CD. However, iTunes does add the song to your Library; instead of creating a file for the song on your Mac, it adds a URL to the song to the Library. Songs that are stored on the Net have the "beam" icon next to their titles, just like Internet radio stations (see Figure 2.8).

Figure 2.8 *You can tell that the highlighted song is actually stored on the Internet by the radio icon next to its name.*

As long as the song doesn't move from its location, you can play the song again from within iTunes just like songs that you have imported. If the song is moved, the URL will break, and you will have to find it again.

If you want to make sure the song remains available to you, download it and add it to your Library as explained in the previous steps. However, you can't always download MP3 songs, so in some cases, you will have to rely on the Internet reference to be able to play them.

Adding Music from the Apple Music Store to Your iTunes Library

With version 4.0 of iTunes, Apple introduced an amazingly cool feature, which is called the Music Store. This is an online source of hundreds of thousands of songs and albums that you can search and browse for music in which you are interested. When you find music you want to add to your Library, you can purchase that music and download it with a couple of mouse clicks. Because you access the Music Store from within iTunes, it is very convenient to use. And since songs are

Making Music with iTunes   Chapter 2   57

only $.99 (and sometimes even less when you purchase albums), adding music from the Music Store is an economical way to build up your Library.

There are two sources that appear in the Source pane related to the Music Store. One is the Music Store itself. When you click this source, the Music Store will appear inside the Contents pane. The other is the Purchased Music playlist; all the music you download is added to this playlist, so you can easily see the music you have purchased (it is also added to your Library).

> **NOTE**
>
> If you use the Shopping Cart preference, the Music Store source contains the Shopping Cart and the Purchased Music playlist.

> ### Minor Catches with Music Store Music
>
> Because of copyright concerns, there are some limitations on the music that you purchase from the Music Store. Fortunately, these limitations aren't likely to ever be noticeable to you. There are really only two meaningful restrictions, which are the following:
>
> - You can only play music you purchase on three Macs at the same time. The Mac on which you play music from the Music Store must be authorized to play it; this is done by configuring a Mac with a Music Store account. You can deauthorize a Mac when you want to use the music on a different machine, sell it, and so on so that it doesn't count against the three-Mac limitation.
>
> - You can only burn the same playlist that contains music you have purchased from the Apple Music Store onto 10 CDs. However, you can always change the playlist and burn it onto additional discs or add a song to a different playlist to put it onto a CD.

> **NOTE**
>
> All music in the Music Store is in the AAC format, which means that standard MP3 players won't be able to play that music. However, the Apple iPod can play AAC music, and putting your music on an iPod does not count against the three-Mac limit.

To find music in the Music Store and add it to your Library, you need to do the following general steps.

1. Configure your Store preferences.
2. Create an Apple Store account or sign in to the Music Store using an existing account.
3. Browse the store and preview songs.
4. Purchase and download songs that you want to add to your Library.

> **NOTE**
>
> In order to work with the Music Store, your Mac must be connected to the Internet.

You can configure your Store preferences on the Store pane of the iTunes Preferences dialog box. All of the options were explained in the previous chapter. The most significant choice you make is which shopping method you want to use:

- With the 1-Click method, you select and purchase songs or albums with a single mouse click (thus, the method's name), and they are immediately downloaded to your Mac. This method is designed for people who use a fast Internet connection, such as DSL or a cable modem.
- With the Shopping Cart method, you select songs and albums, and they are added to your shopping cart. When you are ready to purchase that music, you check out of the store and all of the music in your cart is downloaded to your Mac at the same time. This method is designed for slow Internet connections because downloading music will inhibit shopping for other music at the same time. If you prefer to be able to select music and think about it before purchasing it, this can also be a useful option.

> **NOTE**
>
> The remainder of this section uses the 1-Click method. If you have shopped elsewhere on the Internet, you will have no trouble with the Shopping Cart method.

Making Music with iTunes — Chapter 2

To be able to purchase music from the Music Store, you must sign into the store using an Apple Store account. If you already have an Apple Store account, you can just sign in using that account information (iTunes will remember this until you choose to sign out). If you don't have an Apple Store account, you will need to create one.

Sign In or Create an Apple Store Account

1. Click the Music Store source in the Source pane. The Music Store will fill the Contents pane (see Figure 2.9).

Figure 2.9 *When you choose the Music Store source a world of music (literally) becomes available to you.*

2. Click the Sign In button in the upper-right corner of the Music Store window. You will see the Sign In account dialog box. This dialog box presents two options. In the upper part of the dialog box, you can click the Create Account button to create a new account. In the lower part of the dialog box, you can enter your existing Apple ID and password to sign into your current account.

3. If you need to create an account, click the Create Account button and follow the onscreen instructions to do so.
4. If you need to sign into your existing account, enter your Apple ID and password and click Sign In.

After you have signed into your account, your Apple ID will appear in the Account box to show you the account to which you are current logged in. When you see this information, you are ready to shop.

The Music Store works just like most other Web sites you have seen. You click links, make choices on pop-up menus, and search to move around. You can search for music, browse genres, and so on to find music in which you are interested. When it comes to the Music Store, if you can see it, you can probably click on it to move to some music!

One convenient way to find music is to search for it. After you find music in which you are interested, you can preview that music. Here are the steps to do this.

Searching For and Previewing Music

1. Click on the magnifying glass icon in the Search Music Store box.
2. On the resulting pop-up menu, choose the criteria by which you want to search, such as All (to search all fields), Artist (to search for a specific artist), and so on.

> **TIP**
>
> If you choose Power Search, the Music Store will be replaced by an advanced search window that enables you to perform very precise searches.

3. Type the text for which you want to search in the Search field. As you type, the music that meets your criteria will be shown in the Contents pane (see Figure 2.10). At the top of the Contents pane, you will see albums that correspond to the search, top songs related to the search, and top artists related to the search. In the lower part of the pane, you will see the songs that meet the criteria you entered.

Making Music with iTunes

Figure 2.10 *Here, I have searched for music by Michael Card.*

4. Double-click on a song to listen to a preview.

TIP

You can browse the store by clicking the links that appear at the top of Contents pane. For example, click the House button to move back to the Music Store Home page. As you view specific content, a hierarchical list will appear; you can click any of the links in this list to move to that location, such as all of the music by an artist.

When you find music you want to buy, how you buy it depends on the method you use.

Buy Music with 1-Click

1. Click the Buy Now button next to the song or album you want to buy. The song or album is immediately purchased and will be downloaded to your Library.

Buy Music with the Shopping Cart

1. Click the Add button next to the song or album you want to buy. The song or album you selected will be added to your Shopping Cart.
2. Continue adding songs or albums to the Shopping Cart.
3. When you are ready to purchase the music, click the Buy Now button. All of the music in the Shopping Cart will be downloaded to your Library.

Click the Purchased Music playlist to listen to the music you have purchased. Or you can browse and search in your Library to work with your purchased music. Here are some other points about the Music Store to consider:

- ◆ You move songs you purchased to other Macs by copying them across a network, putting them on a CD, and so on. After you have moved the music to the next Mac, you can add it to the Library by using the Add to Library command. However, to play purchased music on a different Mac, you will need to authorize that Mac. You do this by signing in under the same Apple ID and password that was used to purchase the music originally. You can do this on up to three Macs.
- ◆ If you want to deauthorize a Mac so that it doesn't count against the three-Mac limit, choose Advanced, Deauthorize Computer. That Mac will no longer be able to play the music.
- ◆ If a download is interrupted before all of the music has been downloaded to your Mac, choose Advanced, Check for Purchased Music. This enables you to recover any music you have purchased, but have not downloaded.
- ◆ You can only download music one time! This means that should something happen to the Mac on which your purchased music is stored, you won't be able to download it again without paying for it again. You should always back up your purchased music on a DVD, CD, or on another Mac.

> **TIP**
>
> You can share all the music in your Library, including purchased music, with other Macs on your local network. See the section called "Sharing Music," later in this chapter, for the details.

> **Music on Multiple Macs**
>
> If you have more than one Mac, you might want to install your music Library on each Mac so you can access it from that machine (if your Macs are connected over a network, you can share music from one machine to the others instead). To copy music from one Mac to another, put that music on a CD or DVD and copy it to each Mac. Or you can use file sharing to copy the music files from one machine to another. Then use the Add to Library command to add that music to the iTunes Library on the Mac.

Browsing and Listening to Your Library

After you have built your iTunes Library, you can browse it and then listen to any songs that it contains.

As a source, the Library is unique in that it is designed to hold thousands of songs from hundreds of CDs and other sources (such as the Music Store). Because of this large amount of information it can contain, its Contents pane includes a Browse pane that you can use to view the contents of your Library in an organized fashion.

Browse and Listen to Music in Your iTunes Library

1. Click on the Library to choose it as the source. The contents of your Library will appear in the Contents pane.
2. Click the Browse button (or press ⌘+B) to open the Browse pane.
3. Drag the Resize handle (the small dot in the border between the panes) until the Browse pane and the Contents pane are sized appropriately.
4. In the Browse pane, select the Genre, Artist, or Album in which you are interested (see Figure 2.11). The column to the right of what you select will the contain items relevant to what you have selected. For example, if you select the genre "Jazz," all of the artists that are of that genre will be listed in the Artist column. Similarly, selecting an artist reveals all of that artist's albums in the Album column (see Figure 2.11).

Figure 2.11 *Here, I have selected the genre "Jazz," the artist "Joe Sample," and All for Albums, revealing the two Joe Sample albums in my collection.*

> **TIP**
>
> To show the Genre column in the Browse pane, check the "Show Genre When Browsing" check box in the General tab of the iTunes Preferences window.

The Contents pane will show only the contents of whatever you select in Browse pane. For example, to see all the albums by an artist, click that artist's name. In the Album pane, you will see all of the albums for that artist. In the Contents pane, you will see all of the songs on all of the albums for that artist. To see the tracks on a specific album, click the album name in the Album column. In the Contents pane of the window, you will see all of the tracks on the selected album.

> **TIP**
>
> To see all of the contents of a selected genre, artist, or album again, select All in its column.

5. Select any content to which you want to listen (Genre, Artist, Album, or songs in the Content pane) and click the Play button. The content that you selected will play.

> **NOTE**
>
> In the columns of the Browse pane, you will see All at the top of each list. When you choose All, all the items in that part of the column will be selected (and played if you click the Play button). For example, if you choose an artist in the Artist column, select All in the Album column and click Play; then all of the albums by that artist will be played. Similarly, if you select All in the Album window and then click Play, all of your albums will be played.

The other controls work just as they do for a CD or other source, such as the track check box, Shuffle button, and so on. You can also use the track check box to skip songs and play a song by double-clicking it just as you do when you listen to a CD.

> **TIP**
>
> You can close the Browse pane by clicking the Browse button again or by pressing ⌘+B.

Searching for Music

You can use the iTunes Search tool to search any source—including the Library—for specific songs, artists, genres, or any other information associated with that music.

Search for Music

1. Select the source that you want to search. For example, to search your entire music collection, select the Library.
2. Click the magnifying glass icon in the Search field and choose the criterion by which you want to search. The options are All, which searches all fields, or Artists, Albums, Composers, or Songs (which search just want you expect they would).

> **TIP**
>
> If you want to use the All criterion, you can skip Step 2 because this is selected by default.

3. Type the text for which you want to search in the Search field (see Figure 2.12). As you type, iTunes redraws the list in the Contents pane so that only items whose informations contains what you typed are shown. The information that is searched depends on the selection you made.

Figure 2.12 *You can use the iTunes Search tool to limit the contents shown in the Contents pane to specific songs.*

4. Continue typing until the Contents pane includes only those songs in which you are interested.

> **TIP**
>
> To clear a search so that all the contents of the selected source are shown again, click the Clear, which is the "x" located at the right end of the Search field (this is visible only if you have performed a search).

Removing Songs from the Library

If there are songs that you are sure you will never want to use again, you can delete them from your Library (if you just don't want to hear them anymore, uncheck their check boxes instead). When you delete songs from your Library, the original files are also deleted and will no longer be available on your Mac.

Remove Songs from the Library

1. Select the songs that you want to delete.
2. Press Delete. You will see a warning dialog box.
3. Click Yes. If some of the songs you selected were imported from a CD or other source, you'll see a second warning dialog box explaining that some of the songs you selected are stored in your Music Library folder—meaning that they are files you have encoded.
4. Click Yes. The songs will be removed from the Library, and the related source files will be moved to the Trash. The next time you empty the Trash, the files will be deleted from your Mac.

Classifying and Configuring the Music in Your Library

The iTunes Information window is a powerful tool that you can use to get information about tracks and to control specific aspects of those tracks. For example, in Chapter 1, you learned how to associate an Equalizer preset with a specific song. The Song Information window enables you to do more than just this task.

In the previous section, you learned how to search the Library for specific songs. You can use the Information window to associate a variety of data with a song for searches and other purposes. You can also associate songs with a genre to improve browsing, create your own genres, and so on.

The Information window contains the following panes:

- ◆ **Summary.** Use this tab to get general information about the song, such as title, artist, album, encoding method, and so on

- ◆ **Info.** This tab enables you to apply various tags to the song, such as its artist, album, year, track number, and genre. You can also add comments about the song. The tags are what are searched when you perform a search using the iTunes Search tool.
- ◆ **Options.** Using this tab, you can change the relative volume level of the song, apply an Equalizer preset, and control the start and stop playback time.
- ◆ **Artwork.** On this tab, you will see any artwork that is associated with the song. For example, when you purchase music from the Music Store, the album artwork is downloaded along with the song. You can also add artwork to or remove artwork from a song by using the Add or Delete buttons on the Artwork tab.

> **TIP**
>
> If you click the Artwork button located under the Source pane, a pane will appear. When artwork is associated with the song that is currently playing, it will appear in this pane.

View a Song's Information

1. Select a song.
2. Choose File, Get Info, press ⌘+I, or point to the song, hold the Control key and mouse button down, and choose Get Info from the contextual menu. The Information window will open.
3. Click the Summary tab if it isn't selected already. Information about the selected song will appear (see Figure 2.13).
4. To see the next or previous song in the selected source, click the Next Song or Prev Song button, respectively.
5. Click OK when you are done viewing this information. The Information window will close.

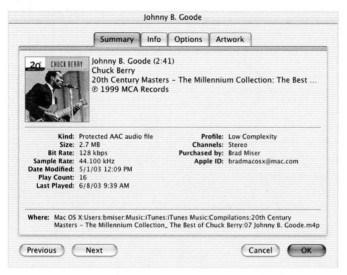

Figure 2.13 *The Summary tab provides detailed information (despite being called the Summary tab) about a song, such as where it is stored and the technical information related to how it was encoded.*

In order to make browsing and searching efficient, you should ensure that your music has appropriate information associated with it. If you need to edit a song's information, use the following steps.

Edit a Song's Info

1. Select a song.
2. Choose File, Get Info, press ⌘+I, or point to the song, hold the Control key and mouse button down, and choose Get Info from the contextual menu. The Song Information window will open.
3. Click the Info tab. You will see the information that is currently applied to the selected song (see Figure 2.14). If you have imported the song from a CD or purchased it from the Music Store, it is likely that the name of the song (which appears at the top of the Song Information window), artist, album, track number, and genre will be filled in. In many cases, that is all the information you need.

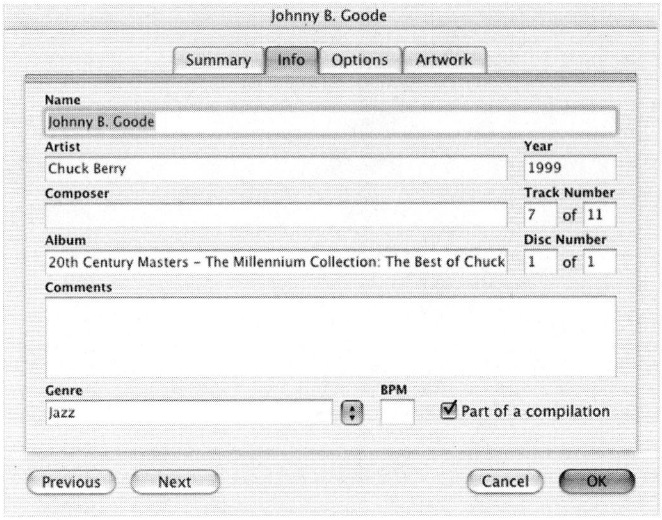

Figure 2.14 *The information associated with this song was downloaded automatically from the Music Store when the song was added to my Library.*

4. To change any of the song's tags, enter or edit the information shown in the various fields. For example, you can change the song's name or add comments about the song in the Comments field.
5. You can associate the song with a genre by choosing the genre on the Genre pop-up menu.
6. Click OK to save your changes.

> **TIP**
>
> You can add your own genres to the Genre pop-up menu. Open the menu and choose Custom. The Genre field will become editable. Type the genre you want to add. It will be added to the menu, and you can associate it with songs just like the genres included by default.

Rate Your Tunes

You can apply a rating to the songs in your Library to indicate how much you like or dislike them. You can use these ratings to sort the Contents pane, and you can use them in smart playlists. To rate a song, select it, hold the Control key down, click the mouse button, choose My Ratings on the contextual menu, and then choose your rating for the song (from one to five stars).

There are a number of options you can configure for a song that impact how it plays.

Configure a Song's Options

1. Select a song.
2. Choose File, Get Info, press +I, or point to the song, hold the mouse button down, and choose Get Info from the contextual menu. The Song Information window will open.
3. Click the Options tab (see Figure 2.15).

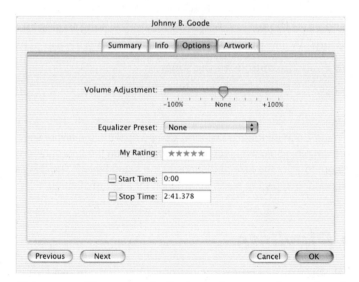

Figure 2.15 *You can use the Options tab to set various options for a song, such as its relative volume level.*

4. To change the relative volume of the song, drag the Volume Adjustment slider to the right to make the song play louder than "normal" or to the left to make the song play quieter than "normal."
5. To apply an Equalizer preset to the song, select the preset you want to use on the Equalizer Preset pop-up menu.
6. To apply a rating to the song, click on the dot in the My Rating field for the number of stars you want to give the song, from one to five.
7. To start playing the song at some point other than its beginning, check the Start Time check box and enter the start time in minutes and seconds. When you play the song, it will start at the time you input.

> **TIP**
>
> Using the Start Time option is a great way to get rid of interviews or talking at the start of a track. This content can be interesting once or twice, but probably not every time you hear the song. Just set the song to start when the talking is done, and you won't ever have to hear it again.

8. To stop playing the song before it reaches its end, check the Stop Time check box and enter the time at which you want the song to stop in minutes and seconds. When the song reaches this point, it will stop playing.
9. Click OK to apply the options to the song.

> **TIP**
>
> Many of the items in the Song Information window can be applied to multiple songs at the same time. For example, you can select several songs, open the Information window, and apply a genre to all of the selected songs at the same time. Doing this saves a lot time when you need to apply the same information for a group of songs.

Playing with Playlists

Ever had a CD that you really liked except for one song that annoyed you? Ever really liked a song and wished that it would play more than once? Ever get tired of hearing only a CD's worth of music at a time? For all these situations and more, you can use iTunes playlists to customize your music to make it what you want.

Earlier, you learned about the iTunes Library source. This source doesn't actually contain any music—its contents consist of pointers to MP3, AAC, and other files that are stored on your Mac.

While the Library source contains all of the music that you have added to your Library, you can also create customized sublibraries, called *playlists*. These playlists act like albums—they contain specific sets of songs. You can create your own playlists and add any songs in your Library to them. You can add the same song to more than one playlist, and you can add a song to the same playlist more than one time. You can make playlists as long or as short as you want.

After you create a playlist, you can listen to it, put it on a CD, or download it to an MP3 player. You will be using playlists quite frequently.

There are two types of playlists: playlists and their smarter relatives, called *smart playlists*. Playlists are collections of songs that you manually place in the group. Smart playlists are created based on a set of criteria that you define.

Making Playlists

Playlists enable you to create your own albums containing as many songs as you'd like in any order that you want. You can repeat individual songs many times in the same playlist and include the same songs in different playlists. After you have created playlists, you can continue changing them by adding more songs, removing songs that you no longer want to be included, changing the playback order, and so on.

> **NOTE**
>
> A "regular" playlist has an icon with a single note on it. These playlists appear towards the bottom of the iTunes Source pane.

Creating a new playlist is very straightforward.

Create a Playlist

1. Click the New Playlist button or choose File, New Playlist (press ⌘+N). You will see a new, untitled playlist in the Source pane.

2. Name your new playlist. Immediately after you create a playlist, the name is in the edit mode, and you can name it.
3. Browse or search your Library to find the songs that you want to include in your playlist.
4. When you find tracks that interest you, drag them from the Contents pane onto the playlist that you created in Step 1. The songs that you drop onto a playlist are added to it. You can drop the same song onto a playlist as many times as you like.

> **TIP**
>
> Some standard Mac selection tricks will help you choose songs for a playlist. You can choose a contiguous set of songs by holding the Shift key down, clicking the first song in the group that you want to select, and then clicking the last song in the group that you want to select. You can select multiple noncontiguous songs by holding the ⌘ key down while you click on each song that you want to select. You can select all of the songs in the Contents pane by clicking that pane and choosing Edit, Select All (press ⌘+A). To unselect all songs, choose Edit, Select None (press Shift+⌘+A).

5. After you have added several songs, click the playlist you created in the Source pane to see its contents in the Contents pane (see Figure 2.16).
6. Drag the songs up and down in the Contents pane to change the order in which they will play.
7. Continue adding and ordering songs until the playlist contains the songs that you want in the order that you want to hear them.

> **TIP**
>
> A fast way to start a new playlist and add songs to it is to select a group of songs and choose File, New Playlist From Selection (or press Shift+⌘+N). A new playlist containing the selected songs will be created.

When you select a playlist in the Source pane, information about that playlist appears at the bottom of the iTunes window. This information includes the number of songs in the playlist, their total playing time, and the size of the files that you have referenced in the playlist. This information is very useful when you want to place the playlist on an MP3 device or when you want to burn a CD. You can

Figure 2.16 *This playlist takes me back to the 60s (since I wasn't old enough to enjoy the music then, I can use iTunes to enjoy it now).*

use the size information to ensure that the playlist will fit in the device's memory. (Playlists themselves contain only file references so they are quite small; however, when you put a playlist on an MP3 player or a CD, the actual source files are moved to that device.)

> **NOTE**
>
> Playlists are listed in the Source pane in alphabetical order. You can't change this order, so if the order in which your playlists appear is important, keep that in mind when you name them.

Listening to a playlist is just like listening to other sources. Select the playlist in the source window and use the playback tools and techniques that you learned earlier in this chapter to listen to it.

There are several ways in which you can change your playlists, including the following:

- You can edit playlist names by clicking on them and waiting for a second or so until the name becomes highlighted. When it is highlighted, you can change the name.
- You can delete songs from a playlist by selecting the playlist as the source, selecting the songs that you want to delete, and pressing Delete. You will see a warning dialog; click Yes to remove the song from the playlist. The song is not deleted from the Library nor is the source file affected, so you can always add it to other playlists again.
- To add more songs to the playlist, select them in the Library's Contents pane and drag them to the playlist.
- You can delete a playlist by selecting it and pressing Delete.

> **TIP**
>
> If iTunes ever loses track of a song in your Library for some reason, a caution icon (an exclamation point) will appear next to the song's title. Double-click the song. A prompt will appear asking you if you want to locate the song. Do so, and move to the song on your Mac (it should be in the album's folder in the iTunes Music folder). Select the song and click Choose. The song will be "found" again. If you aren't able to find the song on your Mac, you will have to import it or download it again.

Making Your Music Smarter with Smart Playlists

A smart playlist is defined by a set of criteria rather than just a set of songs. This means that a smart playlist can continually change to meet the criteria that define it. For example, if you create a smart playlist based on a specific music genre, any new music you add with that genre attached will be added to that playlist automatically. This is really cool because smart playlists are *dynamic,* meaning that their contents can change over time. There are many criteria on which you can base smart playlists, so the possibilities are almost endless.

iTunes comes with a number of predefined smart playlists that appear at the top of the Source pane, just below the Purchased Music source. For example, one of these is called Recently Played. This playlist contains songs that you have recently played, which is a good way to listen to music you have just added to your Library.

> **NOTE**
>
> Smart Playlists have an icon that contains a "snowflake."

Create a Smart Playlist

1. Hold the Option key down and click on the New Playlist button, choose File, New Smart Playlist, or press Option+⌘+N. The Smart Playlist window will appear (see Figure 2.17).

Figure 2.17 *The Smart Playlist window enables you to create a complex playlist based on multiple criteria.*

2. Check the "Match the following condition" check box. The pop-up menus and text box will become active.
3. Select the criterion on which you want to base the condition on the first pop-up menu. For example, choose Genre to base the condition on the music's genre.
4. Choose the operand on which you want to base the condition on the second pop-up menu. The operands that are available depend on the condition that you selected. For example, if you choose a text condition, such as Genre, your choices include contains, is, is not, and so on. If you choose a numeric condition, such as time, your choices include is, is not, is greater than, is in the range, and so on.
5. Enter the text or numbers for the condition in the check box. For example, if you selected Genre, you could enter Jazz or Rock (see Figure 2.18). If you selected time, you could enter the length of the songs you want to be included.
6. Click the Plus sign. Another condition will be added to the smart playlist. A new pop-up menu will appear next to the check box at the top of the window.
7. On the top pop-up menu, choose all if you want all of the criteria to be met or any if only one of the criteria has to be met for a song to be included in the playlist.

Figure 2.18 *So far, this advanced smart playlist will contain songs that are associated with the genre Jazz.*

8. Repeat Steps 3 through 5 to configure the new condition.
9. If you want to add another condition, click the Plus sign again.
10. Repeat Steps 3 through 5 to configure that condition.

> **TIP**
>
> To remove a condition from a smart playlist, click the minus sign next to that condition.

11. Keep adding and configuring conditions until you have added all that you want to include.
12. If you want to limit the playlist to a certain number of songs, amount of time, or file size, check the "Limit to" check box, enter the value that you want to use for the limit, select the parameter by which you want to limit the playlist on the pop-up menu (for example, choose songs to limit it to a specific number of songs), and then choose how you want the songs to be selected on the "selected by" pop-up menu. Suppose that you want to include only 50 songs in the playlist and want them selected by those that are most played. Your input would be 50 songs on the first pop-up menu and those that are most played on the second pop-up menu.
13. If you want the playlist to include songs that you have skipped (by unchecking their check boxes), uncheck the "Match only checked songs" check box. If this check box is checked, skipped songs will also be skipped by the playlist.

14. If you want the content of the playlist to change over time, check the Live Updating check box. Each time you play the playlist, iTunes will select the songs it plays based on the latest information. For example, if the playlist is based on genre and you add a new album from the genre to your Library, that album would be added to the playlist automatically. (If you don't check this check box, the playlist will contain songs based on the music as it existed in your Library when you created the playlist.)
15. Review the conditions to make sure you have defined them like you want them (see Figure 2.19).

Figure 2.19 *This smart playlist will play only Jazz music that I have rated at three stars or better.*

16. Click OK. A new smart playlist will appear in the Source pane.
17. Rename the smart playlist as needed.
18. Select the playlist. Its current contents will be displayed in the Contents pane (see Figure 2.20).

> **TIP**
>
> To change the criteria for a smart playlist, select the playlist you want to change, select and press ⌘+I to open the Smart Playlist window. You can make changes and then click OK to update the playlist. When you do so, the songs that meet the revised criteria will be added to the playlist.

Figure 2.20 *This playlist will continue to grow; every time I rate a Jazz song at three stars or better, it will be added to the playlist automatically.*

After you have created a smart playlist, you can listen to it just like other sources.

> **NOTE**
>
> The Purchased Music source is actually a smart playlist that collects all of the music you have purchased from the Music Store. As you purchase music, each song you buy is added to the Purchased Music playlist automatically.

Sharing Music

You can share music in your iTunes Library with other Macs with which you are networked. You can also listen to music that is being shared with you.

Sharing Your Music on a Network

To share your music with other Macs on your network, you just need to set your sharing preferences.

Share Your Mac's Music

1. Open the Preferences dialog box and click the Sharing button.
2. Check the "Share my music" radio button.
3. Click the "Share entire library" radio button to share all of the music in your Library or click the "Share selected playlists" radio button and click the check box next to each playlist you want to share only those playlists.
4. Give your shared music a name by typing a name in the Shared Name field. This is the name of the source others will select to access your music.
5. If you want to require a password for people to be able to share your music, check the "Require password" check box and enter a password in the field.
6. Click OK.
7. If you required a password, provide it to the people with whom you want to share your music.

After you have shared your music, people can access it using the same steps you use to access music being shared with you.

> **NOTE**
>
> In order for your music to be accessible on the network, your Mac must remain awake. If you turn it off or if it goes to sleep, others won't be able to access your shared music.

Listening to Music Being Shared with You

To search your network for music being shared with you, open the Sharing pane of the iTunes Preferences dialog box and check the "Look for shared music" check box. When you close the Preferences window, iTunes will look for any sources that are being shared with you. When it finds them, they will appear in the Source pane (see Figure 2.21). Shared sources have a blue icon with a single note.

Figure 2.21 *The source called "Mitch Miser's Music" is being shared by another Mac on my network.*

Listen to Shared Music

1. Select the shared source that you want to listen to.
2. If it requires a password, enter the password at the prompt and click OK. The shared source will become available.
3. Click the Expansion triangle next to the source to see the playlists that have been shared with you.
4. Listen to the shared source just like you listen to your own playlists.

> **NOTE**
>
> You can't move music from a shared source into your Library from within iTunes.

Chapter 3

Putting Your iTunes Music on the Move

Having your entire music collection on your Mac is cool. Creating and using playlists to customize your music is even cooler. However, there is no need to limit iTunes' coolness to the confines of your Mac. iTunes enables you to "mobilize" your music (sorry about that, but I just had to write that), in the following ways:

- Burn your own music CDs
- Take your music on the road with an MP3 player
- Use the coolest mobile music player on the planet—the Apple iPod

Burning Your Own CDs

There is nothing like creating your own audio CDs to provide a musical experience that is tailored to your tastes and musical desires wherever you are. As you learned in Chapter 1, iTunes enables you to create different types of music CDs. For example, you can create an audio CD that can be played in any standard CD player, such as the CD player in your car. Or you can create an MP3 CD that contains MP3 versions of your music; of course, you need a player capable of playing MP3 music to play these CDs (the benefit is that you can put a lot more music in the MP3 format on a single CD). Fortunately, many new CD players are capable of playing MP3 CDs, so this is a very useful option.

> **NOTE**
>
> Obviously, to burn your own CDs, you need a drive that is capable of writing to CD. All modern Macs include such a drive. If you are using an older Mac that doesn't include a CD recorder, you can easily add an external USB or FireWire CD-RW drive to your system. For example, you can purchase a nice FireWire CD-RW drive from www.smalldog.com for less than $150.

The following are the four general steps you need to burn your own music CDs:

1. Install and configure your CD recorder.
2. Configure iTunes burning in the audio CD, MP3, or Data CD or DVD format.
3. Create the playlist from which you want to create a CD.
4. Burn the CD.

You only need to do Step 1 once; after you have verified that iTunes is able to recognize your CD burner, you won't have to worry about this step again. You need to do Step 2 every time you want to change the format in which you want to burn CDs. The other two steps are required every time you burn (a CD, that is).

> **NOTE**
>
> Apple maintains lots of good iTunes information on the Web; check it out at `www.apple.com/itunes`. In addition to information, you can also download the latest updates to the application.

Prepping Your Burner

If your CD burner is an internal one that came with your Mac, this part of the process is pretty trivial. Even if you added a CD burner later, there still isn't much to it.

Check and Configure a CD Burner

1. Turn your CD recorder on (if it is an external model).
2. Choose iTunes, Preferences or Press ⌘+,.
3. Click the Burning button. The Burning Preferences pane will appear (see Figure 3.1).

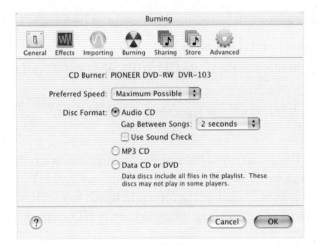

Figure 3.1 *You can check to see if your CD burner is ready to cook on the Burning pane of the iTunes Preferences dialog box.*

> **NOTE**
>
> Any Mac with a SuperDrive, a Combo Drive, or a CD-RW drive is ready to burn CDs.

4. Ensure that your CD recorder appears next to the CD Burner text at the top of the Burning pane. If it does, your Mac recognizes your drive, and you are good to go. If it doesn't, you need to figure out why your Mac is not communicating with the drive (this isn't likely to happen, but is possible if you are using an external drive).

> **NOTE**
>
> For help troubleshooting hardware devices, see my book *Special Edition Using Mac OS X v10.2*.

5. Set the Preferred Speed to the appropriate speed, which in most cases is Maximum Possible. This setting will burn your CDs at the fastest speed your drive supports. If recording doesn't work properly, reduce the speed, for example, to a snail's pace of 2x. Often, this will eliminate problems you might experience during the burning process.

6. Click OK. The hardware part of the process should be ready to roll.

Choosing a Burn Format

If you will be using the CDs that you burn in a CD player that is capable of reading the MP3 format, you should burn in that format because you will be able to get more music on a single CD. If you will be playing the disc on a player that can't handle MP3, you will have to use the Audio CD format. If you are burning the disc for back-up or copying purposes (such as copying to another Mac you own), choose the Data CD or DVD format.

Choose a CD Burn Format

1. Choose iTunes, Preferences or Press ⌘+,.
2. Click the Burning button. The Burning Preferences pane will appear.
3. Click the MP3 CD radio button to burn MP3 CDs, the Audio CD format to burn regular old audio CDs, or the Data CD or DVD radio button to create a data disc.
4. If you chose the Audio CD format, choose the gap between songs on the Gap Between Songs pop-up menu. Your choices range from no gap up to 5 seconds.
5. If you want iTunes's Sound Check feature to be used when you burn an Audio CD, check the "Use Sound Check" check box.
6. Click OK.

Creating a Playlist to Burn

You choose the songs that you want to put on a CD by creating a playlist containing the songs that you want to include in the order in which you want to hear them. See the section called "Playing with Playlists" in Chapter 2 for the details.

When you are creating a playlist for a CD, there is an additional wrinkle that you need to consider, which is how much music you place in the playlist. When you record a CD, you are limited to the maximum storage capacity of the CD media you use. All CD media is rated in terms of playing time and memory size. In most cases, this is about 70 minutes and 750MB. In the standard Audio CD format, this equates to about 70 minutes of music. In the MP3 format, you can store roughly three times as much music on a single CD.

When you prepare your playlist, keep an eye on the time information at the bottom of the iTunes window. When you record a CD in the Audio CD format, you need to keep the playing time of the playlist less than the playing time limit of the CD media on which you record. When you record an MP3 CD, you need to keep the memory to less than the memory capacity of the discs you use.

> **NOTE**
>
> When it comes to CD media, you have two basic choices: CD-R or CD-RW. CD-R discs can be recorded to one time only. You can erase CD-RW discs and record to them many times. When you are recording music CDs, you should generally stick to CD-R discs because CD players are more likely to be able to handle CDs in this format. And, with the cost of a disc being about a quarter, there isn't really any reason not to use them!

Burning a CD

Creating the playlist that you want to put on a CD is the only part of the process that takes any time to do. After your playlist is done, burning isn't difficult.

Burn a CD

1. Select the playlist that you want to put on CD. The Action button will become the Burn CD button.
2. Check the information for the playlist that you have created to make sure it will fit onto the CD media you are using (see Figure 3.2).
3. Click the Burn CD button. You will be prompted to insert a blank CD. The Burn CD button becomes "radio active" to show that your system is ready for action.
4. Insert a blank CD. Your Mac will check the disc you inserted to make sure it is ready to go. You will see the status of this process in the Information window; when all is ready, you will see the number of songs and total time for the disc (see Figure 3.3).
5. Click the Burn CD button again. iTunes will start burning the CD. Depending on the format of the CD that you are creating, the speed of your CD burner, and your Mac's capabilities, the burning process can take just a couple of minutes to a half-hour or so. As the process goes on, you can monitor its progress in the Information window (such as the

Putting Your iTunes Music on the Move — Chapter 3

Figure 3.2 *At just under 70 minutes, this playlist will be just right for a CD in the Audio CD format.*

Figure 3.3 *This disc is ready to burn.*

estimated time to complete the burn). When the CD is done, your Mac will play the done sound, the CD will be shown in the Source pane, and it will begin to play. (The name of the CD will be the playlist's name.)

> **NOTE**
>
> The spinning Burn CD icon gives you a clue as to how fast the data is being transferred to the CD that is being recorded. The faster the icon spins, the higher the data transfer rate is achieved. If the icon slows considerably or stops altogether, you might experience errors because data isn't flowing fast enough to keep the CD burning process fed properly. If this happens, quit all applications that might be accessing any disks on your Mac and make sure that you aren't playing any music in iTunes. This will ensure that the maximum amount of system resources is available for the CD burning process. You can also lower the burn speed to reduce the data flow requirements. Doing so will often alleviate this problem.

Taking Your Digital Music on the Road with MP3 Players

MP3 players are neat because they are really small and can hold the specific music that you want. Many are completely RAM-based, which means that they have no moving parts and can never skip. By using the MP3 format, most MP3 players are capable of two or more hours of music, and you never have to deal with CDs, which can be a pain when you are on the move.

iTunes makes it easy to move music to and from most MP3 players that are available.

Choosing an MP3 Player

There are lots of MP3 players available and explaining all the details associated with these devices is beyond what I have room to cover here. However, the following list provides some guidelines for you:

- **iTunes compatibility.** By default, iTunes comes with the plug-ins required to support a number of MP3 players, including some of the most popular models. You need to check to make sure an MP3 player is both Mac OS X- and iTunes-compatible before you purchase it.

Putting Your iTunes Music on the Move — Chapter 3

- **Memory.** MP3 players come with a built-in amount of memory. The more memory a model has, the more music that you will be able to store and listen to. Typical models come with 64MB of memory or more, which is enough for about an hour or two of music, depending on the encoding method that you use. Most MP3 players also use some form of removable memory, such as CompactFlash media. Being able to use this type of memory is good because you can expand the amount of music that you can take with you by obtaining more memory cards.

- **Size and style.** Most MP3 players are really small (the smallest are the Sony models, which are not much larger than a pen). They have a variety of shapes, colors, and so on. Although the style factors don't affect performance, the size and shape of the unit should definitely be a consideration. The whole idea is to carry the unit with you, so you want one that is comfortable for you.

- **Cost.** The largest factor in the cost of an MP3 player is the amount of memory that it has. You can get capable MP3 players for $150 or less. Before paying much more than this, you should consider getting an Apple iPod (you'll learn more about the iPod later in this chapter).

Moving Your Music to an MP3 Player

To listen to music on an MP3 player, you download the music you want from iTunes to the player.

Download Music from iTunes to an MP3 Player

1. Create a playlist containing the songs that you want to put on your player. Just like when you create a playlist for a CD, use the playlist's information to ensure that the amount of memory required to store the songs in the playlist is equal to or less than the memory available in your MP3 player. For example, if your MP3 player has 64MB of memory, the playlist must be 64MB or less.

2. Connect your MP3 player to your Mac and power the player up. iTunes will automatically recognize your player, and it will be selected in the Source pane.

3. If the player has music on it already, select the songs it contains and press the Delete key to empty the player's memory.

4. Drag the playlist you created in Step 1 onto the player in the Source pane. The music will be downloaded to the player. You can see the progress of the process in the Information window.

5. Select the MP3 player in the Source pane. At the bottom of the Contents pane, you will see a memory gauge that shows you the memory status of the player (see Figure 3.4). You also see additional control buttons that you can use with the MP3 player.

Figure 3.4 *The MP3 player (which happens to be a Rio 500) is selected as the source, and you can see the music it contains.*

Here are some notes to help you work with an MP3 player:

◆ You can drag songs directly from the Library (individual songs or albums) to download them to the player without creating a playlist. However, using a playlist helps you get the most music possible on the player because you can easily see the memory requirements of the playlist versus the memory capability of the player.

◆ When you select an MP3 player as a source, you will see some additional buttons at the bottom of the iTunes window (refer to Figure 3.4). Use the Settings dialog box to rename your player. You can also upgrade its firmware by clicking the Upgrade Firmware button. Some MP3 players enable you to create folders in which to store music. Use the New Folder button to create a new folder on the MP3 player. Use the Erase Player button to delete all songs from the MP3 player's memory.

> **Moving Purchased Music to an MP3 Player**
>
> Because music you purchase from the Apple Music Store is in the AAC format, you can't place it on standard MP3 players because they can't play the AAC format. You need to first convert the AAC formatted files into MP3, and then you can place them on an MP3 player. One way to do this is to burn the songs onto an Audio CD. Then configure iTunes to import songs in the MP3 format and import the songs from the audio CD you created back into your Library. This will create an MP3 version of the music that you can move to a standard MP3 player.

Mastering Your Mobile Music with the iPod

While the Apple iPod is an MP3 player, it is much more than most MP3 players. While many MP3 players are limited to 64MB or 128MB of memory, the iPod includes its own 10GB, 15GB, or 30GB hard drive. Even with the smallest drive, the 10GB model, you can store an entire music collection on the iPod (about 2,500 songs or more), which eliminates the chore of selecting a small subset of your library to take on the road with you. The iPod uses the FireWire interface to communicate with your Mac, which means that data transfers to and from the iPod much more quickly than it does with most other MP3 players (because most use USB, which is much slower than FireWire). And iTunes is designed to make managing your mobile music with the iPod even easier than it is with other MP3 players. For example, you can set the iPod up so that it is automatically synched with your iTunes music collection, including the songs in your Library, your playlists, and so on.

The iPod's only downside is its cost, which is higher than many MP3 players (the iPod currently ranges from $299 for the 10GB model to $499 for the 30GB model). However, if you consider that the iPod is actually a very small FireWire hard drive and includes a 10-hour rechargeable battery, its price doesn't seem as high. Also, keep in mind that you would have to buy many, many memory cards for most players for them to even approach the amount of music you can store on the iPod.

Besides which, the iPod is simply one of the coolest devices around (see Figure 3.5).

Figure 3.5 *Ah, the iPod. If only all devices were this cool and so very functional at the same time.*

> **NOTE**
>
> Another cool feature of the iPod is that its battery can be recharged through the FireWire port. This means that you can recharge your iPod just by connecting it to your Mac; newer iPods include a docking device to make this even more convenient. You don't need to fuss with batteries or a separate charger.

Moving Your Music Collection to an iPod

One of the great things about the iPod is that iTunes is designed to keep the iPod in synch with your music Library. When you connect an iPod to your Mac for the first time, iTunes will copy all of your music and playlists from your Mac and store them on the iPod.

Copy Your Music Collection to an iPod for the First Time

1. Connect the iPod to your Mac using the supplied FireWire cable. Your Mac will recognize the iPod as a new source, and iTunes will begin to download all of the music in your Library to the iPod. During this process, the iTunes Information window will display the progress of the process, as well as warning you *not* to unplug the iPod while the update is in process. As songs are downloaded, the refresh icon next to them disappears.
2. When the process is complete, disconnect the iPod. Your entire iTunes music library is ready to go with you.

> **NOTE**
>
> If your iTunes library contains more music than can be stored on the iPod, you will have to manually configure the music on the iPod. You will learn how to do that in the next section.

> **NOTE**
>
> iTunes contains a complete online help system for the iPod. To access it, choose Help, iPod Help.

Managing Your iPod Music Collection

When your iPod is connected to your Mac, iTunes will recognize it as a source, just like other sources. And like the Library source, you can browse the music on your iPod using the Browse and Contents pane (see Figure 3.6). These tools work just like they do for the Library.

Figure 3.6 *This iPod has 968 songs on it—just try carrying enough CDs to handle all this music!*

TIP

Click the Expansion triangle next to the iPod's icon in the Source pane to show a list of its contents.

As you add music to your Library, create playlists, remove songs, and so on, you will want to keep your iPod current with your iTunes Library. You can control how this is done by clicking the iPod Preferences button (refer to Figure 3.6) and setting preferences using the iPod Preferences dialog box (see Figure 3.7).

NOTE

The iPod supports the AAC format, so you can move your purchased music to it just like music in the MP3 format.

Figure 3.7 *Using the iPod Preferences, you can control how your iTunes music and iPod music are synchronized.*

The options you have are explained in the following bulleted list:

◆ **Automatically update all songs and playlists**. When this option is selected, the entire iTunes music Library will be synchronized with the music on the iPod each time that you connect the iPod to your Mac. This means that the iPod contains a mirror image of the music that you are managing in iTunes. In order to use this option, your Library must not contain more information than the iPod is capable of storing (for example, if you have a 10GB iPod, your iTunes Library must be 10GB or less).

◆ **Automatically update selected playlists only**. When you choose this option, you select the playlists that you want to be updated automatically. When you connect the iPod to your Mac, only the selected playlists are synchronized. This option is useful if there is music in iTunes that you don't really want to carry with you or when you can't fit your entire iTunes Library on the iPod. Create the playlists that you want to keep on the iPod and then have only those playlists synchronized automatically.

◆ **Manually manage songs and playlists**. With this option, you must manually move songs to the iPod; you do this just like you do for "regular" MP3 players or manual playlists. For example, you can drag songs from the Library onto the iPod in the Source pane.

◆ **Open iTunes when attached**. With check box checked, iTunes will open when you attach an iPod to your Mac.

- **Enable FireWire disk use.** You can use your iPod as an external FireWire hard disk. To do so, check this check box and also the "Manually manage songs and playlists" radio button. When you attach the iPod to your Mac, you can work with it just like other hard disks. (You can't use this method to transfer music to the iPod, though; instead you must use iTunes to do that.)
- **Only update checked songs.** This option enables you to prevent songs from being copied to the iPod. Check this check box and then uncheck the check boxes next to any songs that you don't want to be copied to the iPod.

> **TIP**
>
> You can play the music on an iPod through the Mac to which it is connected, just like other sources. Why is this cool? Suppose you are using a Mac that isn't your own. You can connect your iPod to it and play your music though that Mac without having to copy the music to the Mac itself.

That is really all there is to it. The Apple iPod is a rare device that really does work as well as the marketing information claims it will. If you are at all serious about having a mobile music collection, check out the iPod.

> **NOTE**
>
> For more information on the iPod, see www.apple.com/ipod/.

PART II

iPhoto: Not Your Father's Photo Album

4 **Touring Your iPhoto Digital Darkroom**

5 **Building Your iPhoto Photo Library**

6 **Editing the Images in Your iPhoto Photo Library**

7 **Making the Most of Your Images**

Chapter 4

Touring Your iPhoto Digital Darkroom

If pictures are worth a thousand words, then iPhoto is worth at least a dozen word processors. With iPhoto, you can take control over digital images that you capture with a digital camera, scan, and have developed on CD or that you acquire from just about any other source. As you build an image library, you can enjoy these images for their own sake and use them in your iLife projects.

With iPhoto, you can do the following tasks:

- Import images from a digital camera or from other sources
- Organize and catalog your images
- Edit the images by cropping, rotating, removing red-eye, and so on
- Create custom photo books to display your images in creative ways
- Print images
- Display your images in slideshows and Web pages
- Order professionally printed images and photo books
- Share your images through a .Mac account
- Add your images to a DVD or CD

> **NOTE**
>
> This part of the book is based on iPhoto, version 2.0.

> **TIP**
>
> iPhoto's home on the Web is located at www.apple.com/iphoto/. You can visit this site to download the application and updates, learn more about it, and so on.

Working in the iPhoto Window

If you read through the previous chapters on iTunes, then you will have an easier time learning and using iPhoto because the applications are similar in many ways, as you will see in this section.

Like iTunes, iMovie, and the rest of the iLife applications, iPhoto is both powerful and easy to use. In the following sections, you'll get a quick tour of iPhoto.

When you open iPhoto, you will see a three-paned window that looks quite similar to iTunes (see Figure 4.1). Also like iTunes, when you select a source in the Source pane, you'll see the contents of that source in the Contents pane. You use the Contents pane to select the images with which you want to work. Unlike iTunes, iPhoto has four modes, with each mode enabling you to do specific tasks with the images that you have selected in the Source and Contents pane. When you choose a mode, the Tool pane will contain the tools that you use in that mode. Between the Tool pane and the Contents pane, you see iPhoto controls, which include the Mode buttons.

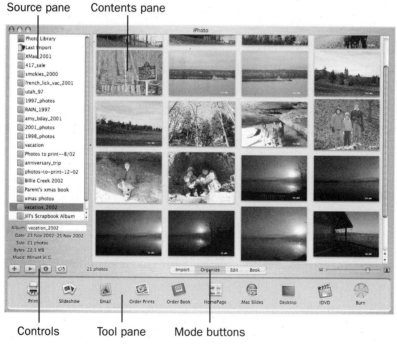

Figure 4.1 *iPhoto helps you make the most of your digital images.*

The iPhoto Source Pane

Images in iPhoto can be organized into albums; iPhoto albums are analogous to "analog" photo albums that contain the images in your photo collection. The iPhoto Source pane shows all of the albums that are contained in your Photo Library, which is the sum total of all the images you have stored in the application.

iPhoto includes two photo albums that are always present: Photo Library and Last Import. The Photo Library album contains all of the images that you have imported into iPhoto (regardless of how you imported them). The Last Import album contains the images that you downloaded during your most recent download session.

To work with an album, you select it in the Source pane, and its contents will be shown in the Contents pane.

> **TIP**
>
> You can resize the Source pane by dragging its Resize handle (the small circle located in the border between the Source and Contents panes) to the left or right.

The iPhoto Contents Pane

The iPhoto Contents pane shows the contents of the source album that is selected in the Source pane. How you see the images in the Contents pane depends on the mode in which you are operating. Depending on the mode you are in, you might see thumbnail views of all of the images in the selected album, a single image that you have selected in the album, or a photo book you are building.

iPhoto Controls

Between the Source and Contents panes and the Tool pane, you see iPhoto controls that are available in all the modes (see Figure 4.2).

These controls are explained in the following list (you'll learn how to use all of the controls throughout this part of the book):

- **New Photo Album.** You click this button to create a new album.
- **Play Slideshow.** Click this button and a slideshow displaying the images in the selected album will play (accompanied by a music soundtrack).
- **Information.** Click this to open or expand the Information area of the Source pane. If the Info area is not displayed, clicking this button once will open it. If it is displayed, clicking this button will expand it. If it is expanded, clicking this button will close it.
- **Rotate.** This one rotates selected images by 90-degree increments.

Touring Your iPhoto Digital Darkroom | Chapter 4 | **105**

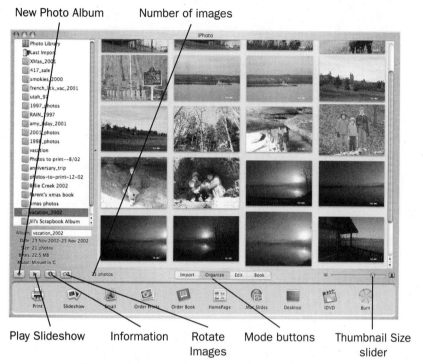

Figure 4.2 *The controls between the Source and Contents pane and the Tool pane are always available to you.*

- ◆ **Number of images.** If you have an album selected, this number shows how many images are in the selected album. If you have images selected, it shows the ratio of selected images to all of the images in the current album.
- ◆ **Mode buttons.** Use these buttons to change the mode in which you are working. When you click a mode button, the Contents and Tool panes will change to reflect the mode you select.
- ◆ **Thumbnail Size slider.** Drag this slider to change the size of the images you see in the Contents pane. Moving the slider to the right makes the thumbnails larger (meaning that you see fewer of them in the Contents pane), while moving it to the left makes the images appear smaller, and you can see more images at the same time. The setting of this slider doesn't actually change the images in any way; it only determines how large the images appear onscreen. For example, compare the size of the thumbnails in Figure 4.2 with the same thumbnails in Figure 4.3.

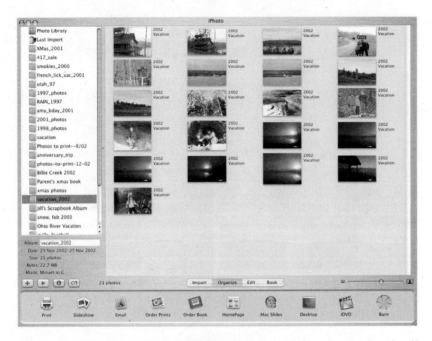

Figure 4.3 *Moving the Thumbnail Size slider to the left makes the thumbnails smaller, which means that you see more of your images on the screen.*

Using iPhoto Modes and Tools

For each iPhoto task, there is a corresponding iPhoto mode. And for each mode, there is a set of tools on the Tool pane. In this section, you'll get a quick overview of each mode and the major tools you will see in that mode. You'll learn how to use these modes and tools throughout the rest of this part of the book.

The iPhoto Import Mode

When you use iPhoto in the Import mode, you import photos into the application, which places the images that you import into your Photo Library. There are two ways to import images into iPhoto: from a digital camera or from other sources.

When you connect a digital camera to your Mac and click the Import button, iPhoto will recognize the camera and show you how many images it contains (see Figure 4.4). When you import images from other sources, you won't see a camera icon, but you will see the other Import tools.

Touring Your iPhoto Digital Darkroom Chapter 4 **107**

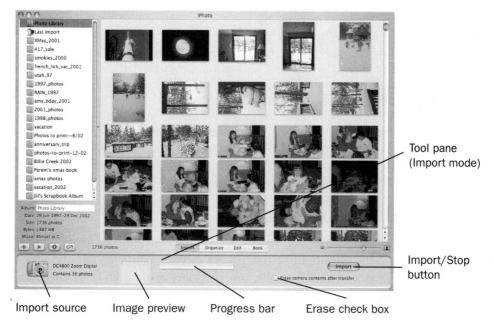

Figure 4.4 *In this figure, you can see that a Kodak DC 4800 camera is connected to the Mac and that there are 36 images available for download.*

In the Import mode, the Tool pane contains the following elements:

- **Import source.** When iPhoto is communicating with a camera, you will see that camera's information, such as its model name. You'll also see how many images are available to be downloaded into iPhoto. When a camera is not connected, you'll see the "No camera connected" message.

- **Image preview.** When you import images, you will see a preview of each image as it is imported.

- **Progress bar.** The progress bar displays the progress of the import process. As images are imported, a blue bar fills the progress bar. When the progress bar is completely filled, the process is complete.

- **Erase check box.** If you check the "Erase camera contents after transfer" check box, the images on your digital camera will be erased after they have been imported into iPhoto.

- **Import/Stop button.** This button is Import when you aren't importing images. When you click the Import button, the import process starts, and the button becomes Stop (which does just what you think it does).

> **NOTE**
>
> Here are two important comments about the Erase check box. First, if you don't have a camera connected to your Mac, it is inactive, so you can't use it. Second, even when it is active, I recommend that you don't use it. You should leave all the images on your camera until you are sure that they have been imported into iPhoto correctly. If something happens to the images while you are importing them and they are erased from your camera as well, they are gone forever. After you have verified that your images have been imported into iPhoto successfully, you can delete them from your camera by using its controls.

The iPhoto Organize Mode

iPhoto continues its straightforward naming conventions with the Organize mode in which you organize the images in your Photo Library, as well as the albums that you create. Typically, you also start tasks, such as editing images or creating books, from the Organize mode.

When in the Organize mode, the Tool pane contains a variety of tools that you can use to do tasks with the images you select (see Figure 4.5).

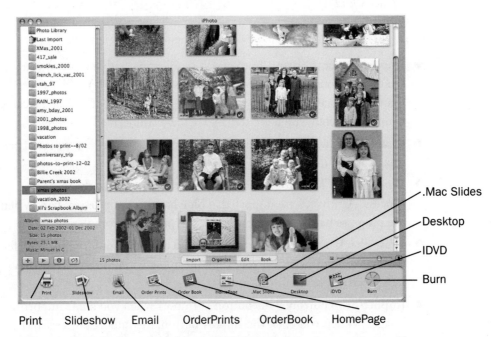

Figure 4.5 *In the Organize mode, the Tool pane contains buttons that enable you to do lots of cool things with your images.*

In the Tool pane, you will see the following buttons:

- **Print**. Click this to print selected images.
- **Slideshow**. Click this to present the images in the selected album in a slideshow.
- **Email**. When you click this, you can email the selected images to someone via your preferred email application.
- **Order Prints**. You click this to order professionally printed copies of selected images in various sizes.
- **Order Book**. After you build a photo book, you can click this button to order a professionally printed copy.
- **HomePage**. Click this button to create and publish selected images to a Web page on your .Mac tools site.
- **.Mac Slides**. Click this to create a set of slides from the selected images that other people can access via .Mac. They can use the images for their own tasks, such as using them as a screensaver.
- **Desktop**. Click this to apply the selected images to your Mac's desktop.
- **iDVD**. Click this to send the selected images to iDVD.
- **Burn**. Click this to place the selected images on a CD.

You'll learn much more about these tools in later parts of this section of the book.

The iPhoto Edit Mode

You can use iPhoto's Edit mode to make changes (hopefully improvements) to your images. While iPhoto is not a full-featured image editing application such as Adobe Photoshop, its tools enable you to make the changes that most people want to make.

To edit an image, you select it and then click the Edit button. The image will fill the Contents pane, and you will see the Edit mode's Tool pane (see Figure 4.6).

> **TIP**
>
> You can also move into the Edit mode by double-clicking on an image.

Figure 4.6 *You can use iPhoto's Edit mode to make changes to your images, such as rotating them or cropping them.*

In the Edit mode, you will see the following tools:

- **Constrain pop-up menu.** Use this pop-up menu to restrict the selection box (that you use to choose a portion of the image that you want to change) to a specific proportion, such as 5 x 7, when you crop it. This feature helps proportion an image for a specific purpose.
- **Crop.** Select part of an image and click this button to crop an image to the area that you have selected.
- **Enhance.** Click this button to have iPhoto enhance the image's color and other properties.
- **Red-Eye.** Click this button to remove the red in the selected area of an image (usually when a subject in the image has those special demon eyes that result from camera flash).
- **Retouch.** Use this tool to clean up specific areas in an image.
- **B & W.** Click this button to convert an image to black-and-white.
- **Brightness/Contrast sliders.** Use these sliders to adjust the brightness and contrast of an image.

◆ **Next/Previous buttons.** Move to the next or previous image in the selected album by using these buttons.

> **TIP**
>
> You can configure iPhoto so that you actually edit images using a different application, such as Photoshop. Instead of using iPhoto editing tools, when you go into the Edit mode, the image that you want to edit will open in the other application automatically. You will learn how to configure this later in the chapter.

Some of the Editing tools, such as Crop and Red-Eye, require you to select part of the image before you use those tools. However, these Edit buttons don't become active until you do so. To select part of an image, first drag in that image. As you drag, the selection box will appear, and you can use it to choose the part of the image with which you want to work.

One "editing" tool remains visible at all times—that is the Rotate button. To rotate images, you select the images you want to rotate and then click the Rotate button. By default, images rotate in the counterclockwise direction, but if you hold the Option key down while you click the Rotate button, they rotate in the clockwise direction instead. (You can set the default rotation direction with an iPhoto preference.)

A nice feature of iPhoto is that it maintains the original version of images that you edit so that you can return to the "pristine" version of the photo at any time. When you do this, you lose any changes you have made to the image, but at least you can recover from your "improvements."

The iPhoto Book Mode

In the Book mode, you can create very nice books of your photos in a variety of formats and styles. You can also choose to display a variety of information next to the photos in the book. After you have created a book, you can print it yourself or order a printed copy.

In the Book mode, the Contents pane contains a preview of the selected book page above thumbnails of each page in the book (see Figure 4.7).

While you'll get more detailed information about creating books later in this part of the book, the following list provides an overview of the tools that you see in the Tool pane:

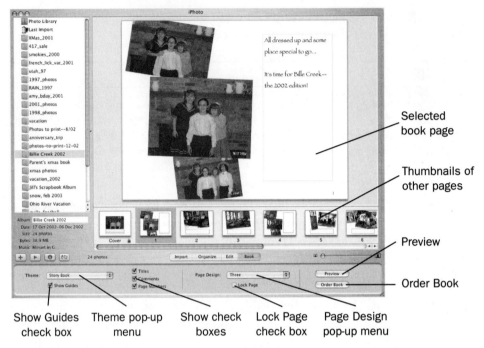

Figure 4.7 *Here, I chose the Storybook theme for the book and am entering comments about the photos on the selected page.*

- **Theme pop-up menu.** Each book that you create can be on one of six themes. The theme determines how images are displayed on each page of the book. For example, if you choose Story Book, images appear at different sizes and orientations on the pages for a more casual look. If you choose the Year Book theme, thumbnail images will appear on each page of the book. Each theme style also has corresponding text boxes in which you can enter commentary of other information for the book.

- **Show Guides check box.** When this check box is checked, you see blue guidelines around the various text boxes on a page.

- **Show check boxes.** These check boxes determine which elements of an image's information—that being titles or comments—appear next to the image in the book. The Page Numbers check box determines if the book's page numbers are displayed. If a check box is checked, then that information will appear on the book page.

> **TIP**
>
> Some themes don't show certain information, even if the check box is checked. For example, the Story Book theme doesn't display any of the image's information, regardless of the check box settings. Instead, that theme provides a separate text box for each page in which you can use text to narrate the book you create

- **Page Design pop-up menu.** Use this pop-up menu to choose a page's design, such as making it the Cover or Introduction, or to choose how many images will appear on that page. If pages are selected when you make a choice on this menu, only the selected pages are affected. If you don't select pages, all the pages in the book are affected. You can choose different designs for each page in the book.
- **Lock Page check box.** When this box is checked, you can't change a page's design. Use this to prevent accidental changes to a page.
- **Preview.** When you click the Preview button, a separate preview window opens, and you can page through your book as it will look when it is printed.
- **Order Book.** This button enables you to order a professionally printed and bound version of a book.

> **TIP**
>
> You can use the Thumbnail Size slider in each mode. For example, when you are editing an image, you can make the image appear larger so that you can make more refined selections. In the Book mode, use the slider to change the size that the pages you work with appear in the Contents pane.

Making Your iPhoto Preferences Known

Configuring iPhoto is relatively simple. Choose iPhoto, Preferences, and you will see the iPhoto Preferences dialog box (see Figure 4.8). These preferences are explained in Table 4.1.

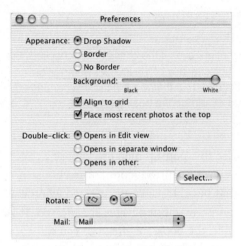

Figure 4.8 *Use this Preferences dialog box to configure your iPhoto preferences.*

Table 4.1 iPhoto Preference Settings

Preference	Options	What the Options Do
Appearance	Drop Shadow	The Shadow option puts a drop shadow behind the thumbnail images in the Contents pane when you are in the Organize mode.
	Border	When you choose this option, each thumbnail appears inside a border.
	No Border	With this preference, thumbnails don't have any border or drop shadow.
	Background	You use this slide to set the color of the background of the Contents pane. Dragging the slider to the right makes the background white; moving it all the way to the left makes it black. Placing it in the middle results in a shade of gray.
	Align to grid	With this option checked, your images remain aligned to the iPhoto grid.
	Place most recent photos at the top	When this check box is checked, the photos that you imported most recently appear at the top of the Contents pane.
Double-click Action	Opens in Edit view	With the Edit view option, when you double-click an image, it opens in the Edit mode.

Table 4.1 iPhoto Preference Settings (continued)

Preference	Options	What the Options Do
	Opens in separate window	With the separate window option, when you double-click an image, it opens in a separate window in which you can view and edit the image. This is very useful, especially because you can customize the toolbar that appears at the top of the window.
	Opens in other	When you choose this preference and then use the Select button to choose an image editing application, the images will open in the editing application that you selected. For example, you might choose to edit your images with a more powerful image editing application such as Adobe Photoshop.
Rotate	Clockwise button	With this button selected, the Rotate button rotates images in the clockwise direction by default (you can hold the Option key down while you click on the Rotate button to rotate images in the opposite direction).
	Counterclockwise button	With this button selected, the Rotate button rotates in the counterclockwise direction by default (you can hold the Option key down while you click on the Rotate button to rotate images in the opposite direction).
Mail	Email application	Use this pop-up menu to choose the email application that you want to use to email images from within iPhoto. For example, if you use Apple's Mail application, choose Mail on the pop-up menu.

Using iPhoto in Your iLife Projects

As you can see, when it comes to digital images, iPhoto is way cool. You can do amazing things with your images from within the application. And, whenever you use digital images in your projects, iPhoto is just the tool you need. Here are a myriad of ways you can use iPhoto:

- ◆ Capture and organize all your images
- ◆ Quickly find images in your collection

- Create and view custom photo albums
- Create cool photo books to display your favorite images
- View images in slideshows
- Email images
- Order prints and books
- Create a Web site for your images
- Add images to iMovie projects
- Put images in a slideshow on DVD
- Add images to your desktop

iPhoto Menu Commands and Keyboard Shortcuts

While some of the commands listed in the following table might not be familiar to you the first time you read through this book, they will make perfect sense when you have read through all of this part of the book. You can use this table as a handy reference whenever you need a quick refresher on a specific command or to find the keyboard shortcut for commands you use frequently.

Table 4.2 Useful iPhoto Menu Commands and Keyboard Shortcuts

Menu	Command	Keyboard Shortcut	What It Does
iPhoto	Preferences	⌘+,	Opens the iPhoto Preferences dialog box.
File	New Album	⌘+N	Creates a new photo album.
File	Import	Shift+⌘+I	Enables you to import images from sources other than a digital camera.
File	Export	Shift+⌘+E	Enables you to export images outside of iPhoto.
File	Show Photo Info	⌘+I	Opens the photo information window that provides detailed information about an image.
File	Duplicate	⌘+D	Creates a copy of selected images.
File	Revert to Original	None	Returns an image that you have edited to its original condition.
File	Move to Trash	⌘+Delete	Moves selected images to the Trash.

Table 4.2 Useful iPhoto Menu Commands and Keyboard Shortcuts (continued)

Menu	Command	Keyboard Shortcut	What It Does
File	Empty Trash	None	Empties the Trash.
Edit	Select All	⌘+A	Selects all the images in the Contents pane.
Edit	Deselect All	Shift+⌘+A	Deselects all images in the Contents pane.
Edit	Rotate>Counter Clockwise	⌘+R	Rotates selected images in the counterclockwise direction.
Edit	Rotate>Clockwise	Shift+⌘+R	Rotates selected images in the clockwise direction.
Edit	Set Title To	None	Enables you to choose the information that you want to be displayed as the selected images' title; the options are Empty (no title), Roll info, File name, and Date/Time. If you choose the Date/Time option, you can select the format of the date and time used in the title.
Edit	Keywords	⌘+K	Opens the Keywords dialog box that enables you to assign keywords to images and to search for images by keywords or other data.
View	Titles	Shift+⌘+T	Displays titles next to the image thumbnails in the Contents pane.
View	Keywords	Shift+⌘+K	Displays keywords next to the image thumbnails in the Contents pane.
View	File Rolls	Shift+⌘+F	Displays film rolls next to the image thumbnails in the Contents pane. (In iPhoto, the film roll is the number of the import session in which you added an image to the Photo Library.)
View	Arrange Photos	None	Enables you to group images in the Contents pane by Film Roll, Date, Title, or Manually.
Help	iPhoto Help	⌘+?	Opens the Help Viewer application, showing iPhoto help.

Chapter 5

Building Your iPhoto Photo Library

Now that you have a good overview of iPhoto, it's time to start using it! To have access to all of your great (and let's face it, some not so great) images, you add those images to your iPhoto Photo Library so that they are always accessible to you. Because you are likely to end up with thousands of images, you need some way to be able to find specific images with which you want to work—that is where iPhoto's labeling and searching tools come in. And you need to organize your images into photo albums that you can use for various types of projects, such as creating a book. In this chapter, you'll learn about the following tasks:

- Add images from a digital camera to your Photo Library
- Import images from other sources to your Photo Library
- Add keywords to your images
- Add titles and comments to your images
- Choose how images appear in the Contents pane while in the Organize mode
- View detailed information for your images
- Find images in your Photo Library
- Create and organize photo albums

Importing Images into the Photo Library

Moving your images into iPhoto is a simple task, whether you are bringing them in from a camera or from image files that you have found from other sources (such as images that you have scanned or that you have downloaded from the Web).

Importing Images from a Digital Camera

One of the great things about using a digital camera is that you can easily import images onto your Mac where you can work with those images in many ways. iPhoto makes importing images from a digital camera extremely simple.

CAUTION

Not all digital cameras are compatible with iPhoto, although most modern cameras are. To see if your current camera or one that you are thinking about buying is iPhoto-compatible, see www.apple.com/iphoto/import.html. If you don't use a camera that is compatible with iPhoto, you will need to download its images to your hard drive (using the software that came with the camera) and then use the steps in the section called "Importing Images from Other Sources" to move those images into iPhoto.

Download Images from a Digital Camera into iPhoto

1. Open iPhoto if it isn't already open.
2. Connect your camera to your Mac.
3. Power up your camera. If this is the first time that you have connected your camera to iPhoto, you will see a dialog box asking you if you want iPhoto to be launched automatically when a camera is attached to your Mac. Unless you use your camera with other applications, which isn't all that likely, click Yes to set that preference.
4. Click the Import mode button—this step won't be necessary if you clicked Yes when prompted about iPhoto being launched automatically when a camera is connected. Your camera will be recognized in the lower-left corner of the Import Tool pane, and you will see how many photos are ready to be downloaded.

NOTE

After you have configured iPhoto to launch automatically when you connect a camera to your Mac, you won't ever need to do Step 4; iPhoto will automatically recognize your camera and move into the Import mode.

5. Click Import. The application will begin moving the images from the camera's memory into your Photo Library. As the process proceeds, you can see its progress in the Progress bar (see Figure 5.1).
6. When the process is complete, disconnect your camera. The message "No camera is selected" will appear in the Tool pane.
7. Click the Last Import album in the Source pane. iPhoto will move into the Organize mode, and you will see the photos that you just imported.

Figure 5.1 *Here, you can see that 36 photos are available for download and that the import process is just about done.*

> **NOTE**
>
> If you choose the "Place most recent photos at the top" preference, the images you import will appear at the top of the Contents pane when you select the Photo Library as the source.

8. Review the images that you just downloaded in the Contents pane to make sure all of the images were downloaded successfully.

9. If all of the images were downloaded successfully, use your camera's tools to delete those images from its memory.

I strongly recommend that you add information (such as keywords and comments) to your images as soon as you import them. If you wait, you aren't likely ever to get around to it, and the photos will not be as easy to work with. Make a habit of labeling and organizing your images as soon as you import them, and your photo collection won't get out-of-hand (organizing one import session's worth of images is much easier and faster than organizing hundreds of images at the same time). See the section "Labeling Your Images," later in this chapter, for the details.

Importing Images from Other Sources

You can also add images from other sources to your iPhoto Photo Library. For example, if you don't have a digital camera that is compatible with iPhoto, then you will have to download images from that camera (such as by using a USB memory card reader) and then import them into iPhoto. Or you might want to add photos that you have scanned to iPhoto so that you can use iPhoto's great tools to work with them. You can also add images that you have downloaded from the Net to your Photo Library. iPhoto can and should be the one place in which you store all of the images that you work with.

> **NOTE**
>
> You can import a wide variety of image file formats into iPhoto, including JPEGs, Photoshop files, and other common image file formats.

No matter the source, you can add images that are stored on your Mac's hard drive to your iPhoto Photo Library by using the following steps.

Import Images from Other Sources into iPhoto

1. Prepare the images that you want to import. For example, scan the photos or download them from a USB memory card reader to your Mac. Or download the images from the Internet.
2. Choose File, Import (or press Shift+⌘+I). You will see the Import Photos dialog box.
3. Move to the files that you want to import and select them (see Figure 5.2). You can select multiple images at the same time by holding the ⌘ key down while you click each image.
4. Click Import (or press Return). The images will be imported into your Photo Library. You can monitor the process by watching the Progress bar—importing images from files is much faster than importing them from a camera, so the process moves along pretty quickly.
5. Click the Last Import album in the Source pane. iPhoto will move into the Organize mode, and you will see the images that you just imported (see Figure 5.3).

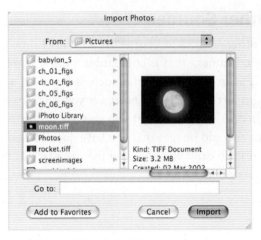

Figure 5.2 *You select the images that you want to import in the Photo Library using the Import Photos dialog box.*

Figure 5.3 *These two images have just been added to my Photo Library.*

After you have imported images, you should label them just as you do for images that you imported from a camera. See the next section, called "Labeling Your Images," for the information you need to label your images.

TIP

To remove images from your Photo Library, select the images and press the Delete button. Click OK in the warning dialog box, and the image will be deleted from iPhoto. Obviously, you should do this only with images that you are sure you will never want again.

Where iPhoto Stores Your Digital Images

When you import images into iPhoto, from either a digital camera or from other sources (such as photos that you have scanned), the images are stored in the following location:

Yourhomefolder/Pictures/iPhoto Library

As iPhoto imports images into your library, it creates several subfolders and data files that it uses to maintain your image collection. Within the iPhoto Library folder, you will see several data files that iPhoto uses to keep your images organized; these files are Library.data, Library.cache, and Dir.data. You won't ever need to work with these files directly. iPhoto also creates a folder called *Albums* in which it stores information related to albums that you create. You'll also notice a folder for each year in which photos that you import are captured. Within each year's folder, you will find one or more subfolders that are given numeric names. Within those folders are a collection of files and folders that include the images themselves along with roll data, thumbnails, and so on. Image files will be named with sequential numbers that iPhoto attaches to the images as you import them.

The organization and naming scheme that iPhoto uses isn't likely to make much sense to you (it sure doesn't to me), but, fortunately, you don't need to deal with it directly very often. You can just rely on iPhoto to manage all of the complexity for you. Still, you can move directly to the images within iPhoto's folders if you want to. View the folders in a Finder window using the Columns view; when you select an image, you will see a preview of it. This helps you know what the content of a specific image file is (the naming scheme certainly won't tell you!). You can copy image files from the iPhoto folders to other locations to use them for other purposes.

Note: Don't move the files from the iPhoto folders because iPhoto will get confused when it tries to access those images. Copy them instead so that the source file always remains within the iPhoto folders.

> However, when you need to use an image outside of iPhoto, you can easily export the images from iPhoto to work with them in other applications or for other reasons.

Labeling Your Images

Because you are likely to accumulate a large number of images, it is imperative that you keep them organized and that you use iPhoto's information tools to help you identify your photos so that you can find them when you need them.

To keep your images organized, you can associate several different kinds of information with your photos. Some of these data are attached by iPhoto automatically while you add or change other data. The labels that are associated with images include the following:

- **Title**. Each image in your Photo Library has a title. When you import images, the title that iPhoto assigns to them is the file name that iPhoto assigns to that image. But you can change this to give an image a more meaningful title.

- **Date**. iPhoto labels each image with the date and time on which it was captured (if the image came from a digital camera) or with a file's date if the image is imported from a hard disk. You can also change this information if you want to.

- **Comments**. iPhoto enables you to add comments to each image. For example, you can provide the context for the image so that when you look at it later, you will understand it better or if you have a poor memory like I do, you can explain where the information was captured. Comments are especially useful when you create books because they can include interesting things you've said about those images.

- **Film roll**. As you import images, iPhoto labels each image session as a "film roll" and attaches that film roll number to the image. (A film roll number is a sequential value.) You can use this information to find images based on the group in which you imported them. You can't change the film roll number. Film roll is only visible when you are working with the Photo Library as the source.

- **Keywords**. Keywords are short phrases that you can assign to images so that you can find the images again by searching for the keywords. The benefit of keywords is that you can define a set of keywords and apply them consistently over time. For example, suppose that you like to take photos of your kids' birthday parties. You can create a keyword "Kids' Bday Parties" and assign that to the images you take. Since you use the same phrase, you can find the images again easily because you don't have to remember how you labeled particular images; instead, you can find them by doing a keyword search.

You can configure the data by which you label and view images so that you can identify and locate specific images among the thousands you are likely to store in your Photo Library. You'll learn how to choose the labels that are displayed in the section called "Configuring the Information You See in the Organize Mode," later in this chapter.

> **NOTE**
>
> In addition to these labels, iPhoto captures all sorts of detailed technical information for each image that you import. You will learn about this in the section called "Viewing Detailed Information for Your Images," later in this chapter.

Adding Titles and Comments to Your Images

You can label images with a title or comments to the images in your Photo Library to make them easier to find or to document something about those images. Titles and comments can also be useful when you are creating some projects, such as when you create a book or a Web site for a group of images.

Add Titles and Comments to Images

1. Click the Organize button if iPhoto is not currently in the Organize mode.
2. Find the images you want to label. One reason I suggested earlier that you should label images immediately after you import them is because it is simpler to find the images that you most recently imported. You can find the group of images that you most recently imported by clicking the Last Import photo album in the Source pane. The images in that group (which is what iPhoto considers a film roll) will be displayed in the Contents pane. If you wait until you have imported images in multiple sessions, it will be more difficult to locate specific images to label.

3. Click the Information button located just underneath the Source pane until you can see the Comments box (see Figure 5.4). Depending on your starting point, you might have to click the button once, twice, or not at all if the Comments box is already displayed.

4. Click on an image's thumbnail to select the image to which you want to attach information. The image will be enclosed in a blue box to show that it is selected. In the Information area, you will see iPhoto's default title for the image (the file name the image was assigned when you imported it), the date and time on which the image was captured (assuming that iPhoto was able to retrieve this information from the source), size (the resolution at which the image was captured and file size), the music associated with the image when it is displayed in a slideshow, and the Comments for the image (see Figure 5.4).

Figure 5.4 *The Comments box enables you to associate text with an image.*

5. If you want to use something other than the iPhoto file name as the image's title, click in the Title field, select the default title, and replace it with a title of your choosing.

6. If you want to change the date that iPhoto has associated with an image, click the in Date field, select the current information, and change it. In most cases, this won't be necessary.

7. Click in the Comments box and enter comments about the image. Comments can be anything you desire, such as a description of the location where the image was captured, something amusing that happened at the same time, and so on.

> **TIP**
>
> When should you add titles and comments? That is a good question. Because they are somewhat labor-intensive to input, you might want to add this data only when you plan to use images in projects later. For example, you can display the title in photo books and on a Web site, so having titles that are more informative than the file name is a good idea for those projects. (Of course, while it is a good habit to add this information immediately after you import images, you can add titles and comments to images at any time.) For general identification purposes and so that you can locate images quickly, keywords are easier to assign and to use to find images.

8. Repeat Steps 4 through 7 for each image to which you want to add information.

One way to title images is to name the event followed by the month and year, as in event, Month, Year. This makes it easy to find images by the event or general date on which the event occurred. Unfortunately, you can't select a group of images and enter the same title and comments for them at once (that would be a nice feature, though!). What you can do is title one, copy the title you enter, and paste it to each image's Title box. Then you can enter the comment in one image's Comments box and paste that into the Comments box for the other images. Using consistent titles and comments makes finding the images again much simpler.

Associating Keywords with Your Images

Keywords help you find photos because you can search a group of images that are associated with specific keywords. You can use keywords to perform fairly complex searches because you can search by multiple keywords at the same time.

Defining Your Own Keywords

iPhoto includes a number of keywords by default. However, you can create your own keywords, and you can change any keywords that are available (whether you added them or they came with iPhoto). After you have set the keywords you want to use, you can associate them with your images and use them to search for specific images.

To get started, create a list of some keywords that you will use to find images. Some examples might include the following:

- Holidays
- Birthdays
- Scenic
- Vacations
- Sports
- Specific years
- People's names

> **NOTE**
>
> Adding each year as a keyword is very useful because you can combine that with other keywords to quickly find individual images. For example, suppose you have defined 2003 as a keyword. If you also use Birthdays as a keyword, you can find images from all of the birthdays in 2003 by searching on 2003 and Birthdays. You could find images from a specific person's birthday by using that person's name as a keyword. Combine all three keywords in a search, and you can quickly zoom in on the images from a specific event.

Add your keywords to the list of keywords that are available in iPhoto by using the following steps.

Add Your Own Keywords to iPhoto

1. Choose Edit, Keywords (or press ⌘+K). The Keywords/Search dialog box will appear.
2. On the Keywords pop-up menu at the top of the dialog box, choose New. You will see a new keyword called "untitled" (see Figure 5.5).
3. Type the keyword that you want to add.
4. Press the Return key. That keyword will be added to the application and will be available for you to assign to images and then use to search for images.
5. Repeat Steps 2 through 4 for each keyword you want to add.

Building Your iPhoto Photo Library Chapter 5

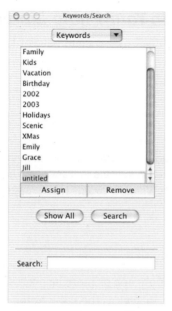

Figure 5.5 *You can add your own keywords to those that are included with iPhoto by default.*

Here are a couple of tips related to configuring keywords in the application:

- You can remove a keyword from the list by selecting it and choosing Delete on the Keywords pop-up menu at the top of the Keywords/Search dialog box.

- You can change a keyword by selecting it, choosing Rename on the Keywords pop-up menu, typing the new name, and pressing Return. This action changes the keyword on the list as well as on any images with which it is associated.

> **NOTE**
>
> You might have noticed that one of iPhoto's default keywords is a check mark. This is the one keyword that you can't change. The check mark is intended to be assigned to images temporarily so that you can perform a specific task for those images. For example, you might want to order prints from only a few photos in an album. You can apply the check mark keyword to each image that you want a print of and then find those images by searching for the check mark keyword. (The check mark actually appears in the lower-right corner of the image itself instead of next to it.) After you order the prints, you can remove the check mark keyword from the images.

Assigning Keywords to Images in Your Photo Library

To be able to use keywords to find images, you need to associate keywords with images. You do this in the same way, regardless if you want to use the keywords that are included with iPhoto or those that you added to it.

> **NOTE**
>
> To work with keywords, make sure they are displayed by choosing View to open the View menu. A check mark should be next to Keywords to indicate that keywords are being displayed. If the check mark isn't there, choose View, Keywords to display keywords.

Assign Keywords to Images

1. Select the images to which you want to apply one or more keywords. You can assign the same keywords to multiple images at the same time.

> **TIP**
>
> You can select multiple images that aren't next to one another by holding the ⌘ key down while you click on each image you want to select. You can select multiple images that are next to one another by holding the Shift key down, clicking the first image you want to select, and then clicking the last image that you want to select; the first and last images as well as all those that are between them will be selected. You can choose all of the images in a selected source by pressing ⌘+A.

2. Choose Edit, Keywords or press ⌘+K. The Keywords/Search dialog box will open.
3. Click on the first keyword that you want to assign to select it. That keyword will become highlighted (see Figure 5.6).
4. Click on Assign. The keyword you selected will be assigned to all the images that you selected in Step 1.
5. Click on the next keyword you want to assign to the selected images.
6. Click on Assign. The keyword you selected will be assigned to all the images that you selected in Step 1.
7. Repeat Steps 5 and 6 for each keyword you want to assign to the selected images. The keywords that you have assigned to the selected images will be highlighted.

Building Your iPhoto Photo Library — Chapter 5 — 133

Figure 5.6 *The keyword "Scenic" is selected; click Assign to associate that keyword with selected images.*

8. Click on the Keywords/Search dialog box's Close button. The Keywords dialog box will close. When you return to the iPhoto window, the keywords that you assigned will appear next to the images that you selected (see Figure 5.7).

TIP

The Keywords/Search dialog box is independent of the iPhoto window, which means that you can leave it open and switch between it and the iPhoto window. This process saves you the steps of opening and closing the dialog box each time you want to assign keywords or search for images.

To remove a keyword from an image, do the following steps:

Remove Keywords from Images

1. Select the images containing the keyword that you want to remove.
2. Choose Edit, Keywords or press ⌘+K. The Keywords/Search dialog box will open.

Figure 5.7 *These images have all had the keywords "2003" and "Scenic" applied to them.*

3. Select the keywords you want to remove from the images. (Only the keywords that are currently applied to the selected images are highlighted.)

4. Click on Remove. The keyword you selected will no longer be associated with the selected images.

After you have configured the keywords for your images, you can use those keywords to find images (see the section called "Finding Images in the Photo Library," later in this chapter, for ways to find specific images.

Configuring the Information You See in the Organize Mode

There are a number of ways in which you can configure the Contents pane when you are working in the Organize mode. You should get familiar with these ways so that you can configure the pane so that it suits your preferences.

Configure the Contents Pane in the Organize Mode

1. Use the Thumbnail Size slider to set the size of the thumbnails you see. Making the thumbnails larger makes it easier to identify images. The trade-off is that you see fewer of them in the pane.

2. Choose View, Titles or press Shift+⌘+T to show image titles if they are hidden or to hide them if they are shown. When you show titles, they appear just below the lower-left corner of the images.

3. Choose View, Keywords or press Shift+⌘+K to show keywords if they are hidden or to hide them if they are shown. When you show keywords, the keywords you have assigned to images appear just to the right of the upper-right corner of the images. (Of course, if you haven't assigned any keywords to images, no keywords will appear next to those images.)

4. If you have selected the Photo Library to work with it, choose View, Film Rolls or press Shift+⌘+F to show film roll information if it is hidden or to hide it if it is shown. (You can display film roll information only when you are working with the Photo Library. If you are working with a photo album, this option is disabled.)

5. Choose View, Arrange Photos to see the Arrange Photos menu. On this menu, you can choose how you want images in the Contents pane arranged. The choices are by Film Roll, by Date, by Title, or Manually.

   When you choose one of these, the images in the selected source will be sorted by the attribute you select, such as by their date to list the images in the Contents pane chronologically.

   When you have selected the Photo Library and choose by Film Roll, the images are grouped by film roll. Next to the film roll title, you can click the Expansion triangle to show or hide the images within that film roll (see Figure 5.8).

   When you have selected a photo album, you can choose Manually (which is disabled when you are working with the Photo Library). This choice enables you to manually organize the images in a photo album, which is essential when you are creating projects (you'll learn how this works later in this chapter).

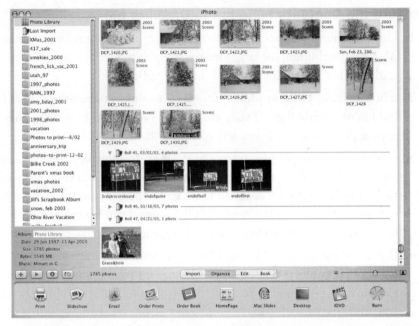

Figure 5.8 *When you choose to view film roll information, images are grouped by their film rolls; here you can see I have collapsed film roll 46, while film rolls 45 and 47 are expanded.*

TIP

You can choose to view each source differently. For example, you can choose to view one photo album by date and another manually. The view settings you choose are specific to each source. However, the Thumbnail Size slider setting applies to all sources.

On Film Rolls

As you read previously, Film Roll is used to mark the import session in which you imported images into iPhoto, regardless of how you imported those images. Film rolls start at 1 with the first group of images you import and are numbered sequentially as you import more images. Within each film roll, individual images are also numbered sequentially. For example, Roll 35, 3 indicates the third image in the 35th import session. The date on which you imported the images in a film roll is also part of the film roll information.

> When you are working with the Photo Library, showing Film Rolls can be a good way to quickly find a group of images. If you used any version of iPhoto prior to version 2, the title of each image defaulted to its film roll and sequential number, as in Roll 39 36 meaning the 36th image in the 39th import session. In iPhoto version 2 and later, the default title is the file name that iPhoto assigns to images when they are imported. If you don't assign titles to images and have used previous versions of iPhoto, you will notice this difference when you show titles and move between images that you imported under earlier versions and those that you imported under version 2 or later.

Viewing Detailed Information for Your Images

iPhoto keeps very detailed information on each image in the Photo Library. You can view this information by using the following steps.

View Detailed Information for an Image

1. Select the image about which you want to get detailed information.
2. Choose File, Show Photo Info or press ⌘+I. The Photo Info window will appear.
3. Click the Photo tab. Information about the image will be shown, such as its size, date, file name and size, and the camera with which it was captured (see Figure 5.9).
4. Click the Exposure tab. On this tab, you will see technical information about the settings with which the image was captured, such as shutter speed, aperture, and so on.
5. Click on another image to view its information. Because the Info window is independent of the iPhoto window, you can leave it open and select the images in which you are interested.
6. Click the window's Close button when you are done using it.

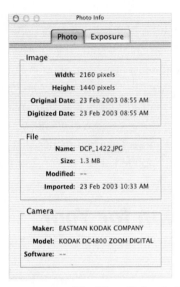

Figure 5.9 *The Photo Info window enables you to get detailed information about images.*

> **NOTE**
>
> The information that is captured for each image depends on the device that was used to capture it and how the image was imported into iPhoto. Some cameras will be able to communicate more information to iPhoto and some less. Likewise, if you import images from a disk instead of a camera, they are likely to have less information.

Finding Images in the Photo Library

After you have added hundreds of images to your Photo Library, finding specific images with which you want to work can be a challenge. Fortunately, iPhoto includes powerful search tools that can help you locate individual images so that you can work with them.

You can search for images by Keyword or by Title or by Comments.

To find images by keywords, do the following steps.

Find Images by Keywords

1. Select the source that you want to search by clicking on it in the Source pane. Select a photo album to search it or select the Photo Library to search all of your images.
2. Choose Edit, Keywords or press ⌘+K. The Keywords/Search dialog box will open.
3. Click on a keyword for which you want to search. It will become highlighted to show you that it is selected.
4. Hold the ⌘ key down and click on the other keywords for which you want to search. When you choose more than one keyword for a search, all of those keywords must be associated with an image for it to be found.
5. Click on Search. Only the images that are associated with the selected keywords will be shown in the Contents pane (see Figure 5.10).

Figure 5.10 *Because I selected the keywords "2003" and "Scenic" and then clicked Search, only images associated with those keywords are shown in the Contents pane.*

6. Click on the iPhoto window. You will see the images you found in the Contents pane.

> **NOTE**
>
> If you close the Keywords/Search dialog box, your search is lost, and you will see the contents of the selected source instead. Leave the dialog box open as long as you want to work with your search results. Since the dialog box is independent of the iPhoto window, you can move it out of the way if you want to.

7. When you are done with your search, close the Keywords/Search dialog box.

> **TIP**
>
> You can show all the images in the selected source again by clicking on the Show All button in the Keywords dialog box.

You can also search for images by title or comments in a similar way.

Find Images by Title or Comments

1. Select the source that you want to search by clicking on it in the Source pane. Select a photo album to search it or select the Photo Library to search all of your images.
2. Choose Edit, Keywords or press ⌘+K. The Keywords/Search dialog box will open.
3. Type the text for which you want to search in the Search box. As you type, the selected source is searched for the images that contain the text you typed (in their Title or Comments fields), and they are shown in the Contents pane (see Figure 5.11).
4. Click on the iPhoto window. You will see the images you found in the Contents pane.
5. When you are done with your search, close the Keywords/Search dialog box.

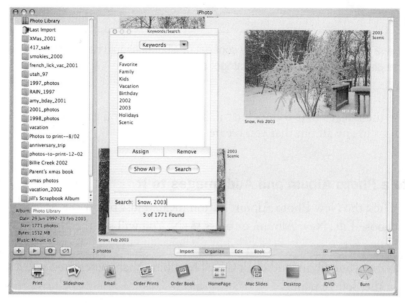

Figure 5.11 *Here, I have searched for images that contain the text "Snow, 2003" in their title or comments information.*

NOTE

Because the search is performed each time you type a letter or a number, typing might be sluggish if you are searching in a source that has lots of images. After these get narrowed down, the speed at which you can type will increase.

Building Photo Albums

A photo album is a collection of images that you can create for any purpose, such as to organize all of the photos related to an event, to gather photos for a slideshow that you want to put on DVD, and so on. When you create a photo album, only small pointers to the images are contained in the photo album, not the images themselves. The "master" image is always maintained in the Photo Library. This means you can create as many photo albums as you want without incurring much of a disk storage penalty. You can place the same image in as many photo albums as you like. You can also safely delete images from a photo album without removing the images from the Photo Library.

> **NOTE**
>
> If you have used iTunes' playlists, the concept of albums should be easy to grasp because playlists and albums are analogous.

You can choose the images that you include in an album, and you can include any number of photos in any album that you create.

Create a Photo Album and Add Images to It

1. Click the New Photo Album button located just below the Source pane, choose File, New Album, or press ⌘+N. You will see the New Album dialog box.
2. Name your album and click OK. The album that you created will appear in the Source pane.
3. Find the images that you want to include in the new album; use the searching techniques that you learned earlier to do so.
4. Select the images that you want to include in the album (select multiple images by holding the ⌘ key down) and drag them onto the new album in the Source pane. As you drag the images onto the album, a red circle containing a number will appear—the number is the number of images that you have selected (see Figure 5.12).
5. Continue finding images and dragging them onto the album.
6. When you are done, select the album in the Source pane, and you will see the images that it contains in the Contents pane (see Figure 5.13).

> **TIP**
>
> A quick way to select all the images shown in the Contents pane is to choose Edit, Select All, or press ⌘+A.

Figure 5.12 *Here, I am placing 21 images in the album called "Ohio River Vacation" (you can see the search I performed to find these images in the Keywords/Search dialog box).*

Figure 5.13 *When you select a photo album in the Source pane, you see the images it contains in the Contents pane.*

Here are some album tidbits:

- Placing images in an album does not remove them from the Photo Library; the Photo Library always contains all of the images that you have imported into iPhoto (unless you have deleted some images from the Photo Library).
- You can create an album by dragging images from the Photo Library or from other albums onto the Source pane. An album called Album-# will be created. You can edit the album name by selecting it and when it is highlighted, changing the name to what you want it to be.
- You can place the same image in as many albums as you'd like.
- To remove an image from an album, select it and choose File, Remove from Album or press Delete. The image will be removed from the album, but not from the Photo Library.
- Changes that you make to an image in an album, such as associating keywords with it or editing it, *do* affect the image in all its locations, including in the Photo Library. When you change an image in one location, it is changed in all locations.

The order in which images appear in a photo album is important because that order is the same in which they will appear in projects that you build within iPhoto, such as slideshows and photo books.

The first image in a photo album is the one in the upper-left corner of the Contents pane. The second image is to its right and so on until the end of the row is reached. Then the first image in the next row is next in order, followed by the one to its right and on down the window from left to right and top to bottom.

You can change the order of images by using the following steps.

Organize the Images in a Photo Album

1. Select the photo album you want to organize. Its images will appear in the Contents pane.
2. Choose View, Arrange Photos and then choose the attribute by which you want the images sorted, such as by Date to have the images listed in chronological order. To set the order of the images yourself, choose Manually.

3. Select the images you want to move in the photo album.
4. Drag the selected images until you reach the location where you want them. As you select and drag images, the number of images you are moving will be shown in a red circle next to the point. A vertical black line shows where the selected images will be located when you release the mouse button.
5. Release the mouse button. The images will slide apart to make room for the images you are moving.
6. Continue moving images until they are in the order you want.

Chapter 6

Editing the Images in Your iPhoto Photo Library

Some of the images you capture might not be perfect out of the camera or off the disk. Fortunately, iPhoto includes a nice set of editing tools that will help you make improvements to the photos you use in your projects.

With iPhoto's editing tools, you can change your images in the following ways:

- Rotate them to change their orientation
- Crop them to remove parts that you don't want to keep
- Enhance them to improve color and clarity
- Remove red-eye to make people or animals in your images look less demonic
- Convert them to black-and-white to make images look like they were taken in the good old days
- Adjust their brightness or contrast to make them look just right

Rotating Images

Images can have one of two orientations: Landscape or Portrait. When you capture images, you are likely to change the camera's orientation to capture the best image possible. For example, landscape shots are often best captured in the Landscape orientation, which is wider than it is tall (hmmm, I wonder how they named that one?). When you are capturing images or people, the Portrait orientation, which is taller than it is wide, is frequently a good choice (another naming coincidence do you suppose?).

Because you are likely to rotate your camera as you take pictures, the pictures that you import will probably be of mixed orientation. For most uses, including simple browsing, slideshows, books, and so on, this is usually not a good thing. iPhoto's Rotation tool comes in handy at this point and enables you to rotate images so that the "bottom" of all your images is toward the bottom of the screen.

Editing the Images in Your iPhoto Photo Library   Chapter 6

> **NOTE**
>
> Rotating images is a very basic aspect of editing your images. In fact, unlike the other editing tools, the Rotate function is always available regardless of the mode in which you are working.

Rotate Images

1. Select the photo album containing the images you want to rotate.
2. Select the images that you want to rotate.
3. Click on the Rotate button. The images you selected will be rotated in a 90-degree increment in the default direction you have configured for the button.

Rotating images is quite simple as you can see. Still, here are some tips to make you an expert in the art of rotation:

- Images will be rotated in a 90-degree increment each time you click on the Rotate button.
- To rotate images in the direction opposite to that set as the default rotation direction, hold the Option key down while you click on the Rotate button.
- You can change the default direction of rotation when you click the Rotate button by using the iPhoto Preferences dialog box.
- You can rotate images in the clockwise direction by selecting them and choosing Edit, Rotate, Clockwise or by pressing Shift+⌘+R.
- You can rotate images in the counterclockwise direction by selecting them and choosing Edit, Rotate, Counter Clockwise or by pressing ⌘+R.

Preparing to Edit Images

Rotating images is so simple that you don't need to do any preparation. Just select and rotate. However, the other editing tasks aren't quite that straightforward and are worthy of some prep work, which is the point of this section.

Deciding to Edit a Copy or the Original

When you edit an image, your changes affect *all* instances of that image in all your photo albums, in the Photo Library and wherever else that image is used within the application. (Fortunately, iPhoto maintains the original image should you ever want to go back to it. See the section called "Restoring an Image to Original Condition," at the end of this chapter, for more information about this.)

This is a problem if you want to have multiple versions of an image, say one cropped and one not cropped or one in black-and-white for a book and another in color for a slideshow. Fortunately, you can create duplicates of images. Each copy becomes a new, independent image just as if you had imported it again. You can create one copy for each "version" of the image you want to use in your projects.

You can create as many copies of an image as you'd like, but remember that each image consumes disk storage space. If you are going to use only one version, there is no need to duplicate it since iPhoto maintains the original version for you. But, if you do want to use multiple versions of the same image, use the following steps.

Create Multiple Versions of an Image

1. Select the images that you want to duplicate.
2. Choose File, Duplicate or press ⌘+D. A copy of the image will be created. The copies will have all of the same information associated with them as the originals, such as keywords, dates, and so on. The only difference is that the word "copy" is appended to the images' titles (see Figure 6.1).

Choosing How You Want to Edit Images in iPhoto

When you edit images within iPhoto, there are two basic ways the Edit window can be configured. There are slight differences between the two ways, but they each work similarly.

One way is to edit images within the iPhoto window itself—this is the default configuration. When you use this configuration and double-click an image (or select it and click on the Edit mode button), the image fills the Contents pane and the edit tools appear in the Tool pane (see Figure 6.2).

Editing the Images in Your iPhoto Photo Library   Chapter 6   151

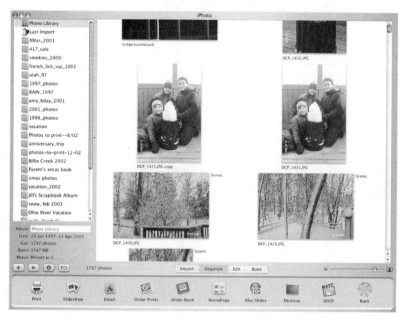

Figure 6.1 *Seeing double? No, I just created a copy so I could have a cropped version and have one version uncropped.*

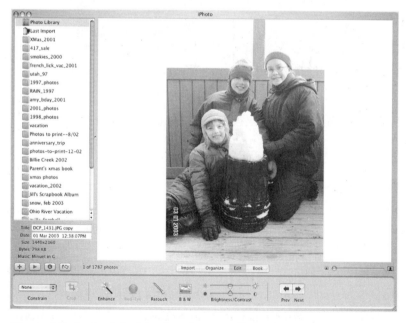

Figure 6.2 *In the default mode, when you edit images, they fill the Contents pane and the editing tools appear in the Tool pane.*

The other way is to have the images you edit appear in a separate Edit window. To enable this method, set the Double-click preference to "Opens in separate window." With this preference set, when you double-click an image, a new, separate Edit window appears (see Figure 6.3). You can use the editing tools that appear in the window's toolbar to edit the image.

Figure 6.3 *When you edit images in a separate window, you can customize the editing tools that appear in the toolbar.*

One of the nice things about this method is that you customize the tools in the window's toolbar so that it contains the tools you use most frequently.

Customize the Tools in the Edit Window's Toolbar

1. Open the Edit window.
2. Click the Customize button. The Customize sheet will appear (see Figure 6.4).
3. To add tools to the toolbar, drag them from the sheet onto the toolbar.
4. To remove tools from the toolbar, drag them off the toolbar.
5. Use the Show pop-up menu to choose how you want the tool icons to appear. Your choices are Icon & Text, Icon Only, or Text Only.

Figure 6.4 *The Customize sheet enables you to add or remove tools from the Edit window's toolbar.*

6. To use small icons (which take up less space on the toolbar), check the Use Small Icons check box.

7. Click Done. The toolbar will contain the tools you selected in the format you chose.

> **NOTE**
>
> Another nice thing about using the separate Edit window is that you can have multiple Edit windows at the same time.

The method that you use to edit images depends on your personal preference. The "edit in the same window" option is especially useful if you want to edit a series of images, such as those in a photo album. You can use the Prev and Next button to quickly move to and edit each image in the selected source. The "edit in a separate window" option is useful because you can develop and use a custom set of tools to make editing easier and faster. Plus, you can move the Edit window around, which is especially good if you use multiple monitors. And you can minimize the Edit window to move it out of your way temporarily.

Both methods are easy to use. I recommend that you configure the application to use the Edit window (by setting the "Opens in separate window" preference). When you want to use the Edit window, double-click the image you want to edit, and it will open in the Edit window. When you want to edit an image within the iPhoto window, select the image and click the Edit mode button; the image will fill the iPhoto window, and you can edit it there.

> **NOTE**
>
> Through the rest of this chapter, you will see examples of editing being done with both techniques.

Selecting Parts of an Image You Want to Edit

The Crop and Red-Eye editing tools require that you select the part of the image to which you want to apply the editing tool. Rather than explaining how to select parts of an image in multiple locations, this section explains how to do it. You can use the selection techniques in this section when you use either of these tools.

> **NOTE**
>
> The Crop and Red-Eye tools are disabled until you select part of an image. The other editing tools are disabled while you have part of an image selected.

When you select parts of an image, you have two basic choices: unconstrained or constrained. When you use the unconstrained option, you can choose any part of the image. When you choose the constrained option, you can only choose part of the image with a specific proportion.

You typically will want to use the constrained option when you crop images and the unconstrained when you are applying the Red-Eye tool.

Select Part of an Image, Unconstrained

1. Open the image in the Edit window or select the image and click the Edit mode button.
2. Move the pointer over the image. The cursor will become a plus sign.

3. Drag in the image. As you drag, the pointer becomes the arrow again, a selection box appears, and the part of the image that you have selected remains clear while the part that is not selected becomes shaded (see Figure 6.5).

Figure 6.5 *The selected part of the image remains clear, while the unselected part is shaded back.*

4. When you have selected the part of the image you want to select, release the mouse button. The cursor becomes a plus sign again.
5. To move the selection box around in the image, move the pointer inside the selection box. The pointer will become a hand icon. Hold the mouse key down and drag the selection box so it contains the part of the image you want to select.
6. To resize the selection box, point to one of its edges and drag.

When you want to ensure that the part of the image you select has a specific proportion, you use the constrained option. When you do so, the selection box always has the proportion that you select. For example, if you are cropping an image for a slideshow you are preparing in iDVD, you want the image to have the 4x3 proportion so that it will scale properly to fit the screen. Similarly, if you want to order an 8x10 print of an image, you would use the 8x10 constraint when you crop the image. There are quite a number of constrain options, which are all listed (and even explained) on the Constrain pop-up menu.

Select Part of an Image, Constrained

1. Open the image in the Edit window or select the image and click the Edit mode button.
2. On the Constrain pop-up menu, choose the option you want, such as 4x3 (Book,DVD).

> **TIP**
>
> If you use the "separate window" editing option, you can add buttons for the constraints you use most frequently to the toolbar.

3. Use Steps 2 through 6 in the previous group to select part of the image. The only difference is that the selection box will remain in the proportion you selected on the Constrain pop-up menu.

> **TIP**
>
> When you use the "edit in a separate window" option, you can enter a custom constraint in the Custom boxes to use a custom constraint.

Zooming on Images for Editing

As you edit images, you will need to zoom in and out to see the results of your changes. How you do this depends on the editing mode you are in.

Zoom an Image in the "Same Window" Editing Mode

1. Select an image and click the Edit button. The image will fill the Contents pane.
2. Use the Thumbnail Size slider to zoom in on or zoom out of the image.

> **TIP**
>
> If you select part of the image before you zoom, iPhoto will attempt to keep that part of the image centered on the screen as you zoom.

Zoom an Image in the "Separate Window" Editing Mode

1. Open an image in the Edit window.
2. Click the Up arrow in the toolbar to zoom in. As you zoom, the current percentage of zoom is shown in the window's title bar (see Figure 6.6).

Figure 6.6 *This image is zoomed to 100% as you can see in the window's title bar.*

3. Click the Down arrow to zoom out.

> **NOTE**
>
> Each click of the Zoom arrows zooms you in or out by a percentage increment, such as from 75% to 100%.

> **TIP**
>
> You can resize the Edit window, just like other Mac windows. To fit an image so that it fills the Edit window, click the Fit button on the toolbar.

Cropping Images

Images often contain extra stuff that doesn't help the image and might distract the viewer from the image's intended subject. You can crop images so that they contain only the material you want to be included. Or you might choose to crop an image to increase the focus on the central subject captured in the image.

When you crop an image, you select the part of the image that you want to keep and get rid of everything else. In addition to removing part of the image, the remainder of the image will appear to be larger since a smaller image fills the same space on the screen during a slideshow.

Crop an Image

1. Select the image you want to crop and then double-click it or click on the Edit mode button. The image will appear in the Edit window, or it will fill the Contents pane.

> **NOTE**
>
> Generally, you should use a constrained selection when you crop an image because it keeps the image in the correct proportion for projects in which you will use the image. For example, if you will include the image in a slideshow for DVD, you should choose the 4x3 proportion because that is the proportion of images that iDVD uses. If you don't crop images using a constrained selection, the "i" applications will size them the best they can so the images can be displayed where you use them. However, this can cause the subject of images to be too small, or it might result in some odd squishing if the original photo is of some odd proportion.

2. If you are going to use a constrained selection, choose the constraint on the Constrain pop-up menu.
3. Use the selection techniques you learned earlier to select the part of the image that you want to keep (see Figure 6.7).

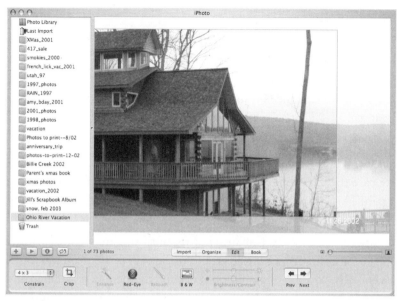

Figure 6.7 *Here, I am cropping an image using the constrained selection of 4x3.*

4. Click on the Crop button. All of the image outside of the selection box will be removed.

5. Hold the Control key down. While you are holding the Control key down, iPhoto will display the uncropped version again.

6. Compare the two versions to make sure the cropped version is the one you want to keep.

TIP

If you decide you don't want to keep the cropped version, open the Edit menu and choose Undo Crop Photo.

Enhancing Images

When an image doesn't look quite right, you can use the Enhance tool to enhance the image. This tool will attempt to adjust colors and contrast so they look better. You will be amazed at how well this tool works. It can do wonders with even not-so-good photos.

Enhance an Image

1. Select the image you want to enhance and then double-click it or click on the Edit mode button. The image will appear in the Edit window, or it will fill the Contents pane.
2. Click on the Enhance button. iPhoto will adjust the photo's colors and contrast.
3. Hold the Ctrl key down. iPhoto will remove the enhancements you have applied and show you the original image.
4. Release the Ctrl key. The enhancements you have applied will be shown again. This enables you to quickly compare the enhanced and unenhanced version of an image.
5. Continue clicking the Enhance button until you are satisfied with the image's appearance. Don't be afraid to click on this button too much. Eventually, you will click once too often, and the image will become worse instead of better. When that happens, choose Edit, Undo Enhance Photo to undo the last enhancement you applied.

Removing Red-Eye from Images

If you take photos of anything with eyes (for example, people or animals) in conditions where you use a flash, you have no doubt seen the dreaded demon eye effect that can sometimes occur. This red-eye can ruin an otherwise good photo. Fortunately, you can use iPhoto's editing tools to "get the red out."

Remove Red-Eye from an Image

1. Select the image you want to change and then double-click it or click on the Edit mode button. The image will appear in the Edit window, or it will fill the Contents pane.
2. Use the zoom tools that you learned about earlier to zoom in on the eyes that have gone over to the dark side.
3. Use the selection techniques to select the eyes from which you want to remove red-eye. Because the Red-Eye tool removes all the red in the area that you select, you should select as small an area as possible. Your goal should be to select only the red part of the eyes (see Figure 6.8).

Editing the Images in Your iPhoto Photo Library Chapter 6 161

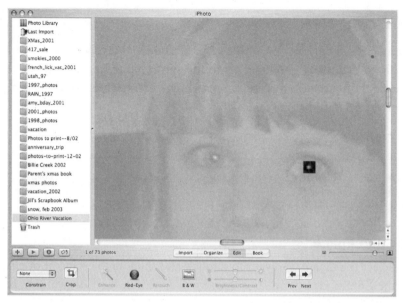

Figure 6.8 *When you remove red-eye, you should select as small an area as you can so you don't remove any red that should be there.*

> **NOTE**
>
> When selecting an area for removing red-eye, you generally want to use an unconstrained selection so that you can make the selected area as small as you can and still get all the red out of the eyes.

  4. Click on the Red-Eye button. The red in the area you selected will be removed, and the selection area will be cleared.
  5. Hold the Control key down to see the red back in again.

> **TIP**
>
> If you decide that the red-eye removal wasn't a success, choose Edit, Undo Reduce Red-Eye to undo the change and try it again.

  6. Keep selecting areas and using the Red-Eye button until you have returned all eyes to their normal condition.

Retouching Images

The Retouch tool enables you to blend in scratched and other unwanted marks from a photo by blending the mark into the surrounding image. You have to use this one carefully because too much retouching becomes very obvious and has a detrimental effect on the image.

> **TIP**
>
> If the blemish is located in an area away from the main subject, consider cropping it out instead of retouching it.

Retouch an Image

1. Select the image you want to retouch and then double-click it or click on the Edit mode button. The image will appear in the Edit window, or it will fill the Contents pane.

> **NOTE**
>
> The Retouch tool does not appear in the Edit window's toolbar by default. You can add it if you want.

2. Use the zooming techniques you learned earlier to zoom in on the area that you want to retouch.
3. Click on the Retouch button.
4. Move the cursor—which will now be a crosshair—over the area that you want to retouch.
5. Press the mouse button down and move the pointer over the area you want to retouch. As you move the pointer, the area will be smudged so that the blemish is blended in with the surrounding area of the image.

> **NOTE**
>
> When you are using the Retouch tool, think of the cursor as a brush that you brush over the area you want to retouch.

Editing the Images in Your iPhoto Photo Library   Chapter 6   **163**

> **TIP**
>
> For best results, press the mouse button down when you are in the part of the image you want to keep and drag it over the blemish. This tends to spread that part of the image over the blemish, which is what you want. If you start in the blemish, you may spread it over the image rather than making it less noticeable.

6. Hold the Control key down to see the image without the retouch effect.
7. Keep selecting areas and using the Retouch tool until you have removed the blemishes from the image.

> **TIP**
>
> If you decide the retouch hurt rather than helped your image, you can choose Edit, Undo Retouch to remove the last changes you made.

Making Images Black-and-White

Sometimes, you just gotta go retro. Or perhaps you like the artistic look and feel of black-and-white images. iPhoto enables you to convert any image into black-and-white.

Make an Image Black-and-White

1. Select the image you want to convert into black-and-white and then double-click it or click on the Edit mode button. The image will appear in the Edit window, or it will fill the Contents pane.
2. Click on the B & W button. iPhoto will process the image and when this is complete, the image will be in black-and-white.
3. Hold the Control key down to see the image in living color again.

> **TIP**
>
> To return an image to color, choose Edit, Undo Convert to B & W.

Adjusting Brightness and Contrast of Images

Contrast is the relative brightness of the darker areas of an image as compared to the lighter areas of an image. Brightness is the overall light level of the entire image. These two controls are lumped together because they tend to work in tandem. When you change the contrast, you lighten the lights or darken the darks, which can make the overall brightness of the image look wrong. Similarly, when you change an image's brightness, you can make the dark areas too dark or the light areas too light. You can use the Brightness/Contrast sliders to make substantial changes in the way an image appears.

> **TIP**
>
> You can often achieve better results more easily by using the Enhance button. Try that tool before you use the Brightness and Contrast tools.

Change an Image's Brightness and Contrast

1. Select the image you want to adjust and then double-click it or click on the Edit mode button. The image will appear in the Edit window, or it will fill the Contents pane.
2. Drag the Brightness slider to the right to make the light level of the entire image brighter or to the left to darken the image. As you move the slider, the brightness level of the image will change so you can see the results of your changes as you make them.
3. Hold the Control key to down to see the image as it was.
4. Drag the Contrast slider to the right to increase the contrast between light and dark areas or to the left to decrease the contrast between the light and dark areas.
5. Hold the Control key to down to see the image as it was.
6. Continue using the sliders to get the image to look the way you want it. You will often find that changing one slider causes you to need to change the other. You might need to spend some time in this balancing act to get the image to look its best (see Figure 6.9).

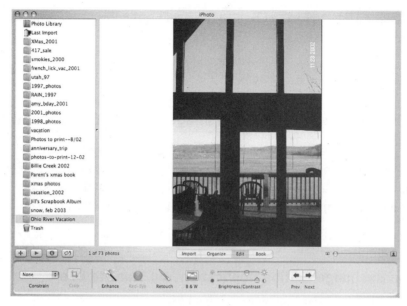

Figure 6.9 *When you have a backlit image like this one, you can sometimes improve it by adjusting the brightness and contrast.*

Restoring an Image to Original Condition

One of the coolest things about iPhoto is that it maintains an original version of all the images that you edit. If you make several different kinds of edits, such as a crop followed by an enhancement and retouch and then decide that you really want the image back to the way it was before you improved it, you can recover the original version of the image quite easily.

> **CAUTION**
>
> Just as when you edit an image, when you restore an image, that image is changed everywhere the image is used, such as in photo albums, books, and so on. Restoring an image to its original condition, just like editing an image, can have unintended results.

Restore an Image to Its Original Condition

1. Select an edited image that you want to restore to original. You can select it in a photo album, in the Photo Library, or display it in the Edit mode.

2. Choose File, Revert to Original. You will see the Revert confirmation dialog box.

3. Click on OK. The image will be restored to the state it was in when you first imported it into iPhoto.

> ### Editing Images with Other Image Editing Applications
>
> While iPhoto includes most the editing tools you are likely to need or want and they have the benefit of being integral to iPhoto itself, you might prefer to use a different image editing application. Fortunately, iPhoto is flexible enough so that you can use any image editing application to edit the images in your iPhoto Photo Library. First, choose the image editing application you want to use.

Choose the Image Editing Application You Want to Use

1. Open the iPhoto Preferences dialog box.
2. Choose the "Opens in other" radio button.
3. Click Select. You will see the Open dialog box.
4. Move to the application you want to use to edit your images.
5. Select that application and click Open. When you return to the Preferences dialog box, you will see the application you selected.
6. Close the Preferences dialog box.

To edit an image, double-click on it. The image editing application you selected will open, and you can use its tools to edit the image. When you save your changes, the image within your iPhoto Photo Library is saved as you edited it.

Chapter 7

Making the Most of Your Images

While building your Photo Library with images that you have edited is fun, the real kicks start when you use iPhoto in your own projects, CDs, DVDs, and in many other ways. Within iPhoto, you can do all sorts of interesting and fun things with your images, including the following activities:

- Print your images
- Email images to other people
- Order professional prints of your images that are delivered to your door
- Create and print custom photo books and order professionally printed and bound copies
- Add images to your desktop
- Put your images on DVD and CD
- Export images for use in other applications and in many other ways

Printing Images

iPhoto and an inexpensive inkjet printer enable you to print copies of your photos that are equivalent in quality to pictures printed by a professional. Of course, when you print photos from within iPhoto, you don't have to wait for your pictures nor do you have to deal with the hassles of taking your images someplace for developing and printing.

Printing images from within iPhoto is similar to printing documents from other applications (although the specific settings you use are more important because of their effect on the quality of the printed images).

One difference between printing images and other documents is that the quality of the paper on which you print is very important to the results you achieve. You should use paper that is designed for printing photos; this paper will make a tremendous difference in the quality of the images that you print.

Print Your iPhoto Images

1. Select the images that you want to print.

> **TIP**
>
> When you are printing images that have the portrait orientation in sizes that fit more than one image per page, you should rotate them to have the landscape orientation before you print them. This will align the long axis of the image with the long side of the paper (which is the width). After you have printed the image, you can rotate it back to "normal." (Because printing images in the 8×10 size fills a page, you don't need to rotate images when you print them in this size.)

2. Click the Print button. You will see the Print dialog box (see Figure 7.1). On the left side of the dialog box, you will see the first page of images that you selected. In the right side of the dialog box, you will see controls you use to configure the print job. At the bottom of the dialog box, you will see various buttons you can use to perform specific actions.

Figure 7.1 *The Print dialog box in iPhoto contains more options than it does in most applications.*

3. Choose the printer on which you want to print the images on the Printer pop-up menu.
4. Use the Presets pop-up menu to select preset settings for the selected printer. For example, most printers have special settings for printing on photo paper.
5. Use the Style pop-up menu to choose the style in which you want to print the images. For example, choose Full Page to print a single image per page; when you choose this, you can use the Margins slider to set the margins around the image. Choose Greeting Card to print the images in

a format designed to be folded into a greeting card; use the Style radio buttons to choose the style of card you want to print. Choose Standard Prints to print images in standard sizes; then choose the size of the prints on the Size pop-up menu (check the "One photo per page" check box if you want only one image to be printed on each sheet).

> **TIP**
>
> Some printers support printing on specialized photo paper that is segmented in the standard print sizes, such as 5x7. You should choose one of these papers if you are printing standard size prints.

6. Use the other controls in the dialog box to adjust how your image will be printed. For example, click on the Advanced Options button to open the full Print dialog box for your printer.
7. When you are done setting options, click Preview. The images will be converted into a PDF document and will open in the application you use to view documents of that type.
8. If the images appear as you want to print them, print the images. If not, move back into iPhoto and make changes to the print settings.

> **TIP**
>
> Each printer has its own set of print options. You should explore the user manual included with your printer so you understand its options and how they impact the quality of images that you print.

Printing images with the highest quality will take some experimentation with your specific printer, printer settings, paper, and so on. Minor changes in settings or using a different type of paper can have dramatic effects on the quality of the images that you print. I recommend that you spend some time printing with different combinations of printer settings and paper until you achieve the best results. Then document the combination that works the best for you so that you can use those same settings the next time that you print images.

> **NOTE**
>
> While printing your own images can be fun, it can also be time-consuming, frustrating, and expensive, especially if you have a hard time finding the settings you need to use to get photos printed with good quality. You should consider ordering prints from Apple instead. In addition to being extremely easy, you might find that ordering images in that way gets you better prints that cost less and are less work for you. Read about this in the section called "Ordering Prints," later in this chapter.
>
> Make sure that when you compare the cost of ordering prints versus ordering them from Apple, you take into account all the costs of printing them yourself. This includes paper and ink, both of which are fairly expensive when you calculate the cost on a per image basis.

Viewing Slideshows

An iPhoto slideshow is a great way to view your images on your Mac. When you display your images in a slideshow, you can choose music to accompany the images and you can configure various other aspects of the slideshow, such as how long the images appear on the screen. You can also save your settings so that you can use them on other slideshows easily.

Configure a Slideshow and Then View It

1. Select a group of images that you want to see in a slideshow. The easiest way to do this is to choose a photo album in the Source pane. (If you have a lot of time or not many photos, you can select your Photo Library to see all of your photos in the same slideshow).

2. Click the Slideshow button in the Tool pane. You will see the Slideshow Settings dialog box (see Figure 7.2).

3. Use the "Play each slide for __ seconds" box and arrows to set the number of seconds that each image will appear on the screen. The default is 2 seconds, which seems about right for most photos. If you like to linger over your photos longer, increase this number. If you are relatively impatient, change this to 1 second. You can change this value by clicking the Up or Down arrows or by typing a number in the box.

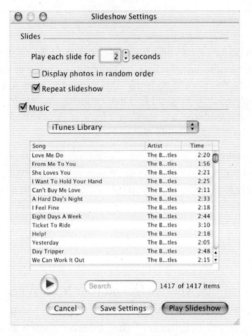

Figure 7.2 *You use this dialog box to configure an iPhoto slideshow.*

4. If you want the images to be shown in a random order, check the "Display photos in random order" check box. If you leave this check box unchecked, the images will be displayed in the order that they are shown in the selected source, such as the photo album.

5. If you want the slideshow to play through once and then stop, uncheck the "Repeat slideshow" check box.

6. If you want music to play while the slideshow is displayed, check the Music check box and do Steps 7 through 9 to choose the music you want to hear. If you don't want to hear music, uncheck the Music check box and skip to Step 10.

7. Choose the source of the music you want to hear on the pop-up menu. You have two fundamental choices: Sample Music contains music that came with iPhoto, while iTunes Library enables you to access all of the music you have in your iTunes Library. Within the iTunes Library, you can select any of the simple playlists that you have created (you can't choose a smart playlist to accompany a slideshow). When you make a

choice on the pop-up menu, you will see the songs in the source you select in the bottom part of the dialog box.

8. Select the song you want to play during the slideshow by clicking it.

> **TIP**
>
> You can preview a song by selecting a song and clicking the Play button (click the Stop button to stop the preview).
>
> You can search for a song by typing the song's information in the Search box. As you type, the list of songs will be reduced to include only those that match your search.

9. If you want to permanently associate the selected song with the source when you view it in a slideshow, click the Save Settings button. If you click on this button, the dialog box will close, and you will return to the iPhoto window. You can skip the rest of the steps in this section. (You can view the slideshow button by clicking the Play Slideshow button located under the Source pane.)

> **NOTE**
>
> When you save a song with a source, the song you selected will appear in the Information area just below the Source pane when you select that source (or when you select an image within that source).

10. Click on Play Slideshow or press Return. Prepare to be impressed as your screen fills with your images and they transition smoothly from one to the next (see Figure 7.3).

11. To stop the slideshow before it finishes or if it repeats, click the mouse button or press the Esc key.

You can also view a slideshow without configuring it first from any mode (such as the Organize or Edit modes). When you view a slideshow in this way, it is displayed with the default settings, such as the default music, or with the settings you have saved by using the Slideshow Settings dialog box.

Figure 7.3 *An iPhoto slideshow is a great way to enjoy your photos.*

View a Slideshow Using Saved Settings

1. Select the source that you want to view in a slideshow. The music that is configured for that source appears in the Information area below the Source pane.
2. Click the Play Slideshow button that is located above the Tool pane. The slideshow will play.
3. To stop the slideshow before it finishes or if it repeats, click the mouse button or press the Esc key.

When you use iPhoto's slideshow function, you create a temporary slideshow just to view the images on your Mac. You can't save the slideshows that you view with this tool (although as you learned, you can save the settings for the slideshow so you use them each time you view it within iPhoto). However, you can use iPhoto to export a series of images as a slideshow and then use other iLife applications to save the slideshow in a variety of ways, such as putting a slideshow on DVD, importing images into iMovie, and so on. You can also send images directly to iDVD from within iPhoto. You'll learn these techniques for each application throughout this book.

Emailing Your Images

You are very likely to want to share your photos with others; sending them via email makes this easy to do. You can use iPhoto's email feature to send images with just a few mouse clicks.

First, you need to set the email application you want to use to send photos. Then you can send images with a single mouse click.

> **NOTE**
>
> By default, iPhoto is configured to use Apple's Mail application to email images. If you use Mail, you don't need to do the following steps.

Set the Application You Use to Email Images

1. Open the iPhoto Preferences dialog box.
2. On the Mail pop-up menu, choose the application you want to use. Your choices are America Online, Eudora, Mail, or Entourage.
3. Close the dialog box.

Email Images

1. Select the images that you want to email to someone.
2. Click on the Email button in the Tool pane. You will see the Mail Photo dialog box (see Figure 7.4).

> **TIP**
>
> When you send images, consider the connection that the recipient uses to retrieve email. If the recipient uses a dial-up connection, be careful not to overload their connection with high-resolution images or even with lots of low-resolution images. Even if the recipient uses a broadband connection, their email account might have a file size limit for attachments to email messages. If you want to transfer lots of images, consider posting them to a .Mac Web site instead.

Figure 7.4 *Using the Mail Photo dialog box, you can configure the images you send to people via email.*

3. Choose the resolution of the images you email on the Size pop-up menu. The higher the resolution you choose, the better the quality of the images, but the file sizes will be larger as well. The choices on the pop-up menu range from Small to Full Size (which is the resolution with which the images were captured). Use the Estimated Size value to assess whether the size of the files will be too large for the recipient to reasonably receive. For example, sending 5MB of images to someone who uses a dial-up connection is probably not a good thing to do.

4. If you want the titles and comments to be included with the images, check the Titles and Comments check boxes, respectively.

5. Click on Compose. A progress window will appear as iPhoto prepares the images. When this process is complete, the email application you selected will open, and a new message will be created. The images you selected will be attachments to the email message (see Figure 7.5). By default, the subject of the message will be *X* great iPhotos where *X* is the number of images you selected.

6. Address the message, add some text to it, and send it as you would any other email you write.

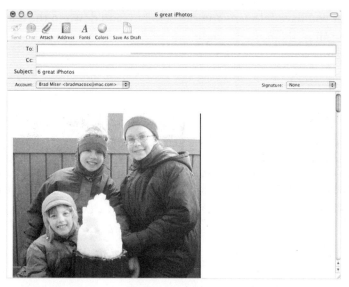

Figure 7.5 *Sending images from iPhoto is simple; all that remains is to address the message and add some text!*

Ordering Prints

While most Mac users have an inkjet printer that is capable of printing fairly nice photos, printing photos can be a bit of a pain, and the results you get aren't always the best. Plus, if you want to share those photos with other people, you have to go through the hassle of mailing them, which might be enough to stop you from sharing them.

To save you the hassle of printing or mailing images, you can order prints from Apple (the prints are actually provided by Kodak). The first time that you order prints, you will use or create an Apple account; after that, you can order prints with a single click by using the appropriately named 1-Click service.

Order Prints of Your Images

1. Select the photos for which you want to order prints (such as by selecting an album).
2. Click the Order Prints button. You will see the Order Prints dialog box (see Figure 7.6). Along the top left side of the dialog box, you will see the

photos that you have selected. You can scroll up and down in the dialog box to view all of them. In the right side of the window, you will see the list of available sizes, prices, and the quantity box.

> **NOTE**
>
> The first time you order prints, you will need to set up or configure your Apple account. This is the same account that you use to purchase music through iTunes or to make purchases at the Apple online store. To set up a new account or configure an existing one, click on the Set Account button in the Order Prints dialog box. Follow the on-screen instructions to configure your account in iPhoto. After you have done that once, you can order prints or a book with a single click.

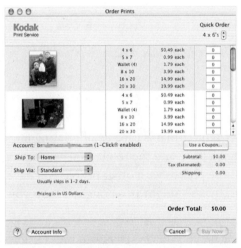

Figure 7.6 *Ordering prints is a great way to share your photos with others.*

3. Enter the quantity of each size of photo that you want to order. The total cost of your order will appear at the bottom of the dialog box.

> **TIP**
>
> You pay a single shipping charge for each order you make. Because of that, you should order groups of images rather than just a picture or two at a time.

4. If you haven't used this service before, open the Ship To pop-up menu, choose Add New Address, and create an address. Add addresses for everyone to whom you will send photos.

5. Choose the address to which you want the current order sent on the Ship To pop-up menu.

6. Choose the shipping method on the Ship Via pop-up menu. Your choices are Standard or Express. Obviously, Express is faster and is also more expensive.

7. When you are ready to order, click the Buy Now button.

8. Follow the on-screen instructions to complete the order. Your photos will be printed and shipped. Apple keeps you notified of the status of your order via email.

In the Order Prints dialog box, you will see the cost of each size of print that you can order. Most of these costs are quite reasonable when compared to the cost of the ink and paper required to print images on an inkjet printer. The shipping costs are also reasonable given that you don't have to do any work to get the order shipped anywhere you'd like. However, because it is so easy to order prints, you might find yourself going overboard the first time or two that you order. So before you hit the Buy Now button, take a moment to double-check what you are ordering.

Low Resolution Images

If images in a group that you select in an album or individually are of low resolution, they will have the low-resolution warning icon placed on them; this icon is a yellow triangle with an exclamation point inside it. An image with this icon might or might not print well in prints or in a book that you order. Be cautious about including low-resolution images in your orders, or you might be disappointed with the results.

Creating, Printing, and Ordering Photo Books

With iPhoto's Book tools, you can create really nice photo books to display your images. You can then print these books yourself or order a professionally printed copy from Apple. Exploring all the details of designing and creating books is beyond the scope of this chapter; however, the following sections will get you started.

Creating a Photo Book

Creating a photo book is a fun and interesting process and gives you a good chance to unleash your creativity.

Create a Photo Book

1. Create a photo album containing the images that you want to include in the photo book.
2. Make the order of those images in the album the same as the order in which you want them to be in the book you are creating (starting from the top left, which will be the first image in the book to the bottom right, which will be the last image in the book). (see Chapter 5 for the steps to create and organize a photo album.)
3. Edit the images in the photo album to make them the best they can be. (see Chapter 6 for the steps to edit images.)
4. Click the Book mode button. The Content pane will include two panes; at the top, you will see the first image in the book, which will be its cover. In the lower part of the pane, you will see thumbnails of each page in the book (see Figure 7.7).
5. Choose a theme for the book on the Theme pop-up menu. The book will be redesigned into the theme you select. For example, if you choose Classic, large images will be placed on the pages in a neat and orderly fashion. Choosing Catalog results in thumbnails of each image.
6. Check the Show Guides check box to mark the borders of text boxes with blues lines.
7. Use the Show check boxes to turn various text on or off. For example, to hide the book's page numbers, uncheck the Page Numbers check box. Not all text appears in all book themes (for example, Titles don't appear in the Story Book theme, but they do in the Year Book theme).
8. Select the first page in the book, which is the cover, by default. You will see a large size version at the top of the pane.

Making the Most of Your Images — Chapter 7

Figure 7.7 *When you move into Book mode, you see the detail for a page in the book in the upper part of the Contents pane and thumbnails of the other pages in the lower part of the pane.*

9. Choose a page design for that page on the Page Design pop-up menu. Typically, you will leave the first page as the Cover page design, but you can change it if you'd like.

10. Edit the text on the page by clicking in the text boxes that appear on the page. When you do, the page view will be magnified so that it is easier to edit. I recommend that you leave the Show Guides check box checked because the guides make the location of text boxes obvious.

11. Choose the next page in the book by clicking its thumbnail image. You will see its preview in the upper part of the pane.

12. Choose a page design from the Page Design pop-up menu. For example, choose the number of images that you want to be displayed on that page. The choices that you have on this menu are determined by the theme of the book.

13. Edit the text that appears on the selected page.

14. To change the order in which images appear on a page or to change the page on which specific images appear, switch to the Organize mode and

change the order of the images in the album from which you are creating a book. The images will be reshuffled in the book to match the order of the images in the album. Depending on the number of pages in the book and the page design you use, it can be a bit tricky to get specific images on a specific page, but with a little trial and error, you can do it.

> **TIP**
>
> When you include multiple images on a page, the orientation of those images can be important. Use the order of the images in the photo album to determine how those images appear on the page. For example, if you have two landscape images and one portrait image, place the two landscape images next to each other so they will appear next to one another on the page while the portrait image appears by itself (see Figure 7.8).

15. Continue working through the rest of the pages until you have selected a page design, ordered the images in the photo album so the right images appear on each page, and added text to each page (see Figure 7.8).

Figure 7.8 *This page has the Classic theme applied and includes three images.*

> **TIP**
>
> As you "finish" pages, check the Lock Page check box. This prevents the images on that page from being changed, even when you move images around in the photo album. You should lock pages as you complete them, but realize that if you lock a later page and then change an earlier one, you can add odd pages to the book. Start locking pages from the front and work toward the back.

Here are some additional comments about creating photo books:

- While I suggested in the previous steps that you add text to the pages in the book as you design them, this was mostly for instructional purposes. A more efficient approach is to design all of the pages first (by choosing the page design for and the images that appear on each page) and then go back and add text. This approach works better because your page design can affect the text that is appropriate for a page. For example, if you use the Story Book theme, changing a page design can change your narrative text for a page. Designing the pages first and then adding text will prevent you from having to make so many text changes later.

- Unfortunately, iPhoto does not allow you to check the spelling of the text you type. You should carefully read all of the text before you print or order a book. An even better idea is to have someone else read your book before you print or order it. You don't want to find out that there is a typo in your book after you have invested the resources to print or order it!

- Books remain with the albums from which they were created. You can't save a book as an entity outside of iPhoto; however, you can save a PDF version of the book (you won't be able to change this version, though, without a PDF editing application, such as Adobe Acrobat). If you change a book that you have created, the previous version is lost. If you want to keep a book, keep the album from which you created it (don't make any changes to the album or you will change the book). If you want to have multiple versions of a book for the same set of images, create a new photo album for each version of the book that you want to keep.

- Books that you order from Apple should include at least 10 pages. If you have fewer than 10 pages in a book that you want to order, add more images or change the theme or page design so that you have at least 10 pages. Otherwise, the book you receive will have blank pages in it—you still have to pay for pages whether they contain images or not.

Previewing a Photo Book

You can use the Preview tool to see your book as it will be printed before you actually print it.

Preview a Photo Book

1. Click Preview. A preview window will appear (see Figure 7.9).

Figure 7.9 *Use the Preview tool to preview your books before you print them.*

> **TIP**
>
> You can resize the Preview window by dragging its Resize handle.

2. Uncheck the Show Guides check box if you don't want to see the text guides on the pages (you should generally leave this check box checked).
3. Click the page forward and page backward arrows at the top of the window to preview each page in the book.

> **TIP**
>
> You can jump directly to a page by typing its number in the page number box and pressing the Return key.

4. Make a note of any problems you see, such as wrong photos appearing on a page, typos, and so on.
5. Close the Preview window when you are done previewing the book.
6. Fix any problems you found in Step 4 by using the steps in the previous section.
7. Continue previewing and fixing the book until it as good as you can make it.

Printing a Photo Book

After you have created a book, you can print it yourself. You can do this to produce a book that you want to keep, or you might want to print it before you order it to make sure it is "right" before you spend money to find out that it isn't (right, that is).

Print a Book

1. While you are in the Book mode and the book you want to print is displayed, choose File, Print or press ⌘+P. The Print dialog box will appear (see Figure 7.10).

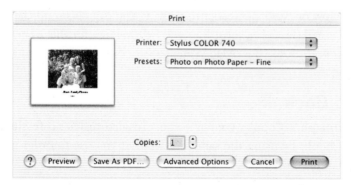

Figure 7.10 *Printing a book is a must before you order it.*

2. Choose the printer you want to use on the Printer pop-up menu.
3. Choose the presets on the Presets pop-up menu.
4. To perform other configurations, click the Advanced Options button and use the resulting dialog box to configure the print job.

> **TIP**
>
> If you are printing the book to proof it, use the Draft black-and-white mode on your printer and use plain paper the first time you print the book. This process will minimize the amount of ink or toner and the paper expense for the proof copy. After the book is right, you can print it with high-quality settings and paper if you want to.

5. Click on the Print button. The book will be printed.

While you can't save a book outside of iPhoto so that you can edit it, you can create a PDF of your book.

Create a PDF Version of a Photo Book

1. Configure the book for which you want to create a PDF.
2. Open the Print dialog box.
3. Click on the Save As PDF button. You will see the Save to File dialog box.
4. Name the book file, choose a save location, and click the Save button. The book will be saved as a PDF file in the location you selected.

After you have created a PDF version of a book, you can use a PDF reader application, such as Preview or Acrobat Reader to view it. You can also send the book to other people via email (however, most files will be too large for this to be practical) or post the book PDF to your .Mac Web site.

Ordering a Photo Book

While you can print photo books yourself, you can also order professionally printed and bound books by using the same service that you use to order prints. The process is also quite similar.

Making the Most of Your Images Chapter 7 **187**

> **TIP**
>
> Before you order a copy of the book from Apple, print it yourself first (even if you only have a black-and-white printer). Books are expensive to order, and you should use your printed copy to make sure that the book you create is worth the cost and that it doesn't have any mistakes.

Order a Professionally Printed and Bound Photo Book

1. Build the book (see the section called "Creating a Photo Book," earlier in this chapter, for details).
2. Print your book and check it. Use the draft or black-and-white mode of your printer to make the process faster and less expensive.

> **NOTE**
>
> The first time you order a book, you will need to set up or configure your Apple account. This is the same account that you use to purchase music through iTunes or to make purchases at the Apple online store. To set up a new account or configure an existing one, click on the Set Account button in the Order Prints dialog box. Follow the on-screen instructions to configure your account in iPhoto. After you have done that once, you can order a book with a single click.

3. When you are *sure* that your book is right, click the Order Book (you must be in the Organize mode to see this button). Your book will be assembled. Depending on the number of images and pages in your book, this process can take a few minutes. If your book contains low-resolution images, fewer than 10 pages, or some other problems, you will be warned. (You can choose to continue without fixing the problems, or you can stop the process and fix the problems before continuing.) When the process is complete,

> **NOTE**
>
> The cover of a book is actually page 1; iPhoto numbers the second page as 1. This can be confusing when you order a book because you will see one less page number than there are actual pages in the book. For example, if a book has 19 numbered pages, there are actually 20 pages in the book (because the cover counts as one page).

Figure 7.11 *The Order Book dialog box enables you to choose a cover and order your book.*

you will see the Order Book dialog box (see Figure 7.11). This dialog box is very similar to the Order Prints dialog box and works in the same way.

4. Select a cover for your book on the Cover Color pop-up menu.
5. Choose the number of books you want to print via the Quantity tool.
6. Use the Ship To and Ship Via pop-up menus to enter the shipping information.
7. When you are ready to order, click the Buy Now button and follow the on-screen instructions. In a few days, the book will be delivered to the address you selected.

Be aware that ordering books is a relatively expensive proposition. The first 10 pages cost $29.99, additional pages are $3 per page. Shipping for a book is also relatively expensive at $7.99. You also must pay sales tax if applicable. Take plenty of time to design and check your book before you order it unless you don't mind $40 "experiments."

Building a Photo HomePage

You can use iPhoto to create a HomePage Web site through an Apple .Mac account.

> **NOTE**
>
> Before you can post images to a .Mac Web site, you need to have created a .Mac account.

Post Images to Your .Mac Web Site

1. Select the images that you want to place on the Web (such as selecting a photo album on the Source pane).
2. Click the HomePage button in the Tool pane. You will see the Publish HomePage dialog box (see Figure 7.12).

Figure 7.12 *Using iPhoto's HomePage button, you can create a Web page for your photos in mere seconds.*

3. Select the title text at the top of the page and edit it. By default, the Web page's title will be the name of the photo album, but you can change it to be anything you'd like.
4. Select the page text just below the title text and edit it. For example, you can include a few sentences to explain the images you are posting on the site.
5. Select the title of the first image on the page and edit it, if necessary. By default, images are titled with the title they have within iPhoto. You can change this text as you desire (changing the titles on the Web page does not change the titles within iPhoto).

6. Repeat Step 5 for each image on the page.

> **TIP**
>
> You can use the dialog box Scroll tools to see all of the images on the page.

7. Click a frame style to apply that frame to all of the images on the page.
8. Choose the .Mac account to which you want to publish the page on the Publish to pop-up menu.
9. Choose the number of columns of images you want to include on the page by clicking the 2 Columns or 3 Columns radio button.
10. Check the "Send Me a Message" check box to include a link to your email address on the Web page. A visitor can click this link to send you an email message.
11. Check the Counter check box if you want the page to include a counter that counts the number of visitors to the Web page.
12. Click Publish. iPhoto will connect to the Internet and transfer your photos to your .Mac account. When the process is complete, you will see a completion dialog box that provides the URL to the page that you just created.
13. Click the Visit Page Now button and enjoy (see Figure 7.13).

> **TIP**
>
> When you publish your photos via HomePage, make sure that you have meaningful titles for your images. Otherwise, you get titles like those shown in Figure 7.13—probably not what you want!

On the Web page you create with the HomePage tool, you can click an image or click on the Start Slideshow link to display the images in a slideshow. In the resulting slideshow, you can click on images to see larger versions in separate Web browser windows.

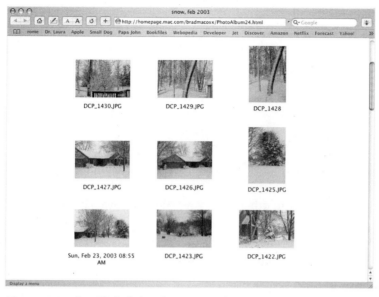

Figure 7.13 *I published these images on a Web page in about one minute.*

Creating .Mac Slides

You can present a set of images as a .Mac slideshow—this enables other people to use your slideshow as their screen saver.

To make a slideshow available, you publish it to your iDisk.

> **NOTE**
>
> Before you can post images as .Mac slides, you need to have created a .Mac account.

Publish a Set of .Mac Slides

1. Select the images that you want to publish (such as selecting a photo album on the Source pane).
2. Click the .Mac Slides button in the Tool pane. You will see a warning dialog box asking if you are sure you want to publish a set of .Mac slides.
3. Click on the Publish button. You will see a progress window that shows each image as it is uploaded. When the process is complete, you will see the confirmation dialog box (see Figure 7.14).

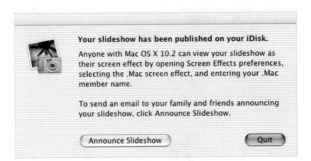

Figure 7.14 *When you see this dialog box, your .Mac slides are online.*

4. If you want to inform others that your slides are available, click on the Announce Slideshow button, and you'll see an email message that contains information about how the slides can be accessed. If not, click on the Quit button and skip the next step.

5. Address the email message and send it.

Anyone who uses Mac OS X version 10.2 or later will be able to use your slides as their screen saver by subscribing to it. As you make changes to the slides by republishing them, the changes you make will be made for everyone who has subscribed to the slideshow automatically.

Adding Images to the Desktop and as a Screen Saver

You can easily add images in your iPhoto Library to your desktop. The images you add are used both as the desktop image and as the screen saver.

> **TIP**
>
> You can optimize images for your desktop by cropping them using the Desktop option on the Constrain pop-up menu.

Adding iPhoto Images to the Desktop and as a Screen Saver

1. Select the images you want to use on the desktop, such as by selecting a photo album on the Source pane, and click the Desktop button. You will see the Screen Effects dialog box (see Figure 7.15). The image source that you selected will be shown on the pop-up menu.

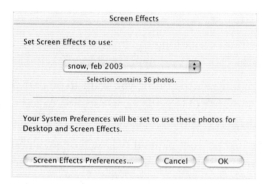

Figure 7.15 *You use this dialog box to configure the images you apply to your desktop.*

2. If you don't want to use the image source shown on the pop-up menu, open it and choose a different source. On this menu, you will see each photo album you have created along with the All Albums choice that takes photos from all of your photo albums. (You can't select your Photo Library.)
3. Click on the Screen Effects Preferences button.
4. Use the Screen Effects pane to configure your screen saver.
5. Move back into iPhoto and click on the OK button to close the Screen Effects dialog box.

> **NOTE**
>
> If you use multiple monitors, the images you select are applied to your main monitor only.

Your desktop will be filled with an image from the group you selected and will rotate among these images according to the settings in the Desktop pane of the System Preferences application. When your screen saver activates, it will use images from the same source.

Putting Images on DVD

From within iPhoto, you can move a set of images to iDVD to create a slideshow on DVD that you can view on a computer or in a standard DVD player connected to a TV. To do so, you use the following steps.

Putting iPhoto Images on DVD

1. Create and select a photo album containing the images that you want to put as a slideshow on a DVD.
2. Use the slideshow tools to configure the music you want to be part of the slideshow when you place it on DVD (see the earlier section called "Viewing Slideshows" for help doing this).
3. Click on the iDVD button on the Tool pane. iDVD will open, a new iDVD project will be created, and the images in the source you selected in Step 1 will be added to the new iDVD project. The project's main menu will have a default design and will contain a link to the slideshow you have added. The name of this link will be the name of the photo album you selected in Step 1 (see Figure 7.16).

Figure 7.16 *The slideshow called "Snow, Feb 2003" was imported into iDVD when I selected that photo album and clicked the iDVD button.*

4. Use iDVD's tools to configure the slideshow, add more content to the DVD, and to design its menus. See Part IV of this book for detailed information about using iDVD.

> **NOTE**
>
> It is just as easy to select an iPhoto photo album from within iDVD as it is to use the iDVD button from within iPhoto. Because you will likely want to add more than one slideshow to a DVD, I recommend that you start a DVD from within iDVD and use its tools to add content rather than starting from within iPhoto.

Putting Images on CD

Putting images on an iPhoto CD is a great way to share them with someone else who uses iPhoto, especially if that person doesn't have a broadband connection to the Internet and can't receive images over email very well. You can also archive or back up your photos on a CD. When you burn a photo album on a CD, iPhoto re-creates the files on the CD just as it stores them on a hard disk.

Put Images on a CD

1. Select the images that you want to put on a CD, such as selecting a photo album to put its images on a disc.

> **TIP**
>
> You can select multiple photo albums to burn them to a CD at the same time.

2. Click on the Burn button. It will become active (it fills with a colored radioactive symbol). You will be prompted to insert a blank disc.
3. Do so and click OK. The Burn button will begin to pulse, indicating that you are ready to burn the disc.
4. Click the Burn button again. The Burn Disc dialog box will appear. In this dialog box, you will see the number of albums and photos you have selected to burn (see Figure 7.17).

Figure 7.17 *When you see this dialog box, you are ready to burn images to a CD.*

5. Click on the Burn button. A progress window will appear, and you can use it to monitor the process. When the CD has been burned and verified, the progress window will disappear, the disc will be ejected, and you will hear the disc complete tone.
6. Insert the CD in your Mac. iPhoto will open if it isn't already open, and the CD you burned will appear in the Source pane.
7. Select the CD as the source, and you will see the photos it contains (see Figure 7.18).

> **TIP**
>
> You can click the Expansion triangle next to the CD icon to expand it. When you do, you will see all of the photo albums it contains.

If you provide the disc you burned to someone who uses iPhoto, they can mount the disc and access the photos it contains from the iPhoto Source pane. For example, they can drag the images from the CD onto their Photo Library to import them into their own Photo Library. The files can also be accessed directly from the Finder by opening the CD in a Finder window if the recipient doesn't have or use iPhoto. (Be aware that the somewhat confusing naming and hierarchy structure that iPhoto uses to store images makes this process somewhat cumbersome. If the recipient doesn't use iPhoto, consider exporting the images as a Web site, which you will learn how to do in the next section).

Making the Most of Your Images — Chapter 7

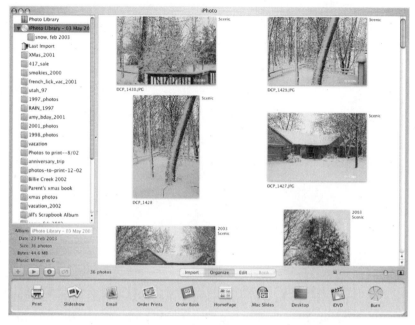

Figure 7.18 *These images were burned to the CD from within iPhoto.*

Exporting Images Outside of iPhoto

There are a number of ways that you can export images from iPhoto for different purposes. You can export images as separate files so that you can work with them in other applications. Or you can export a set of images as a Web site. Another option is to export a set of images as a QuickTime movie.

Exporting Photos as Separate Files

If you want to use iPhoto photos in other applications, you need to export those images as individual files.

Export iPhoto Images as Individual Files

1. Select the images that you want to export as files, such as by selecting a photo album.
2. Choose File, Export or press Shift+⌘+E. You will see the Export Photos dialog box (see Figure 7.19).
3. Click the File Export tab if it isn't already selected.

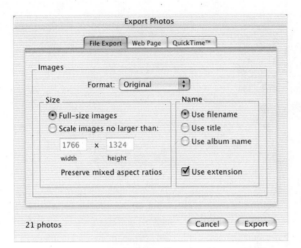

Figure 7.19 *The three export options you have appear as tabs in the Export Photos dialog box.*

4. Choose the format in which you want the files exported on the Format pop-up menu. Your choices are Original (which exports the files in the same format in which they were imported), JPG, TIFF, or PNG. The option you choose should depend on how you are going to use the images. In most cases, Original is probably the best choice.

5. Click the "Full-size images" radio button to export the files at their current resolution or click the "Scale images no larger than" radio button and enter the resolution with which you want the image files to be exported. Using the "Full-size images" option results in the maximum quality, but also in the largest file size. If you want to decrease the file size, you can enter the maximum resolution in the two boxes. If you have images that are less then the resolution you enter, they won't be scaled.

NOTE

The first image's original resolution is shown in the boxes under "Scale images no larger than" radio button.

6. Choose the name option for the files by clicking one of the Name radio buttons. The "Use file name" option causes iPhoto to use the file name it created when you imported the images as the exported file's file names.

The "Use title" option causes the images' titles to be used as the file names. The "Use album name" causes the album name and a sequential number to be used as the file name.

7. If you want the appropriate file name extension to be included in the file name, check the "Use extension" check box. You should usually use this option so other applications can more easily recognize the format of the files you export.

8. Click Export. You will see the Export sheet.

9. Move to the location in which you want to store the image files and click OK. The images will be exported to the location you selected (see Figure 7.20).

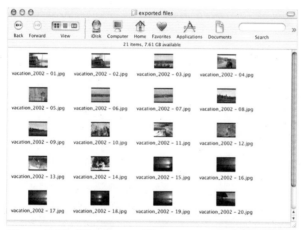

Figure 7.20 *These image files were exported from iPhoto and can be used just like any other image files.*

Exporting Images as a Web Site

Earlier, you saw how easy it is to create a Web site containing photos via .Mac HomePage. It is also quite easy to create a separate Web site for your photos so that you can view them on your hard drive, publish the site on a local network, or publish it to a Web site you host with a Web hosting service other than .Mac.

Export Images as a Web Site

1. Select the images that you want to include in the Web site, for example, by selecting an album.

2. Choose File, Export or press Shift+⌘+E. You will see the Export Photos dialog box.

3. Click the Web Page tab of the Export Photos dialog box (see Figure 7.21).

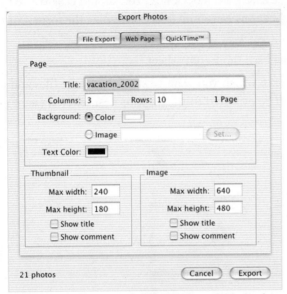

Figure 7.21 *You can export images as a Web site for various purposes, such as to post on a local network.*

4. Enter the title of the page you are creating in the Title box. By default, this is the name of the photo album that you selected in Step 1.

5. Choose the number of rows and columns in which you want the images to be displayed on the Web page.

6. Use the Color radio button and bar to set the page background to a color (it is white by default) or the Image radio button and Set button to choose an image as a background for the page.

7. Use the Thumbnail Max width and Max height boxes to set the maximum size of the thumbnails of each image.

8. If you want the titles displayed next to the thumbnails on the Web page, check the "Show title" check box in the Thumbnail section.

9. If you want the comments displayed next to the thumbnails on the Web page, check the "Show comment" check box in the Thumbnail section.

10. Use the Image boxes to set the maximum size of the images the viewer will see when she clicks on the thumbnails.
11. If you want the titles displayed next to the images on the Web page, check the "Show title" check box in the Image section.
12. If you want the comments displayed next to the images on the Web page, check the "Show comment" check box in the Image section.
13. Click Export. You will see the Export sheet.
14. Select a location where you want to save the Web site and click OK. The Web page will be created in the location you specified. You can monitor the process with the Exporting progress window that appears while the export is occurring.
15. Open the folder you selected in Step 14 and open the *foldername*.html file, where *foldername* is the name of the folder you selected in Step 14. You will see the page in a Web browser (see Figure 7.22). You can view individual images by clicking their thumbnails. The image will be displayed in a new Web browser window, and navigation links will appear to enable you to view all of the images on the Web page.

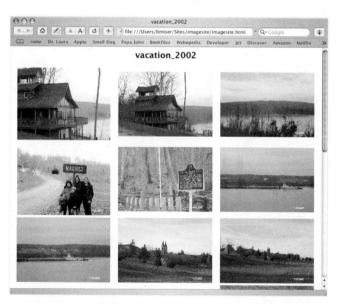

Figure 7.22 *This Web page took all of one minute to create.*

You can use the iPhoto Web sites you export as stand-alone sites, or you can add them to other Web sites you have created.

Exporting Images as a QuickTime Movie

You can also export images as a QuickTime movie, which creates a stand-alone version of a slideshow that you can view and use in a number of ways.

PART III

iMovie: The Swiss Army Knife of Digital Video Software

- 8 **Touring Your iMovie Movie Studio**
- 9 **Building a Movie in iMovie**
- 10 **Building a Better Video Track in iMovie**
- 11 **Building a Soundtrack That Rocks**
- 12 **Producing Your Movies**

Chapter 8

Touring Your iMovie Movie Studio

With due respect to the other "i" applications, iMovie is the application that ignited the iLife revolution, and it remains the most powerful of them all. iMovie was, and is, revolutionary. Before iMovie, editing video was a task that only people who were either professionals or had lots and lots of time on their hands could do. Video editing applications were complex, and their tools were difficult to learn and use. iMovie changed all that.

iMovie blends power and ease-of-use in a truly remarkable way. With a DV camcorder and a few minutes of time, you can create amazingly sophisticated movies that include titles, transitions, special effects, multiple soundtracks, and much more. And with the range of tools that it provides, iMovie is the heart of the digital lifestyle. You can use it to work with content from other applications, whether you intended to use that media in a movie project or not. For example, you can use iMovie to create sound effects for your desktop. Or you can use it to make soundtracks for slideshows that you create in iPhoto. There is no limit to what you can do with iMovie and a bit of imagination.

What's more, using iMovie is just plain fun. Here's just a sampling of what you can do:

- Import video clips from a digital camcorder
- Edit those clips
- Apply special effects to clips, such as the Sepia Tone effect that makes everything look old
- Build a movie from the clips you have imported and edited
- Add amazing transitions such as wipes and warps
- Insert titles to give yourself or someone else the appropriate credit
- Add iPhoto pictures to a movie
- Build amazing soundtracks that include music, sound effects, and narration
- Export your movies to DVD, QuickTime, and videotape

> **NOTE**
>
> This part of the book was written to version 3.0.3 of iMovie.

Working in the iMovie Window

Unlike other video editing tools, you can be up and creating movies in just a few minutes. However, just because you can get started quickly, that doesn't mean iMovie is a basic tool; it empowers you to do many amazing things with your projects. It's just that the iMovie interface is so well designed that you don't have to spend hours learning how it works.

iMovie provides an amazing array of tools for you to use. Even better, these tools use a consistent interface so that once you are versed in iMovie, its tools will quickly become second nature to you.

The iMovie Window

The iMovie window contains five main areas, only four of which you can see at the same time (see Figure 8.1).

In the upper-left corner of the window is the Monitor. Here, you preview and edit your movie, as well as the clips from which you build that movie. In the upper-right, you will see the iMovie Tool pane. At the bottom of the pane, you will see seven buttons, with each button opening a palette of tools in the pane. Just under the Monitor, you will see the controls area that includes various buttons that you use to control playback and editing functions. Underneath that area, you will see the two viewers, the Clip Viewer and the Timeline Viewer (you can only see one viewer at a time). In the bottom-right corner of the window are the disk space tools that you use to manage the disk space associated with your project.

iMovie Modes

iMovie has two basic modes in which you operate: Camera or Edit. The mode you are in is determined by the position of the Camera/Edit mode switch that is located in the Controls area (see Figure 8.1). When the switch is to the left (toward the camera icon), iMovie is in the Camera mode. In this mode, you work

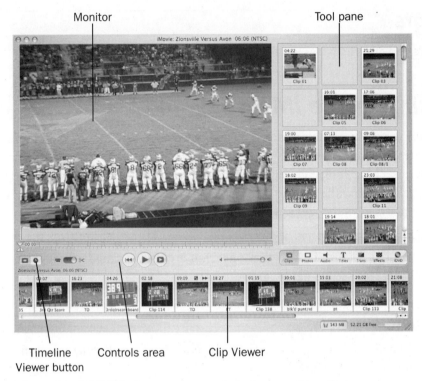

Figure 8.1 *With iMovie, you can create just about anything that you can conceive.*

with a DV camera that is attached to your Mac to import video clips from which you will build your movie. When the switch is to the right and iMovie is in the Edit mode (the scissors icon), you work with video clips to preview them, edit them, and so on. You will spend most of your iMovie time in the Edit mode.

> **NOTE**
>
> You seldom actually have to move the Camera/Edit mode switch. When iMovie detects that a camera is connected to your Mac, it selects the Camera mode automatically. When you select a video clip to work with it, iMovie switches to the Edit mode automatically.

The Monitor

The Monitor serves two purposes. One is to enable you to view clips and your movie as you edit them by removing frames, pasting frames, splitting clips, and so on. The other is to enable you to view and import content on a digital camcorder. The controls that you see in the Monitor depend on the mode in which iMovie is operating.

The Monitor in Edit Mode

Since you will spend most of your time in the Edit mode, take a few moments to learn about the Monitor's controls when iMovie is in this mode (see Figure 8.2). Table 8.1 explains the elements of the Monitor window that you need to understand.

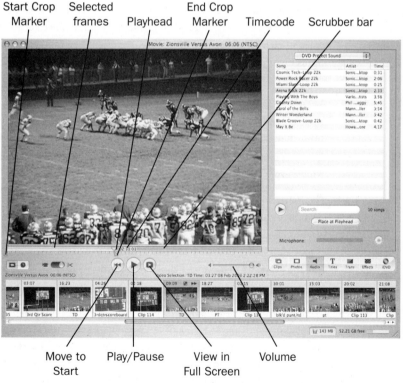

Figure 8.2 *When you are in the Edit mode, the Monitor contains controls you use to edit your clips.*

Table 8.1 Features of the Monitor in Edit Mode

Element	Purpose
Scrubber bar	The Scrubber bar is a visual representation of the timeline for a clip, a group of clips, or your movie (depending on what you have selected).
Timecode	The precise location of the Playhead is shown by the timecode that "floats" next to the Playhead. As its name implies, the timecode provides information about the time aspects of a clip or movie. Timecodes appear in the following format:
Minutes:Seconds:Frames	If a clip or movie is less than a minute, you will see only two sets of numbers: Seconds and Frames.
	The Frames part of the timecode is a counter that measures the number of frames in a single second of the clip. Most clips that you capture with a camcorder have 30 frames per second, which results in smooth on-screen motion. Within each second of the clip, the frames are numbered from 00 to 29 (for a total of 30 frames). The Frames part of the timecode tells you where in each second of the clip you are. For example, a timecode of 36:21 means that the clip is 36 seconds long and has gone 21 frames into the 37th second (so it is actually almost 37 seconds long).
	As you start editing, the timecode becomes very useful, especially when you are able to interpret it immediately. The first few times it can be a bit confusing, but just keep remembering that the last number in the timecode is the frame number; timecodes will become second nature to you as you gain iMovie experience.
Playhead	The Playhead is a pointer on the Scrubber bar that shows you the relative location of the frame that currently appears in the Monitor. You use the Playhead to determine where you "are" in a clip or in your movie. As a clip or movie plays, the Playhead moves across the Scrubber bar. You can also drag the Playhead to move in a clip or in your movie.
Start Crop Marker Stop Crop Marker	As with most Mac applications, you select the material that you want to change in some way (in this case, frames of a video clip) and then perform some action on them, such as cutting them out of a clip. You use the crop markers to select the frames with which you want to work. The Start Crop Marker indicates the first frame that you select, while the Stop Crop Marker indicates the last frame in the selection.

Table 8.1 Features of the Monitor in Edit Mode (continued)

Element	Purpose
Selected frames	The selected frames are indicated by the gold highlighting between the two markers. The action you select will be performed on these frames. For example, if you choose Cut, the selected frames will be removed from the clip or movie.
Move to Start	Clicking this moves you to the start of your movie and unselects any selected clips.
Play/Pause	Click Play to watch and hear selected clips. Click Play again to pause the action. You can also start and stop play by pressing the Spacebar.
View in Full Screen	Plays the selected clips in full-screen mode in which you only see the clips; the iMovie interface disappears.
Volume	This slider adjusts the playback volume. Note that this only affects the current volume of the clip or movie and in no way changes the clip or the movie itself.

> **NOTE**
>
> By the way, movies produced by Hollywood studios use a frame rate of 24 fps, which is slightly lower than the rate used by camcorders for television productions.

One of the most important iMovie skills you need is the ability to move around in a clip quickly and precisely in order to preview and edit clips. The following are the most important ways to move around:

◆ Click on the Playhead and drag it to the right to move forward in the clip (or to the left to move backward in the clip). When you release the mouse button, the Playhead is at the exact position that you left it. The current frame will be shown in the Monitor, and you can see the exact position at which the Playhead is located by the timecode displayed next to it. Use this method for large but quick movements in the clip, such as moving from the beginning to the middle.

- You can move the Playhead much more precisely by using the keyboard; this is essential when you get to detailed editing because you can move by increments as small as a single frame. To move the Playhead one frame at a time, use the Left and Right arrow keys. As you can probably guess, the Right arrow key moves the Playhead forward one frame, and the Left arrow key moves you backward one frame. Use this method to position the Playhead very precisely.

- You can move the Playhead forward or backward 10 frames at a time by holding the Shift key down while you press the Left or Right arrow keys. This movement technique is also very useful when you are doing detailed editing because it enables you to move quickly to a precise location in the clip, but you get there a bit faster than by moving one frame at a time.

The Monitor in Camera Mode

When iMovie is in the Camera mode, the features of the Monitor are less complex because importing clips is a relatively simple task (see Figure 8.3 and Table 8.2). The cool thing about using an iMovie-compatible camera is that iMovie's controls actually control the camera itself so that you can do everything you need from within iMovie.

Table 8.2 Features of the Monitor in Camera Mode

Element	Purpose
Camera status information	When a camera is connected to your Mac, you see information about its status. For example, when you rewind the camera, you see the message "Camera Rewinding." This information helps you control your camera from within iMovie more easily. (In Figure 8.3, you see the output of the camcorder from which a clip is being imported. The camera status information appears when the camcorder is not playing.)
Rewind/Review	When the DV camcorder is not playing, the Rewind button rewinds the tape at top speed. When the tape is playing, it plays the tape backward. In the Review mode, you have to "hold" the button down to keep the review going (in other words, if you let up on the button, it goes back into Play mode).
Import	Clicking the Import button starts or stops the import process. When you click this button, iMovie plays the DV camera and begins importing video clips.
Pause	Puts the camera in Pause mode.

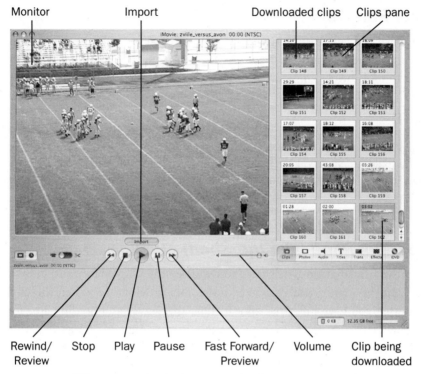

Figure 8.3 *When you are in the Camera mode, the Monitor contains the controls you use to control your DV camera and to import clips from it.*

Table 8.2 Features of the Monitor in Camera Mode (continued)

Element	Purpose
Play	Plays the camera.
Stop	Stops the camera.
Fast Forward/ Preview	When the tape is not playing, the Fast Forward button moves the tape forward at top speed. When the tape is playing, it plays the tape forward at a high speed.
Volume	Drag the slider to the right to increase the volume and to the left to decrease it. Note that this affects only the playback volume and doesn't actually change the movie at all.
Clips pane	This area contains the clips that you have downloaded from the camera. As you import clips, each clip is placed in a "slot" on the palette. The clip that you are currently importing is highlighted in blue.

The Tools Palette

The iMovie Tools Palette contains the tools that you use to build a movie from the clips, images, and sounds that you import into your iMovie project. You select a palette of tools by clicking one of the buttons along the bottom of the palette.

> **NOTE**
>
> One of the nice things about iMovie is that although it provides lots of tools on the various palettes, they work similarly. After you have learned to use a couple of them, you can use the others quite easily because they use a consistent framework (even more evidence of the elegance of iMovie's design).

The Clips Pane (aka the Shelf)

When the Clips button is selected, you will see the Clips pane (also know as the Shelf). In this mode, the Palette contains lots of "slots" in which the clips and images that you have imported appear. This area serves as a holding area for your clips; they remain here until you place them in your movie (see Figure 8.4). Along the right side of the Shelf, you will see the scroll bar that you use to move up and down the Shelf to locate clips you want to use.

Figure 8.4 *The Shelf lives up to its name; as you build a movie, you grab the clips and images stored on the Shelf.*

The Photos Palette

When you click the Photos button, you will see the Photos palette (see Figure 8.5). This palette enables you to access the images stored in your iPhoto Photo Library so that you can use those images in an iMovie project. See Table 8.3

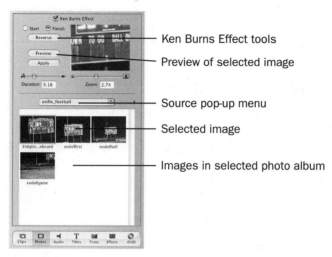

Figure 8.5 *The Photos palette enables you to use the images you have stored in iPhoto in your iMovie projects.*

Table 8.3 Features of the Photos Palette

Element	Purpose
Ken Burns Effect tools	These tools enable you to apply a zooming and motion effect to photos to make them more visually interesting. You can use the controls to configure and apply the effect to an image. When that image appears in a movie, the effect will be seen.
Preview of selected image	When you select an image in your iPhoto Photo Library, you will see a preview of the image. As you apply the Ken Burns Effect to the image, you will see the results in this preview. (You can also preview the image in the Monitor.)
Source pop-up menu	This pop-up menu enables you to choose any photo album in your iPhoto Photo Library. (You can also choose Photo Library to view all of your images.) When you select a photo album, thumbnails of the images contained in that source are shown in the lower part of the palette.

Table 8.3 Features of the Photos Palette (continued)

Element	Purpose
Selected image	When you want to work with an image, you select it. It becomes highlighted to show you that it is the current image.
Images in selected photo album	When you select a photo album as the image source, you see thumbnails of each image in the lower section of the palette.

The Audio Palette

Ah, what would a movie be without sound? A silent movie, of course. The Audio palette provides tools you can use to add music, sound effects, and recorded sound to your movie (see Figure 8.6). Table 8.4 provides an overview of the tools on the Audio palette.

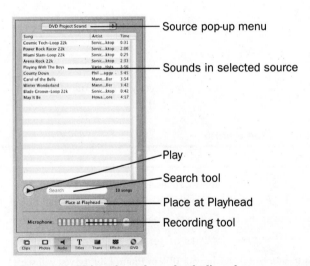

Figure 8.6 *Using the tools on the Audio palette, you can make your movie sing, laugh, cry, bark, or make just about any other noises that you desire.*

Table 8.4 Features of the Audio Palette

Element	Purpose
Source pop-up menu	This pop-up menu enables you to choose the source of sound you want to use. There are three fundamental options: iTunes Library, which lets you access the music and sounds you have stored in iTunes (you can choose a playlist to work with the songs it contains); iMovie Sound Effects, which enables you to add sound effects to a movie; and Audio CD, which enables you to record audio from a CD.
Sounds in selected source	When you select a source on the Source pop-up menu, the sounds contained in that source are listed in the center part of the palette. For example, when you select a playlist, the songs in that playlist are shown. You can select a sound (such as a song or sound effect) to work with it.
Play	Click this button to hear a sound that you have selected.
Search tool	Use this tool to search for sounds. As you type text in the Search box, the list of sounds is reduced to include only those items that contain the text you type.
Place at Playhead	When you select a sound and click this button, that sound is inserted at the location of the Playhead.
Recording tool	You can use this tool to record sound, such as from a microphone that is connected to your Mac. An obvious use of this tool is to add narration to a project. However, you can also connect other devices, such as a tape recorder, to record sound from that source.

The Titles Palette

The Titles tools enable you to add all sorts of text to your movies. Although adding on-screen text is called *titling*, this term refers to much more than just the movie's name. Basically, titling is iMovie's term for overlaying all sorts of text on the screen. The titles that you might want to use in your movies include the following:

- ◆ **Captions**. You can use "clip captions" to add information to the images that are appearing on the screen. You might want to add some explanation of what is happening onscreen, the date on which the clip was captured, or you can even add subtitles if you want to.

♦ **Credits.** I'm sure that you are quite familiar with credits, because most modern movies have several minutes of credits at the end. Credits are just what the term implies: the opportunity to take, or give, credit for something in the movie.

♦ **Titles.** Titles are introductory text that can introduce a movie, a scene, or anything else you think warrants an introduction. Titles normally appear at the beginning of something, whether it be a movie or a clip.

To work with titles, you click the Titles button to reveal the Titles palette (see Figure 8.7). The elements of the Titles palette are explained in Table 8.5.

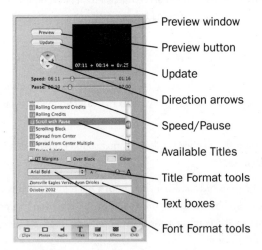

Figure 8.7 *The Titles tools enable you to add many types of text to your movies.*

Table 8.5 iMovie's Titles Tools

Tool	What It Does
Preview window	When you click a title style, you see a preview of that title in the Preview window.
Preview button	When you click this button, you see a preview of the selected title in the Monitor.
Update	If you make changes to a title that you have already placed in your movie, click this button to update the title to include the changes that you have made.
Direction arrows	Some titles let you set the motion of the title. You choose a direction for that motion by clicking one of the direction arrows.

Table 8.5 iMovie's Titles Tools (continued)

Tool	What It Does
Speed/Pause sliders	All titles have a set amount of time that it takes for the title effect to occur. You use the Speed slider to set this time. Drag it to the left to make the title faster or to the right to make it slower.
	If there is a pause element in a title's motion, you use the Pause slider to control how long that pause lasts. Drag the slider to the right to make the pause last longer or to the left to make it a shorter pause.
Available Titles	This list shows the titles that are available to you.
Title Format tools	These tools enable you to set the general format of the title.
	A QuickTime movie has different proportions than a standard TV screen. For title styles that appear on the bottom edge of the screen, this can be a problem because those titles can get cut off when the movie is viewed on a TV. Unchecking the QT Margins check box moves the title up on the screen so that it won't be cut off when you show the movie on a TV. Checking it moves the title back down again so that it appears in a better location on the screen when viewing the movie in QuickTime Player.
	If you prefer the title to appear over a black background instead of appearing on a clip, you can check the Over Black check box. Instead of being applied to a clip in your movie, the title appears in a new black clip that is added to your movie wherever you drop the title.
	You can use the Color button to change the color of the text in the title (it also affects the stripe color in Stripe Subtitle).
Font Format tools	You use these tools to format the text in the title.
	The Font Family pop-up menu enables you to choose a font family for a title.
	The Font Size slider enables you to make the selected font larger (drag it to the right) or smaller (drag it to the left).
Text Boxes	You type the text for a title in the text blocks that appear on the palette. You see two or more styles of text box, depending on the title you use. Most styles use single lines of text. Others use a larger text block into which you can place a fair amount of text.
Add/Remove Text Boxes	Some titles can contain multiple text blocks. When you select one of these, the Add (+) and Remove (-) text blocks buttons will appear. Click the Add button to add text blocks to your title. Click Remove to remove text blocks.

The tools and options that you see on the Titles palette depend on the title style that you use. Some styles (for example, Centered Multiple) allow you to add more lines or blocks of text. With these styles, the Add button is active. Other styles (for example, Scrolling Block) involve motion for which you can set the direction; the Direction Arrows are active for these types.

The Transitions Palette

The segment between two clips in a movie is called the *transition*. You can use different transitions to smooth the flow from one clip into the next so that your series of individual clips doesn't look like a series of clips, but rather a movie that flows smoothly from one scene to the next. All movies use transitions of one sort or another.

The three most common types of transitions are the *Straight Cut, Cross Dissolve,* and *Fade To* or *From Black*. The Straight Cut isn't a transition that you have to apply; this is what happens if you don't add a transition between two clips. A Straight Cut transition occurs when one scene runs right into the next one. As long as the adjacent scenes are similar enough, the Straight Cut seems very natural, and you don't even notice it. The Cross Dissolve is also very common; in this transition, one scene dissolves into the next. This transition can be useful when the adjacent scenes are somewhat similar, but different enough that a straight cut is a bit jarring. The Fade To or From Black are two of the more useful transitions. With the fade, a clip fades to black or fades in from a black screen.

You can apply these and other transitions to a movie by using the tools on the Transitions palette that appear when you click the Trans button (see Figure 8.8). An overview of the Transition tools is provided in Table 8.6.

Table 8.6 iMovie's Transitions Tools

Tool	What It Does
Preview window	When you select a transition on the list of available transitions, a preview of that transition will play in the Preview window. You can use this to get a quick idea of what the transition looks like. You will see the transition applied to the clip that you have selected; if you don't have a clip selected, you will see that transition applied to the first clip in your movie.

Table 8.6 iMovie's Transitions Tools (continued)

Tool	What It Does
Preview button	When you click the Preview button, you will see a preview of the selected transition in the Monitor. This makes the effect of the transition easier to see because it appears much larger, but it also takes longer to preview.
Update	You use this button to change a transition that has been placed in a movie. You select the transition clip, use the Transitions tools to make changes to it, and then click the Update button to apply those changes to the transition clip in the movie.
Direction arrows	When a transition has a directional component, such as a push effect, you use the direction arrows to set the direction of the transition. For example, when you use the Push transition (where one clip "pushes" the previous one off the screen), you click the arrow for the direction in which you want the push to occur.
Speed	You use this slider to control the amount of time over which the transition effect is displayed. Moving the slider to the left makes the transition last a shorter amount of time. Moving it to the right stretches the transition out so that it takes longer to play. After you release the slider, you immediately see the transition in the Preview window.
Available Transitions	This list shows the transition effects that are currently available to you. To work with a transition, you select it on the list.

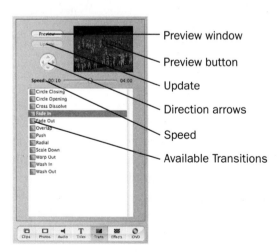

Figure 8.8 *The Transitions tools enable you to smooth the digital flow of your movies.*

> **On Rendering**
>
> Titles and transitions are sophisticated effects, and they require your Mac to do a lot of work to apply them to a clip. The process of applying a transition or title to a clip is called *rendering*. When your Mac renders a clip, it applies the proper amount of title or transition effect to each frame of the clip. When you apply complex titles or transitions with a long duration, this can take a while. Fortunately, you can continue to work while your Mac renders your movie in the background.

The Effects Palette

The sixth tool button is the Effects button; Effects is short for special effects and that is precisely what this palette enables you to apply to your movies (see Figure 8.9).

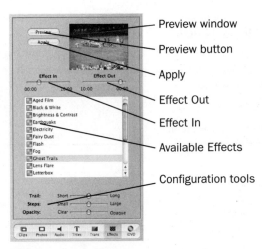

Figure 8.9 *The Effects palette is special indeed.*

Unlike the Transitions and Titles palettes, the effects available on the Effects palette are related to each other only in that they are special effects and they all appear on the same palette. Each effect is unique, and the controls that appear for one effect may or may not be the same as those that appear for another. For example, the Adjust Colors effect includes sliders for Hue Shift, Color, and Brightness, while the Sepia Tone effect doesn't have any tone adjustments. Fortunately, though, all the effects do work similarly even though the controls you see for various effects might be a bit different.

Table 8.7 provides an overview of some of the tools common to many of the effects.

Table 8.7 iMovie's Effects Tools

Tool	What It Does
Preview window	When you select an effect, you see a preview of it in the Preview window.
Preview button	Click this button to see a preview of the selected effect in the Monitor.
Apply	Click this button to apply the selected effect to the selected clip.
Effect In	The Effect In slider controls the number of frames over which the effect is applied. When the slider is all the way to the left, the effect is applied in full force from the start of the clip. As the slider is moved to the right, the effect "fades in" and is applied gradually over the time selected on the slider up to the maximum amount of time on the slider (10 seconds). For example, if you wanted to apply the black-and-white effect to a clip that is surrounded by two color clips, you might want the color of the clip to slowly fade away so that the transition to black-and-white isn't jarring.
Effect Out	The Effect Out slider controls the time over which the effect "fades out." When the slider is all the way to the right, the effect remains in full force until the end of the clip. As the slider is moved to the left, the effect begins to fade out from the point at which the slider is set (the maximum amount is 10 seconds before the end of the clip).
Available Effects	This area contains the list of effects from which you can choose. You can use the scroll tools to see all the available effects.
Configuration tools	Various sliders appear when you select certain effects; these sliders enable you to change some aspect of the effect. For example, when you choose the Ghost Trails effect, you see three sliders that enable you to configure that effect. Some effects don't have configuration tools; these effects are either on or off.

The iDVD Palette

You will want to put many of the movies that you create on DVD so that you can view them on your Mac or on most standard DVD players. Fortunately, iMovie and iDVD are tightly integrated, just like the rest of the iLife applications. The iDVD palette, which you reveal by clicking the iDVD button, enables you to do two tasks related to putting a movie on DVD (see Figure 8.10).

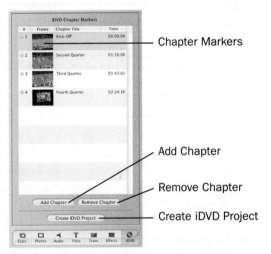

Figure 8.10 *With the iDVD palette, adding an iMovie to a DVD is a snap (or should that be click).*

If you have ever watched a commercially produced movie on DVD, you have no doubt seen the chapter selection menu that enables you to jump quickly to specific scenes in the movie. This is very handy when you want to watch certain scenes again or to find the place where you stopped watching the movie at some point. iMovie and iDVD enable you to add chapter selection menus to your movies on DVD; these work just like they do on the DVDs that come out of Hollywood. To create these menus in iDVD, you use the iDVD tools to add chapter markers to a movie. Each chapter marker you add to a movie becomes a button on the chapter selection menu on a DVD; the viewer can click a button to jump to that scene.

From the iDVD palette, you can also create a new iDVD project and add the current iMovie project to it with a single click of the mouse button.

An overview of the tools on the iDVD palette is provided in Table 8.8.

Table 8.8 iMovie's Effects Tools

Tool	What It Does
Chapter Markers	When you add a chapter marker to a movie, that marker is added to the list of chapter markers at the top of the iDVD palette. In addition to a thumbnail of the frame where the marker is placed, you will see the name of the marker (which is the name of the related button on the chapter selection menu) and the timecode of the frame at which the marker is located.
Add Chapter	This button adds a new chapter marker to the movie at the current location of the Playhead.
Remove Chapter	When you select a chapter marker shown on the list and then click this button, that marker is removed from the movie.
Create iDVD Project	When you click this button, a new iDVD project is created and the current iMovie project is added to it.

The Clip Viewer

Just below the Monitor and Tools palette are the two Viewers; the viewer that you can see depends on which Viewer button is selected. When the Clip Viewer button is selected, the Clip Viewer appears (see Figure 8.11).

The Clip Viewer is where you build your movie. After you have placed clips on the Shelf, you drag them onto the Clip Viewer to place them in the movie. You do the same for transitions and titles to add them to a movie. The Clip Viewer enables you to view thumbnails of each clip in your movie in the order in which they appear. Conveniently, you can also change the order in which clips appear in a movie by rearranging the clips on the Clip Viewer.

Clip Viewer   Clip Viewer button   Selected Clip   Selected Clip in the Monitor

Figure 8.11 *The Clip Viewer is where you build the video track of your movie.*

The Timeline Viewer

When you click the Timeline Viewer button, the Timeline Viewer appears (see Figure 8.12).

As you can probably guess, the Timeline Viewer shows you the timeline for your movie. While the Clip Viewer is designed for the gross (meaning large, not disgusting) assembling of your movie, the Timeline Viewer shows you all of your movie's details. It includes the three tracks that your movie can have, which are the video track plus two audio tracks. You also have tools that you can use to create your movie's soundtrack and synchronize the elements of your movie with one another. An overview of the tools on the Timeline Viewer is provided in Table 8.9.

Touring Your iMovie Studio   Chapter 8   227

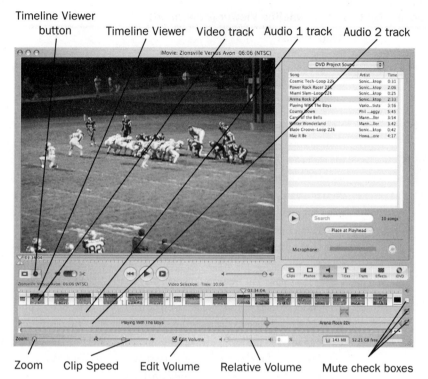

Figure 8.12 *The Timeline Viewer enables you to view all of the tracks of your movie at one time.*

Table 8.9 Tools on the Timeline Viewer

Tool	What It Does
Timeline Viewer button	Click this button to show the Timeline Viewer.
Timeline Viewer	This viewer shows all the details of a movie's contents and enables you to configure them.
Video track	The top track on the Timeline Viewer displays the video track for the movie. You can see each clip in the movie, including video clips, transitions, and titles. This information is exactly the same as in the Clip Viewer, although it looks a bit different. The video track also includes the audio that is part of the video.
Audio 1 track	You can place any sound on the Audio 1 track, including sound effects, sound that you record, and music. The sound on the track is represented by blue blocks when the sound is a sound effect or by an orange bar when the sound is recorded sound or music.

Table 8.9 Tools on the Timeline Viewer (continued)

Tool	What It Does
Audio 2 track	The Audio 2 track is the same in function as the Audio 1 track. Its purpose is to make working with multiple sounds easier because you can separate sounds on the audio tracks to make them easier to manipulate.
Zoom	You can choose the magnification of the Timeline Viewer by using the Zoom slider. When the slider is to the left, you see more of the movie's timeline, but the elements you see are smaller and more difficult to work with. When you move the slider to the right, you "zoom in," and you can see elements in greater detail. As you edit a movie, you can use this slider to change the view to be appropriate for the task you are doing. For example, when you are synchronizing sound, you might want a close-up view so you can position objects in precise relative positions. When you are recording sound from an audio CD, you might want to see more of the movie so that you can see how much longer the sound you are recording will play relative to the movie's length.
Clip Speed	This slider enables you to change the speed at which a clip plays. Moving the slider to the left toward the rabbit) makes the clip play faster and provides a fast forward effect. Moving the slider in the other direction (toward the turtle) makes the clip play more slowly in a slow motion effect. When the slider is in the center, the clip plays at its original speed.
Edit Volume	When this check box is checked, a line representing the volume level of an audio clip appears in the clip. You can change the volume level of the clip by moving the line up or down at various points. For example, to fade the sound out, you drag the line to the bottom of the clip. The angle of the line indicates how rapid the fade out is. You can change the volume at multiple points in any clip.
Relative Volume	This slider and text box enable you to set the relative volume of clips. For example, you might want narration in your movie to be louder than the music score. You move the slider or enter a percentage in the box to set the relative volume levels of various audio elements. Unlike the Volume slider in the Monitor, this slider *does* change the movie. It is called Relative Volume because you change only the relative volume levels of elements in your movie, not the actual volume of the movie itself (which is controlled by the viewer when your movie is played).
Mute check boxes	The Mute check boxes determine whether the audio contained in a track is audible or silent. When a track's Mute check box is checked, the sound contained in that track is heard. Conversely, to mute a track's sound, you uncheck its Mute check box.

> **TIP**
>
> Here's a little secret for you. You can do everything in the Timeline Viewer that you do in the Clip Viewer, plus a lot more. You don't ever really have to use the Clip Viewer, although it is easier to use it to initially build your movie.

The Disk Gauge

iMovie projects are big, really big. DV clips consume tremendous amounts of disk space, and you can expect a movie's files to consume several GBs of disk space even for a relatively short movie. The Disk Gauge, which is located in the bottom-right corner of the iMovie window, is a tool you use to monitor the disk space that is available on the disk on which the iMovie project is stored (see Figure 8.13).

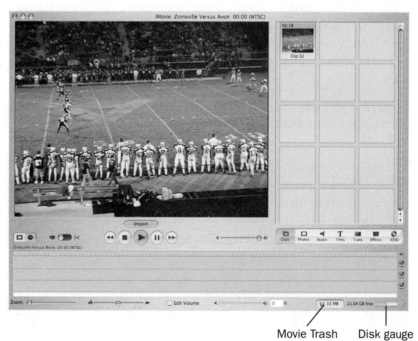

Figure 8.13 *This disk currently has 23.54GB of space available—probably plenty even for a relatively long movie.*

Along with the numeric value shown, the gauge uses a color code scheme to keep you informed about the available disk space for your project. When the gauge is green, iMovie thinks you have plenty of room left. When the gauge turns yellow, the disk is starting to fill up, and you need to keep a close eye on the situation. When the gauge turns red, the disk is either full or getting very close, and your project is about to come to a grinding halt because you won't have any more room to store more clips, transitions, audio, and other elements of your movie.

The iMovie Trash

iMovie has its own Trash. When you delete clips, cut frames from clips, and otherwise dispose of material, iMovie moves that material to its Trash (refer to Figure 8.13). For example, when you cut frames from a clip, they are moved to the Trash. The material remains here until the Trash is emptied. This enables you to undo things you have done, up to the last 10 actions you have performed.

> **NOTE**
>
> Unlike the Mac OS Trash, you can't drag items from the iMovie Trash back into your project. You can only retrieve them by using the Undo command.

While being able to undo actions is good, items in the Trash do consume disk space. When you are running low on disk space, you should empty the iMovie Trash to free up more room on the disk. To empty iMovie's Trash, choose File, Empty Trash. Be aware that iMovie empties its Trash whenever you quit the application so make sure that nothing is there that you will need again before you quit iMovie.

Making Your iMovie Preferences Known

There are three areas for setting preferences to control how iMovie works: General, Import, and Advanced. Similar to all Mac OS X applications, you set your iMovie preferences by choosing iMovie, Preferences. The iMovie Preferences window has three areas, which not coincidentally, correspond to the three areas I listed previously (refer to Figure 8.14).

The iMovie preferences are explained in Table 8.10.

Touring Your iMovie Studio Chapter 8 **231**

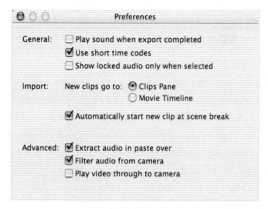

Figure 8.14 *There aren't many iMovie preferences that you will want to change in the beginning, but you might want to make some changes as your iMovie expertise grows.*

Table 8.10 iMovie's Preferences

Area	Preference	What It Does
General	Play sound when export is completed check box	When this check box is checked and you export a movie from iMovie, a sound will play when the export process is complete. This can be useful because iMovie exports can take a long time. This sound lets you know when the process is complete, even if you aren't sitting in front of your Mac at the time.
General	Use short time codes check box	When checked, iMovie won't display the leading zeros in a timecode. However, I recommend that you uncheck this to cause iMovie to display the full timecode so that it appears consistently, thus making it easier to interpret.
General	Show locked audio only when selected check box	You can lock audio clips to specific points relative to the Playhead's position in a movie. When you do this, you can move other elements around in the movie, and the audio remains in sync with the element to which you locked it. When this check box is checked, you see the locked icon only when an audio clip that has been locked has been selected. I like to leave this off since it can be helpful to see which audio is locked when you are looking at a movie in the Timeline Viewer, regardless of whether you have an audio clip selected or not.

Table 8.10 iMovie's Preferences

Area	Preference	What It Does
Import	New clips go to radio buttons	By default, iMovie places clips that you import on the Clips pane (the Shelf) from which you can drag them to the Clip Viewer or Timeline Viewer to place them in your movie. If you choose the Movie Timeline radio button instead, iMovie places clips on the Clip Viewer/Timeline Viewer instead of the Shelf, and you build a movie as you import clips. I recommend that you leave Clips Pane selected because it makes building a movie easier.
Import	Automatically start new clip at scene break check box	By default, this check box is checked. As iMovie imports video clips from a DV camera, it starts a new clip each time there is a break in the video coming in; basically, a clip starts when you pressed the Record button on the camera and stops when you pressed the camera's Record button again to stop recording. If this check box is unchecked, iMovie imports the video as one clip (up to 2GB, at which point iMovie starts a new clip anyway). Usually, you want iMovie to break the clips for you automatically so you should leave this check box checked.
Advanced	Extract audio in paste over check box	You can paste video over an existing video segment. When this check box is checked, the audio track for the video over which you are pasting a clip is extracted so that it remains as a separate sound on one of the Audio tracks. This means that the sound that was originally part of the video over which you paste a new video clip remains in the movie undisturbed, even though you replace part of the video. For example, suppose that you have a clip containing narration that you want to maintain, but you want to replace part of the video that you shot with another clip. With this option on, when you paste in the new segment, the underlying narration is extracted and moved to one of the Audio tracks, where it remains intact. With this option off, the audio of the clip in which you are pasting is also pasted over with the audio from the video clip that you are pasting over the original video.
Advanced	Filter audio from camera check box	With this option on, iMovie filters the sound that it imports from a DV camera. Unless you have a very specific reason that you don't want this to happen, you should allow this to happen because the quality of your audio will be better.

Table 8.10 iMovie's Preferences

Area	Preference	What It Does
Advanced	Play video through to camera check box	If you have a DV camera connected and powered up while you edit a movie, when you play clips or the movie, this preference causes what you play to be displayed on the DV camera as well as on the Mac's screen. For example, you might want to do this to preview what you play in your DV camera's monitor to give you a better perspective of how the video will appear on a television screen.

Using iMovie in Your iLife Projects

In addition to enabling you to create all sorts of cool movies, iMovie is a very useful tool for other tasks as well. In fact, iMovie is likely to be the digital lifestyle application that you use most often for your projects. Just some of the things you can do with it are the following:

- Build cool movies that include titles, transitions, and special effects
- Create complex soundtracks that include music, sound effects, and narration
- Add chapter markers to a movie so that you can easily create a chapter menu when you place the movie on DVD
- Add still images to a movie or video to a slideshow
- Capture video and audio clips from movies or television shows to use in your projects
- Create soundtracks for slideshows and other projects for which you create the video track by using other applications.

Table 8.11 iMovie Menu Commands, Other Commands, and Keyboard Shortcuts

Menu	Command	Keyboard Shortcut	What It Does
iMovie	Preferences	⌘+,	Opens the iMovie Preferences dialog box.
File	New Project	⌘+N	Creates a new iMovie project.
File	Open Project	⌘+O	Opens an existing iMovie project.

Table 8.11 iMovie Menu Commands, Other Commands, and Keyboard Shortcuts (continued)

Menu	Command	Keyboard Shortcut	What It Does
File	Save Frame As	⌘+F	Saves the frame currently displayed on the Monitor as an image file outside of iMovie. This enables you to capture frames from a movie as a graphic.
File	Import	Shift+⌘+I	Enables you to import content into an iMovie project, such as graphic files, audio files, and so on.
File	Export	⌘+E	Enables you to export an iMovie project to videotape, QuickTime, or for DVD.
File	Show Info	⌘+I	Opens the Clip Info window that provides information about a selected clip.
File	Empty Trash	None	Empties the iMovie Trash.
Edit	Select All	⌘+A	Selects all of the clips in the Clips pane or on one of the viewers.
Edit	Select None	⌘+D	Unselects any selected clips; this causes your entire movie to be shown in the Monitor.
Edit	Crop	⌘+K	Removes all frames that are outside of the Crop Markers.
Edit	Split Video Clip at Playhead	⌘+T	Creates two clips from the current clip. The clips are separated at the location of the Playhead when the command is used.
Edit	Create Still Frame	Shift+⌘+S	Creates a still image of the current frame and places that image on the Clips pane from where you can add it to a movie.
Advanced	Extract Audio	⌘+J	Extracts the audio track from a selected video clip and places it on one of the Audio tracks where it becomes just like any other audio; for example, you can move it on the timeline, crop it, and so on.

Table 8.11 iMovie Menu Commands, Other Commands, and Keyboard Shortcuts (continued)

Menu	Command	Keyboard Shortcut	What It Does
Advanced	Paste Over at Playhead	Shift+⌘+V	Pastes selected frames over frames in the selected clip starting at the current location of the Playhead. Use this command to replace some of the video in a clip.
Advanced	Lock/Unlock Audio Clip at Playhead	⌘+L	Locks an audio clip to the current loca tionof the Playhead, such as when you place it at the beginning of a video clip when you want the audio to always remain in synch with the video clip, even if you move the video clip on the timeline. If you select a locked audio clip and use the command, the clip becomes unlocked again.
Advanced	Reverse Clip Direction	⌘+R	Causes the selected clip to play in the opposite direction.
Advanced	Restore Clip	None	Causes a clip to which you have applied special effects to be returned to the condition it was in when you imported it into iMovie (except for any edits you made, such as removing frames).
None	Decrease Volume	Down arrow	Decreases playback volume.
None	Fast Forward (Camera mode)	Cmd+]	Makes the camera play in fast forward.
None	Increase Volume	Up arrow	Increases playback volume.
None	Move audio clip backward by 1 frame	Click audio clip; then Left arrow	Enables you to move the location of audio clips precisely.
None	Move audio clip backward by 10 frames	Click Audio clip; then Shift+ Left arrow	Enables you to move audio clips in 10 frame increments.

Table 8.11 iMovie Menu Commands, Other Commands, and Keyboard Shortcuts (continued)

Menu	Command	Keyboard Shortcut	What It Does
None	Move audio clip forward by 1 frame	Click audio clip; then Right arrow	Enables you to move an audio clip forward by one frame.
None	Move audio clip forward by 10 frames	Click audio clip; then Shift+Right arrow	Enables you to move an audio clip forward by 10 frames.
None	Move backward 1 frame	Left arrow	Moves the Playhead back one frame.
None	Move backward 10 frames	Shift+Left arrow	Moves the Playhead back by 10 frames.
None	Move Crop Marker backward by 1 frame	Click Crop Marker; then Left arrow	Moves the selected Crop Marker back one frame, which adds one frame to the currently selected frames if you select theStart Crop Marker or removes it if you select the End Crop Marker.
None	Move Crop Marker backward by 10 frames	Click Crop Marker; then Shift+ Left arrow	Moves the selected Crop Marker back 10 frames, which adds 10 frames to the currently selected frames if you select the Start Crop Marker or removes 10 frames if you select the End Crop Marker.
None	Move Crop Marker forward by 1 frame	Click Crop Marker; then Right arrow	Moves the selected Crop Marker ahead one frame, which adds one frame to the currently selected frames if you select the End Crop Marker or removes it if you select the Start Crop Marker.
None	Move Crop Marker forward by 10 frames	Click Crop Marker; then Shift+ Right arrow	Moves the selected Crop Marker ahead 10 frames, which adds 10 frames to the currently selected frames if you select the End Crop Marker or removes 10 frames if you select the Start Crop Marker.
None	Move forward 1 frame	Right arrow	Moves the Playhead forward by one frame.

Table 8.11 iMovie Menu Commands, Other Commands, and Keyboard Shortcuts (continued)

Menu	Command	Keyboard Shortcut	What It Does
None	Move forward 10 frames	Shift+Right arrow	Moves the Playhead forward by 10 frames.
None	Move Playhead to beginning of clip/movie	Home	Moves the Playhead to the beginning of a clip if a clip is selected or to the beginning of the movie if no clip is selected.
None	Move Playhead to end of clip/movie	End	Moves the Playhead to the end of a clip if a clip is selected or to the end of the movie if no clip is selected.
None	Play/Stop (Edit mode)	Spacebar	Starts or stops playback of a clip if one is selected or of the movie if no clips are selected.
None	Rewind (Camera mode)	Cmd+[	Rewinds the camera.
None	Start/Stop Import (Camera mode)	Spacebar	Starts or stops the import process.

Chapter 9

Building a Movie in iMovie

Creating a watchable movie involves more than just slamming video clips into your Mac and plopping them on the Clip Viewer. If you really want to create movies that people (including you) will actually want to watch, you should use a disciplined process that consists of the following steps:

1. Plan your movie by deciding what content you are going to include.
2. Build a basic video track by importing video clips and images, editing video clips, configuring still images, and placing them in the movie.
3. Improve the video track by adding transitions, titles, and special effects.
4. Build a soundtrack by adding music, sound effects, recorded sound, and then mixing that sound.
5. Polish the movie by doing final editing.
6. Export the movie for videotape, QuickTime, or DVD.

This chapter covers Steps 1 and 2 of this process. The rest of the steps are covered in the remaining chapters in this part of the book.

Planning a Movie

In a cruel twist of irony, while planning your movie is the most important step in the whole process, I don't have room in this chapter to give it more than a very basic treatment (this chapter is about using iMovie rather than making movies). I have room only to tell what planning you *should* do and to explain how to prepare an iMovie project. If you are serious about making movies, you should learn more about the planning tasks associated with the movie-making process.

> **NOTE**
>
> If you want to learn more about making movies with iMovie, including planning them, see my book *The Complete Idiot's Guide to iMovie 2*. While some of the tools you have used have changed because iMovie is now in version 3, the planning information remains the same.

Deciding What Your Movie Will Be

There are two general kinds of movies you will make: *spontaneous* and *scripted*. In spontaneous movies, you usually have a set of clips that you have captured with a camcorder and you want to make a movie from those clips. In scripted movies, you actually have a script that controls the contents of the movie, by defining what happens on the screen, who says what, and so on. Creating a scripted movie is not what most people do with iMovie, so I'll focus on spontaneous movies.

Most of the time, you will be using iMovie to create a movie from a video that you have taken at some event, but some of the best movies can be made from videos taken during those "everyday" moments that we all take for granted.

While the contents of the video you capture might not be "known" before you capture it, your movie's contents should be known before you crank up iMovie and start building the movie in iMovie. Create a rough plan for your movie by doing the following steps.

Plan a Movie

1. Decide the general content of the movie. For example, if you took video during a vacation, decide what parts of the vacation you want to include in the movie. You might want to include the whole vacation, or you might want to create movies about specific activities that you did during the vacation.
2. Watch the raw video that you captured.
3. As you view the video, create a log that generally describes the contents of the video at various timecodes. This log is essential while you make your movie, but it is even more important for cataloging the raw footage in your collection so that you can find it again later.
4. In your log, include a notation for clips that contain footage that you think you will want to include in your movie. This notation will help you avoid spending time importing clips that you were never going to use anyway.

When you shoot the clips for a movie, keep the following tips in mind:

- When you shoot at any specific time (such as an event), try to keep the total amount of video to 30 minutes or less (preferably less). The more video footage that you have to work with, the longer the movie will take to create and the more effort you'll have to spend doing it. This makes it harder to get the movie done, and projects can linger forever and never get finished. For example, if you have one hour of raw footage, it will take quite a while just to preview that video to see what you actually have. It's better to have a shorter but finished movie than a longer one that is never seen.

- When you shoot, try to vary camera locations so that you have shots from different perspectives that can be put together. A movie shot from the same perspective can be less interesting than one that includes a variety of shots.

- Try to keep camera motion while you are shooting to a minimum. When you move the camera, stop shooting while you are moving, unless it is essential to move and shoot at the same time. Footage that you capture on the move is not likely to be pleasant to watch. For the same reason, you should also avoid using the camera's Zoom control while you are shooting. Stop taping, change the camera position or zoom, and resume taping again. Try to use a tripod whenever possible.

Preparing the iMovie Project

When you have planned your movie, you are ready to get into iMovie and start making the movie by creating an iMovie project.

Create an iMovie Project

1. Open iMovie. If you have not used iMovie before, you will see a dialog box with three buttons: New Project, Open Project, and Quit. In this dialog box, click the New Project button. (If you have previously worked with iMovie, it remembers your last project and automatically opens it for you. In that case, start a new project by choosing File, New Project.)

> **TIP**
>
> To open a project on which you have worked recently, choose File, Open Recent, and select the project that you want to open on the list of recent projects.

2. In the Create New Project dialog box, name your project. Move to the volume on which you are going to store it and click Create.

   When you choose a location in which to store a project (by selecting a location in the Create New Project dialog box), make sure that you choose a volume with plenty of free space. If you have a partitioned hard disk, you might need to move outside of your Home directory to store your project in order to have enough room. In an ideal situation, you will have a dedicated hard disk or volume on which to store your project. If your movie will be more than a couple of minutes, you should have at least 2GB available for your project. Running out of disk space will put a major crimp in the movie-making process.

   When you create a new iMovie project, iMovie creates a folder on the drive you selected with the name you gave your project. Within that folder, you'll find a file and another folder.

3. Move to the Finder and open the project folder that you just created, and you will see two items: a folder called *Media* and an iMovie file that has the same name as the project you created (see Figure 9.1). The Media folder is used to store the clips, images, additional sounds (such as a music track), and other components that you use in your project. The iMovie file is a small pointer file that contains references to all the files in the media folder that you are using. If you want to open your project by double-clicking something, this is the icon that you double-click.

Figure 9.1 *Within your iMovie's folder, you will see the Media folder and an iMovie file.*

> **NOTE**
>
> The steps in the remainder of this chapter assume that iMovie is configured with the preferences as I like them and as described in the section called "Making Your iMovie Preferences Known" in the previous chapter. If you set your preferences differently, the steps you need to use might be slightly different than what is shown in this chapter and what you see on your screen might look different. For example, if you have imported clips placed on the Clip Viewer instead of the Clips pane, you won't end up with clips on the Shelf like my steps do. While you are learning iMovie, keep your preferences the same as mine. After you know your way around the application, you can change your preferences to suit your, well, preferences.

Building a Basic Video Track

After you have planned your movie and created an iMovie project, your next step is to create the basic video track. To do this, you perform the following general steps:

1. Import the video clips and images that you will use in your movie.
2. Edit the clips you imported.
3. Build the basic video track from your edited clips and images.

Stocking the Shelf (aka the Clips Pane) with Clips and Images

As you learned in the previous chapter, the Clips pane (aka the Shelf) is a holding area for clips and other content that you use to create a movie. The following are the three sources of content that you will store on the Clips pane:

- Video clips from a DV camera
- QuickTime clips
- Still Images (that aren't stored in your iPhoto Library)

Importing content from each of these sources requires slightly different tasks.

Stocking the Shelf with Video Clips from a DV Camera

The really neat part about an iMovie-compatible DV camcorder is that you can control your DV camcorder by using iMovie's controls. The Play, Fast Forward, Stop, and other buttons in the iMovie Monitor actually control your DV camcorder. Importing clips from a DV camcorder is a snap.

> **NOTE**
>
> This chapter assumes you are using a digital camcorder that is compatible with iMovie. If you are, you can control the camera from within iMovie. If you aren't using an iMovie-compatible camcorder, some of the information in this chapter won't be correct for you. To see if your camcorder is compatible with iMovie, see www.apple.com/imovie/compatibility/camcorder.html.

Import Clips from a DV Camcorder

1. Open your iMovie project.
2. Turn the DV camera on and set it to its output setting (this is sometimes labeled VCR or VTR).
3. Connect the FireWire cable to the DV camcorder and your Mac. iMovie will switch into the Import (Camera) mode, and you will see a message in iMovie's Monitor window confirming that iMovie is in touch with your DV camcorder. In addition to the "Camera Connected" message, the Import button appears just under the Monitor, and you see buttons you can use to control the camera, such as Rewind, Fast Forward, and so on.

> **TIP**
>
> If iMovie doesn't switch into the Camera (Import) mode automatically, move the Mode switch button to the left (toward the camera icon).

4. Use iMovie's Play and other buttons to control the DV camera to move to the first segment on the tape that you want to import into your project; this is where the log you created when you planned your movie comes in. Use your log to get to a point just before the clip that you want to import starts.

5. Click the Import button (or press the Spacebar); iMovie will start the camcorder and begin capturing the clips. It stores the first clip in the first available slot on the Clips pane. When it gets to a scene break (the point at which you hit the Stop Recording button when you captured the clip with the DV camcorder), it ends that clip and immediately begins capturing the next scene, which it places in the next available slot on the Shelf. iMovie names each clip *Clip #* where # is a sequential number.

iMovie continues this process until it runs out of video to import or out of disk space to store clips, whichever comes first (see Figure 9.2).

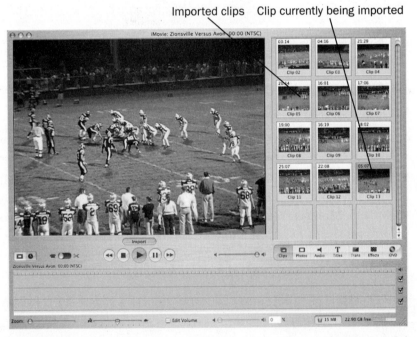

Figure 9.2 *Capturing clips from a DV camera is easy because iMovie does the work for you.*

6. If you don't want to wait that long, click Import again to stop the import process (or press the Spacebar).
7. Use the iMovie controls to move the tape to the next set of scenes that you want to capture and begin again.
8. Continue this process until you have imported all the scenes that your movie plan calls for. Your Shelf now has some nice clips (and probably some not-so-nice ones) ready for you to edit and use in your movie.

> **TIP**
>
> As you import clips, keep an eye on the Disk Gauge. If it turns yellow or red, you need to make more room on the disk on which your project is stored before you can import more clips.

9. When you have captured the clips you need for your movie, disconnect your camera and turn it off.

> **NOTE**
>
> If you don't use an iMovie-compatible camcorder, you might still be able to import clips, but you won't be able to control your camera by using iMovie's controls. You will have to control the camera with its buttons and manually start and stop the import process using iMovie's Import button.

Stocking the Shelf with QuickTime Clips

A great source of material for your iMovie projects is QuickTime movies that you create or that you obtain from other sources, such as those you download from the Web. You can add any QuickTime movie to the Shelf and then use that QuickTime movie in your iMovie project.

> **NOTE**
>
> In order to download many QuickTime movies from the Web, you must be using the Pro version of QuickTime. For detailed information about QuickTime Pro, see my book *Special Edition Using Mac OS X v10.2*.

Import a QuickTime Movie into iMovie

1. Choose File, Import (or press Shift+⌘+I). The Import sheet will appear.
2. In the Import sheet, move to the QuickTime that you want to add to the Clips pane.

3. Select the QuickTime movie and click Open. The Import Files progress window will appear (see Figure 9.3). When the import process is complete, the clip appears on the Clips pane, and it is automatically selected so that you see it in the Monitor. From this point on, it behaves in the same way as any other clip on the Shelf, such as those you imported from your DV camera.

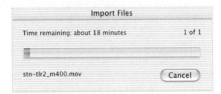

Figure 9.3 *Importing even a relatively small QuickTime movie can take a while, but sometimes the results are worth the wait.*

Stocking the Shelf with Still Images

You might want to use still images in your movie (a strategically placed still image can make a nice transition between scenes), or you might want to include still images related to a particular clip. You can import images in the usual image file formats, such as JPEG, TIFF, and so on, into your iMovie project and store them on the Clips pane. From there, you can place them in your movie.

> **NOTE**
>
> If the images you want to use in an iMovie project are stored in your iPhoto Photo Library, you don't need to bother with the steps in this section because as you learned in the previous chapter, you can access all of your iPhoto images from the iPhoto palette. See the section called "Adding iPhoto Images to the Video Track", later in this chapter, for the details.

Import Still Images into iMovie

1. Prepare the images that you want to import outside of iMovie. For example, you might find some cool images on the Internet that you want to download and edit for use in your iMovie project.
2. Jump back into your iMovie project and choose File, Import. The Import sheet will open.

> **NOTE**
>
> You must be in the Edit mode to import images. If iMovie is in the Camera mode, disconnect your camcorder or move the Camera/Edit switch to the Edit position.

3. Move to the folder in which you saved the photos that you prepared in Step 1.
4. Hold the Shift key down (to select a series of images next to each other) or the key down (to select individual images) and click all the images that you want to import.
5. When the images that you want to import are selected, click Open. A progress window will appear. After a few moments, you will see the images on the Clips pane (see Figure 9.4). You can work with images just like you do video clips; for example, you place an image in your movie by dragging it to the Clip Viewer.

Figure 9.4 *Here you can see that I have imported two TIFF images into an iMovie project.*

> **NOTE**
>
> When you import an image or a QuickTime movie into an iMovie project, its clip name is the file name of the file you imported.

> **Images in iMovie**
>
> Images that you import into iMovie will be converted into the 640x480 format in the landscape orientation. If you import images larger than this, iMovie will do the conversion itself, and the results might not look very good. For best results, you should use an image editing application to put your images in the 640x480 format before importing them into iMovie. For portrait-oriented photos, you might want to place the image over a 640 x 480 background and save the combined image. Otherwise, iMovie will stretch a narrower image to fill the screen, and that probably won't look very good either.
>
> When you import an image into iMovie, in addition to it being resized as explained in the previous paragraph, it is also converted into a "clip" in which each frame is exactly the same. By default, image clips have a duration of 5:22 meaning that they remain on the screen for 5 seconds and 22 frames. You can change this duration as you will learn later in this chapter.

Hacking (aka Editing) Your Clips

After you have your source material (your clips) stored on the Clips pane, you should edit them. Your goals should include the following:

- Preview clips on the Clips pane to see which clips you actually want to use in the movie.
- Delete any clips you won't use.
- Rename clips that will appear in your movie and get information about them.
- Split clips into parts so you can work with each part individually.
- Edit any clips you will use in your movie.

> **NOTE**
>
> In this section, I refer to all the content on the Clips panes as "clips," even still images. In iMovie, a still image is just a clip in which each frame is the same.

Previewing Clips

When iMovie adds clips to the Clips pane (regardless of how they got there), you will see a thumbnail of the first frame in each clip in its slot on the Clips pane. In the upper left-corner of the clip's slot, you will see its duration, in the timecode format (see Figure 9.5). For example, a duration of 17:01 would indicate that a clip is 17 seconds and 1 frame long. At the bottom of the clip, you will see the clip name that iMovie assigned to the clip (you can change this as you will learn shortly).

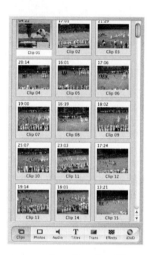

Figure 9.5 *On the Clips pane, you can see the duration of each clip along with its name.*

To preview a clip, do the following steps.

Preview a Clip

1. Select a clip by clicking it on the Clips pane. The clip is highlighted with a blue border, which means that the clip is selected. More telling is the first frame of the clip that shows in the Monitor (see Figure 9.6).

Figure 9.6 *Clip 01 has been selected, so it appears in the Monitor where you can preview it.*

> **TIP**
>
> If you are in the Import (Camera) mode when you select a clip on the Clips pane, notice that when you select a clip, iMovie moves into the Edit mode automatically. If iMovie isn't in the Edit mode, slide the Camera/Edit switch to the right (toward the camera icon).

2. Click the Play button (or press the Spacebar). The clip will play, and you can watch it in the Monitor. Let the clip play to its end or click the Play button again to stop it.

> **TIP**
>
> One of the fastest ways to preview a clip is by dragging the Playhead through the clip. This can give you a good idea of what the clip contains in just a few seconds. For the initial preview, using the Playhead to fast forward through the clip is often the best technique.

3. Decide if the clip has usable material in it or not.

Deleting Clips

When you identify clips that don't have any content you are going to use in a movie, it is best to get rid of them right away so that they aren't wasting previous disk space.

Delete a Clip

1. Select the clip.
2. Press the Delete key. The clip will be moved to the Trash.

> **TIP**
>
> You can also delete a clip by selecting it and choosing Edit, Clear or by dragging it to the iMovie Trash

3. Continue deleting clips until you have rid your project of the useless clips.

After you have deleted all the clips that you want to get rid of, you should empty the iMovie Trash to actually delete the files from your disk. Choose File, Empty Trash to do so. Click OK in the resulting warning dialog box, and the files will be removed from your Mac.

> **TIP**
>
> It is best to get rid of the clips you won't be using (by emptying the Trash) before you start editing clips and building a movie. I recommend this practice because iMovie stores all of the data it needs for you to be able to undo things you have done, such as applying special effects to a clip, in the Trash. When you empty the Trash, these data are lost, and iMovie will no longer be able to undo your actions. If you get rid of clips early, you can save disk space by emptying the Trash, but you won't lose the ability to undo your actions because you won't have taken any yet.

Viewing and Changing a Clip's Information

iMovie enables you to view detailed information for clips and to rename them so that they have more meaningful names than those assigned by iMovie.

View a Clip's Information and Rename It

1. Select a clip on the Shelf.
2. Double-click the clip, choose File, Show Info, or press ⌘+I. The Clip Info window will appear (see Figure 9.7). At the top of the window, you will see the clip's current name. Below that, you will see other information about the clip, such as its Media File name, size, when it was captured, and its duration.

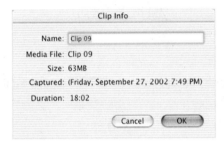

Figure 9.7 *The Clip Info window gives you the scoop on a clip and enables you to rename it.*

> **NOTE**
>
> When iMovie imports a clip, it stores that clip in the Media folder with the project's folder. The name of the file that iMovie creates is the same as the original clip name. When you rename a clip, the original file name does not change. If you should ever need to find the file in the Finder, such as to import it into a different iMovie project, you can locate that file by viewing its Media File information shown in the Clip Info window.

3. If you want to rename the clip, select its current name so that it becomes highlighted and type the clip's new name.
4. Click OK to rename the clip and close the Clip Info window. When you return to the Shelf, the clip will have the name you gave it.

> **TIP**
>
> You can also rename a clip on the Clips pane by clicking in the clip name area and selecting the current name so that it becomes highlighted. Then type a new name for the clip.

Splitting Clips

In certain situations, you might want to split a clip so that you can work with each part independently. When you split a clip, the two resulting clips behave just like clips you have created by capturing them from a DV camera or by importing them.

Split a Clip

1. Select the clip that you want to split. It will appear in the Monitor.
2. Drag the Playhead to the point at which you want to split the clip.
3. Choose Edit, Split Video Clip at Playhead or press ⌘+T. The clip will be split into two clips at the point in the clip at which the Playhead was located. A new clip with "/1" will be appended to the first segment's name and will be added to the Clips pane (for example, if the clip's name was Clip 43, the new clip will be named Clip 43/1). You can treat the two clips independently because they are now separate clips.

Editing Clips

Editing your clips is one of the most important tasks you will do. When you edit a clip, you remove everything from that clip that will detract from, rather than add to, your movie. Editing your clips is fundamental to creating good movies.

You can edit clips at any time, but in my opinion you are better off if you edit your clips *before* you place them in a movie. Building a movie from edited clips gets you to a completed movie faster because you deal with less material when you actually build your movie.

> **NOTE**
>
> Even if you edit your clips before you place them in your movie, you should expect to have to do some minor editing on some clips after you build your movie. However, you can get clips very close to their final condition before you even place them in a movie.

One of the most fundamental tasks is removing frames from a clip, such as removing them from the beginning or end of a clip. However, you can remove frames from anywhere in a clip with the same steps.

Remove Frames from a Clip

1. Click the clip on the Clips pane that you want to edit to select it; the clip appears in the Monitor.
2. Preview the clip and locate a part of the clip that should be removed.
3. Click on the End Crop Marker and drag it to the approximate point at which you want to stop removing frames from the clip (see Figure 9.8). When you click on the Crop Marker, it becomes dark blue to indicate that it is selected, and the Playhead will "stick" to it, and you will see the frame at which both are currently located in the Monitor. The gold bar that appears between the Crop Markers indicates the frames you have selected. As you drag a Crop Marker, you can see the frames you are moving through.

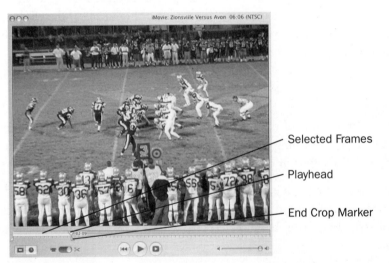

Figure 9.8 *When selecting frames for editing, you use the End Crop Marker to indicate the last frame in the selection.*

> **NOTE**
>
> You have to move the End Crop Marker first because it butts up against the Start Crop Marker.

4. While the Playhead is "stuck" to the End Crop Marker, you can move it one frame at a time by pressing the Right arrow key to add one frame to the selection or by holding the Shift key down and pressing the Right arrow key to add 10 frames to the selection. Similarly, if you press the Left arrow key, you will remove 1 or 10 frames from the selection. Use this technique to position the End Crop Marker on the exact end frame that you want to select.

   Next, you will position the Start Crop Marker.

5. Click the Start Crop Marker (it becomes highlighted in dark blue, and the Playhead will jump and stick to it) and drag the Start Crop Marker to the approximate location at which you want to start selecting clips. (If you want to start selecting frames at the first frame, you don't need to move the Start Crop Marker because it is positioned there by default.)

> **TIP**
>
> The timecode that appears next to the Playhead makes it much easier to tell how many frames you have selected because it counts each frame as you selected it. Keep a close eye on the timecode as you select frames to become adept at selecting exactly the frames you want.

6. While the Playhead is "stuck" to the Start Crop Marker, you can move it one frame at a time by pressing the Right arrow key to remove one frame to the selection or by holding the Shift key down and pressing the Right arrow key to remove 10 frames to the selection. Similarly, if you press the Left arrow key, you will add 1 or 10 frames from the selection. Use this technique to position the Start Crop Marker on the exact start frame that you want to select (see Figure 9.9).

7. To remove the selected frames from the clip, choose Edit, Cut (or press ⌘+X). The Crop Markers are reset to the beginning of the clip and the selected frames are removed from the clip.

8. Play the clip to see how it is without the frames that you just removed. If you don't like the result, you can undo it by choosing Edit, Undo (⌘+Z) and selecting a different set of frames to remove.

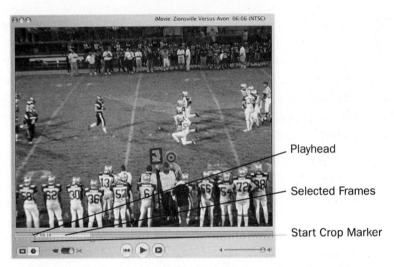

Figure 9.9 *The first frame in the section is now at timecode 00:18.*

> **TIP**
>
> You can also remove frames by selecting them and pressing the Delete key or by choosing Edit, Clear. The Clear command removes selected frames without placing them on the Clipboard. Technically speaking, you should use Clear rather than Cut because then memory resources aren't wasted by placing the selected frames on your Mac's Clipboard. However, I prefer to use Cut because it has a keyboard shortcut, whereas Clear does not. And practically speaking, you won't notice any performance problems if you leave frames on your Clipboard.

9. Preview the edited clip and continue editing it until you have removed all the chaff from it.

> **NOTE**
>
> By the way, copy, paste, and other editing commands work in iMovie just like they do in other Mac applications. If you select a series of frames and choose Copy instead of Cut, the frames are left in the clip and copies are moved to the Clipboard, and you can paste them in the same clip or in another clip.

You can also crop a clip to remove everything from it *except* the frames you have selected. This is a good way to remove frames at the beginning and end of a clip at the same time.

Crop a Clip

1. Use the selection techniques you learned in the previous steps to select the frames that you want to *remain* in the clip.
2. Choose Edit, Crop (or press ⌘+K). The frames that were not included in the selection will be removed from the clip.
3. Preview the clip. If you don't like the results of the crop, undo it.

Continue editing the clips you will use in the movie until they are as close as possible to how you want them to be in your movie. It's usually a good idea to leave a couple of spare frames at each end of the clips so that you have some "extra" to work with when you apply titles and transitions and do the final editing. Your goal should be to have a set of edited clips from which to build a movie. When you are done editing clips, you should have shorter and fewer clips than you did after you imported all the clips into the project.

Building the Basic Video Track

After you have gathered your content and edited your clips, you are ready to build a movie from those clips. You assemble your movie by placing video clips and images that you have stored on the Clips pane and images that you have stored in iPhoto on the Clip Viewer. Then you put that content in the order that you want it to be viewed in the movie.

Adding Video Clips and QuickTime Movies to the Video Track

Adding video clips and QuickTime movies to an iMovie movie is a matter of drag-and-drop. (Since both kinds of content behave in the same way, they are both referred to as clips from here on.)

Place Video Clips and QuickTime Movies in an iMovie Movie

1. Click the Clip Viewer button to bring the Clip Viewer to the front (it will probably be in the front already).
2. Drag the first clip from the Clips pane onto the Clip Viewer. When you release the mouse button, you will see the clip's thumbnail on the Clip Viewer. This means that the clip is now part of the movie (see Figure 9.10).

Figure 9.10 *This clip is now part of the movie.*

3. Drag the next clip from the Clips pane onto the Clip Viewer and place it before or after the first clip that you placed there.
4. Continue moving clips and QuickTime movies from the Clips pane to the Clip Viewer until you have placed all of the clips that you want to use in your movie (see Figure 9.11).

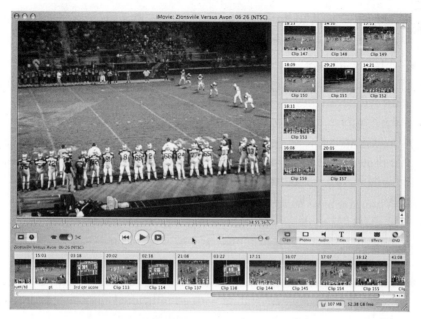

Figure 9.11 *Here, you can see that I moved many of the clips from the Clips pane to the Clip Viewer.*

> **TIP**
>
> If you want to place a clip between two clips that are already on the Clip Viewer, just drag the clip to where you want it to be. The clips on each side will slide apart to make room for the new clip. If you get to the end of the Clip Viewer, use the scroll bar to create more space on the Clip Viewer for additional clips. The Clip Viewer will continue to expand so that you can place as many clips on it as you have hard disk space to store them.

5. Preview the movie by playing it. Make sure that no clips are selected (choose Edit, Select None or press Shift+⌘+A) and press the Play button. The movie will play; you haven't added any transitions yet, so all the clips run right into one another (the Straight Cut). Sometimes, this will look fine; sometimes, it won't. You will add transitions later in the process.

As you add video clips and QuickTime movies to build your basic video track, keep the following points in mind:

- When you select more than one clip on the Clip Viewer or when you have no clips selected (so that the whole movie is shown in the Monitor), the Monitor will show the clips that you have selected. Vertical lines in the Scrubber bar mark the boundaries of each clip.
- As you add clips to the Clip Viewer, the total playing time for the movie is shown just above the Clip Viewer and just under the Clip Viewer and Timeline Viewer buttons.
- When you have built your movie, choose Edit, Select None (or press Shift+⌘+A) to deselect any clips that are selected. Press the Home key to move to the start of your movie. To preview your movie, press the Spacebar. Your movie will play.
- You can use the same movement and editing techniques with an entire movie as you can when dealing with an individual clip (such as dragging the Playhead, using the Arrow keys, and so on).
- You can play or edit a single clip again by selecting it on the Clip Viewer. The timecode shown next to the Playhead in the Monitor for the selected clip becomes the timecode for the clip's first frame in the movie and shows you the location of that clip in the movie.
- You can remove a clip from your movie and place it back on the Clips pane by dragging it from the Clip Viewer to the Clips pane. You can move it back to the Clip Viewer to add it to the movie again.
- You can delete a clip from the movie and from the project by selecting it and then pressing the Delete key.
- To see your movie in full-screen mode, click the View in Full Screen button. Your movie plays back so that it takes up the entire screen. This helps you focus on your movie without any distractions from the iMovie interface. To stop your movie and return to iMovie before your movie has finished, click the mouse button or press the Spacebar.

Continue placing clips in the Clip Viewer until you have all the clips that you want to appear in your movie. You don't have to use all the clips on the Clips pane; you can leave clips there for later use or delete them when you are sure that you won't use them in this movie.

Adding Images from the Shelf to the Video Track

Adding images that are stored on the Clips pane to a movie isn't a lot different than adding video clips or QuickTime movies.

You learned earlier that you can easily add images to the Clips pane to include them in your movies. Rather than using a frame rate, still images use a duration, which is how long the image appears on-screen. By default, this is something slightly longer than 5 seconds, meaning that the still image appears on the screen for that period of time. You can change the duration for a still image when you add it to your movie.

Add Images Stored on the Clips Pane to a Movie

1. On the Clips pane, select the image that you want to add to the movie.
2. Drag the image onto the Clip Viewer. (If you move the image between two clips already there, those clips will slide apart to make room for the image.)
3. When the image is in the position where you want it, release the mouse button.
4. Select the image, click the Photos button to open the Photos palette, and use the techniques explained in the next section to configure the image, by configuring the Ken Burns Effect and setting the duration and zoom for that image.

Adding iPhoto Images to the Video Track

You can still add your iPhoto images to a movie, or you can create a movie consisting entirely of iPhoto images to create a slideshow. When you add images from iPhoto to a movie, you can configure motion effects for the images you add; in iMovie, these effects are called the Ken Burns Effect. This effect—taken from the treatment of images that Ken Burns uses in his excellent documentaries, such as *Civil War*—applies motion and zoom effects to the image. You can configure the effect for each image you add to the movie, from no effect at all to a maximum effect.

For all images you add, whether you choose to use the Ken Burns Effect or not, you can set the image duration and zoom. The image's duration setting determines how long the image appears on the screen. The zoom determines which part of the image is displayed.

Add an iPhoto Image to a Movie and Configure Its Ken Burns Effect, Duration, and Zoom

1. Click on the Photos button to open the iPhoto palette.
2. On the Source pop-up menu, choose the iPhoto source, such as a photo album, that contains the images that you want to add to the movie on the pop-up menu. The images contained in the selected photo album will appear in the Preview window in the lower part of the palette (see Figure 9.12). To the right of the pop-up menu, you will see the number of images that are contained in the selected photo album.

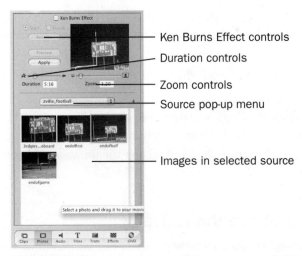

Figure 9.12 *When you choose an iPhoto source on the Source pop-up menu, you will see the images that source contains in the lower part of the iPhoto palette.*

TIP

If you are configuring an image that you placed in a movie from the Clips pane, you don't need to do Steps 2 and 3. Just select the image in the Clip Viewer before you click the Photos button. When you click the Photos button, the image you selected will appear in the Preview window, and you can work with it just like an image that is located in your iPhoto Photo Library.

3. Select the image that you want to add to the movie. A preview of the image with the current motion effects will appear in the image Preview window located at the top of the palette.

4. If you want to apply the Ken Burns Effect to the image, click the Ken Burns Effect check box. The Ken Burns Effect controls will become active, and you will see a preview of the image with the effect applied in the Preview window. If you don't check this check box, only the Duration and Zoom controls will be active.

5. Click on the Start radio button. This enables you to configure the starting location of the motion effect. Skip this step if you aren't using the Ken Burns Effect.

6. Use the Zoom slider to set the amount of magnification that will be applied to the image at the start of its clip if you apply the Ken Burns Effect or throughout the image clip if you don't apply the effect. Drag the slider to the left to show more of the photo or to the right to show less of it.

7. Move the pointer over the image in the Preview window. The cursor will turn into a hand.

8. Hold the mouse button down and drag the image until the part of the image that you want to be shown at the start of the image clip (with the Ken Burns Effect applied) or throughout the image clip (without the effect) is shown in the Preview window (see Figure 9.13).

> **NOTE**
>
> Skip Steps 9 through 12 if you aren't applying the Ken Burns Effect to the image.

9. Click on the Finish radio button. The image will jump to its ending location and zoom settings.

10. Use the Zoom slider to set the amount of magnification that will be applied to the image at the end of its clip. Drag the slider to the left to show more of the photo or to the right to show less of it.

Figure 9.13 *When the Start radio button is selected, you set the zoom and area of the image at the beginning of its clip.*

> **TIP**
>
> You can also enter the zoom and duration values by typing a duration (in the timecode format) or zoom (in zoom amount) directly in their respective boxes.

11. Move the pointer over the image in the preview window. The cursor will turn into a hand.

12. Hold the mouse button down and drag the image until the part of the image that you want to be shown at the end of the image clip is shown in the Preview window.

13. Use the Duration slider to set the length of time for the image clip. Drag the slider to the left to make the clip shorter (which makes the motion effect faster if you have applied it to the image) or to the right to make the clip last longer (to make the motion effect slower if you have applied it to the image). If you don't apply the Ken Burns Effect to an image, setting its duration only changes the length of time that image appears on the screen. When you release the mouse button, a preview of the image and motion effect will appear in the Preview window (see Figure 9.14).

Figure 9.14 *When the Finish radio button is selected, you configure the image at the end of its clip; you use the duration to set the amount of time the clip will appear on the screen.*

14. Click on Preview. You will see the image clip as you have configured it in the Preview window. (If you don't apply the Ken Burns Effect, the Preview button is inactive because there is no point in previewing a static image—what you see is what you get.)

TIP

If you want the motion effect to be applied in the opposite "direction," click on the Reverse button. A preview of the motion effect moving in the opposite direction (zooming in instead of zooming out) will be shown in the Preview window.

15. Repeat Steps 4 through 14 to make changes to the image clip until you are satisfied with it.
16. Click on Apply. The motion effect, duration, and zoom settings will be applied to the image, and the image clip will be placed at the end of the Clip Viewer. When the image appears on the Clip Viewer, the image will be rendered and selected so that it appears in the Monitor.
17. Drag the image clip to the location on the Clip Viewer at the point in the movie where you want it to appear.

> **TIP**
>
> If you want to change the motion effect, duration, or zoom for an image after you have added it to the Clip Viewer, delete it from the Clip Viewer and repeat the previous steps to reconfigure the image clip.

> ### Rendering
>
> Most of the effects that you apply to a video or image clip must be rendered when the clip is placed in a movie. During the rendering process, iMovie applies the appropriate amount of effect to each frame in the clip. Depending on the speed of your Mac, the effect you are using, and the length of the clip, this process can take some time to complete. Fortunately, you can continue to work while your Mac renders clips. As a clip is rendered, you will see a red progress bar at the top of the clip's thumbnail on the Clip Viewer. You can mostly ignore this process as your Mac handles it for you. For example, you can move a clip while it is being rendered. And your Mac can render several clips at the same time. There are a couple of things that you can't do while clips are being rendered. One is saving the project; sometimes you can't preview a clip that is being rendered in the Monitor.
>
> When you are configuring an effect, you can see the result of that effect in the Preview window in the Tools palette . This prevents you from having to wait for the rendering process to be completed before you can see the effect. The rendering process is done only when you place the effect on the Clip Viewer.

Arranging the Clips in a Movie

After you have placed all the image content in the Clip Viewer and thus added it to the movie, you need to organize that content so that each clip and image appears in the proper spot on the movie's timeline.

Set the Order in Which Content Appears

1. Select a video or image clip on the Clip Viewer.
2. Drag that clip to a new location on the Clip Viewer. When you pause between two clips, they slide apart to make room for the clip you are moving. (Repeat Steps 1 and 2 for each clip that needs to be moved.)
3. Preview the movie and make any changes in the order of clips that are needed.

Chapter 10

Building a Better Video Track in iMovie

Now that you have the basic video track for your movie, it's time to polish your movie's video track by adding titles, transitions, and special effects; and you can add some iMovie trick effects to really liven things up. While building a basic movie is interesting, this is where using iMovie really gets to be fun and your own creativity comes into the movie-making process.

Explaining Yourself with Titles

In the section called "The Titles Palette," back in Chapter 8, you learned about how you can use iMovie's titling tools to add all sorts of text to your movie, such as opening and closing credits, captions, and so on. And you were provided with an overview of the Title tools that are available on the Titles palette. While these tools vary a bit among the various styles of titles, the general steps to apply any title to a movie are the same.

1. Decide on the type of text you want to add (such as caption, credit, date, or title) and whether you want to apply that title to a clip or over a black background.
2. Based on the kind of text you add and where you apply it, decide on a title style to use. See Table 10.1 for a description of the title styles available in iMovie.
3. Open the Titles palette and click the title style you chose in Step 2 to select it. You will see a preview in the Preview window.
4. Type the text for the title in the text boxes for that style. Use the Add button (if available) to add more text blocks to the title.
5. Use the QT Margins check box to set QuickTime margins (if applicable).
6. If you want to apply the text over a black background rather than a clip, check the Over Black check box.
7. Choose a font, color, and size for the title text.
8. Set the direction of the motion (if applicable).
9. Set the speed and pause (if applicable) of the title.

10. Set the other properties of the text by using its sliders. For example, when you choose one of the Bounce styles, you can use the Wave slider to set the amount of "bounce" the title has.
11. Preview the title in the Preview window and by clicking the Preview button (to preview it in the Monitor).
12. Make adjustments to the title until it is what you want.
13. Place the title in your movie.

Table 10.1 Title Styles Available on the Titles Palette

Title	Description
Bounce Across	Two lines of text flow across the center of the screen in wavy lines.
Bounce Across Multiple	Same as Bounce Across except you can add multiple lines of text.
Bounce In To Center	One line of text moves from the top and bottom sides of the screen toward the center.
Cartwheel	Two lines of text move onto the screen while the letters in that text rotate.
Cartwheel Multiple	Same as cartwheel except that you have multiple lines of text.
Centered Multiple	Multiple lines of text fade into the center of the screen in groups of two lines of text.
Centered Title	Same as Centered Multiple except there is only one group of two lines of text.
Converge	Expanded letters converge from the side of the screen to the center of the screen to form two lines of text.
Converge Multiple	Same as Converge except you can add multiple lines of text.
Converge to Center	Expanded letters converge from both sides of the screen to the center to form two lines of text.
Converge to Center Multiple	Same as Converge to Center except you can add multiple lines of text.
Cross Through Center	Two lines of text appear in a mirror effect and rotate until they become visible in the center of the screen.
Cross Through Center Multiple	Same as Cross Through Center except you can add multiple lines of text.

Table 10.1 Title Styles Available on the Titles Palette (continued)

Title	Description
Drifting	Two lines of text fade onto the screen and drift around there.
Flying Letters	Two lines of text appear on the screen by each letter flying onto the screen.
Flying Words	Two lines of text appear on the screen by each word flying onto the screen.
Gravity	Two lines of text start at one edge of the screen as a jumbled group and then "fall" to the center of the screen.
Gravity Multiple	Same as Gravity except you can add multiple lines of text.
Music Video	A block of text appears in the lower-left corner of the screen.
Rolling Centered Credits	Multiple lines of text scroll across the screen from the top or bottom. The lines of text are centered on the screen.
Rolling Credits	Multiple lines of text scroll up or down the screen. Each line of text is connected to its mate by dotted lines (like the credits you usually see at the end of a movie).
Scroll with Pause	Two lines of text scroll from the edge of the screen to the center, pause there, and then scroll off the other edge.
Scrolling Block	A block of text scrolls from the top to the bottom or from the bottom to the top of the screen.
Spread from Center	The letters in two lines of text appear in a clump at the center of the screen and spread out until they form two lines of text.
Spread from Center Multiple	Same as Spread from Center except you can have multiple lines of text.
Stripe Subtitle	Two lines of text appear in a stripe of color at the bottom of the screen.
Subtitle	Two lines of text appear at the bottom of the screen.
Subtitle Multiple	Same as Subtitle except you can have multiple lines of text.
Twirl	Two lines of text appear on the screen and then each letter spins around its base until they return to the starting position.
Typewriter	Two lines of text appear on the screen letter by letter as if they are being typed.

Table 10.1 Title Styles Available on the Titles Palette (continued)

Title	Description
Unscramble	Two lines of text appear in a jumble and unscramble themselves so they become legible.
Unscramble Multiple	Same as Unscramble except that you can have multiple lines of text.
Zoom	Two lines of text appear at a very small size and zoom to fill the screen.
Zoom Multiple	Same as Zoom except you can have multiple lines of text.

> **NOTE**
>
> With the two Bounce styles, the Wave slider will appear just under the Pause slider. You use the slider to control the amount of wave (or bounce) that the lines of text have.

Using any of these title styles is very similar, and once you have used one or two of them, you will be able to use the others just as easily. In the next two sections, you will see the detailed steps to create two specific kinds of titles. If you work through these steps, you will learn all you need to know to create titles of any of the other styles. Following those sections, you will learn how to change a title that is already part of a movie, such as to fix a typo.

Adding Opening Credits

Most movies contain opening credits that introduce the movie. The Scroll with Pause style can be a good choice for this purpose (of course, you should experiment with the other choices to see if you prefer a different style).

Add Opening Credits to a Movie

1. Click the Titles button to open the Titles palette.
2. Click the Scroll with Pause style to choose it. You will see a preview of the title in the Preview window (the text will be some filler that iMovie has inserted for you).
3. If you want the text to appear over a black background instead of over a clip, click the Over Black check box.

> **NOTE**
>
> If the title style you are using is located at the bottom of the screen, such as the Music Video style, you should check the QT Margins check box if you intend to view the movie only on a computer using QuickTime. This setting will slide the text down to the bottom of the screen. If you are going to view the movie on a TV screen (via videotape or DVD), leave this unchecked or the text might be cut off when you view it. For titles that don't appear at an edge of the screen, you don't need to set this check box.

4. If you want the title to appear over a clip, select the clip on the Clip Viewer to which you want to apply the title. If you checked the Over Black check box, you can skip this step.

5. Type the title text in the text boxes (with the Scroll with Pause style, you have two lines of text).

> **NOTE**
>
> If you use one of the Multiple styles, you can click the + button to add lines of text in groups of two. You can click the – button to remove lines of text in groups of two.

6. Choose a font for the title on the Font pop-up menu.

7. Choose a size for the title by using the Font Size slider.

8. Choose the color of the text by using the Color button. When you click this button, the Color Picker tool will appear, and you can use it to choose the color of the text. (White is the default color and is usually a good choice unless you are applying the text to a light background.)

> **NOTE**
>
> Each time that you make a change, a preview of the title appears in the Preview window to show you the effect of your change.

9. Use the Direction Arrow buttons to set the direction of the text's motion. For the Scroll with Pause style, you can click one of the arrows to set the direction of the scroll. For example, if you click the Up arrow, the lines of text scroll up from the bottom of the screen.

> **NOTE**
>
> The Direction Arrow buttons aren't applicable to all styles nor are all the directions available for the styles that do use some sort of motion effect. When a Direction button is not applicable, it is grayed out to indicate that you can't use it.

10. Use the Speed slider to set the title's duration. The Speed slider determines how long the title appears on the screen. Moving the slider to the right causes the title to appear on the screen for a longer period of time. In the case of the Scroll with Pause style, appearing longer means that the text takes longer to scroll across the screen and so moves more slowly.

> **TIP**
>
> If you apply a title over a clip and the duration of the title is longer than the clip over which you apply it, the title will "spill over" onto the next clip. You won't see this in the preview window because you have to click the Preview button to see the title in the Monitor in order to see how the title will actually appear in the movie.

11. Use the Pause slider to set the amount of time the text actually appears on the screen. With the Centered Title style, the text fades in and then fades out. The farther to the right you place the Pause slider, the longer the text appears on the screen relative to the length of the title clip.

    The Pause slider is not active for all title styles; when a style does not include a pause, the Pause slider will be grayed out.

> **NOTE**
>
> As you configure the Speed and Pause sliders, the total length of the title clip appears at the bottom of the Preview window. If the style includes a pause, this will have two components. The first is the speed setting, while the second is the amount of pause. These two values are added to give you the total length of the title clip.

12. When you think that the title is getting close to being ready, click Preview to preview it in the Monitor. If you have a clip selected, the title will appear in that clip in the Monitor. If you have the Over Black check box checked, the title will appear over a black background.

13. Continue making changes to the title until you are satisfied with it (see Figure 10.1).

Figure 10.1 *Here, I am previewing the title I have configured in the Titles palette.*

14. When you are ready to add the title to the movie, drag the title style from the Titles palette to the Clip Viewer. If you are applying the title over a clip, drag it to the left side of the clip to which you want to apply the title. If you checked the Over Black check box, drag the title to the point in the movie at which you want it to appear. When you release the mouse button, the title clip will be added to the Clip Viewer. If you applied the title to a clip, that clip will be separated into two clips. One clip will contain the clip with the title applied, while the other will contain the remainder of the clip without any title effect.

In any case, when you place the title clip on the Clip Viewer, it will be rendered. While the rendering process is occurring, you can continue to work on your movie (however, you might not be able to view the title, nor will you be able to save the movie until all rendering has been completed).

When the rendering is complete, the title clip will include the Title Clip icon at the top to indicate it is a title clip; this icon is a "T" inside a box (see Figure 10.2).

Title clip

Figure 10.2 *The first clip in the Clip Viewer is a title clip.*

15. Select the title clip on the Clip Viewer and press Play to preview it.

Adding a Caption to a Clip

Another example of a commonly used title effect is a caption, which means that text appears on a clip (presumably to place the clip in context or to explain it).

Add a Caption to a Clip

1. On the Clip Viewer, select the clip to which you want to add a caption.

2. On the Titles palette, select the Stripe Subtitle title style. The Preview window will show the selected clip with the title applied to it. The title will contain the last text you typed or iMovie's placeholder text if you haven't created any titles during the current work session.

> **TIP**
>
> If you want the caption to appear on a black screen before the clip instead of over it, check the Over Black check box.

3. Enter the caption's text in the text boxes (the Stripe Subtitle style also allows two lines of text; the top line will appear larger than the bottom line).
4. Use the Font pop-up menu and the Size slider to configure the text.
5. Use the Color button to set the color of the stripe within which the text appears. With this title style, the text is always white; you can change the color of the stripe to make the text legible.
6. Use the Speed slider to set the amount of time that the caption appears on the screen.
7. Click Preview to preview the title in the Monitor.
8. If you are going to watch the movie only on a computer via QT, check the QuickTime Margins check box. This will move the strip caption to the lower-left corner of the screen. If you view the movie on a Timeline Viewer, the title will likely be cut off in this position, so check this check box only if you won't be watching the movie on a Timeline Viewer.
9. Continue refining the title until it is ready for your movie.
10. Drag the title to the left of the clip to which you want to apply it (which should be the clip that you selected in Step 1). The selected clip will be split in two, and the part containing the title will be rendered. The name of the segment of the clip containing the title will be part of the title's text.
11. After the title clip has been rendered, select it and press Play to view it (see Figure 10.3).

Figure 10.3 *A Stripe Subtitle title has been applied to this clip.*

> **NOTE**
>
> Title clips behave just like other clips on the Clip Viewer. You can move them around, delete them, and so on. Of course, if you have applied a title to a clip (such as a caption), moving the title to a different clip can have unanticipated effects.

Changing a Title Clip That Had Been Placed in a Movie

Sometimes, you will want to make changes to titles that have already been placed in a movie. (If you are like me, most of the time this will be because you made a typo when you created the title. If only iMovie included a spell checker!) Making changes to a title clip that has been placed in a movie is similar to creating the title clip in the first place.

Change a Title Clip Included in a Movie

1. Select the title clip that you want to change.
2. Use the tools on the Titles palette to make changes to the title, such as changing its text, speed, font, and so on.

3. When you are satisfied with the changes you have made, click the Update button to apply the changes to the title clip. It will be rendered again, and the changes you have made will become part of the movie.

Smoothing the Digital Flow with Transitions

Back in the section called "The Transitions Palette" in Chapter 8, you learned about iMovie's powerful transitions tools that you could use to add transition effects to your movies. Similar to titles, while there are many kinds of transitions available to you, you apply them using the same general steps.

1. Select the clip to which you want to apply the transition.
2. Select the transition that you want to apply; you will see a preview in the Preview window. See Table 10.2 for a description of the transitions available to you.
3. Use the Speed slider and Direction Arrow buttons to configure the transition.
4. Drag the transition into the movie and place it between the clips that you want to transition between.

Table 10.2 Transitions Available on the Transitions Palette

Transition	Description
Circle Closing	A circle collapses on one clip revealing the next clip outside the collapsing circle.
Circle Opening	A circle opens over one clip while revealing the next clip inside the expanding circle.
Cross Dissolve	One clip dissolves into the next.
Fade In	The clip fades in from a black screen.
Fade Out	The clip fades out to a black screen.
Overlap	The two clips overlap each other for a time.
Push	One clip pushes the next off the screen.

Table 10.2 Transitions Available on the Transitions Palette (continued)

Transition	Description
Radial	One clip is replaced by the next as a hand sweeps around the screen like a second hand sweeps around a clock face.
Scale Down	One clip shrinks in the window revealing the next clip.
Warp Out	An expanding bubble reveals the next clip while removing the current clip from the screen.
Wash In	A clip fades in from a white screen.
Wash Out	A clip fades out to a white screen.

Because the transitions are so similar, after you have used one or two of them, you will be able to use any of them. In this section, you will learn how to apply two of the most useful transitions; reading these steps will enable you to apply any of the other transitions just as easily. You also need to know how to change an existing transition, which is explained after the two example transition sections.

Adding a Fade Out Transition

One of the more useful transition effects is the fade out where a clip fades to a black screen. This transition is great for those times when there is a substantial change between two clips or at the beginning or ending of a segment of your movie. The fade gives the viewer a clear indication that a change is coming, but does so in a smooth way.

Add a Fade Out Transition

1. Click the Trans button to open the Transitions tool palette.
2. Select a clip on the Clip Viewer to choose which clip is used to preview the transition. When you preview a transition, it is applied to the clip you select.
3. Click the Fade Out transition. You will see a preview in the Preview window.
4. Set the speed of the fade by using the Speed slider. Moving the slider to the right makes the transition last longer, which means the clip to which

> **NOTE**
>
> Because some transitions will actually be applied to two clips when you add them to the movie, this preview isn't entirely accurate because it causes the selected clip to transition to itself. Still, the preview will give you a pretty good idea of how the transition will look.

you apply it fades out more slowly. Moving the slider to the left makes the clip fade out more quickly.

5. Click the Preview button to preview the fade in the Monitor.
6. Continue adjusting the Speed slider until you are happy with the results (see Figure 10.4).

Figure 10.4 *This transition will cause a clip to fade to a black screen as you can see it doing in the Monitor.*

7. When the transition is what you want it to be, drag the transition to the right side of the clip on the Clip Viewer that you want to fade out (see Figure 10.5). The transition clip appears as a green box with arrowheads that indicate the direction of the transition. The transition will be rendered and will become part of the movie. A rendering progress bar

appears in the bottom of the clip's icon to show you how the process is moving along.

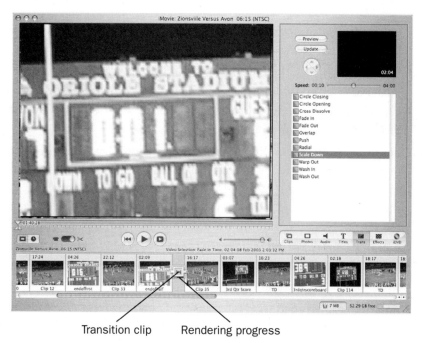

Figure 10.5 *Transition clips appear as green boxes between the clips that they transition between.*

Like titles, when you add a transition to a clip, the clip to which you apply the transition is actually split into two parts. One segment contains most of the clip to which you apply the transition, while the other clip contains a portion of the original clip with the transition effect applied to it.

Even though they look a bit different than video or image clips, transition clips can be handled in the same way. For example, you can apply a transition clip to a different clip by moving it to a new location on the Clip Viewer. And you can delete a transition clip by selecting it and pressing Delete.

Adding a Push Transition

Another useful transition is the Push during which one clip is "pushed" off the screen by the next clip. This is useful for major scene breaks or to indicate the passage of time while maintaining the relationship between the two scenes.

Apply a Push Transition

1. In the Clip Viewer, select the clip where you want the Push transition to take effect.
2. Open the Transitions palette and click the Push transition to select it; then watch the preview in the Preview window.
3. Set the direction of the push by clicking one of the Direction Arrow buttons. For example, to have a clip pushed off the right edge of the screen, click the Right Direction Arrow button. A preview of the push will be shown in the Preview window.
4. Set the transition's duration with the Speed slider; try placing the slider in the middle of its range. If that is too long or too short, use the slider to set the proper amount of time for the transition. In the case of the Push, the speed setting determines how fast one clips pushes the next one off the screen. Drag the slider to the right to make the push slower or to the left to make it faster.
5. When the timing looks close, click Preview to see how it looks on the Monitor (see Figure 10.6).
6. After you are satisfied with the transition, drag the transition from the Transitions palette to the Clip Viewer and drop it between the two clips that you want to transition between. The transition will be added to the movie and will be rendered.

Changing a Transition That Has Been Placed in a Movie

Changing a transition after it has been placed in a movie is just like changing a title clip that is part of a movie.

> **NOTE**
>
> The amount of time over which a transition can be applied depends on the length of time of the clip to which you apply it. A transition effect can't last longer than the clip to which it is applied. If you try to add a transition that is longer than the preceding clip, you will see an error message and will have to shorten the transition or apply it to a longer clip.

Building a Better Video Track in iMovie Chapter 10 **285**

Figure 10.6 *The Monitor shows a preview of the Push transition.*

Change a Transition Clip

1. Select the transition clip that you want to change.
2. Use the transition tools to change the transition, such as changing its duration. You can even change the transition style if you want to.
3. When you are done making changes, click the Update button to implement your changes in the movie. The transition clip will be rendered again.

◆ You can place two transitions adjacent to one another. For example, to have one clip fade out and then the next fade in, place a Fade Out and a Fade In between two clips.

Some Transition Rules to Create By

Transitions are fun to add to a movie, but there are some general guidelines you should follow so your movies make good use, but not overuse, of transition effects.

- Don't feel as though you need to have a transition effect before and after every clip in your movie. Sometimes (dare I say most of the time?), the default straight cut works just fine. This is where your creativity comes in, so experiment until you achieve an outcome that is pleasing to you.
- Certain transitions tend to cause viewers to expect certain things. For example, a fade transition usually implies a longer break in the action, such as a major scene change. A cross dissolve is usually used where a minor scene change is taking place. A straight cut should be used when you want to call as little attention to the transition as possible. Keep these guidelines in mind when you use transitions so you don't stray too far from your viewer's expectations.
- Don't use transitions just for the sake of using them. Adding transitions is fun, and you might be tempted to put them everywhere. When transitions are done properly, the viewer shouldn't even notice them. If you find yourself or your audience being wowed by your transitions, something isn't right. Also, avoid the so-called ransom note effect resulting from applying every kind of transition in a movie—just because you can.

Making Your Movie Special with Special Effects

Special effects are a good way to enhance the quality of your movie's clips or to add artistic touches to your movie. Like the titles and transitions tools, there are a large number of special effects available to you, and the tools that you use to configure them work in a similar manner. However, because the types of special effects are more specialized than titles or transitions, you'll notice a wider variation in the tools that you use for special effects.

The general steps you follow to apply a special effect to a clip are the following:

1. Select the clip to which you want to apply a special effect.
2. Choose the special effect you are going to apply to the clip. See Table 10.3 for a description of the special effects available to you.
3. Use the Effect In and Effect Out sliders to set the start and end points for the effect.

4. Use the other configuration tools to adjust the effects settings. These vary from effect to effect.
5. Preview the effect in the Preview window and in the Monitor.
6. Apply the effect to the selected clip.

Table 10.3 Special Effects Available on the Effects Palette

Effect	What It Does	When To Use It
Adjust Colors	Enables you to adjust the hue, color, and lightness of a clip.	When a clip has poor color or seems somewhat dingy.
Aged Film	Makes the clip look old by adding scratches, jitters, and other artifacts that appear in video capture with old cameras.	For artistic effects.
Black and White	Converts a clip into black-and-white.	For artistic effects.
Brightness & Contrast	Enables you to adjust the brightness and contrast of a clip.	When a clip is too dark, too bright, or has poor contrast.
Earthquake	Causes the clip to "shake."	For artistic effects.
Electricity	Causes an "electric" line to appear at the top of the clip as if it is being hit by lightning or a Tessla Coil.	For artistic effects.
Fairy Dust	Causes a trail of "fairy dust" to move across the screen.	For artistic effects.
Flash	Makes a flash of light wash out the clip for a time.	For artistic effects.
Fog	Shrouds the clip in digital fog.	For artistic effects.
Ghost Trails	Causes the clip to be ghosted so that objects are trailed by faint copies of themselves as they move.	For artistic effects.

Table 10.3 Special Effects Available on the Effects Palette (continued)

Effect	What It Does	When To Use It
Lens Flare	Causes a spot of light to appear as if the camera were pointed toward the Sun when the clip was captured.	For artistic effects.
Letterbox	Places black bars at the top and bottom of the screen to simulate the Letterbox format. This effect actually cuts off the top and bottom part of the clip rather than reformatting it into the true Letterbox format.	For artistic effects.
Mirror	Makes the clip appear with a mirror image of itself.	For artistic effects.
N-Squares	Makes the clip play in each of multiple squares on the screen; you set how many squares appear on the screen.	For artistic effects.
Rain	If rainy days and Mondays get you down, you won't like this one.	For artistic effects.
Sepia Tone	Applies a "wood grain" texture to the clip.	For artistic effects (often used to make a clip appear as if it were filmed in the past).
Sharpen	Adjusts a clip's sharpness.	When a clip is too "fuzzy."
Soft Focus	Applies a blur to the images in a clip.	For artistic effects.

As with titles and transitions, a couple of examples of how to apply special effects will enable you to apply the others. Unlike the titles and transitions, you will probably have to experiment more with the various special effects because of the greater diversity in the controls you use to configure each effect. If you decide that you don't like what you have done to a clip, you can change the effect that you applied, or you can restore the clip to its original condition.

Making New Clips Look Old

A useful special effect is the application of Sepia Tone to a clip, which gives the clip a beige-tinged, wood grain effect that viewers will interpret as the clip being old. This technique is often more effective for implying age than converting a clip to black-and white would be.

> **NOTE**
>
> If you want to maintain a clip's color while you age it, use the Aged Film effect instead.

Add Sepia Tone to a Clip

1. Select the clip to which you want to apply the Sepia Tone effect.
2. Click the Effects button and from the list of available effects, click Sepia Tone. You will see a preview of the effect in the Preview window.
3. Use the Effect In slider to set how long the effect takes to transition in; if you want the whole clip to be in Sepia Tone, leave the slider set all the way to the left. The farther to the right that you drag the slider, the longer it takes for the full effect to kick in.
4. Use the Effect Out slider to determine when the effect begins to go away, thus returning your clip to its previous appearance. If you leave the slider all the way to the right, the clip remains in Sepia for its duration. The farther you move the slider to the left, the earlier in the clip the effect begins to disappear.
5. When you think that you are close to where you want to be, click Preview. You will see a preview of the affected clip in the Monitor.
6. Continue refining the effect until you are happy with it.
7. When you are satisfied with the effect, click Apply, and the effect will be applied to the clip. As with other effects, the clip must be rendered while the effect is applied to it; you will see the progress of this process by the

progress bar that appears at the top of the clip. Clips to which a special effect has been applied have the Special Effect icon (a box with two corners shaded) at the top of their thumbnails (see Figure 10.7).

Figure 10.7 *If this book were printed in color, you would be impressed with the look of this clip to which the Sepia Tone effect has been applied.*

8. When the rendering process is complete, select the clip and click the Play button to view it with the effect applied.

> **NOTE**
>
> Because some of the effects are very intensive for your Mac to apply, the preview in the Monitor might be quite jerky. Don't be concerned about this. After the effect has been applied to the clip and rendered, it will play smoothly.

Improving a Clip's Brightness and Contrast

You can adjust a clip's brightness and contrast for artistic effect or to correct problems with the clip.

Adjust a Clip's Brightness and Contrast

1. Select the clip that you want to correct.
2. Click the Brightness & Contrast effect. You will see a preview in the Preview window.
3. Use the Effect In slider to set how long the effect takes to transition in; if you want the whole clip to be affected, leave the slider set all the way to the left. The farther to the right that you drag the slider, the longer it takes for the full effect to kick in.
4. Use the Effect Out slider to determine when the effect begins to go away, thus returning your clip to its previous appearance. If you leave the slider all the way to the right, the clip will remain as you adjust it for its duration. The farther you move the slider to the left, the earlier in the clip the effect begins to disappear.
5. Use the Brightness slider to change the clip's brightness. Moving the slider to the left makes the overall brightness of the clip darker while moving it to the right makes the overall clip's brightness brighter.
6. Use the Contrast slider to change the clip's contrast. Moving the slider to the left decreases the difference between the light and dark areas of the clip. Moving it to the right increases the difference between the light and dark areas.

> **NOTE**
>
> Brightness and Contrast are always grouped together because changing one often leads you to change the other to achieve the best balance between them. You usually will have to make several adjustments to each slider to get the clip "just right."

7. Click Preview to see the changed clip in the Monitor.
8. Continue adjusting the effect until you are happy with it.
9. Click Apply to apply the effect to the clip. The clip will be rendered with the effect.

10. When the rendering process is complete, select the clip and click the Play button to view it with the effect applied.

> **NOTE**
>
> Because effects are processor-intensive to apply, the rendering process for them will take longer than for titles or transitions. However, since you can continue to work while clips are being rendered, this shouldn't be a problem.

Changing a Special Effect

You change a clip that has an effect applied to it by updating the effect.

1. Select the clip that has an effect applied to it. You will see the clip in the Monitor.
2. On the Effects palette, select the effect that you want to change and use the Effects tools to configure the effect.
3. Click on Apply. The effect will be applied to the clip, and it will be rendered again.

Restoring a Clip

When you apply an effect to a clip, iMovie renders that clip using the effect that you apply. However, it also saves the original clip so that you can go back to it if you want.

1. Select the clip that has an effect applied to it.
2. Choose Advanced, Restore Clip. The clip will be restored to its previous condition.

> **NOTE**
>
> You can only restore a clip until you empty the iMovie Trash. This is because the original version of the clip is stored in the Trash when you apply an effect to it. When the original version is removed from iMovie (by emptying the Trash), it is no longer available to be restored. Make sure you don't empty the iMovie Trash until you are sure that you won't want to restore any of the clips you have modified to their original condition.

> **More on Special Effects**
>
> Feeling special about iMovie's special effects? Here are some more points to ponder:
>
> - You can apply multiple special effects to the same clip. When you apply two or more special effects to the same clip, the number of effects you have applied is indicated by the number next to the special effects icon.
>
> - If you apply multiple special effects to a clip and want to restore it to its original condition, you have to use the Restore Clip command once for each effect you applied to the clip to get it back to its original condition. For example, if you applied two effects to a clip, you will have to use this command twice to restore the clip to its original state.
>
> - As with transitions, you shouldn't add special effects just because you can—which might be a temptation because they are fun to play with. A few special effects go a long way.

Using Cool iMovie Tricks to Liven Things Up

Several iMovie tricks will help you make your movie even more interesting. These include changing the speed at which clips play, changing the direction in which a clip plays, adding an instant replay to a movie, and adding a freeze frame.

Speeding Clips Up or Slowing Them Down

iMovie enables you to change the rate at which a clip plays; you make clips play faster than "normal" or slow them down in a slow motion effect. For example, you might choose to speed a clip up to make it move along faster when the actual content isn't so compelling. Or you might want to slow a clip down to make its detail easier for the viewers to spot.

Change the Speed a Clip Plays

1. Click the Timeline Viewer button to reveal the Timeline Viewer.

2. Use the Zoom slider to choose a viewing magnification that is comfortable for you (the default value might be just fine). For this task, you should be able to see a whole clip's section so it is easy to select.
3. Select the clip whose speed you want to change.

TIP

You can select the clip on the Clip Viewer and then open the Timeline Viewer if you prefer.

4. Move the Clip Speed slider to the left (toward the rabbit) to make the clip play faster or to the right (toward the Turtle) to make it play more slowly (see Figure 10.8). The clip will lengthen or shorten on the Timeline Viewer, depending on whether you slowed it down or sped it up, respectively.

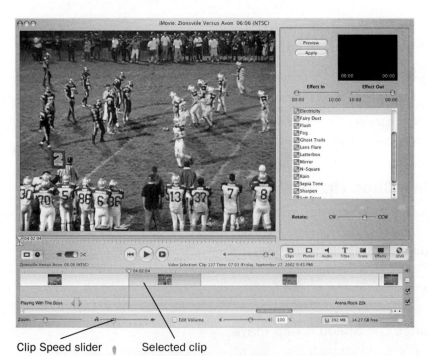

Clip Speed slider   Selected clip

Figure 10.8 *You can use the Clip Speed slider to change the speed at which a clip plays (in this case, the clip will play at a higher rate since the slider is moved toward the rabbit).*

> **NOTE**
>
> When you view a clip whose speed has been changed in the Clip Viewer, a speed change marker will appear on the clip. If you speed up a clip, the fast forward symbol will appear at the top of the clip's thumbnail.

5. With the clip whose speed you changed still selected, preview it in the Monitor.
6. Continue adjusting the speed until you have achieved the effect that you desired.

> **TIP**
>
> Changing a clip's speed also changes its audio. If you don't want the audio to be affected by the speed change, extract the audio from the clip first (you'll learn how to do this in the next chapter) because changing a clip's speed does not affect audio in one of the Audio tracks.

To return a clip to its original speed, repeat the previous steps, except this time place the slider in the center of the range, which is marked with a vertical line. This will return the clip to its original speed.

Changing the Direction Clips Play

You change the direction in which clips play by using the following steps.

Change a Clip's Direction of Play

1. Select the clip whose direction you want to change.
2. Choose Advanced, Reverse Clip Direction (or press ⌘+R). On the Clip Viewer, the clip will be marked with a reverse direction marker (the Rewind symbol) and will play in the opposite direction. In both the Clip Viewer and the Timeline Viewer, the clip's thumbnail will become its last frame instead of its first.
3. Preview the clip in the Monitor.

> **NOTE**
>
> Just like speed changes, when you change a clip's direction, the clip's audio is also changed. But audio on the Audio tracks is not changed. If you want to preserve the direction of the clip's audio, extract it before you change the clip's direction.

Adding Instant Replay

You can combine the previous two tricks to create an instant replay effect.

Create Instant Replay

1. Select the portion of the clip that you want to replay and copy it; to make the most realistic effect, include the very end of the clip in your selection.
2. Move to the Clip Viewer and use the Paste command twice so that you have the three clips in a row. The first clip should be the original, while the next two should be the segment that copied in Step 1 and that will be replayed.
3. Choose the middle clip (the first replay segment) and make it play in reverse.
4. Use the Clip Speed slider to make the clip play very fast. Since the clip is playing in the reverse direction, it will appear to rewind really quickly.

When you play this section of your movie, it will appear as if a segment of the clip is rewound at high speed before replaying, thus looking just like instant replay.

Creating a Freeze Frame

An interesting transition effect is to "freeze frame" the last image in a clip before the transition to the next clip.

Add a Freeze Frame Effect

1. Select the clip that you want to freeze-frame.
2. Move to the end of the clip by dragging the Playhead to the end of the Scrubber bar.
3. Choose Edit, Create Still Frame (or press Shift+⌘+S). A still image clip of the frame that was visible on the Monitor will be created on the Clips

pane in the first empty slot. Its name will be *Still #*, where # is a sequential number.

4. Double-click the image clip you created in Step 3. Its Clip Info window will open (see Figure 10.9).

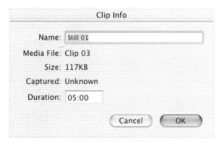

Figure 10.9 *You can set the duration of a freeze frame by using the Clip Info dialog box.*

5. Enter the amount of time you want the image to appear on the screen in the Duration box. The default is 5 seconds.

NOTE
Timecode is used even for still images. To enter 3 seconds, you would type in 03:00, which is 3 seconds and no additional frames.

6. Click OK to close the Clip Info window.
7. Drag the image clip from the Clips pane to the right of the clip from which you created it. When you play this section of the movie, the scene will "freeze" for the duration of the image clip before moving into the next clip.

TIP
You can apply transitions and titles to image clips just as you can to other clips. For example, inserting a freeze frame and then applying a fade out or cross dissolve transition to it makes a very interesting transition.

> **TIP**
>
> You can export any frame in a movie as an image file by moving to that frame in the Monitor and choosing File, Save Frame As (or press ⌘+F). In the resulting dialog box, choose a save location, file name, and format (JPEG or PICT). Click Save, and the frame will be exported from iMovie, and you can work with it just like other image files you have.

Pasting Over a Clip

There might be situations in which you want to replace some or all of the frames in one clip with frames from another clip. For example, suppose that you have shots of the same scene that are taken from different perspectives. You can use one shot as the master and paste in scenes from the other perspective over them.

Paste Over a Clip

1. Select the frames that you want to paste into another clip and copy or cut them.
2. Select the clip into which you want to paste the frames that you copied or cut.
3. Place the Playhead at the point at which you want the paste over to start. You can also use the Crop Markers to select the area in which to paste the copied or cut frames.
4. Choose Advanced, Paste Over at Playhead (or press Shift+⌘+V). The frames that you cut or copied will be pasted over the selected area in the original clip.

Chapter 11

Building a Soundtrack That Rocks

Sound is a very important part of any movie; in fact, a good soundtrack can make a so-so movie good and can make a good movie great. Your iMovie soundtracks can include the following kinds of sound:

- **Native sound.** When you import clips into iMovie, any sound that was part of those clips comes in, too. If your clips had sound, you've already heard it numerous times while you were assembling your movie from those clips. You can use iMovie tools to control some aspects of your movie's native sound.

- **Sound Effects.** You can add sound effects to your movie to bring it to life. You can use iMovie's built-in sound effects, and you can import other sound effects to use.

- **Music.** The right music makes a movie a better experience. You can import music to your movies from many sources, such as your iTunes Music Library, audio CDs, MP3 files, and so on.

- **Narration and other recorded sound.** If you want to explain what is happening in a movie or add your own commentary, you can record narration for your movie. You can also use the narration tool to record sounds from a tape player or other audio device.

While you can work with a movie's video track in either the Clip Viewer or the Timeline Viewer, when you work with sound, you use the Timeline Viewer exclusively. As you have seen, the Timeline Viewer includes three tracks. The top track represents the video track and the native sound of the video included in the movie. The lower two tracks are for audio that you add to your movie, such as sound effects, music, recorded sound, and so on.

After you have added sound to each of these tracks, you mix those sounds so that they all sound just right.

Going Native (Native Sound That Is)

Most of the video that you import into iMovie will contain native sound that presumably goes along with the video since it was recorded at the same time. You can do several tasks to make the most of the native sound included in your video track.

When you edit a video clip that contains native sound, the sound is also edited. For example, if you remove frames from a clip, the audio from those frames is removed too. When you crop a clip, copy frames and then paste them in another clip, or other tasks, the audio in the clips is affected in the same way as the video. For this reason, you should also listen to clips while you edit them to make sure that you aren't removing or changing audio in unanticipated ways. If you want to maintain the sound that came in with video clips so that your edits of the video clip don't change the sound, you can extract the sound as you will learn later in this section.

> **NOTE**
>
> Many of the techniques you will learn for one kind of sound, such as for the native sound, work in the same way for other kinds of sound. To save space in this chapter, you won't find each technique repeated in each section. You should read through this chapter in its entirety so you learn all the techniques you can use when working with sound.

Muting Native Sound

The most basic change that you can make is to mute the Native sound so that you don't hear it when the movie plays. For example, the quality of the sound you recorded with your video camera might not be very good—it might be too choppy because of the edits you made to the video clips, or it simply might not be valuable for the movie. To mute the native sound so that you don't hear it, uncheck the Mute check box located on the right end of the Video track in the Timeline Viewer (see Figure 11.1). Now when you play your movie, you won't hear any of the sound that is part of the video clips in the Video track.

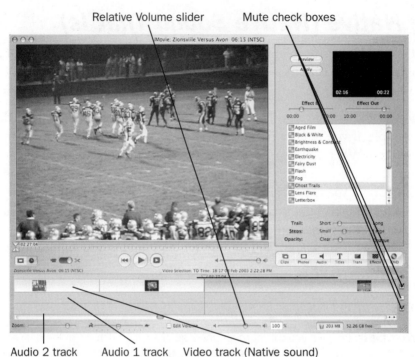

Figure 11.1 *With this configuration of Mute check boxes, the sound in the Video track and Audio track 2 would be heard when the movie played while the sound in the Audio 1 track would not (be heard that is).*

To hear the native sound again, check the Mute check box.

TIP

When you mute a check box and then export your movie, such as exporting it for QuickTime, the sound that you mute is not included in the exported version. This means that the soundtrack that you muted is not heard in the exported version of the movie. When you export the movie to QuickTime, this also makes the resulting file size smaller because you include less data in the movie's file.

Changing the Relative Volumes of Native Sound Clips

Because the clips in the Video track probably came from different sources or were recorded under different conditions, the sound level from one clip to the next might vary quite a bit. Although some variation is natural (you expect the roar of a jet plane to be louder than a cat walking across the road), too much variation (or the wrong variation, such as if the cat is louder than the airplane) can be annoying or distracting. You can use the Relative Volume slider to set the relative sound levels of the various sound clips that make up the Native soundtrack.

Set the Relative Volume Level of the Native Sound in a Movie

1. On the Native track (the top track on the Timeline Viewer), select a clip that should be at the "average" volume level of your movie; after you do so, the clip's bar on the track becomes highlighted in blue to show that it is selected.
2. Make sure the Relative Volume slider is set to the 100% position, which is marked by a vertical line through the slider. This sets the volume level of the selected clip at the "average" level.

> **TIP**
>
> You can also set the relative volume levels as percentages by typing a number in the percent box next to the slider. The position of the slider is always indicated by the percentage displayed in the box. When you move the slider, the percentage changes and when you input a percentage, the slider moves correspondingly.

3. Select another clip in the Video track.
4. Use the Relative Volume slider to set its volume, relative to the "average" clip that you selected in Step 1. If you want the sound of the selected clip to be louder than the sound level of your "average" clip, drag the Relative Volume slider to the right of the 100% position; you can make the sound as loud as 150% of the average sound. If you want it to be quieter, move the slider to the left of the 100% position. Or, if you want it to be about the same, leave the slider in the 100% position, which is the default for all sound.

> **TIP**
>
> You don't have to set the sound level of the "average" clip at 100%. You can set the average point at any slider location or percentage that you choose. The 100% position is easy to recognize, and it is the default level for all sound so it is usually the best choice.

5. Repeat Steps 3 and 4 for each clip in the Video track.
6. Preview your movie to hear the results of your work. Hopefully, all the sound makes sense. Loud sounds should be loud, while quiet sounds should be quiet. If not, continue with the previous steps until the native soundtrack is what you want it to be.

> **TIP**
>
> You can change the relative sound levels for several clips at once by holding the Shift or ⌘ key down while you select the clips. With the clips selected, move the Relative Volume slider. The relative volume of all the selected clips will be set at the level you choose.

Fading Native Sound

You can use iMovie's Edit Volume tool to make the sound of a clip fade in or out smoothly. If you make a clip's sound fade in, it starts completely silently and smoothly increases to the level you set. Similarly, if you fade out a sound, its volume smoothly becomes quieter until, by the end of the clip, it has faded to silence.

Fading sound from clip to clip can make your movie flow more smoothly if it includes native sound, because the sound of each component clip fades in and out rather than going through a jarring transition as one clip's sound runs into the next.

> **NOTE**
>
> If you add a Fade Out or Fade In transition to a clip, its sound also fades, so you don't need to use the Edit Volume tool to fade the sound for that clip.

Fade a Sound In or Out

1. Select the sound clip that you want to fade, such as one of the clips on the Video track that contains sound.
2. Check the Edit Volume check box. The Volume Level bar will appear through each clip in the track that you selected (see Figure 11.2). This line represents the volume level at each point in each sound clip in that track. By default, this line is at the 100% position (relative position ,that is).

Building a Soundtrack That Rocks Chapter 11 **305**

Figure 11.2 *You use the Volume Level bar to set the relative volume level at any point in a clip, such as to fade a clip's sound out at the end.*

TIP

When doing detailed editing work, such as when editing the volume, use the Zoom pop-up menu to expand the clips to make editing the volume easier.

  3. Click on the Volume Level bar at a point at the end of the clip whose sound you want to fade out. A handle (a yellow dot) will appear, and a segment of the Volume Level bar will be highlighted in yellow to indicate what portion of the clip will be affected by the change you make. A smaller dot will appear at the start of the segment to show you where the fade will begin.

NOTE

It can be difficult to get a marker to appear exactly where you want it to be. If the Volume Level bar moves at the start of the next clip instead of the end of the one you are trying to fade, you clicked in the wrong clip. Press ⌘+Z to undo the marker creation and try again.

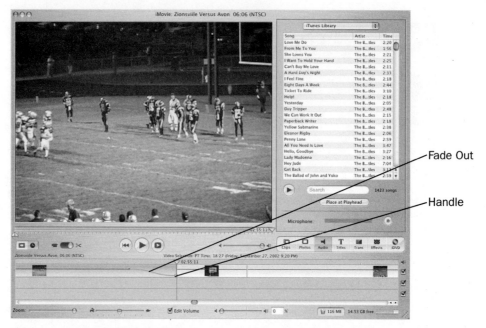

Figure 11.3 *The Volume Level bar in the selected clip indicates the sound in this clip will fade out smoothly.*

4. Drag the yellow handle until it is at the bottom of the clip; this represents the zero volume level (see Figure 11.3). A nice fade out effect will be created, and the clip's volume will smoothly fade out at the end of the clip.

> **TIP**
>
> Instead of dragging the marker, you can use the Relative Volume slider to set the location of the marker, or you can type a percentage in the percentage box (such as 0 to make the sound silent).

5. Move to the beginning of clip whose sound you want to fade in.
6. Click on the Volume Level bar at the beginning of the clip. A marker will appear.
7. Drag the handle to the bottom of the clip, move the Relative Volume slider all the way to the left, or type 0 in the percentage box. The clip's sound will now be silent at the start.
8. Click on the Volume Level bar at the point at which you want the clip's volume to reach its 100% level. Another handle will appear.

NOTE

Before you can move a marker, you must select it. When a marker is selected, it is yellow. When it isn't selected, it is purple.

9. Drag the handle to the 100% point, move the Relative Volume slider to the 100% line, or type 100 in the percentage box. The clip's sound will now fade in smoothly (see Figure 11.4).

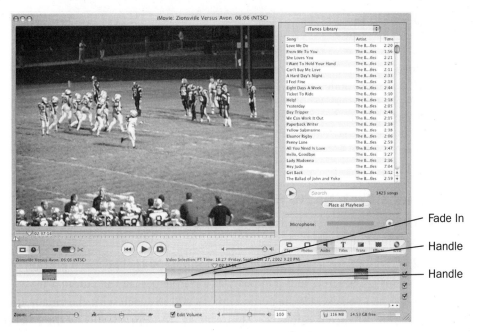

Figure 11.4 *This clip's sound will now fade in smoothly.*

TIP

To remove a marker (thus returning the Volume Level bar to its previous location), select the marker and press the Delete key.

NOTE

You can use the Relative Volume bar to set the relative volume level at an unlimited number of points in your movie. You will learn more about this tool in the section called "Bringing All That Sound Together", later in this chapter.

Extracting Native Sound

You can extract the audio portion of a clip that contains native sound so that you can work with that sound independently from the video clip. For example, you might want to remove some frames from a clip while keeping the underlying sound intact. You can extract the sound from that particular clip and then edit the video without changing the sound that you extracted. Extracting the audio from a clip also enables you to move the sound relative to the video clip. This is useful if you don't want to use all of the audio, but want to keep all of the video in the clip.

> **TIP**
>
> One of the best uses for the extracting audio feature is when you have a clip containing background music that should be at least somewhat synchronized with the video, such as a ballet performance. You can extract the audio, and then you can edit the video part of the clip without hacking up the music that goes with it. You can then "spread" the extracted music so that the single music clip covers all of the video. Although the music may not exactly match what is happening in the video anymore, this is much less distracting than music that jumps around as the edited scenes play.

Extract a Clip's Native Sound

1. Select the video clip from which you want to extract sound on the Timeline Viewer.
2. Choose Advanced, Extract Audio or press ⌘+J. The audio portion of the clip is extracted, and it appears as a purple bar on the Audio 1 track. When you extract the audio clip, it's still in synch with the video clip from whence it came (see Figure 11.5). You can tell this by the Locked icons that appear at the beginning of the video and audio clips. You'll learn more about locking and unlocking audio clips to video in the section called "Bringing All That Sound Together," later in this chapter.

After the audio clip is extracted, you can use the audio editing techniques that you will learn about in the rest of this chapter to work with it. For example, you can move it around, crop it, and so on. After the audio has been extracted, it behaves just like other sounds that you add to your movie.

Building a Soundtrack That Rocks Chapter 11 **309**

Locked icon   Extracted audio

Figure 11.5 *The audio shown in the Audio 1 track was extracted from the clip called "TD" and so is labeled TD – Audio.*

More on Extracted Audio

When you extract audio from a video clip, the audio actually is copied to the audio track rather than being removed from the video clip. The relative volume of the audio that is part of the video clip is also set to zero so that you never hear it again. Does this matter? Not really, but you shouldn't extract an audio clip unless you really need to. Because it is not actually removed from the video clip, a movie file will be larger than if you didn't extract the audio (because iMovie will carry two versions of that sound around) when you export it. If you only want to mute the audio associated with a video clip, set its relative volume to zero instead of extracting it.

This also means that you can hear the sound of a video clip from which you have "extracted" the sound by selecting that clip and using the Relative Volume slider to increase the sound of the clip again. You can use this for some interesting sound effects because you can have multiple versions of the clip's sound playing at the same time—you could also make each version slightly out of synch with the others.

Livening Up Your Movie with Sound Effects

One of the more fun aspects of making a movie is adding sound effects to it. There are two ways to add sound effects to a movie: You can add iMovie's built-in effects, or you can create your own sound effects and add them to an iMovie project.

> **NOTE**
>
> The only difference between a sound effect and other sounds in iMovie is that sound effects are relatively short (usually just a few seconds).

Adding iMovie's Built-In Sound Effects

iMovie includes quite a number of interesting sound effects that are built into the application. You can access these on the Audio palette. To add a built-in sound effect to your movie, do the following steps.

Add a Built-In Sound Effect to a Movie

1. Click the Audio button to reveal the Audio tools.
2. Choose iMovie Sound Effects on the Source pop-up menu at the top of the Audio tools. You will see the list of sound effects that are built into iMovie (see Figure 11.6). These are organized into two groups: Skywalker Sound Effects and Standard Sound Effects. The sounds in these groups work in the same way.
3. Scroll down the list until you find a sound effect that you want to hear.

> **TIP**
>
> You can search for sound effects by name by typing text in the Search box. As you type, the list of sound effects will be reduced so that it includes only those sound effects that include the text you type.

4. Select a sound you want to hear.
5. Click the Play button. You will hear the sound.

Figure 11.6 *When you choose iMovie Sound Effects on the Source pop-up menu on the Audio palette, you will see iMovie's built-in sound effects.*

6. Drag the sound effect onto Audio track 1 to the point at which you want the sound effect to play. As you drag the sound, a yellow line will appear where the sound will be placed when you release the mouse button. When you release the mouse button, the sound will be placed at the location of the cursor. It will appear as a purple bar whose title will be the name of the sound effect (see Figure 11.7).

7. Drag the Playhead to a point just before the sound effect.

8. Click on Play to preview the movie; when the Playhead reaches the sound effect, you will hear it.

9. To change the location of the sound effect, simply drag it to a new location. You can also move it precisely by using the keyboard techniques you learned earlier in the book (for example, select the sound effect and press the Right Arrow key to move it one frame to the right).

Figure 11.7 *The Audio 1 track now has a sound effect placed on it.*

> **NOTE**
>
> You can add sound effects to either audio track. They work the same way no matter which track you place them in. The purpose of providing multiple soundtracks is that you can more easily work with a variety of sounds in your movie, such as sound effects, music, and narration because you have more room in which to work. Because music tends to be long, it can be difficult to include both sound effects and music in the same track. Generally, you should use one track for music and the other for sound effects and other sound. It doesn't really matter which track you use for which purpose, but by default, iMovie will add music to Audio Track 2, so it makes sense to use Audio Track 1 for sound effects and other sound.

Want some more tips about working with sound effects? Check out the following list:

- ◆ You can crop a sound effect using the Crop Markers that appear at each end of the sound effect's bar. You will learn how to crop sounds in the section called "Bringing All That Sound Together," later in this chapter.

- You can change the relative volume of a sound effect just like you do for other sounds in the movie, such as the native sound. You can also check the Edit Volume check box to use the Sound Volume bar to fade the sound effect in or out and to change its volume at any location.
- To delete a sound effect from a movie, select it and press Delete. This only removes the sound effect from the current movie. You can always select it on the Audio palette to add it again in the current movie or in another one.
- You can add the same sound effect as many times to the same movie as you'd like.
- You can also overlap sound effects. To do so, simply drag one effect on top of another. For example, to have lots of people cheer during a movie, drag the Outdoor Cheer sound effect to the Timeline Viewer several times. At those moments where the sound effects overlap, all the overlapped sound effects will play. You can more easily manage overlapped sound effects by placing some in the Audio 1 track and others in the Audio 2 track (assuming you don't have music in that track, of course).
- To keep a sound effect in synch with the video, you should lock the sound effect in place. You'll learn how later in this chapter.

Adding Your Own Sound Effects

iMovie's built-in sound effects are cool, but you can add just about any audio file as a sound effect in a movie. This includes WAV, AIFF, and other common audio file formats. For example, you can download WAV files from the Internet and add them to a movie project.

Add an Audio File as a Sound Effect

1. Move the Playhead to the location in the movie at which you want the sound to play.
2. Choose File, Import. The Import sheet will appear.
3. Move to and select the sound file you want to import and then click on Open. The sound you imported will be added as an orange bar to Audio track 2 at the location of the Playhead (see Figure 11.8).

Figure 11.8 *Here, I have imported a sound effect that I downloaded from the Internet; it appears on the Audio 2 track.*

4. Press the Arrow keys to move the sound effect by one frame or 10 frames at a time (hold down the Shift key) to position the sound effect precisely.
5. Drag the sound effect onto the Audio 1 track if you prefer all of the sound effects to be on that track. When you do so, the sound effect's bar will become purple, just like sound effects you add from the Audio palette.
6. Move the Playhead to a point before the sound effect you added.
7. Play the movie to hear the sound effect you added.

You can edit sound effects that you import just like other sounds in your movie, such as moving it, cropping it, and so on.

Making Your Movie Sing with Music

Music is one of the best things that you can add to a movie (just imagine *Star Wars* without its music, and you'll understand instantly the value of adding music to a movie). There are three ways that you can add music to an iMovie project: You can

> **NOTE**
>
> You can import MP3 and other music files just like any other audio file. See the section called "Adding Your Own Sound Effects," earlier in this chapter, for the steps to do so.

add music from your iTunes Library, you can import MP3 or other music files, or you can record music directly from an audio CD.

Adding Music from Your iTunes Library

Living the iLife is easy because of how well the applications are integrated. Adding music from your iTunes Library to a movie project is a perfect example.

Add iTunes Music to a Movie

1. Click the Audio button to open the Audio Palette.
2. Move the Playhead to the location in the movie at which you want the music to start playing.
3. On the Source pop-up menu, choose iTunes Library or choose the playlist that includes the music you want to add to the movie. In the Content window, you will see a list of every song in your iTunes Library or the contents of the playlist you selected, respectively.

> **TIP**
>
> Under the iTunes Library selection on the Source pop-up menu, you will see each of the standard playlists you have created. When you select a playlist, only the songs in that playlist will appear in the Contents pane of the Audio palette.

4. Scroll or search in the Contents pane to find the music you want to add to the movie. Searching works just like it does in other areas.

> **TIP**
>
> You can double-click on a song or select it and click on the Play Sound button to hear it. To stop the music, click on the Play button again.

5. Click on Place at Playhead. The music will be imported into iMovie and will be placed on Audio track 2 at the location of the Playhead. You will see the name of the song in the music clip (see Figure 11.9).

Figure 11.9 *I've added the song "Playing with the Boys" to the beginning of this movie.*

6. Play the movie. You will hear the music playing as the movie does.

> **NOTE**
>
> Generally, all the music that you listen to, unless you created it yourself, is protected by some sort of copyright. Mostly, these copyrights prohibit you from distributing the copyrighted work as your own or profiting from its distribution. Be aware of any copyright issues related to the music you use in your movies. Generally, as long as you keep your movies to yourself or distribute them to just a few other people, you will be okay copyright-wise. However, if you distribute your movie to many people or use it for any sort of profit-generating work, make sure that you have sufficient licenses to cover the use of that music.

Just like other sounds, you can change the location of music, crop it, lock it in place, and so on. You will learn these techniques in the section called "Bringing All That Sound Together", later in this chapter.

Adding Music from an Audio CD

In the rare case that you want to use music from an Audio CD that you don't want to store in your iTunes Library for some reason (perhaps the music you want to use is from a sound effects collection that you will never want to listen to for its own sake), you can add music directly from an Audio CD to place that music in a movie.

Add Music from an Audio CD to a Movie

1. Open the Audio palette.
2. Insert an audio CD into your Mac's CD drive.

> **NOTE**
>
> iTunes will probably launch and attempt to identify the CD and play it. You can stop the music in iTunes if this happens.

3. On the Source pop-up menu, choose the name of the CD you inserted if your Mac was able to identify the CD or choose Audio CD if it wasn't able to do so. The CD's contents will appear in the Contents pane on the Audio palette.
4. Now move the Playhead to the point in your movie at which you want the music to begin. You don't have to be terribly precise here because you can always move the music around on the audio track later.
5. Select the track that you want to add to the movie.

> **TIP**
>
> You can preview tracks by selecting them and clicking the Play button or by double-clicking the song title you want to hear. You can also search the CD's contents.

6. Click Place at Playhead. The track will be added to the Audio 2 track.

> **TIP**
>
> You can also drag a track from the CD window on the Audio palette onto either of the Audio tracks to add that track to your movie.

7. Use the editing techniques you will learn in the section called "Bringing All That Sound Together" to make any changes that are needed, such as cropping, fading, and so on.

Recording Your Own Sounds

Using the Audio palette's Recording tool, you can record your own sounds to play during your movie. One obvious use for this is to add narration to various parts of your movie, but you can also record your own sound effects.

To be able to record sound from an external source, you need to have some sort of microphone attached to your Mac. Some Mac's have built-in microphones. Other Macs have microphone jacks (although these sometimes require that you use a PlainTalk microphone). One of the best ways to record sound is to use a USB microphone. To record narration, use a headset type microphone, such as those included with voice recognition software. Or add a USB sound input device that enables you to connect a standard microphone to it (many headphone type microphones include such a port).

> **NOTE**
>
> If the audio device you use has an audio in port (sometimes you can use the microphone jack), you can connect the output of an audio device, such as a cassette tape player, to it to record sound from that audio device.

Record Narration or Other Sounds for a Movie

1. Click the Audio button to open the Audio palette. At the bottom of the palette, you will see the recording tool. It includes an input level monitor and the Record button.

2. Drag the Playhead to the point in your movie at which you want to begin recording.

3. Test your microphone setup by speaking into it or making the other kind of sound you will be recording, such as by playing a tape player that is connected to your Mac. If everything is working, you'll see a sound level bar in the input level monitor that shows you the level of the sound that is being input. This bar should be moving to levels at least above halfway across the bar, but it should remain in green. If the level gets into the yellow, the input level is probably too high. If it gets in the red, it is definitely too high.

> **TIP**
>
> You can configure the audio input device, such as a USB microphone, on the Input tab of the Sound pane of the System Preferences application. For example, you can set the input level of the device by using the Input volume slider and monitor that level with the Input level bar.

4. Click the Record button (the button with the red dot in it). Your movie will begin playing. Speak into the microphone or make the sound that you are recording, such as by playing an external audio device. A purple bar will appear on the Audio 1 track to represent the sound you are recording (see Figure 11.10). The sound you record will be labeled *Voice #*, where # is a sequential number (each time you click on the Record button, this number is increased by one).

5. When you have recorded all the sound you want, click Record.

6. Edit the recorded sound using the same techniques that you use for other sound, such as native sound and music. You'll learn more of these techniques in the next section.

Figure 11.10 *The Audio 1 track contains two recorded sounds; Voice 03 is currently being recorded.*

Bringing All That Sound Together

After you have added various sounds to your movie, you are likely to have quite a cacophony of sound. The final step in creating a soundtrack is to edit individual sounds and to mix volume levels so your movie sounds the way you want it to.

When you mix a soundtrack, you want to make sure that the following characteristics are true:

- Sounds start and stop at the right time.
- Relative volume levels are correct.
- Sounds enhance one another (instead of detracting from one another).
- Sounds fade in and out smoothly.
- The soundtrack complements the video track (for example, sound effects occur at appropriate moments).

Play your movie from start to finish and pay careful attention to the sound. Evaluate the soundtrack and make notes where improvements are needed. Then use the techniques you will learn in this section and have learned earlier in this chapter to make any changes that are needed.

Changing the Location of Sound Within a Soundtrack

You can change the point in the movie at which a sound plays by dragging its clip on the Timeline Viewer. You can also select the clip and use the Arrow keys to position a clip more precisely.

Cropping Sound

When a sound is too long, you can crop that sound. Each sound clip on the Audio tracks includes a Crop Marker at each end. You can use these markers to select the part of the sound clip that you want to hear when the movie plays. You can also remove the audio that you don't want to be included in the movie by cropping it.

Crop a Sound Clip

1. Select the sound that you want to crop. It will become highlighted.
2. Drag the Crop Marker at the end of the audio clip to where you want the sound to stop. The Playhead will stick to the crop marker so that you can easily see where it will end (and you can use the Arrow keys to position it precisely). The sound that will remain will be shown by the darkened area while the sound that is not selected is indicated by the light part of the sound clip bar (see Figure 11.11).
3. Move the Playhead to the point just to the left of the Crop Marker.
4. Play the movie to hear where the sound stops.
5. Adjust the crop marker if needed.
6. Repeat Steps 2–5 for the Crop Marker at the beginning of the sound clip if you want to crop sound from the beginning as well.
7. Choose, Edit Crop. The sound outside of the Crop Markers will be removed from the clip and from the movie. The clip will shorten to indicate that the sound has been removed.

> **NOTE**
>
> You don't actually have to use the Crop command if you want to leave the sound clip intact for some reason. Any sound outside of a clip's Crop Markers won't be heard when you play or export the movie. However, you should crop out unused sound clips to save disk space after you are sure you won't need that sound any more.

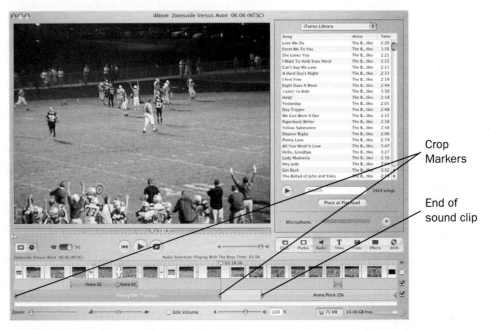

Figure 11.11 *You can use the Crop Markers in an audio clip to crop the sound.*

Fading Sound

You can use the Edit Volume tool to fade a sound in or cause it to fade out (for example, when you crop a sound, you should fade it at the crop point so it ends or starts smoothly). You can fade any sound clip just like you fade Native sound. See the section called "Fading Native Sound" earlier in this chapter for the steps to fade a sound in or out.

Adjusting Relative Volume Levels of Audio Clips

As with the clips in the Native soundtrack of a movie, you want all the sound in a movie's soundtrack to play at an appropriate relative volume level. Typically, you want the music to play more quietly than other sounds so that it doesn't drown out the other sound in the soundtrack. You can use the Relative Volume tools to mix the volume levels of each element of a movie's soundtrack to ensure that each sound plays at an appropriate relative level. Setting the relative volume level of clips among all of the Audio tracks in a movie's soundtrack is done just like setting the relative volume level of clips in the Native Audio track. See the section called "Changing the Relative Volumes of Native Sound Clips" earlier in this chapter for the detailed steps to do this.

Adjusting Relative Volume Levels Within Audio Clips

There might be points in the soundtrack at which you want to lower or raise the relative volume level *within* a sound clip (rather than changing the relative volume level of the entire clip). For example, you might want to lower the relative volume of music when narration is playing so that the narration can be heard clearly. When the narration is not playing, you might want the music to become louder again. You can use the Edit Volume tool to accomplish this.

Change the Relative Volume Level at Any Point Within a Sound Clip

1. Check the Edit Volume check box. The Volume Level bar will appear in each sound clip.
2. Click the Volume Level bar at the point in a clip at which you want to start to change the relative volume level. A handle will appear at the point on which you clicked.

TIP

The currently selected handle is yellow. Unselected handles are orange.

3. Click at the point of the clip's Volume Level bar at which you want to change the relative volume level again. The area between the two markers represents the area of the clip over which you want to change the relative volume level.

4. Drag the first handle down to lower the clip's relative volume at that point or drag it up to increase the clip's relative volume at that point. The section of the Volume Level bar that you are changing will move up or down to indicate the change you have made (see Figure 11.12).

Figure 11.12 *Here, I have lowered the relative volume of the music in Audio Track 2 during the period where narration is playing in Audio Track 1.*

> **TIP**
>
> You can also select a handle and use the Relative Volume slider to change its relative volume level. You can also enter a percentage in the percent box to input a precise relative volume level.

5. Play the section of movie over which you have changed the clip's relative volume.

6. Make changes as needed. For example, you can change the relative volume by dragging the markers up or down.

You can add handles anywhere on the Relative Volume bar in any clip by clicking on it. You can then use these handles to change the relative volume level over the segment defined by two markers.

> **TIP**
>
> To remove a handle, select it and press the Delete key.

Locking Sound in Place

As you continue to work on your movie, you are likely to make some minor adjustments to it (or even some major ones). If these changes involve changing the video track, sounds that you have carefully placed in your movie can become unsynchronized.

You can lock audio to a specific point in a video clip so that when you move the video or when it moves because of edits you make elsewhere in the movie, the audio goes along for the ride and always remains in synch with the video.

To lock a sound in place, do the following steps.

Lock Sound in Synch with Video

1. Select the sound that you want to lock (you can select any type of sound clip).
2. Place the Playhead at the point at which you want to synchronize the sound.
3. Choose Advanced, Lock Audio Clip at Playhead (or press Cmd+L). The Locked icons will appear (see Figure 11.13). One icon appears at the beginning of the locked audio, and the other appears at the point in the video track to which the audio is locked.

Figure 11.13 *Locked Audio icons indicate that audio has been locked to specific points in the video track.*

If audio has been locked to a Playhead position, then when the movie plays and that position is reached, the audio will play, even if you change the video track (such as by removing frames from a clip). In other words, as you make changes to the video track, the locked audio clip "moves" with the point at which you locked it so that it always plays at that point in the video track.

TIP

To unlock an audio clip again, select it and choose Advanced, Unlock Audio Clip (or press ⌘+L).

On the other hand, if an audio clip is not locked to a Playhead position, when you make changes to the video clip, the audio clip remains in its current location on the timeline, regardless if the video it "goes with" moves because of edits you made.

> **NOTE**
>
> Interestingly, you can't change the name of sound clips. You can select a sound clip and open the Info window, but you will see that the name field is empty. Even if you type a name in, that name won't appear in the sound clip.

Chapter 12

Producing Your Movies

After a movie has a great video track that is complemented by an equally impressive soundtrack, it is time to put the wraps on it. First, you should do a final edit of the movie to make sure it is all it can be. Then you can export the movie in a number of ways so that you can enjoy the fruits of your labor.

Polishing a Movie Until It Shines

After you have "finished" a movie, you should do a final edit of the movie to make sure it is what you want it to be. Make any changes you need to if you find problems that should be fixed.

Perform a Final Edit of a Movie

1. Make sure no clips are selected (if they are, choose Edit, Select None).
2. Click on the Start of Movie button.
3. Play the movie.
4. Use the techniques you learned throughout this part of the book to make any of the following changes to the movie if they are needed:

- Edit clips to remove material from clips that are too long.
- Remove clips that you don't want in the movie.
- Add, delete, or change titles, transitions, and effects.
- Add, delete, or change sounds.
- Remix the audio tracks.

Exporting a Movie to Videotape

Putting your iMovie projects on videotape is a good way to store and distribute them for the following reasons:

- **Almost every home has a VCR.** Because VCRs are ubiquitous, you can count on being able to distribute your projects on videotape to just about anyone. Unlike other distribution methods, such as DVD or over the Web, you don't have to be concerned with whether the person to whom you are sending the videotape will have the equipment needed to view it.

- **Videotape is inexpensive**. You can purchase blank videotapes for less than $1. That makes them a very inexpensive media to use to record your projects.

- **No technical savvy is required to play videotapes**. Using a VCR is very basic, and there aren't any technical issues associated with playing one. You don't have to be concerned that the person receiving your videotape won't know what to do with it.

Videotape also has some drawbacks. One is that the resolution at which a standard television and VCR works is fairly low, so you can't expect the same viewing quality that you can achieve on your Mac. Another is that videotape is linear; your viewer is locked into viewing the tape in a specific order (unlike other means, such as DVD, by which the viewer can choose the order in which to view your content).

To get an iMovie project on videotape, you export the movie to your DV camcorder and then record it onto videotape.

Recording an iMovie Project on a DV Camera

You can export any iMovie project to videotape by using the following steps.

Record an iMovie Project on a DV Camera

1. Put a tape on which you want to record your movie in your DV camera.

2. Connect your DV camera to your Mac's FireWire port, turn the camera on, and put it in the "VCR" mode (often called VTR).

3. In iMovie, choose File, Export Movie (or press Shift+⌘+E). The iMovie: Export dialog box will appear (see Figure 12.1).

4. In the Export Movie dialog box, choose To Camera on the Export pop-up menu (it will probably be selected by default).

5. If your camera takes longer than 5 seconds to get ready to record (it probably doesn't), increase the value in the "Wait" box.

6. Input the amount of black screen before your project starts playing in the "Add __ seconds of black before movie" box. The default value is one

Figure 12.1 *Exporting an iMovie project to videotape really is as simple as this dialog box makes it appear.*

second, but you might want to have more "empty" space before your movie starts. This can make it slightly easier to record on a VCR later.

7. Input the amount of black space after your movie by entering a value in the "Add __ seconds of black to end of movie" box. This black space makes a nice buffer between elements recorded on the same tape.

8. Click Export. iMovie will start your camera recording, pause the amount of time you entered in Step 5, play a black screen for the amount of time you entered in Step 6, and then begin recording your iMovie project on the DV camera. When the project has been recorded, iMovie will add the amount of black space that you entered in Step 7 and then stop the DV camera. Your project will be recorded on the DV's tape just as if you had recorded it through the DV camera's lens.

> **TIP**
>
> Some DV camcorders have a pass-through mode that passes the camcorder's input to its output ports. This is very useful because you can connect the camcorder to your Mac and a VCR at the same time, which enables you to record the movie on a VHS tape at the same time you are exporting it from iMovie. Using this mode also results in a higher quality tape because you are recording the movie only once rather than twice (first on the camcorder's tape and then on the VHS tape).

Recording from a DV Camera to VHS

After your project is on a DV tape, you can easily transfer it to a VHS tape.

Transfer a Project from a DV Camera to VHS

1. Connect the standard video and audio ports of your DV camera to input ports on the VCR; many VCRs have ports on the front to make this connection easier. Most DV cameras ship with the cable you need to make this connection.

> **NOTE**
>
> Some DV cameras require that you use a VTR, VCR, or dubbing mode to record the camera's output onto a VCR. If your camera requires this, place the camera in the appropriate mode when you connect it to the VCR. If you don't know which mode to use, see the user manual for your camera.

2. Set the VCR's input mode to be the ports to which you connected the DV camera in Step 1.
3. Move the DV camera to the black space before your iMovie project starts.
4. Put the VHS tape that you are going to record your iMovie project on in the VCR and get it in the position at which you want to begin recording.
5. Start recording on the VCR.
6. Play the tape in the DV camera.
7. When the project has finished, stop the DV camera and the VCR. Your project will be on the VHS tape, and you can view it on any VCR.

Exporting a Movie to DVD

Putting an iMovie on DVD is cool for several reasons. First, DVDs are much easier to handle and store than VHS tapes. Second, when you put an iMovie project on DVD, you can add chapter markers so that the viewer can jump to any scene in your movie without having to fast forward or rewind it. Third, you can include all sorts of other content on a DVD, such as slideshows. And, finally, because you can use iDVD to create interesting menus, a movie on DVD is just plain cool.

Adding Chapter Markers

When you export a movie for DVD, you should add chapter markers to it. These markers make it possible for viewers to use the DVD controls to jump to specific points in the movie to view them by using the chapter menu (also called a scene index). Each chapter marker you add to a movie will become a button on the DVD's chapter menu; viewers can jump to that point by clicking the scene's button. You can add up to 36 chapters markers to a movie.

> **NOTE**
>
> You don't have to add chapter markers to put an iMovie project on DVD; they are simply a tool to make viewing a movie more convenient.

Add Chapter Markers to an iMovie Project

1. Click on the iDVD button. You will see the iDVD palette.
2. Move the Playhead to the point where you want to place the first chapter marker.
3. Click on Add Chapter. The new marker will be shown at the top of the iDVD palette. For each marker, you will see the first frame, the chapter title, and the timecode at which the chapter starts.

> **TIP**
>
> You can add chapter markers from either the Clip Viewer or the Timeline Viewer. When you are working in the Clip Viewer, you can select a clip to place a chapter marker at the start of the clip.

4. Edit the chapter's title. This is the text that will appear next to the chapter on the DVD (see Figure 12.2).

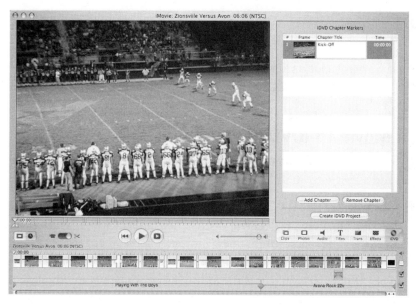

Figure 12.2 *This movie now has one chapter marker.*

5. Repeat Steps 2 through 4 for each chapter you want to create (see Figure 12.3).

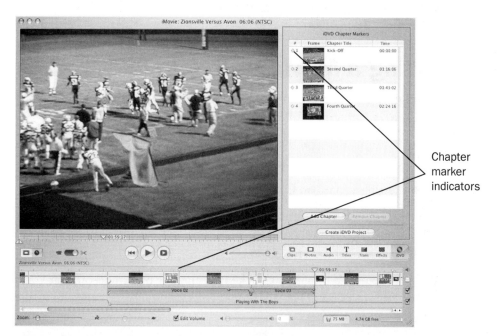

Chapter marker indicators

Figure 12.3 *Now it has a chapter marker for each quarter in the game.*

> **NOTE**
>
> In the chapter marker list, you will see a yellow diamond next to the chapter markers. This same symbol appears in the Timeline Viewer to show you where the chapter markers are currently located (refer to Figure 12.3).

Moving a Movie to iDVD

After you have added chapter markers (if you are going to add them, of course), you can add a movie to an iDVD project in the following two ways:

- **Click the Create iDVD Project button.** When you click this button on the iDVD palette, iDVD will open, a new project will be created, and the movie will be placed in that new project. Then you can use iDVD's tools to design the menus and configure the buttons. This option is most useful when the iMovie project is the only content you are going to place on a DVD.
- **Import the movie into an existing iDVD project.** You can add any iMovie project to an iDVD project by importing it into the project (and there are a couple of ways to do that).

You'll learn how to use iDVD in Part IV of this book.

Exporting a Movie to QuickTime

You might want to export an iMovie project as a QuickTime movie for a number of reasons, including the following:

- Posting movies on the Web
- Sending movies via email
- Putting movies on CD

Because all Macs and most Windows PCs can play QuickTime files (QuickTime is also a standard on the Windows platform), most computer users can view the QuickTime movies you create.

When you export a movie to QuickTime, there is one trade-off that you always have to keep in mind. That is *file size versus quality*. Improving the quality of a movie that you export *always* increases its file size. When you choose less compression or increase the quality level of the compressor that you select, the image and sound quality of the QuickTime movie will be better, but the file size will also be larger.

File size is critical to the method you will use to distribute the QuickTime movie you create. For example, you should limit movies that you email to other people to 2MB or less (unless you are sure they use a broadband connection to the Net; even then, most email gateways limit the size of file attachments that can be received). If you are going to put the movie on a Web site, its file size can be larger, but you still can't get carried away; even professionally produced trailers for movies are usually 25MB or less (in their largest format presentation). If you want to put a movie on a CD, the QuickTime file can be 650MB or so.

When you export a movie as QuickTime, you choose the quality of the resulting movie while keeping in mind how you will distribute that QuickTime file (thus, the file size).

There are two basic ways to set the quality/file size of a QuickTime movie that you export. You can use one of iMovie's standard format options, or you can use the Expert settings.

Exporting a Movie Using a Standard Format

Exporting an iMovie project using one of iMovie's predefined formats is usually the best way to go because it is simple to do and these formats are optimized for the various ways you might want to distribute a movie.

> **TIP**
>
> You can export as many QuickTime versions of a movie as you'd like. For example, you might want to create one version for emailing and another for the Web.

Export an iMovie Project as a QuickTime Movie Using a Standard Format

1. Open the iMovie project that you want to convert into a QuickTime movie.

2. Choose File, Export (or press Shift+⌘+E). The iMovie: Export dialog box will appear.
3. In the Export Movie dialog box, choose To QuickTime on the pop-up menu (see Figure 12.4).

Figure 12.4 *Don't let the simple appearance of this dialog box fool you; exporting an iMovie project as a QuickTime movie is very useful.*

4. Choose the standard format that you want to use on the Formats pop-up menu. On this menu, you will see the following options (listed in order of smallest file size/lowest quality to largest file size/highest quality):
   - Email
   - Web
   - Web Streaming
   - CD-ROM
   - Full Quality DV

   You will also see the Expert Settings option, which you will learn about in the next section.

   Choose the format that is appropriate for the way in which you are going to distribute the movie, such as Web Streaming for a movie that you will post on a Web site that supports streaming, such as a .Mac Web site.

> **NOTE**
>
> Choosing a standard format is no guarantee that the resulting QuickTime file will actually be sized appropriately. For example, if you choose the Email format when you export a long movie, the file size might be way too large to actually send to someone over email. These formats are configured appropriately for the distribution method, but the actual file size depends on the format and the length and content of the movie.

5. Click Export. The Save sheet will appear.
6. Choose a location in which to save the movie, name it (leave the .mov file name extension), and click Save. You will see a progress bar that provides you with an estimate of how long the process will take.

> **NOTE**
>
> Exporting a relatively long movie can take a very long time. Applying the various compression formats to a movie processor intensive, and your Mac has to do lots of work to get the job done.

After the movie has been exported, you can view the resulting QuickTime movie and distribute it via email by putting it on the Web, and so on.

> **NOTE**
>
> If the resulting file size is too large for the way in which you want to distribute the movie, export it again with one of the other formats or use the Expert settings so that you get a smaller file.

Exporting a Movie Using Expert Settings

Most of the time, choosing one of the standard QuickTime format export options is the way to go. However, if you want to experiment by setting the various options yourself, you can use the Expert Settings format option to do so.

The compressors and other options that are available to you in the Expert Settings dialog box are fairly complex and are beyond the scope of this book. Most of the time, one of the standard formats will be what you end up using anyway. However, you can experiment with some of the expert settings if you really want to fine-tune your movies.

You can configure a custom combination of settings used to export a movie by doing the following steps.

Use Expert Settings to Export an iMovie Project

1. Open the iMovie project that you want to convert into a QuickTime movie.
2. Choose File, Export (or press Shift+⌘+E). The iMovie: Export dialog box will appear.
3. In the Export Movie dialog box, choose To QuickTime on the pop-up menu.
4. Choose Expert Settings on the Formats pop-up menu.
5. Click Export. You will see the "Save exported file as" dialog box (see Figure 12.5).

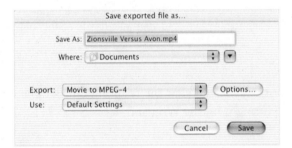

Figure 12.5 *This simple dialog box enables you to access many complex controls you can use to save an iMovie project in a wide variety of file formats and options.*

6. Choose the export option on the Export pop-up menu. This determines the file format of the resulting file. (Some examples are explained after these steps.)
7. Choose to use a standard configuration for the selected file type on the Use pop-up menu or click the Options button to customize the settings used to export the file.
8. Name the file (don't change the file name extension that is added when you choose the format of the exported file).
9. Choose the location in which you want to store the exported file.

Producing Your Movies   Chapter 12   341

10. Click Save. The file will be exported in the format and with the settings that you selected.

While the details of the file format choices you have and the configuration options for each are beyond the scope of this book, some examples might help you understand the breadth of the options you have.

You can export an iMovie project in a number of file formats; you select the format you want to use on the Export pop-up menu. Some of the more useful choices are the following list.

> **NOTE**
>
> If you haven't upgraded to QuickTime Pro, you might not see all of the options in the following list.

- **Movie to AVI.** This option creates an avi file, which is a dominant video standard for Windows computers.
- **Movie to MPEG-4.** The MPEG-4 format is the most modern compression scheme and results in the best quality versus file size ratio. Not all computers will be able to view content in this format (a player must support this format to be able to view MPEG-4 content; for example, QuickTime Player version 6 or later can do this).
- **Movie to QuickTime Movie.** This option creates a movie in the QuickTime movie format, and you can customize the compression and quality settings that are used.
- **Sound to AIFF.** This option saves the movie's soundtrack as an AIFF file that you can use in various ways, such as a background sound for a DVD menu in iDVD.

After you have selected the file format you want to export the movie in, you configure the settings for that format; the settings that are available depend on the format you select. There are two ways to select export settings. You can use the Use pop-up menu to select standard settings, or you can use the Options button to use custom settings.

On the Use pop-up menu, you will find standard settings for the file format you select on the Export pop-up menu. For example, Figure 12.6 shows the standard settings that are available when you export a movie in the MPEG-4 format.

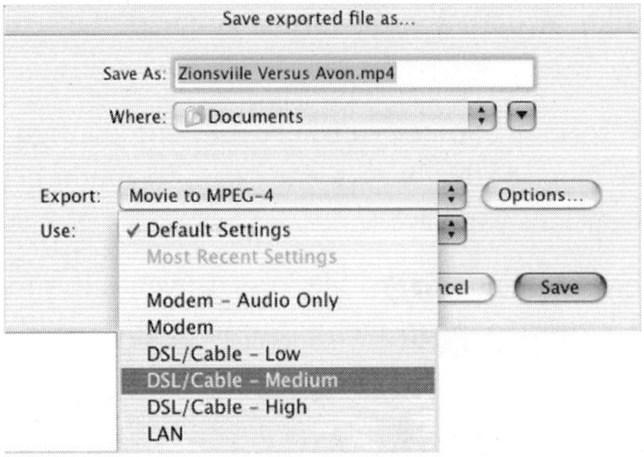

Figure 12.6 *The standard settings for the MPEG-4 format are designed for various connection methods.*

If you click the Options button instead, you will see a dialog box that enables you to customize each setting. The options you have are also driven by the file format you select. Some formats have simple options, while others have very complex settings. For example, Figure 12.7 shows the MPEG-4 Settings dialog box that enables you to configure many aspects of the MPEG-4 files that you create.

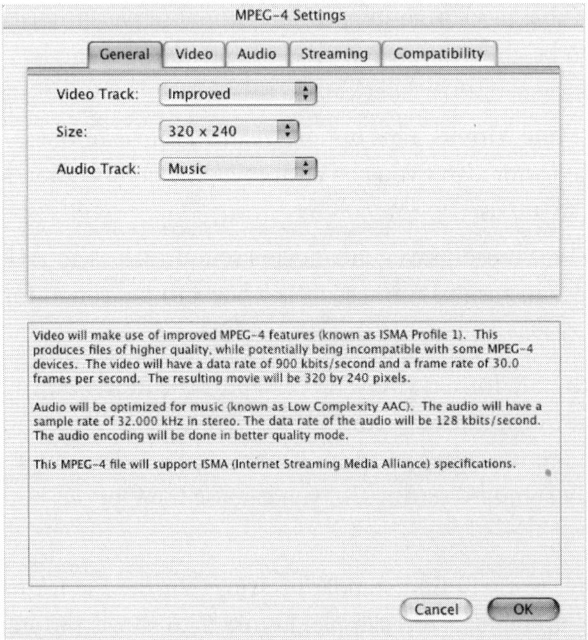

Figure 12.7 *With the MPEG-4 file format, you can perform a very detailed configuration of the format's setting options.*

PART IV

iDVD: The Power of a Movie Production Studio in Your Mac

13 **Touring Your iDVD Production Powerhouse**

14 **Building a DVD**

15 **Designing a DVD**

16 **Previewing, Fixing, and Burning A DVD**

Chapter 13

Touring Your iDVD Production Powerhouse

The Mac is the premiere digital media platform precisely because it has a set of "jaw-dropping, holy-cow-that-is-way-cool" applications that are groundbreaking in many ways. iDVD is another amazing application in that set. With iDVD, you can put your projects on DVD for playback on your Mac or, even better, on most standard DVD players. This enables you to move your projects from the computer room to the living room.

Since DVD players are almost as common as VCRs these days and most households now have them, putting your great (and even not-so-great) projects on DVD is a fantastic way to share those projects with other people.

What's amazing is that with iDVD, not only can you place your projects on DVD, but the DVDs you create can contain custom motion menus and buttons, just like those that appear on commercially produced DVD movie discs. What's even more amazing is that using iDVD is mostly a matter of drag-and-drop, so you can create these amazing DVDs in just a few minutes.

> **NOTE**
>
> iDVD is the one digital lifestyle application that requires specific hardware. That hardware is a DVD Recordable (DVD-R) drive that you use to write to DVD-R discs. In fact, if you don't have a DVD-R drive, iDVD will not even open. The good news is that almost all Macs now have the Apple SuperDrive as an option; this drive includes a DVD-R drive. There are also third-party DVD-R drives available (although for maximum compatibility, an Apple SuperDrive is your best option). If you don't have a DVD-R drive, reading this chapter might provide the motivation you need to get one! (Besides, you were looking for a reason to get a new Mac anyway!)

Working in the iDVD Window

Looking back over the hundreds of applications that I have used in my Mac life, iDVD is among the few that took my breath away when I first saw it (talk about being happy to be a Mac user!). iDVD is a picture of power and elegance wrapped up in a very attractive package.

Touring Your iDVD Production Powerhouse   Chapter 13   347

On the surface, iDVD appears to be relatively simple, which is a good thing because this makes creating DVDs easy and fun. In the background, iDVD manages the complexity of encoding and writing DVDs for you so that you can focus on the more creative aspects of the process.

> **NOTE**
>
> This part of this book is based on version 3.0 of iDVD.

The iDVD Window

When you launch iDVD, you see the iDVD window (see Figure 13.1). Like iMovie, iDVD automatically opens the last project on which you worked. If you haven't used iDVD before, you can create a new project.

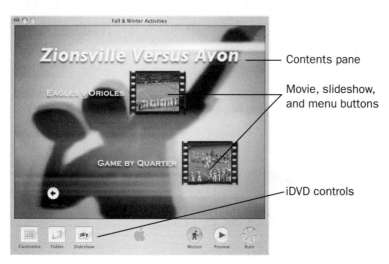

Figure 13.1 *The iDVD window is elegantly designed; it combines simplicity with power.*

The top and largest pane of the window is the Contents pane. What you see and do in this area depends on the mode in which iDVD is operating (you'll learn more about these modes in the next section). When you are in the Design or Preview mode, the Contents pane shows a menu on the DVD; a menu is a container that holds buttons. Buttons represent each project that has been placed on the DVD, or they can lead to another menu. When viewing a DVD, you click a button to view the content or menu with which it is associated. Each menu can include up to six buttons.

Each menu also has a theme that determines how the menu looks and sounds. At the most basic, a theme is simply a static image that is the menu's background. However, menus can contain motion, which means that a movie can play as the menu's background while the menu appears on the screen (if you have watched DVD movies, you have no doubt seen examples of motion menus). Motion menus can include a movie with sound, a movie without sound, or a static image with sound. You can apply one of iDVD's default themes to your menus, and you can create and save your own themes.

Buttons can also have motion, which means that the content that is accessed by that button plays within the button itself while the button is being viewed. This type of motion provides a preview of the content without the viewer having to actually open it. (Again, if you have viewed commercially produced DVD movies, sometimes the chapter buttons contain motion and show you part of the chapter associated with the button.)

iDVD Controls

Along the bottom of the iDVD window is the toolbar that contains six buttons (see Figure 13.2). Each of these enables you to perform a specific task.

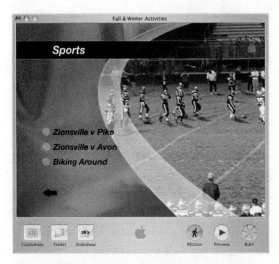

Figure 13.2 *The iDVD window includes six buttons in its toolbar.*

- **Customize.** This button opens the iDVD Drawer (also called the Customize Panel). You'll learn more about this in the next section.
- **Folder.** You click this button to add a folder button. A folder button represents a menu on the DVD. After you add a folder, you can place content on the menu that the folder button represents.
- **Slideshow.** You click this button to add a slideshow to the menu you are currently viewing.
- **Motion.** This button turns background and button effects, called motion effects, on or off. When the button is green, motion effects are on and will be displayed on the screen. When the button is gray, motion effects are off and won't be displayed.
- **Preview.** When you click this button, iDVD moves into the Preview mode (you'll read more about this mode later in this chapter).
- **Burn.** When you are ready to create a DVD, you click this button to write the project to a DVD.

The iDVD Drawer (aka the Customize Panel)

When you click the Customize button, the iDVD Drawer appears (see Figure 13.3). The Drawer contains controls and information that you use while you design and build a DVD.

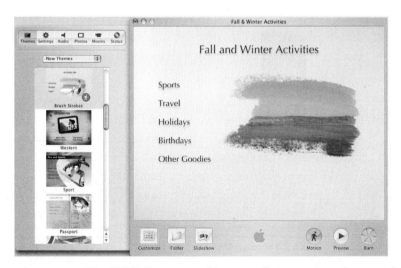

Figure 13.3 *The iDVD Drawer enables you to design various elements of a DVD, add content to it, and monitor various aspects of the burn process.*

> **NOTE**
>
> The iDVD Drawer is also called the *Customize Panel* (which is why the button name is *Customize*). *Drawer* is the more generic term for an interface element that "slides out" of a window, so that is the term I tend to use. Within iDVD, you will see this called the Customize Panel. These two terms refer to the same element.

Along the top of the iDVD Drawer, you will see six buttons, which are the following:

- ◆ **Themes.** Themes are a set of formatting options that you can apply to a menu by clicking the theme that you want to use. A number of standard themes are provided with iDVD for you to use. You can also create and save your own themes so that you can use them just like iDVD's standard themes.
- ◆ **Settings.** The Settings tools enable you to customize the appearance of a menu from adding background images or movies and sound to formatting the menu's title to formatting the buttons' locations and titles.
- ◆ **Audio.** You use the Audio tools to access the music stored in your iTunes Music Library. You can add this music as background to any menu on a DVD, and you can also use it to add soundtracks to slideshows on a DVD.
- ◆ **Photos.** You use the Photos tools to access the images stored in your iPhoto Photo Library. You can use these images as backgrounds for any menu on a DVD, and you can create slideshows from them.
- ◆ **Movies.** You can use the Movies tools to add iMovie and QuickTime movies to a DVD.
- ◆ **Status.** The Status tools enable you to assess the status of the content that you place on a DVD. This includes both the movies you add to the DVD as well as any other files you want to include on it, such as high-resolution versions of the images contained in a DVD's slideshows. You also use the Status tools to add content to the DVD-ROM portion of a DVD (the additional files that can be used when the DVD is inserted into a computer).

You'll learn how to work with each of these tools throughout this part of the book.

> **NOTE**
>
> You can learn about iDVD in more detail in my book *iDVD 3 Fast & Easy*.

iDVD Modes

iDVD has different modes for different parts of the DVD creation process. The following sections give you an overview of each of these modes.

Design Mode

The Design mode is the one in which you add movies and other content to a DVD. You also use this mode when you are designing the "look and feel" of a DVD by applying background images, background sounds, titles, motion effects, and so on to a DVD on which you are working. Some of the major elements of the iDVD window in design mode are shown in Figure 13.4 and explained in the following list:

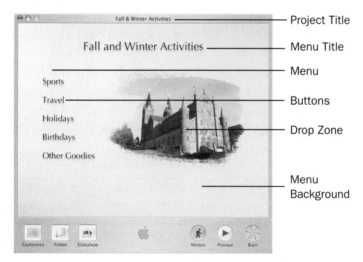

Figure 13.4 *In the Design mode, you design a DVD (clever name, huh?)*

- ◆ **Project Title**. The project title is the name under which you save the iDVD project file. This is the name of the file you open to open a project. It does not actually appear when the DVD is viewed.

> **NOTE**
>
> When you create a DVD using iDVD, you create an iDVD project. This project contains the information that makes up the DVD including its content, background images and sounds, formatting, and so on.

- **Menu.** The Contents pane of the iDVD window represents a menu that will appear on the screen when the DVD is being viewed.
- **Menu Title.** Each menu can have a title to identify that menu. You can format menu titles in a variety of ways.
- **Menu Background.** Each menu can have an image as its background. Or you can use a movie as a background; when the menu appears on the screen, the background movie will play. You can also add background sounds to any menu.
- **Buttons.** On-screen buttons represent movies, slideshows, or other menus on a DVD. Buttons can be text (as in Figure 13.4), images, or previews of the content to which a button points, such as a movie.
- **Button Titles.** Each button is identified by a title. When a button contains an image or preview, the title appears next to the button; when a button is text only, the button title is the button itself. You can format button titles in a number of ways.
- **Drop Zone.** Some menus contain a Drop Zone in which you can place images or movies that are displayed while the menu that contains the Drop Zone is on the screen.

> **NOTE**
>
> The difference between adding an image or movie to a background and adding an image or movie to a Drop Zone is that the when you add an image or movie to a background, that item fills the entire menu. When you add such an item to a Drop Zone, it is displayed only in the Drop Zone itself.

DVDs that you produce with iDVD, just like those that are produced commercially, can include multiple levels of menus. Each menu can contain content buttons (such as for movies or slideshows) or menu buttons that lead to other menus. All DVDs contain at least the main menu, which is the menu that appears when the DVD is played. The main menu is also the one that appears when you open an iDVD project.

You can add menus to the main menu and then add submenus to those menus to build a multitiered structure for a DVD.

Each menu can contain up to six buttons, with each button representing either content (a movie or slideshow) or a submenu. A DVD can contain up to 36 menus—you aren't likely to want to actually include that many, however.

In the Design mode, you can move among menus by using folder, Back, and Forward buttons.

Slideshow Mode

In the Slideshow mode, you can create slideshows from images that are contained in your iPhoto Photo Library or anywhere else on your Mac. You can control the order in which the images appear, the amount of time each image appears on the screen, and the soundtrack that plays while the slideshow does. In Slideshow mode, the iDVD window provides the tools you need to create your slideshows, as shown in Figure 13.5 and explained in the following list:

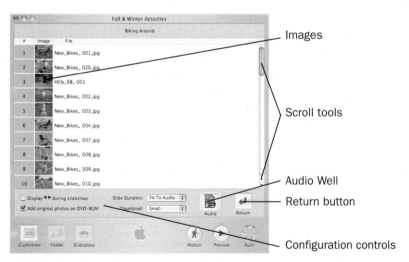

Figure 13.5 *Creating slideshows on DVD is a great way to view your photos.*

- **Images.** The images that are contained in the slideshow are displayed in the upper part of the window in the order in which they will appear during the slideshow.
- **Scroll tools.** You can use the scroll tools to browse the images shown in the window.
- **Configuration controls.** You use these controls to configure specific aspects of the slideshow (you'll learn about these in detail later in this part of the book).
- **Audio well.** You place the sound file you want to use as the slideshow's soundtrack here.
- **Return button.** Click on this button to move back to the menu on which the slideshow is contained; it also returns iDVD to the Design mode.

Preview Mode

iDVD enables you to preview a DVD before you burn it. In the Preview mode, iDVD behaves just like a DVD player; it even presents an on-screen remote control that you use to control the DVD. You use the Preview mode to "watch" a DVD before you actually burn it to a disc. Previewing a DVD enables you to find and fix mistakes so that you don't waste time and money burning discs that have problems. In the Preview mode, the iDVD window looks like that shown in Figure 13.6 and contains the elements explained in the following list:

- **Content window.** This window contains the content that will be displayed on the screen when the DVD is played on a standard DVD player or on a computer.
- **Remote Control.** The iDVD remote control simulates the remote controls used by many DVD players and includes most of the primary controls you will use to view the DVD.
- **Menu controls.** These buttons perform menu tasks; for example, click on the Menu button to move to a DVD's main menu.
- **Playback controls.** Use these buttons to play a DVD.
- **Cursor controls.** Use these controls to make selections in the DVD window. You can use the direction arrows to move the cursor and the Enter button to choose what you have selected.
- **Volume slider.** Drag this to the right to increase the volume or to the left to decrease it.

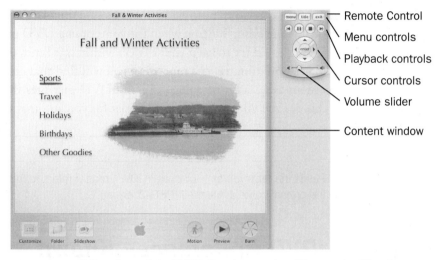

Figure 13.6 *Liberal use of the iDVD Preview mode will prevent a liberal waste of DVD discs.*

Burn Mode

This is the mode you use when you burn a DVD. In this mode, the iDVD window displays a progress bar that shows you the current status of the burn process.

iDVD Projects

Similar to iMovie, when you create a DVD, you first create a project. The project determines what content will appear on the DVD as well as its look and feel.

The content that you place on a DVD will consist of either movies or slideshows. Because you can place any iMovie or QuickTime content on DVD, there is really no limit to the movie content that you can place on a DVD. You can create slideshows from still images in the usual image formats, such as JPEG, TIFF, and so on. Again, because iDVD supports all the standard formats, you can add just about any image to an iDVD slideshow.

When you place content on a DVD (by adding to a project), it is encoded into the MPEG-2 format, which is the standard for DVD. MPEG-2 provides very high quality with relatively small file sizes (thus making digital movies on DVD possible). Fortunately, iDVD manages the encoding process for you and does so automatically. You'll learn how to assess the encoding status of the content on a DVD that you are creating later in this part.

A DVD created with iDVD can contain up to 90 minutes of content. However, iDVD uses a higher-quality encoding scheme when the content in a DVD project is 60 minutes or less—you should try to keep your DVDs within this limit, if possible. (You might think that 60 minutes isn't much, but you will find that creating 60 minutes of *good* content takes a bit of doing.) Again, iDVD manages this for you; the application chooses the 90-min or 60-min format for you automatically.

> **NOTE**
>
> Just like iMovie, iDVD uses the term *render*. However, in iDVD, render refers to the process of encoding the project content into the MPEG-2 format.

Making Your iDVD Preferences Known

As with other applications, iDVD includes a set of preferences that you can configure to suit your needs. You can set iDVD preferences by choosing iDVD, Preferences (or by pressing ⌘+,). The iDVD preferences window contains three buttons in its toolbar that enable you to set preferences in the following areas: General, Slideshow, and Movies (see Figure 13.7). The preferences available to you are explained in Table 13.1.

Figure 13.7 *The iDVD Preferences window enables you to set your preferences in three areas: General, Slideshows, and Movies.*

Table 13.1 iDVD Preferences

Preference Area	Preference	What It Does
General, Project Settings	Show Drop Zones check box	Drop Zones are areas of a menu on which you can place images or video to customize that part of the menu. When you check this check box, you will see the borders of any Drop Zones on a menu. With this unchecked, the borders of a Drop Zone are invisible. Generally, you should leave this checked because it makes working with Drop Zones easier.
General, Project Settings	"Show Apple logo watermark" check box	This setting shows or hides the Apple logo that appears in the lower-right corner of the iDVD window. While being proud that you use a Mac to create DVDs is a good thing, I find the logo to be in the way most of the time, so I recommend you uncheck this check box. (Perhaps you can convince Apple to pay you a royalty if you leave this watermark on!)
General, Project Settings	"Enable background encoding" check box	This control enables iDVD to encode the material you place on a DVD in the background. You will learn more about encoding later in this book; for now, trust me that background encoding is a good thing. I recommend that you check this check box.
General, Project Settings	"Delete rendered files after closing a project" check box	AS you learned earlier, iDVD has to render the content you place on a DVD. If you check this check box, the application will delete the rendered files when you close a project. Generally, you don't want that to happen until you are completely done with a project, so I recommend that you uncheck this check box. (You can delete files manually from the Finder when you have completely finished with a project.)

Table 13.1 iDVD Preferences (continued)

Preference Area	Preference	What It Does
General, Video Standard	NTSC or PAL radio button	There are two primary video standards. NTSC, which stands for National Television Standards Committee, is the primary video format in the U.S., Japan, and some other non-European countries. PAL, which stands for Phase Alternating Line, is the primary video format in Europe. Each format has its own parameters, such as frame rates and such, but you really don't need to worry about the details. If you are creating projects that will be displayed on U.S. equipment, choose the NTSC radio button. If you are creating projects for display on European systems, choose PAL. If you change format, the change you make will apply only to new projects, so make a preference choice before you start a new iDVD project.
Slideshow	"Always add original slideshow photos to DVD-ROM" check box	You can add image files to the DVD-ROM portion of a DVD—this is the part of the disc that can only be accessed by a computer. There are two reasons you might want to do this. One is that you want the recipients to be able to use the images on their own computers; providing the images as separate files is how you can do this. The second reason has to do with the resolution of the images. When you add photos to a slideshow within iDVD, the application matches the resolution of those images to that used by standard DVD players and TVs. This resolution is typically quite a bit lower than the resolution at which you capture images. This means that the images that are part of the DVD are low-

Table 13.1 iDVD Preferences (continued)

Preference Area	Preference	What It Does
		resolution. If you want the recipient to have access to high-resolution images, then you can provide those image files on the DVD. Because it is very easy to add specific image files to the DVD-ROM part of a disc, you should usually leave this check box unchecked. (You'll learn more about this topic later in this part of the book.)
Slideshow	"Always scale slides to TV Safe area" check box	Computers use a different display proportion than do TVs. Because of this, things that look fine when displayed on a computer can be cut off when displayed on a TV. The TV Safe Area is a box that iDVD places on the screen, so you can be sure the content you place on a DVD won't be cut off when you play the DVD on a TV. If you check this preference, iDVD will scale images to fit within this TV Safe Area automatically. This is usually a good thing, so you should leave this check box checked.
Movies, When importing movies	"Automatically create chapter marker submenu," "Never create chap-importing movies chapter marker submenu," or "ask each time" radio button.	As you learned in the previous chapter, you can add chapter markers to an iMovie project to create chapter menus (also called scene indexes) on a DVD. This preference determines if such menus are created automatically, are never created, or are created only after you indicate they should be when prompted when you add a movie to a DVD menu. You might not want all of your movies to have these menus, so I recommend that you select the "Ask each time" radio button.
Movies, Look for my movies in these folders	List of Folders	When you add a movie to a DVD, you can click the Movies button to display the contents of each folder that you add to the list

Table 13.1 iDVD Preferences (continued)

Preference Area	Preference	What It Does
		of folders (the Movies folder within your Home folder is on the list by default). You can add or remove folders from this list to make them available or hidden when using the Movies palette (you'll learn more about this later).

> **NOTE**
>
> There is another video format that will eventually overtake the two that iDVD currently supports. That is High-Definition Television or HDTV format. This format provides much higher image quality than the others and is designed to use the same screen proportions that movies in the theater do (16x9). While iDVD does not yet support this format, it probably will someday—hopefully soon!

Making DVDs with iDVD

Making DVDs with iDVD should be more than just dropping movies and images on a new iDVD project. To get the best results, you should use a structured process consisting of the following general steps:

1. Create a project plan.
2. Create the DVD's menu structure.
3. Create a new iDVD project.
4. Create the movies, music, and images that you will put on the DVD.
5. Add content to the DVD.
6. Design the DVD's menus and buttons.
7. Preview the DVD and fix any problems you find.
8. Burn and label the DVD.

You will learn how to accomplish each of these steps in the remaining chapters in this part of the book.

Using iDVD for Your iLife Projects

iDVD is an amazing tool that you can use to put all the cool projects you create using iMovie, iPhoto, iTunes, and other tools on DVDs that you can view with your Mac or with most standard DVD players. Because you can add such interesting and fun elements to the DVD, your projects will look even better when you see them on DVD. Additionally, you can use iDVD to add all sorts of files to a DVD for other purposes, such as to back up the images and movies you have added to a DVD.

> **iDVD Menu Commands and Keyboard Shortcuts**
>
> While some of the commands listed in the following table might not be familiar to you the first time you read through this book, they will make perfect sense when you have read through all of this part of the book. You can use this table as a handy reference whenever you need a quick refresher on a specific command or to know the keyboard shortcut for commands you use frequently.

Table 13.2 iDVD Menu Commands and Keyboard Shortcuts

Menu	Command	Keyboard Shortcut	What It Does
iDVD	Preferences	⌘+,	Opens the Preferences dialog box.
File	New Project	⌘+N	Creates a new iDVD project.
File	Open Project	⌘+O	Opens an existing iDVD project.
File	Open Recent	None	Opens a previous project on which you have recently worked.
File	Save Project	⌘+S	Saves the current project.
File	Save Project As	Shift+⌘+S	Saves the current project under another name.
File	File, Import, Video	None	Imports a movie file onto the current menu.
File	File, Import, Audio	None	Imports an audio file to use as a slideshow soundtrack or as the background sound for a menu.
File	File, Import, Images	None	Imports images to use in a slideshow or as the background for a menu.

Table 13.2 iDVD Menu Commands and Keyboard Shortcuts

Menu	Command	Keyboard Shortcut	What It Does
File	File, Import, Background Video	None	Imports a movie file as the background of the current menu.
File	Burn DVD	⌘+P	Burns the current project onto DVD.
Edit	Select All	⌘+A	Selects all the items (such as buttons on a menu) on the screen.
Edit	Deselect All	Shift+⌘+A	Deselects any selected items.
Project	Project Info	⌘+I	Opens the Project Info window that you can use to see the status of all the files used in an iDVD project.
Project	Hide/Show Customize Panel	Shift+⌘+B	Opens or closes the iDVD Drawer; this does the same thing as clicking the Customize button.
Project	Add Folder	Shift+⌘+N	Adds a new folder button to the current menu.
Project	Add Slideshow	⌘+L	Adds a new slideshow button to the current menu.
Project	New Menu from Selection	None	Creates a new menu containing the selected items.
Project	Go Back	⌘+B	Returns you to the previous menu.
Advanced	Show/Hide TV Safe Area	⌘+T	Displays or hides the box that represents the YV Safe Area.
Advanced	Motion	⌘+J	Turns motion effects on or off; this does the same thing that clicking the Motion button does.
Advanced	Apply Theme to Project	None	Applies the current theme to every menu in an iDVD project.
Advanced	Apple Theme to Folders	None	Applies the current theme to all folders (menus) that are submenus to the current menu.

Chapter 14

Building a DVD

Now that you have a firm grasp of iDVD and have configured your preferences, it's time to get cranking on your own DVD projects. In this chapter, you will learn the fundamental tasks you need to do to create an iDVD project, add content to it, and develop the content and menu buttons that will appear on the DVD. Your goal in this part of the process is to get all of a DVD's content in its iDVD project and to organize and label that content appropriately. In the next chapter, you'll learn how to format the entire DVD by applying themes, setting menu backgrounds, configuring motion effects, and so on.

Planning a DVD

Doing a DVD the right way is more than just launching iDVD, dropping files on the iDVD window, and clicking the Burn button. To create a DVD that makes sense to viewers and looks good to them, you should plan an iDVD project so that it is one you intentionally create rather than being a collection of files that are haphazardly thrown onto a disc. In addition, a simple plan makes creating that DVD much easier and faster. The major elements of planning a DVD are the following:

- Understand the structure of DVDs you create
- Plan a DVD
- Create an iDVD project
- Create menus in the iDVD project to organize it

Understanding a DVD's Structure

DVDs use a nested menu structure to organize their contents (see Figure 14.1). The "top-level" menu on a DVD, more commonly called the *main menu*, is the first one that appears when the DVD is played. It contains buttons that cause content to be played or that lead to other menus "lower" down in the DVD's structure. The other menus on a DVD can also contain buttons that play content or that lead to menus even lower down in the structure. All menus, except the main menu, have a button that leads back to the previous menu.

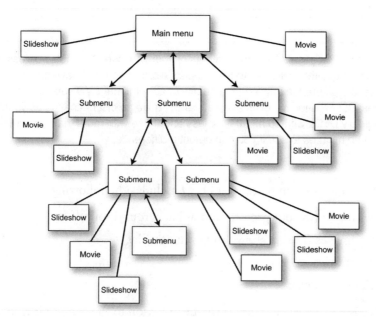

Figure 14.1 *DVDs are organized using a nested structure; levels can contain one or submenus (except the top level that contains the main menu).*

Using iDVD, your DVDs can have up to 36 menus. Each menu can have up to six buttons on it (where a button can point to content, such as a movie or a slideshow, or to a submenu). In iDVD logo, a menu is also called a *folder*. When you add a folder to a menu, you are actually creating a menu on a level below the current one (a submenu).

Usually, each menu should contain content that has a similar theme, such as events, dates, and so on (except the main menu, which leads to all the content on the DVD). This approach organizes a DVD's contents and helps viewers understand where to go to view the content they want to see.

Planning an iDVD Project

The first and most fundamental step is to decide what you want to put on the DVD. While it might seem like a trivial task, it is actually the most important part of the project. You have up to 90 minutes of "room" on a DVD. Although this might not seem like a lot, after you start creating individual projects to put on a DVD, you might discover that it takes a lot of work to develop this much content.

> **NOTE**
>
> Apple claims that you should limit the contents of your DVDs to 60 minutes or less for the best possible quality. I will have to take Apple's word on this as I have never been able to detect the difference between the quality of a 60-minute DVD versus one that is 90 minutes. But perhaps my eyes and ears aren't quite as discriminating as yours, so you should try DVDs with 60 minutes or less and those with more than 60 minutes but less than 90 minutes to see if you can detect a difference.

The type of content you can place on a DVD includes the following:

- iTunes music (in your projects and as background sound)
- iPhoto images (in slideshows and as image files)
- iMovie movies
- QuickTime movies

The best DVDs will have some sort of rhyme or reason to the content included on them. For example, you wouldn't expect a DVD that has videos and slideshows of family activities to also include your own attempt at a Sci Fi thriller. Decide on the theme for your DVD and let that theme drive the creation of the projects you put on it.

Organizing and Outlining a DVD's Content

To get started, organize your content by menu; think about a menu as being a folder for specific content, and you'll get the idea. Each menu will appear in its own window on the DVD. For example, you might choose to group projects related to specific time periods on different menus, or you might want to put all of a DVD's movies on one menu while its slideshows appear on another. As you plan, remember that each menu can have up to six buttons, where each button can either lead to content (such as a movie or slideshow) or to submenus.

You should prepare a planning document for your DVD that will guide you as you create its structure and then add content to that structure. One way to create this plan is to use a word processor and create a table with the following columns:

- **Menu Name.** Each menu on a DVD should have a name; this name appears on the menu to identify it when it is viewed. Generally, menu names help viewers identify the content on that menu.
- **Button.** List each button that will appear on each menu that you listed in the previous column.
- **Description.** Describe each button you listed in the previous column. This description will list the name of the menu to which the button points or will describe the content to which the button points, such as a movie or slideshow.
- **Music and Sound.** Use this column to plan the music or sound that you will use as background sound when the menu appears on this screen or as a soundtrack for content, such as a slideshow.
- **File Location.** Finally, list the location on your Mac where each file you will need for the DVD is located. For music or photos that reside in the respective iTunes or iPhoto libraries, list the appropriate library as the file location.

This task might seem a bit tedious, but it will pay off handsomely when you create a DVD. Having a detailed plan will enable you to create a better DVD and to create that DVD faster. Of course, a plan is just that, a plan; you can make changes on-the-fly as you develop an iDVD project. But a good plan will lead you to a great DVD much faster than just winging it (see Figure 14.2).

> **TIP**
>
> If you like to plan graphically, consider creating a plan using a diagram such as that shown in Figure 14.1. Instead of the generic box labels shown in that figure, you can actually put the menu and button names in the boxes on the diagram. This might help you better visualize the structure of the DVD you are creating.

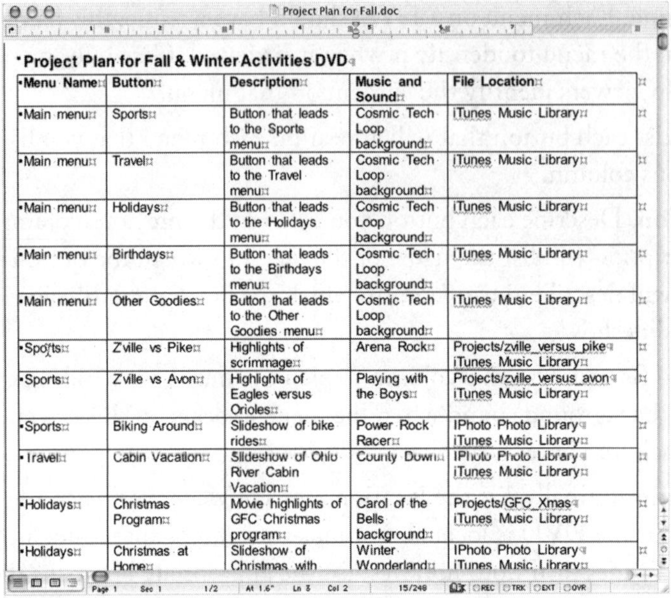

Project Plan for Fall.doc

Project Plan for Fall & Winter Activities DVD

Menu Name	Button	Description	Music and Sound	File Location
Main menu	Sports	Button that leads to the Sports menu	Cosmic Tech Loop background	iTunes Music Library
Main menu	Travel	Button that leads to the Travel menu	Cosmic Tech Loop background	iTunes Music Library
Main menu	Holidays	Button that leads to the Holidays menu	Cosmic Tech Loop background	iTunes Music Library
Main menu	Birthdays	Button that leads to the Birthdays menu	Cosmic Tech Loop background	iTunes Music Library
Main menu	Other Goodies	Button that leads to the Other Goodies menu	Cosmic Tech Loop background	iTunes Music Library
Sports	Z'ville vs Pike	Highlights of scrimmage	Arena Rock	Projects/zville_versus_pike iTunes Music Library
Sports	Z'ville vs Avon	Highlights of Eagles versus Orioles	Playing with the Boys	Projects/zville_versus_avon iTunes Music Library
Sports	Biking Around	Slideshow of bike rides	Power Rock Racer	IPhoto Photo Library iTunes Music Library
Travel	Cabin Vacation	Slideshow of Ohio River Cabin Vacation	County Down	IPhoto Photo Library iTunes Music Library
Holidays	Christmas Program	Movie highlights of GFC Christmas program	Carol of the Bells background	Projects/GFC_Xmas iTunes Music Library
Holidays	Christmas at Home	Slideshow of Christmas with	Winter Wonderland	IPhoto Photo Library iTunes Music Library

Figure 14.2 *A DVD plan will help you create better DVDs faster.*

When it is complete, print your plan because you will be referring to it constantly as you develop the iDVD project.

And Now, a Few More Words on Copyright ...

As you develop your DVD, you might want to include material that other people have produced in the projects that you place on it. The most obvious application is music from audio CDs that you own, which you could use for soundtracks of movies or slideshows. However, you might also want to include QuickTime movies that you downloaded from the Internet, clips from movies, or images that someone else has created. Almost all material that someone else has created is copyrighted.

Most copyrights allow you to use the material for your own viewing but prohibit the redistribution of that material in any form. This means you can use copyrighted material in your productions as long as you don't plan on distributing the end product to other people (especially for profit, but that is not the issue).

You can usually stretch this a bit if you are just sending DVDs to a few people you know, such as your family and some friends. However, if you go beyond this, you should NOT use any copyrighted material in your productions.

> Be especially careful about projects you create and then post on the Web. When you post something on the Web, you are, in reality, distributing it to the world and that will violate the copyright on most copyrighted material. Again, as long as you don't have a Web site that lots of people visit, you aren't likely to run into trouble. But you should be very careful about posting content that contains copyrighted material unless you have a license to use it in that way.
>
> If you do plan on distributing a DVD to lots of people, you need to obtain a license for any material that you don't create yourself. While you probably can't afford to license music from the audio CDs in your collection, there are many types of royalty-free music and images that you can purchase that do allow you to use that content in your own projects and don't restrict your right to distribute the projects you create.
>
> To locate sources of royalty-free content, search the Internet. You will find many sources from which you can purchase content that you can use in your projects without restrictions.
>
> Most people use iDVD to create DVDs for themselves and just a few other folks, so I won't spend any more time on copyright issues in this book. If you are going to distribute the DVDs you create to more than a handful of people, you should get very familiar with copyright implications if you use material other than that you create yourself.

Creating an iDVD Project

Each DVD that you create with iDVD begins with an iDVD project file. This file contains all the content (movies, slideshows, images, and files) that will eventually wind up on a disc along with all of the information about how that content will be presented to the viewer—namely, the format of the menus, background images and sound, and so on. One thing about iDVD project files is that they are big—really big! You will need lots of hard disk space when you create a new project so that it has room for all of the information that is required to create a DVD.

Armed with your DVD plan, you are ready to jump into iDVD and create the iDVD project.

Create a New iDVD Project

1. Launch iDVD.
2. Choose File, New Project. The Save sheet will appear.

> **NOTE**
>
> If you haven't used iDVD before, you don't need to do this step because a prompt asking you if you want to create a new project will appear automatically. Choose the New Project option and then proceed with the next step.

3. Name your project. You can name your project anything you'd like because the name you choose won't appear when the DVD is played (names of individual menus on the DVD do appear). The project name is simply the file name of the iDVD project file.
4. Choose a location in which to save the project. It's important to choose a location in which to save an iDVD project that has enough room to store the project's content. This does not need to be the same place where you store the content for the project; for example, you might create the content for the DVD on a different disk than the one on which you store the iDVD project itself. Make sure that the location where you save your iDVD project has at least 5GB of free space on it. If you have very little content for the DVD, you can get away with less, but 5GB of free space will ensure that you don't run out of disk space while creating a project, which you definitely don't want to happen.
5. Click Save. iDVD will create your project, and you will see the iDVD window, which will show the DVD's main menu. The name of your project will appear at the top of the window. Within the main menu window, you will see one of Apple's menu designs that appears by default if you haven't used iDVD before or the most recent menu design you used if you have worked with iDVD before (see Figure 14.3).

> **NOTE**
>
> The name of the main menu will be the name of the theme that is applied to it. You will fix this in a moment.

6. Click the Motion button. This will turn off any motion effects that are part of the menu's design. These effects can be distracting, not to mention annoying, until you are ready to design the DVD's appearance, which you will get to later in the process.

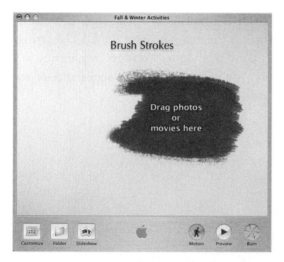

Figure 14.3 *A new iDVD project might not be much when you create it, but you will fix that as you work through the DVD creation process.*

Creating the Menus on a DVD

After you have developed your project plan and have created a new iDVD project, you can create the framework for that project. This framework involves creating a menu on the DVD for each menu listed in your project plan (except the chapter menus for your iMovie projects—you will add those menus when you add the iMovie projects to the DVD). The framework provides all the containers into which you will place the content that will go on the DVD.

Create the Menu Structure for a New iDVD Project

1. Open the project for which you want to create a structure if it isn't open. You will see the main menu that has one of iDVD's themes applied to it already. However, the theme that is applied might be distracting, so apply a less distracting theme for the time being.
2. Click on the Customize button. The Drawer will appear on the left side of the window.
3. Click the Themes button if it isn't selected already.
4. Scroll down in the drawer until you see the Brushed Metal Two theme.

5. Click on the Brushed Metal Two theme. It will be applied to the menu that you are viewing, which is the main menu of the DVD (see Figure 14.4). This is a relatively plain theme that won't get in your way as you create the menu structure. You will customize the appearance of your menus later in the process.

Figure 14.4 *Now that the Brushed Metal Two theme has been applied, there is nothing to get in your way as you build the DVD.*

6. Click on the text "Brushed Metal Two," which is both the name of the theme and the name of the main menu. The text will become editable.

7. Refer to your project plan to get the name of the DVD's main menu and type that name over the selected text. This process will rename the menu to be what your plan calls for.

> **TIP**
>
> Remember to save your project as you work. iDVD doesn't save projects automatically; if it happens to crash while you are working, you will lose any unsaved changes. Fortunately, like all other Mac applications, you can save an iDVD project by pressing ⌘+S.

8. Refer to your project plan to get the number and names of the menu buttons that will appear on the main menu.//
9. Click on the Folder button, choose Project, Add Folder, or press Shift+⌘+ N. A new folder button, entitled My Folder, will appear, which represents a submenu on the DVD.

> **NOTE**
>
> Remember, iDVD refers to submenus as folders. It works this way because menus contain other things, just like folders on the desktop do.

10. Click on the button title that appears at the bottom of the button. The button will be highlighted to show that it is selected, and the preview slider will appear at the top of the button's icon.
11. Click on the button title again. The text will become highlighted so that you can edit it.
12. Type the name of the first menu button on the main menu as listed on your project plan.
13. Click outside of the submenu button. The name of the button will become what you typed in the previous step (see Figure 14.5).

Figure 14.5 *The main menu now contains one menu button, which is called Sports.*

14. Repeat Steps 9–13 for each submenu on the main menu as defined in your DVD plan. The main menu will have a button that represents each of the submenus that you listed for it in your project plan (see Figure 14.6).

Figure 14.6 *If you compare this to the project plan in Figure 14.2, you will see I have created a folder button for each menu button on the main menu.*

> **NOTE**
>
> Don't worry about the location of the buttons or the appearance of the menu. For example, the name of menus you create will default to the name of the theme applied to that menu. You will design how the DVD looks after you place and organize all of the content on it.

15. Double-click on the first submenu's button on the main menu. That submenu will open and will replace the main menu in the iDVD window. The name of the menu will be the name of the theme applied to it, such as Brushed Metal Two.

> **TIP**
>
> You can tell you are on a submenu by the appearance of the Return button in the lower-left corner of the menu's window. (This button always contains a left-facing arrow, but it can look different for different themes applied to the menu.)

16. Select the menu name and type the menu name listed in your project plan. Usually, this will be the same as the name of the button that leads to the menu, but that doesn't have to be the case.
17. Click on the Folder button, choose Project, Add Folder, or press Shift+⌘+ N. A new folder button, entitled My Folder, will appear. This represents a submenu on the menu currently being displayed.

> **NOTE**
>
> Not all menus will have submenus. In fact, many menus will contain only content buttons. For such menus, you don't need to add any folder buttons.

18. Click on the button title that appears at the bottom of the button. The button will be highlighted to show that it is selected, and the preview slider will appear at the top of the folder's icon.
19. Click on the button title again. The text will become highlighted so that you can edit it.
20. Refer to your project plan and type the name of the first submenu listed for the menu on the screen.
21. Click outside of the submenu button. The name of the button will become what you typed in the previous step.

> **TIP**
>
> To remove a button from a menu, click the button to select it and press the Delete key. The button will disappear in a puff of smoke.

22. Repeat Steps 17–21 for each submenu on the current menu. The menu will have a button that represents each of the submenus that you listed in your project plan.

23. Click on the Back arrow to move back to the previous menu (in this case, the main menu).
24. Repeat Steps 15–23 until you have added each menu called for in your project plan.

The framework of the DVD will be ready for you to start adding content. By creating this structure and naming each menu that will appear on the DVD, you have created a place for each movie and slideshow that you will place on the DVD.

Building a Slideshow on DVD

If your project plan calls for slideshows, you will need to add those slideshows to the DVD.

There are two basic ways to add a slideshow to a DVD. One is to use iDVD tools to build the slideshow. The other is to create a slideshow outside of iDVD and then import the slideshow into iDVD. Each method has advantages and disadvantages.

Because you can access your iPhoto Photo Library from within iDVD, using iDVD's tools to build a slideshow is the simplest and fastest way to add a slideshow to a DVD, so that is the method explained in this chapter. Along with iPhoto images, you can also easily use music in your iTunes Library as soundtracks for the slideshows you create.

Image Resolution and iDVD Slideshows

While you don't have to be too concerned about the file format of the images you include in an iDVD slideshow, you do need to be aware of the resolution of the images that you include. iDVD will scale your images to the 640x480 resolution when it creates a slideshow. If an image does not have this proportion, black bars might appear at the top and bottom or left and right sides of the image when it appears on the screen. If the image does not have this proportion, iDVD will scale it so that it does. This can cause images to become distorted and look squished in one direction or the other (or both).

If this bothers you, you should resize your images to the 640x480 resolution before you place those images in iDVD. You can use an image editing application to do this, such as iPhoto. See Chapter 6 to learn how to resize images in your iPhoto Photo Library.

The first step is to identify the slideshows that you want to place on the DVD you are creating. Open the DVD plan and find a slideshow listed on your plan.

After you have identified the slideshows you want to include, the general steps to add a slideshow to an iDVD project are the following:

1. Create a slideshow button on the appropriate menu.
2. Add images to the slideshow from iPhoto or from the Finder.
3. Develop the slideshow by setting the order in which images appear, setting its duration, and so on.
4. Add a soundtrack to the slideshow.
5. Add high-resolution versions of the images to the DVD—or not.

Adding a Slideshow Button to a Menu

To add a slideshow to a menu, you first create a slideshow button on the appropriate menu.

Add a Slideshow Button to a DVD Menu

1. Open the menu on which you want to place a slideshow. You open menus by clicking their folder buttons. If the menu you are looking for is a submenu, you might have to move one or more levels to get to it.
2. Click on the Slideshow button, choose Project, Add Slideshow, or press ⌘+L. A slideshow button (titled "My Slideshow" by default) will be created on the menu (see Figure 14.7).

NOTE
If you are going to view the DVD you create on a TV as well as on a computer, you should set iDVD preferences so that images are scaled to fit the TV Safe Area. This prevents images from being cut off when you view the DVD on a TV. See Chapter 13 to learn how to set this preference.

Figure 14.7 *This menu now has a slideshow button.*

Adding Images to a Slideshow

After you have added a slideshow button to the DVD, you need to add images to the slideshow itself. You can do this in two ways: You can add images from an iPhoto photo album, or you can add images from the Finder.

Adding Images to a Slideshow from iPhoto

Because access to your iPhoto Photo Library is built into iDVD, adding images from your iPhoto Photo Library to an iDVD slideshow is a snap.

> **TIP**
>
> The best way to create a slideshow from iPhoto images is to create a photo album containing the images that you want in the slideshow. See Chapter 5 to learn how to create photo albums.

Add Images from the iPhoto Photo Library to an iDVD Slideshow

1. Open the iDVD Drawer if it isn't already open (click the Customize button or press Shift+⌘+B).

2. Click on the Photos button at the top of the Drawer. In the top pane in the Drawer, you will see all of the sources in iPhoto, including the entire Photo Library, the Last Import album, and any photo albums you have created. In the lower part of the Drawer, you will see the images in the source that is selected in the upper pane.

3. Select the photo album that contains the images you want to place in the slideshow. The images in that photo album will appear in the lower pane (see Figure 14.8).

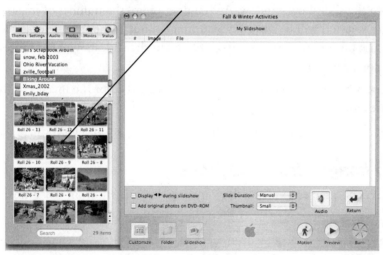

Figure 14.8 *When you choose a source in the upper part of the Drawer, you will see the images contained in that source, such as the images in a photo album.*

TIP

You can use the Search box to search for images in the selected source. To search among all the images in the Photo Library, choose Photo Library as the source and type the text for which you want to search in the Search box.

4. Select the images you want to place in the slideshow. The images you select will be highlighted by a blue box.

> **TIP**
>
> You can select multiple images at the same time. To select a group of images that are next to one another, hold the Shift key down while you click an image; while still holding the Shift key down, click the last image you want to select. The two images on which you clicked and all the images between them will be selected. You can also hold the key down while you click multiple images to select them. Finally, you can press +A to select all of the images in the selected source.

5. Drag the images you want to place in the slideshow from the Drawer onto the slideshow window. As you drag them, the number of images you have selected will be shown next to the pointer. When you release the mouse button, the images will be placed in the slideshow. The images will be sorted by file name.
6. Repeat Steps 3 through 5 until you have added all of the images to the slideshow.
7. Use the Scroll tools to browse all of the images in the slideshow.

Adding Images from the Finder

You can also add images to a slideshow by importing them from the Finder. You can do this by drag-and-drop or by importing them from within iDVD.

To add images by the drag-and-drop method, use the following steps.

Add Images from the Finder to an iDVD Slideshow

1. Open the slideshow to which you want to add images. The slideshow window will appear, and you will see any images that are already in the slideshow.
2. Open the Finder window containing the images you want to add to the slideshow.
3. Select the images you want to add in the Finder window.
4. Drag the images from the Finder window onto the slideshow window (see Figure 14.9). A rectangular box will appear to show you where the images you are dragging will be placed when you release the mouse button. Images will slide apart as needed to make room for the images you

are dragging onto the window. Release the mouse button when you are over the slideshow window and are pointing to the location in which you want to place the images.

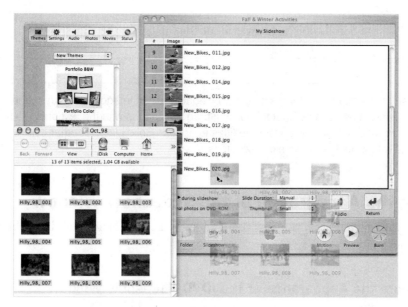

Figure 14.9 *You can drag images from a Finder window onto the iDVD slideshow window to add those images to a slideshow.*

5. Repeat Steps 2 through 4 until you have added all of the images to the slideshow.
6. Use the Scroll tools to browse all of the images in the slideshow.

You can also import images into a slideshow by using the following steps.

Import Images from the Finder into an iDVD Slideshow

1. Open the slideshow to which you want to add images. The slideshow window will appear, and you will see any images that are already in the slideshow.
2. Choose File, Import, Image. The Open sheet will appear.
3. Move to the folder containing the images you want to add to the slideshow.
4. Select the images you want to add to the slideshow.

5. Click on Open. The images you selected will be added to the end of the slideshow.
6. Repeat Steps 2 through 5 until you have added all of the images to the slideshow.
7. Use the Scroll tools to browse all of the images in the slideshow.

> **TIP**
>
> You can create title slides for a slideshow by adding text to images using an image editing application such as Photoshop. Just drag the images with the text onto the slideshow window where you want the titles to appear. Solid black (or other color) screens with white text make nice title slides.

Changing the Appearance of the Slideshow Window

To suit your preferences, you can change how large the image thumbnails in the slideshow windows appear.

Configure the Appearance of the iDVD Slideshow Window

1. Open the slideshow window. You will see thumbnails of each image in the slideshow.
2. Click on the Thumbnail pop-up menu. The menu will appear.
3. Click on Large. The thumbnails in the slideshow window will become larger. This enables you to see the images better, but it also means that fewer of them are displayed in the window.

> **TIP**
>
> Choose Small on the Thumbnail pop-up menu to return the thumbnail sizes to the previous setting.

Changing the Order of Images in an iDVD Slideshow

You can change the order in which images appear in an iDVD slideshow by changing the order in which they appear in the slideshow window. The first image in the slideshow is number 1 and appears at the top of the window. The next one is number 2 and is just below the first one, and so on.

Determine the Order in Which Images in a Slideshow Appear

1. Select the images that you want to move. The images will be highlighted with a blue box.
2. Drag the images to their new location in the window. As you drag up and down in the window, the window will scroll so you can drag the images as far as you'd like. When you stop moving the pointer, the location above which the images will be placed when you release the mouse button is shown by a black box (see Figure 14.10). Release the mouse button when you are over the location in which you want to place the images. The images will appear in the new location and will also be in that spot in the slideshow; they will also be contained within blue bars to highlight their new location.

Figure 14.10 *When you reorder images in the iDVD slideshow window, you change the order in which those images appear when the slideshow is viewed.*

3. Use the scroll tools to review the new order of images in the slideshow.
4. Repeat Steps 1 through 3 to move the images in the slideshow until you are happy with the order in which they appear.

Removing Images from an iDVD Slideshow

You can easily remove images that you don't want to be included in an iDVD slideshow.

Remove Images from an iDVD Slideshow

1. Select the images that you want to remove from the slideshow.

> **NOTE**
>
> Deleting images from a slideshow does not affect the image files themselves, whether they are stored in the Finder or within iPhoto. It only removes them from the iDVD project.

2. Choose Edit, Delete or press the Delete key. The selected images will be removed from the slideshow.

Previewing an iDVD Slideshow

As you develop a slideshow, you can preview it to check the progress of your work.

Preview an iDVD Slideshow

1. Open the slideshow that you want to preview.
2. Click on the Preview button. If it is open, the Drawer will close, the DVD Controller will appear, and you will see the first slide in the slideshow in the DVD window (see Figure 14.11).

> **NOTE**
>
> If you selected the "Always scale slides to TV Safe area" preference, a black border will surround the images. This is because the image is scaled so that it won't be cut off when you view the image on a TV. If you want the image to fill the screen when the DVD is viewed on a computer, turn this preference off.

Building a DVD Chapter 14 **385**

Figure 14.11 *You can preview a slideshow in the iDVD window to check it as you develop it.*

3. Click on the Step Forward button on the Controller to advance the slideshow by one image.
4. Click on the Step Backward button to move the slide back by one image.

TIP

You can also advance the slideshow by one image by pressing the Right Arrow key on the keyboard. The Left Arrow key moves the slideshow back one image.

---

5. Click on the Preview button when you are done previewing the slideshow. You will return to the slideshow window.

Setting the Playback of a Slideshow

You can set an iDVD slideshow to play automatically (in which case, you determine how long each image appears on the screen, or you set the length of the slideshow to match its soundtrack) or manually (in which case, the viewer must manually advance the slideshow by clicking on-screen buttons).

> **TIP**
>
> One of the best ways to set a slideshow's duration is to match the slideshow's length to the soundtrack you will include. If you want to do this, skip ahead to the section called "Adding a Soundtrack to a Slideshow."

Set the Duration of Images in an iDVD Slideshow

1. Open the slideshow window.
2. Choose the length of time that you want each image to appear on the screen when the slideshow is played on the Slide Duration pop-up menu. You can choose from 1 second, 3 seconds, 5 seconds, 10 seconds, Fit To Audio (covered later), or Manual.

> **TIP**
>
> If the images in the slideshow don't contain much detail, use a shorter duration. If they contain more detail, use a longer duration so that viewers will be able to see that detail. Generally, it is better to use shorter durations; it is amazing how little time it takes for a person to view an image. Making the duration too long can result in a boring slideshow.

3. Preview the slideshow again. If you selected a time on the Slide Duration pop-up menu, the images will advance automatically. If you selected Manual on the Slide Duration pop-up menu, use the on-screen arrows to control the slideshow.

> **NOTE**
>
> The benefit of manual playback is that the viewer can choose how long to see each image. The downside is that it is impossible to match a soundtrack to the slideshow because you don't know how long it will take to view.
>
> If you choose the Manual duration for a slideshow check the "Display <> during slideshow" check box; when the slideshow plays, left and right arrows will appear on the screen. The viewer can click these arrows to move the show back or ahead one image, respectively.

Adding a Soundtrack to a Slideshow

Slideshows are dramatically better when you add a soundtrack to them. After you have added a soundtrack, you can easily match the length of the slideshow to the length of its soundtrack.

> **NOTE**
>
> Choosing the music for a slideshow's soundtrack can be difficult, especially if you have lots of music in your iTunes Library. Hopefully, you selected the music for each slideshow when you created the DVD plan. If so, all you have to do is select the music you planned.

Similar to adding images to a slideshow, there are two ways to add a soundtrack to an iDVD slideshow. One is to use music from your iTunes Library. The other is to add audio files from the Finder.

Using iTunes Music as a Soundtrack for an iDVD Slideshow

A great way to add music to a slideshow is to use music in your iTunes Library.

Add iTunes Music as a Soundtrack for an iDVD Slideshow

1. Open the slideshow to which you want to add music.
2. Open the Drawer and click the Audio button. Your iTunes Library will be displayed. At the top of the window, you will see all of the sources in iTunes, from the entire Library along to all the simple playlists you have created.

   You can search for any music in your Library by selecting the area you want to search, such as the Library, and entering the text for which you want to search in the Search field at the bottom of the Drawer. The music that matches what you type will be displayed in the lower pane. Click on the X button to clear the search.

> **TIP**
>
> You can change the width of the columns displayed in the lower pane by dragging the right side of the column heading box.

3. Select the playlist that contains the music you want to use. The contents of that playlist will be displayed in the lower pane (see Figure 14.12).

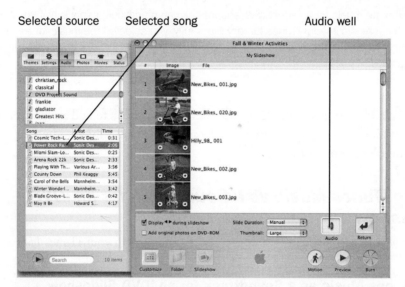

Figure 14.12 *You can access any music in your iTunes Library to add it as a soundtrack for an iDVD slideshow.*

> **TIP**
>
> You can preview a song by selecting it and clicking the Play button.

4. Drag the song you want to use as a soundtrack from the Drawer onto the Audio well in the slideshow window.

> **NOTE**
>
> When you add music to the Audio well, the Slide Duration pop-up menu is set to Fit To Audio automatically. When this duration is selected, the length of time each image appears on the screen is adjusted so that the slideshow will last the same time as the music does. When you add a soundtrack to a slideshow, you should usually leave this setting because it makes everything match. However, you can still select any of the other settings if you prefer.

5. Preview the slideshow again. This time, when the slideshow plays, you will hear the soundtrack, too.

> **TIP**
>
> To remove a soundtrack, drag its icon from the Audio well. When you release the mouse button, it will disappear in a puff of smoke. This action does not affect the actual music file; it only removes it from the DVD project.

Adding Audio Files from the Finder as a Soundtrack for an iDVD Slideshow

You can use almost any sound file, such as AIFF or WAV files, that you have available in the Finder as a soundtrack.

Add an Audio File from the Finder to an iDVD Slideshow

1. Open the Finder window containing the sound file you want to use as a soundtrack.
2. Drag the file that you want to use as a soundtrack from the Finder window onto the Audio well in the slideshow window.
3. Preview the slideshow to see and hear it.

> **TIP**
>
> You can also import a sound file to use it as a soundtrack. Choose File, Import, Audio. The Open sheet will appear. Move to the file you want to use, select it, and click Open. The file you selected will be placed in the Audio well.

Naming a Slideshow Button

You should add a title to slideshow buttons so that viewers will know what the button is (the title will help you keep track of it, too).

Name a Slideshow's Button

1. If you are viewing the slideshow's window, click the Return button to move back to the menu on which the slideshow's button is contained. If you aren't viewing the slideshow's window, open the menu that contains the slideshow's button. You will see that the slideshow's button is currently entitled "My Slideshow."
2. Select the slideshow's button. It will be highlighted, and you will see the preview selection slider at the top of the button.
3. Click on the button's title. It will become highlighted, indicating that you can edit it.
4. Type the button's name (if you created a DVD plan, the button name should be listed on your plan).
5. Press the Return key. The slideshow button will be renamed (see Figure 14.13).

Figure 14.13 *The slideshow's button is now called "Biking Around."*

> **NOTE**
>
> You can also configure the image that appears in the slideshow's button.

Placing High-Resolution Images from a Slideshow on a DVD

If you use a digital camera that has even a modest resolution, such as 2 megapixels, you might notice that the images in a slideshow placed on a DVD look kind of fuzzy and lose some of the detail when compared to viewing those same images within iPhoto. When iDVD imports images into a project in a slideshow, it matches the resolution of those images to the resolution at which TVs display content. A TV's resolution is typically much lower than the resolution of most digital cameras and the Macs on which you display the images. For the sake of being able to display the content you add to an iDVD project with a standard DVD on a TV, a compromise in image quality is made.

When you place images in a slideshow on a DVD, those images become part of that slideshow and are no longer individual files. If you or someone else wants to use individual images for some reason, such as to add to the desktop, there is no way to access the image files included in the slideshow.

To address both of these issues, iDVD enables you to place a high-resolution version of each image contained in the slideshow on the DVD along with the slideshow. These images can be accessed when the DVD is mounted on a computer, just like any other files that are placed on a CD or a DVD-ROM. People who have your DVD can view the images individually in their native resolution, and they can use those images in their own projects, such as to print them, add them to the desktop, and so on.

> **NOTE**
>
> Adding high-resolution versions of the images in a slideshow also provides a backup of those images so you can recover them should something happen to the hard disk on which they are stored.

To place the high-resolution versions of the images in a slideshow on the DVD, do the following steps.

Add High-Resolution Versions of a Slideshow's Images on DVD

1. Open the slideshow whose images you want to include on the DVD as separate files.
2. Check the "Add original photos on DVD-ROM" check box. This will cause iDVD to add each image in its native resolution to the DVD.

> **TIP**
>
> If you always want to include high-resolution images from the slideshows on the DVDs you create, open the Preferences dialog box, click on the Slideshow button, and check the "Always add original slideshow photos to DVD-ROM" check box. Each time you add images to a slideshow, high-resolution versions of those images will also be added to the DVD-ROM part of the DVD. The disadvantage of this is that you will have less room on the disc for other content.

You can view the files that are included on the DVD by doing the following steps.

View the High-Resolution Images Included on a DVD

1. Click on the Status button in the Drawer. You will see the Status tools.
2. Choose DVD-ROM Contents on the pop-up menu. You will see the folders and files currently contained on the DVD. You will see the name of each item along with its size. One of the items you will see is a folder called Slideshows.
3. Click on the Expansion triangle next to the Slideshows folder's icon. The contents of the folder will be displayed. You will see a folder for each slideshow you have placed on the DVD.
4. Click on the Expansion triangle next to a slideshow's folder. You will see a file for each image in the slideshow (see Figure 14.14). These files will be accessible when the DVD is mounted on a computer.

Figure 14.14 *When you select a slideshow's folder in the DVD-ROM Contents pane, you will see the high-resolution versions of the images contained in that slideshow.*

Adding iMovie Movies to a DVD

Putting your iMovie projects on DVD is a great way to store and watch those movies. Using a DVD also enables you to add a scene index, which makes watching movies more convenient.

Unlike iTunes and iPhoto, iMovie is not directly integrated into iDVD. However, like those applications, it isn't hard to add iMovie movies to an iDVD project.

There are two ways in which you can add an iMovie project to a DVD from within iDVD. One is to use the iMedia browser, which you actually already used if you added iPhoto photos to a project. The other is to import the movie directly. Because the iMedia browser is easier and more convenient, you should generally use that technique. However, sometimes it can be useful to import a movie directly.

You can also add an iMovie project to an iDVD project from within iMovie.

Adding iMovie Projects to the iMedia Browser

The iMedia Browser makes finding movies to add to a DVD project simple because you configure the location of those movies within the browser, so finding them and adding them to a project is simple.

To add the location of your movie projects to the iMedia Browser, do the following steps.

Configure the Location of iMovie Projects in the iMedia Browser

1. Choose iDVD, Preferences. The Preferences dialog box will open.

> **TIP**
>
> If you store all of the movies you create in the Movies folder in your Home folder, you won't need to do the following steps. iDVD locates the movies that are contained at the top level of the Movies folder and places them in the iMedia Browser automatically. For iMovie movies stored in other locations, you need to tell iDVD where to look to locate those movies.

2. Click on the Movies button. At the bottom of the window, you will see the list of movie locations that have been added to the iMedia Browser. If you haven't added any, the list will be empty, and your Movies folder will be the only place iDVD looks for iMovie projects.
3. Click the Add button. The Open dialog box will appear.
4. Move to the location of an iMovie project on your DVD plan.
5. Select the folder in which that iMovie project is located.

> **TIP**
>
> If you select a volume or disk, all of the movies located at the root level of the volume or disk will be moved onto the iMedia browser. However, movies located within folders on that disk or volume won't be displayed in the browser. Movies that are contained within folders in a location that you select won't be displayed on the browser either. You have to select a folder or volume that contains an iMovie at its root level for that movie to appear in the browser.

6. Click Open. You will return to the iDVD Preferences dialog box, and the folder you selected will be added to the list of folders in which iDVD should look for movies (see Figure 14.15).

Figure 14.15 *The movies located in the folder shown in the list at the bottom of the Preferences dialog box will appear in the iMedia Browser.*

 7. Repeat Steps 3 through 6 to add each folder that contains a movie you want to put on the DVD to the iMedia browser (see Figure 14.16).

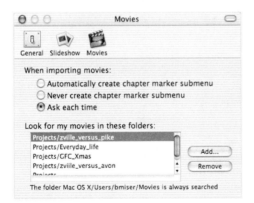

Figure 14.16 *Now several locations have been added; the movies stored in these folders will be available in the iMedia Browser.*

 8. Close the Preferences dialog box when you are done adding locations to it.

Using the iMedia Browser to Add Movies to a DVD

To add a movie from the iMedia browser, do the following steps.

Add Movies to a DVD Using the iMedia Browser

1. Open the menu to which you want to add a movie.
2. Open the iDVD Drawer and click the Movies button. The iMedia Browser will appear. In the top pane, you will see the list of folders that you configured using the iDVD Preferences dialog box; the Movies folder in your Home folder is always on the list.
3. Select the folder containing the movie you want to add to the DVD project. The movies contained in that folder will be shown in the lower pane (see Figure 14.17).

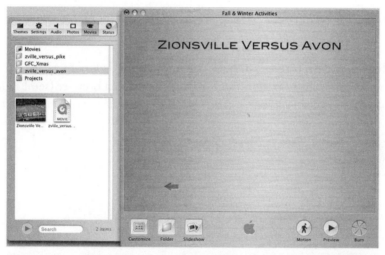

Figure 14.17 *The folders shown in the top pane of the Drawer have been added to the iMedia Browser, and you can quickly add any movies contained in them to an iDVD project.*

TIP

To see a preview of a movie, select its icon (the one containing an image from the movie) and click the Play button. The preview will play within the icon. Click the Play button again to stop the movie. You can search for movies in the selected folder by using the Search tool located at the bottom of the Drawer.

4. Drag the movie's icon onto the DVD menu. As you drag the movie, a number will indicate how many movies you have selected. If you added chapter markers to the movie, when you release the mouse button, the Chapter Marker Import prompt will appear. If the movie doesn't have chapter markers, it will be added to the menu, and you can skip the next step.

> **NOTE**
>
> Drag the icon showing an image from the movie, not the one with the QuickTime logo. If you try to add that one to a DVD, you will see an error message.

5. Click Yes if you want to add a scene selection menu to the DVD or No if you don't. The movie will be added to the menu. If you elected to add a scene selection menu, you will see two buttons on the menu. One will be called "Play Movie" and will be the button on which you click to view the movie. The other will be called "Scene Selection" and will lead to the scene selection menu (see Figure 14.18). If you chose not to add chapter markers, a single button will appear and will have the same name as the movie that you dragged onto the menu.

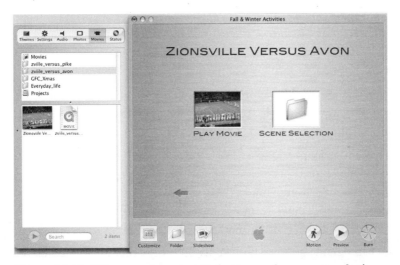

Figure 14.18 *When you choose to add chapter markers, a scene selection menu will be created.*

6. Double-click the movie button (called Play Movie if you added chapter markers, or the movie's name if you didn't) to watch it in the iDVD window. Click in the iDVD window to stop playing it.
7. If you added chapter markers, double-click the Scene Selection button. The scene selection menu will appear (see Figure 14.19). The menu will contain a button for each chapter marker in the movie, and the name of each button will be the name given to that marker within iMovie.

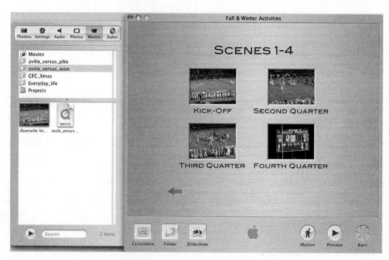

Figure 14.19 *Four chapter markers were added to this movie; each appears as a separate button on the scene selection menu.*

Following are some other notes about adding iMovie movies to a DVD:

♦ If you change an iMovie project after you have added it to the DVD, you need to delete the movie from the DVD and add it again to have the most recent version included on the DVD when you burn it.

♦ After you add a movie to a DVD, the movie and scene selection buttons are independent. This means you can treat each button individually, such as by renaming it, moving it, deleting it, and so on. Each chapter marker becomes an independent movie button on the DVD. For example, you can double-click a chapter marker button to view that part of the movie.

♦ You can rename a movie button just like any other button. Click once on the button; then click the button title, and it will become editable. Type the new name of the button.

Importing Movies to a DVD

You can also import a movie directly into iDVD if you prefer not to use the iMedia Browser or if the folder containing the movie you want to add has not been added to the Preferences dialog box.

> **NOTE**
>
> You can place only one movie that contains a scene selection menu on a menu when you use the import method. If you want to place more than one movie that has a scene selection menu, use the iMedia Browser method instead because that method automatically creates a menu for each movie with a scene selection menu that you add to the DVD.

Import an iMovie Movie into an iDVD Project

1. Open the menu on which you want to add a movie.
2. Choose File, Import, Video. The Import sheet will appear.
3. Move to the movie that you want to add to the DVD.
4. Select the movie's .mov file.
5. Click on Open. If the movie has chapter markers, the Chapter Marker Import prompt will appear. If it doesn't have chapter markers, the movie will be added to the menu, and you can skip the next step.
6. Click Yes to add a scene selection menu or No if you don't want to add one. The movie will be added to the menu and will behave just like movies you add through the iMedia Browser.

Adding iMovies to a DVD from Within iMovie

You can also add an iMovie to a DVD from within iMovie itself. When you do this, iMovie launches iDVD, creates a new project, and adds the movie to it—which makes adding an iMovie to a DVD a one-click process.

Add an iMovie Movie to DVD from Within iMovie

1. Open the iMovie project you want to add to DVD.
2. Click the iDVD button to open the iDVD palette.
3. Click the Create iDVD Project button. iMovie will open iDVD. iDVD will create a new project, and the movie will be added to it. The name of the project will be the name of the iMovie project (see Figure 14.20). If you added chapter markers to the movie, the Chapter Marker Import prompt will appear. If the movie doesn't have chapter markers, it will be added to the menu, and you can skip the next step.

Figure 14.20 *Here, you can see iMovie in the background, the window telling you that iMovie has launched iDVD, and the iDVD window that shows a new project.*

4. Click Yes to add the scene selection menu or No if you prefer not to add it. The movie will be added to the main menu of the new project (see Figure 14.21).

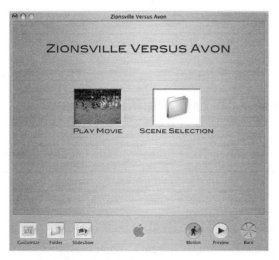

Figure 14.21 *With iLife, you can create a new iDVD project and add a movie to it with a single mouse click.*

Want a few tidbits about adding movies to iDVD from within iMovie? I thought you'd never ask.

- ◆ The iDVD project that you create from within iMovie is just like any other iDVD project you create, except that it already has a movie in it, of course. You can add more content to the DVD, add menus, change its design, rename its buttons, and so on.
- ◆ The movie is always added to the DVD's main menu.
- ◆ The theme of the new DVD project is the one you used most recently. Just like other iDVD projects, you can change its appearance in many different ways.

Adding QuickTime Movies to a DVD

QuickTime content is plentiful, and the QuickTime format is used for many types of projects, including video, audio, and other content. Using QuickTime Pro, you can convert almost any content into the QuickTime format if it isn't in that format already. You can place any QuickTime content on a DVD, no matter what the source of that content is.

Similar to iMovie projects, you can add QuickTime movies to the iMedia Browser and then add them to an iDVD project, or you can import them into a project.

Adding a QuickTime Movie on the iMedia Browser to a DVD

Adding a QuickTime movie from the iMedia browser to the DVD is a snap.

> **NOTE**
>
> You add the folders containing the QuickTime movies you want to add to an iDVD project to the iMedia Browser in the same way that you add folders containing iMovie movies to it. See the earlier section called "Adding iMovie Projects to the iMedia Browser" for the details.

Add a QuickTime Movie from the iMedia Browser to an iDVD Project

1. Navigate to the menu on which you want to place a QuickTime movie.
2. Open the Drawer and click the Movies button.
3. Select the folder in which the movie you want to add is stored. The contents of the folder will be displayed in the lower pane.
4. Drag the QuickTime movie onto the menu. The movie will be added to the menu and to the DVD.

Importing a QuickTime Movie to DVD

You can also import QuickTime movies to a DVD without adding them to the iMedia Browser first.

Import a QuickTime Movie to an iDVD Project

1. Navigate to the menu on which you want to place a QuickTime movie.
2. Choose File, Import, Video. The Open sheet will appear.
3. Move to and select the movie file you want to add.
4. Click Open. The movie will be imported into the project and will be added to the current menu.

> **TIP**
>
> You can also add a QuickTime movie to a DVD by dragging it from a Finder window and dropping it on the menu being shown in the DVD window.

Removing Movies from a DVD

You can easily delete movies from an iDVD project when you don't want those movies to be placed on the DVD.

Remove a Movie from an iDVD Project

1. Open the menu containing the movie you want to delete.
2. Select the movie's button. It will be highlighted with a blue box to show that it is selected.

> **TIP**
>
> If the movie has a scene selection menu, make sure you select the folder button that contains both the movie and the scene selection menu so that you delete both items from the DVD. You can also select the movie button and the scene selection button individually to delete them.

3. Choose Edit, Delete or press the Delete key. The selected items will be removed from the project in a puff of smoke.

Understanding Encoding

As you add movies to a DVD, iDVD automatically begins encoding those movies into the MPEG-2 format, which is the format used for DVD movies. iDVD manages the encoding process for you and encodes movies in the background as you work (assuming you haven't disabled that preference, of course). As long as a DVD project is open, iDVD will be encoding it. When you close a project, iDVD saves the encoded files and will resume where it left off the next time you open the project.

To assess the current encoding status of a project, you can do the following steps.

See the Progress of Encoding the Movies in an iDVD Project

1. In the Drawer, click the Status button. You will see the Status tools.
2. Choose Encoder Status on the pop-up menu if it isn't selected already. Each movie that you have placed on the DVD will be listed. Next to each movie, you will see the current status of the encoding process. When a movie has been encoded, you will see the word "Done." When the movie is being encoded, you will see a blue bar that shows the current progress of the process. When a movie had not been encoded, you will see an empty progress bar (see Figure 14.22).

Figure 14.22 *One movie has been encoded, one is being encoded, and two still have to be encoded.*

All the projects on a DVD must be completely encoded before you can burn that DVD.

At the top of the Drawer, you will see the current length of the contents you have placed on the DVD. For maximum quality, you can place up to 60 minutes of content on a DVD. However, you can add up to 90 minutes of content and still achieve excellent quality (in fact, you might not be able to tell the difference between DVDs less than 60 minutes and those more than 60 minutes).

When you add content that will exceed 60 minutes, you will be prompted to choose which mode you want to be in. If you want to remain in the "60-minute" mode, you will need to remove some content from the DVD before you can burn it.

> **NOTE**
>
> When you switch between the 60-minute and 90-minute modes, each movie has to be encoded again.

Adding Other Files to the DVD-ROM Portion of a DVD

Earlier in this chapter, you learned that you could add image files that are contained in the slideshow to a DVD so that they can be used when the DVD is mounted on a computer. In a similar way, you can actually add any file to a DVD project. When the DVD is mounted on a computer, users will be able to open the files you add, copy them to their computers, and so on.

> **NOTE**
>
> Files that you add to the DVD-ROM part of a DVD are not accessible when the DVD is viewed using a standard DVD player.

Add Files to the DVD-ROM Part of a DVD

1. Open the Drawer and click the Status button.
2. Choose DVD-ROM Contents on the pop-up menu. You will see the list of folders and files that are currently on the DVD-ROM portion of the project.
3. Click on the New Folder button. A new, untitled folder will appear on the list.
4. Double-click on the folder's name. It will become highlighted so that you can edit it.
5. Type a new name for the folder and press Return.
6. Open a Finder window containing a file you want to add to the DVD.
7. Drag the file from the Finder window onto the folder that you created in Step 3.
8. Use the Expansion triangles to show or hide the contents of folders (see Figure 14.23).

Figure 14.23 *This DVD will have some additional files on it; some of these are included in the folder called "Bonus Files."*

Following are a few tips regarding putting files on the DVD-ROM part of an iDVD project:

◆ You don't have to create a folder before placing files on the DVD. You can drag them directly onto the DVD-ROM Contents pane to place them at the root level of the DVD-ROM portion of the DVD.

◆ When you place a file into a folder that already contains files, a black line appears above or below the existing files to show you where the new file will be placed.

◆ You can drag files around in the DVD-ROM Contents pane to change their location, such as to move them into or out of folders.

◆ To remove a file from the DVD-ROM portion of the DVD, select the file you want to remove and press the Delete key.

Chapter 15

Designing a DVD

After you have created the structure of a DVD and filled out that structure with great content, you can finish the package by designing the appearance of the DVD's menus and buttons. This might be the most fun part of the process, and you will be amazed at the cool things you can do with the design tools that iDVD provides.

Understanding the Art of Designing a DVD

Making a DVD look good is lots of fun, and iDVD includes an impressive set of tools that enable you to be very creative when you design your DVDs. Before you jump into designing your own DVDs, take a few moments to understand the design elements with which you can work.

Working with Themes

A *theme* is the set of formatting options that you apply to a menu. The purpose of a theme is to make the DVD more enjoyable to watch by organizing the content on a DVD and providing something interesting for the viewer to see when making a selection from a DVD's menu.

Each menu on a DVD can have the same theme applied to it, or you can apply a different theme to each menu on the disc. There are two fundamental types of themes: built-in and custom.

You can apply built-in themes to a menu with a single mouse click, and iDVD includes a number of built-in themes that you can apply to your DVD projects. Custom themes are those that you create by changing the elements of a built-in theme. You can even add your own themes in iDVD so that they are "built-in" as well.

Whether they are built-in or custom, all themes can contain the following elements:

- **Background image or movie.** All themes have a background, which is the area that fills the screen when the DVD plays and the menu is displayed. A menu's background can be a static image, such as a photo, graphic, a graphic containing geometric shapes and colors, or even a single color that fills the screen. A menu's background can also be a movie that plays while the menu appears. You can use any QuickTime movie as a background, such as those you create in iMovie or by using QuickTime Player Pro.

- **Background sound.** A menu can include sound that plays while the menu appears on the screen. This sound can be music from your iTunes Library, or it can include any sound that you have in an audio format, such as MP3, WAV, or AIFF.

- **Title location.** All menus can have titles, which is the text that identifies that menu when it appears on the screen. You can place the title anywhere on the screen. By default, titles are located in the top center, right, or left of the menu, but you can drag a title anywhere else on the screen.

- **Title format.** You can choose the font, color, and size of the title's text.

- **Button style.** You can choose the style of the buttons that appear on a menu. The simplest button style is just the button's text. Other button styles include various shapes, from simple boxes to more complex shapes that include colors and drop shadows.

- **Button location.** Buttons can be located on a menu according to the invisible grid that ensures buttons are evenly spaced on the menu, or they can be placed in any location you'd like.

- **Button title location.** All buttons can have a title, which is text that identifies that button when it appears on the screen. You can change the location in which the button titles appear relative to the buttons themselves; options are included on the center of the button, at the bottom of the button, and so on.

- **Button title format.** You can also choose the font, color, and size of the text used for button titles.

Working with Drop Zones

Some of the built-in themes include one or more Drop Zones. A Drop Zone is an area on a menu in which you place images, slideshows, or movies that will appear inside the Drop Zone when it appears on the screen (see Figure 15.1). When a theme includes more than one Drop Zone, you can place different content in each Drop Zone.

Unlike buttons, you can't click on a Drop Zone to view the movie or slideshow that plays within it. Drop Zones appear only when you view the menu on which they are located.

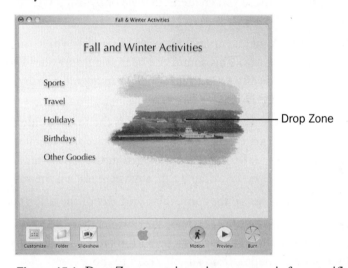

Figure 15.1 *Drop Zones contain an image or movie for a specific part of a menu (unlike the background which fills the screen).*

While they might seem similar, there are several differences between backgrounds and Drop Zones. One difference between a Drop Zone and a background is that backgrounds fill the entire screen while a Drop Zone fills only a portion of it. Another difference is that you can't add audio to a Drop Zone; you can add audio only to a background. A third difference is that all themes have a background, but not all themes include a Drop Zone.

Working with Motion Effects

When a menu has a background movie, sound, or a Drop Zone with a movie in it, that menu has *motion effects*. Motion effects are cool to look at when you view a DVD, but they can be annoying when you are designing a DVD. You can use the Motion button to turn motion effects off or on. When the button is green, motion effects are on. When the button is gray, they are off.

Usually, you should turn motion effects off while you design a menu. When you have the major elements designed, turn motion on again to check out your design and then turn motion off again to keep working.

> **NOTE**
>
> When you turn motion off, all motion is stopped, including that in any Drop Zones that are part of a menu. This can freak you out at first because some Drop Zones use motion to display the zone itself (such as the Drop Zone in the Brush Strokes theme) and might look like they are empty when motion is off. If this happens, just turn motion on again to see the Drop Zone in all its glory.

Let me offer a word of caution here. Just because you can have all sorts of motion effects on a menu doesn't mean that you should use them all the time. You can also have motion in the buttons on a menu; using motion effects in both places can be overwhelming. Usually, it is better to make your menus static when you use motion in the buttons or use motion in the menus when you use static buttons. Occasionally, no motion at all is the best choice. Only very rarely will using motion in the menu background and in the buttons be a good idea.

> **TIP**
>
> You can quickly turn motion on or off by pressing ⌘+J.

Using the TV Safe Area

As you learned earlier, TVs offer different display areas than computers do; computers display larger areas than TVs. The full iDVD window represents what can be displayed on a computer. As you design a DVD, you need to keep the intended viewing platform in mind. If you intend the DVD to be viewed *only* on a computer, you don't need to worry about ensuring that nothing gets cut off because what you see in the iDVD window is what you will see when you play back the DVD. On the other hand, if you intend to view the DVD on a TV, you should work in iDVD's TV Safe Area. The TV Safe Area is a box that iDVD puts on the screen to represent the display area available on a TV. Everything inside the box will be displayed on the screen. Anything outside of the box might be cut off when the DVD is viewed on a TV. To display the TV Safe Area, choose Advanced, Show TV Safe Area or press ⌘+T. The TV Safe Area will appear on the screen as a red box on the screen (see Figure 15.2). If you design a DVD for TV viewing, keep everything you want the viewer to see inside the box.

Figure 15.2 *If you keep all the elements of the DVD within the TV Safe Area, you can be sure that they will be displayed as you see them when a DVD is shown on a TV screen.*

> **NOTE**
>
> If you look carefully at Figure 15.2, you'll notice that some of the text on one of the button titles extends beyond the TV Safe Area. If this DVD were played on a TV, that text outside of the box would not appear on the screen.

Designing Menus

As you learned in the previous chapter, menus provide the structure of a DVD and provide the context for the content on a disc. When a DVD is viewed, the menus also provide the interface for the DVD and can be as simple or as complex as you want them to be. When you design a DVD's menus, you can do the following tasks:

- Name the menus
- Apply a standard theme to a menu
- Add content to Drop Zones that appear on a menu
- Apply the same theme to all the menus on a DVD
- Create a custom theme by applying a background image, movie, or sound
- Save custom themes so you can reuse them easily
- Apply a custom theme to every menu on a DVD

Naming Menus

Each menu on a DVD can have its own title, which is the text that appears when the menu is viewed. A menu's title enables viewers to put the content included on the menu in context.

> **NOTE**
>
> The default title for a menu is the name of the theme that is applied to the menu. This title will remain until you change it. After you change a title, the title will remain what you changed it to even when you apply different themes to the menu.

Name a Menu

1. Open the menu to which you want to add a title.
2. Click on the menu's current title. It will become highlighted to show that you can edit it.
3. Type the menu's new title and press Return. Each time the menu appears on the screen, it will include the title you entered (see Figure 15.3). For now, don't worry about the format of the title. You will determine that when you design the theme's appearance.

Figure 15.3 *This menu, which happens to be the main menu on the DVD, has been entitled "Fall and Winter Activities."*

> **TIP**
>
> The title you use for a menu is not tied to the title of the button that takes you to the menu. Although it can make sense to give the same title to a menu and the button that opens that menu, you might choose to name them differently.

If you don't want a menu to have a title, do the following steps.

Cause a Menu to Have No Title

1. Open the menu that you don't want to have a title.
2. Open the iDVD Drawer.
3. Click on Settings. The Settings tools will appear.
4. Choose No Title on the Position pop-up menu in the Title section. The title will be removed from the menu.

Designing a DVD   Chapter 15   **415**

> **NOTE**
>
> When you remove a title from a menu using the previous steps, the title actually remains with the menu, but you just can't see it. When you apply a different theme to the menu, the title you previously entered will reappear. If you never want the title to appear, make the title consist of only a single space. Then it won't matter if you change themes because the title won't have any text in it anyway.

Using Built-In Themes to Design Menus

Applying iDVD's built-in themes to the menus on a DVD is pretty simple; the only hard part is choosing from among the many neat themes included with iDVD. Applying a theme that includes a Drop Zone includes an additional step of adding movies or images to the Drop Zones.

Applying a Built-In Theme to a Menu

iDVD includes quite a number of built-in themes that you can apply to a menu with a single mouse click.

Apply a Built-In Theme to a Menu

1. Open the menu to which you want to apply a theme. That menu will appear using the theme you selected when you created the DVD project.
2. Open the Drawer if it isn't open already.

> **TIP**
>
> When you are trying out built-in themes, make sure that motion effects are on so you can experience the motion effects that are part of the themes you try.

3. Click on the Themes button. The Themes tools will appear.
4. Choose All on the pop-up menu at the top of the Drawer. All of the built-in themes will appear on the themes list.

> **NOTE**
>
> You can use the pop-up menu to choose the set of themes that you want to see on the list. All shows you all of the built-in themes. New Themes shows you those themes that were added when iDVD 3 was released. Old Themes shows the themes that were included with previous versions of iDVD. Favorites shows the custom themes you have created and saved. Use the All selection until you become familiar with all of the built-in themes.

5. Use the scroll tools to browse the thumbnails of the themes. Each thumbnail shows you a preview of the theme. The theme that is currently applied to the menu will be highlighted.

6. Click on a theme. The menu will be reformatted according to the theme you selected (see Figure 15.4). If the theme contains motion effects and Motion is turned on, they will start to play. If the theme includes one or more Drop Zones, you will see those areas—the text "Drag photos or movies here" appears in the Drop Zones to show you where you can place the content that you want to display in them.

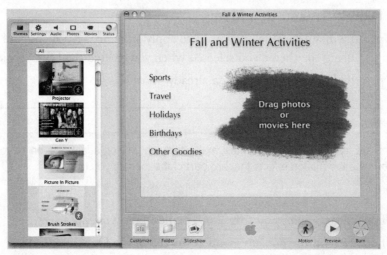

Figure 15.4 *This is the Brush Strokes theme that includes one Drop Zone.*

> **NOTE**
>
> Themes that include motion effects are marked with the Motion icon, which is a smaller version of the Motion button.

7. Repeat Steps 5 and 6 to try other themes. Each time you click on a theme's thumbnail, the current menu will be formatted with the theme on which you click (see Figure 15.5).

Figure 15.5 *This is the same menu as shown in the previous figure, but now it has the Sky theme applied to it.*

Adding Content to Drop Zones

If the theme you apply to a menu includes one or more Drop Zones, you need to add the movie, slideshow, or image you want to be displayed in the Drop Zone.

Add a Movie to a Drop Zone

1. Open a menu containing one or more Drop Zones.
2. Open the Drawer and click the Movies button. The folders containing movies that you have added to the iMedia Browser will be displayed.

3. Click on the folder containing the movie you want to add to the Drop Zone. The movies contained in the folder you selected will be displayed in the lower pane.

4. Drag the movie you want to add in the Drop Zone from the iMedia browser onto the Drop Zone. As you move over the Drop Zone, the borders of the Drop Zone will be displayed; release the mouse button when the borders are highlighted (see Figure 15.6). The movie will be placed in the Drop Zone and will begin playing.

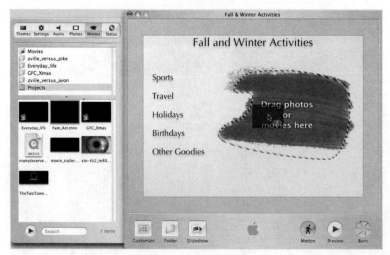

Figure 15.6 *When you drag a movie over a Drop Zone, its borders become highlighted to show you that you are in the right spot.*

> **TIP**
>
> If you want to use a movie in a Drop Zone that has not been added to the iMedia Browser, you can import it. To import a movie into a Drop Zone, move the pointer inside the Drop Zone, hold the Control key down, click the mouse button, and choose Import from the pop-up menu. Use the Open sheet to move to a movie and select it. Click Open, and the movie will be added to the Drop Zone.

5. Move the pointer over the movie you placed in the Drop Zone. The pointer will become a hand.

6. Hold the mouse button down. The movie will be "grabbed."

7. Drag the movie around until the portion you want to be displayed in the Drop Zone is shown (see Figure 15.7). When motion effects are on, the movie will play inside the Drop Zone.

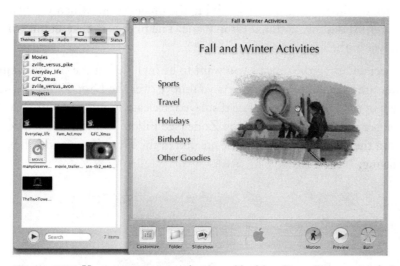

Figure 15.7 *You can move a movie around inside a Drop Zone to determine the part of the movie's images that are displayed.*

TIP

To remove a movie, slideshow, or image from a Drop Zone, move the pointer inside the Drop Zone, hold the Control key down, click the mouse button, and choose Clear from the pop-up menu.

By default, the first 30 seconds of a movie are shown in the Drop Zone. While you can't choose which segment of a movie is shown, you can cause fewer than 30 seconds of the movie to be shown by changing the duration of background motion using the Settings tools. You'll learn how in a later section.

You can also add a slideshow to a Drop Zone so that the slideshow plays when the Drop Zone appears on the screen.

Add a Slideshow to a Drop Zone

1. Open a menu containing one or more Drop Zones.

2. Click the Photos button in the Drawer. You will see your iPhoto photo albums listed in the upper pane; the images contained in the source selected in the upper pane will be shown in the lower pane.
3. Click on the photo album containing the images from which you want to create a slideshow within a Drop Zone. The photos in that album will be shown in the lower pane.
4. Select and drag the images you want to be included in the slideshow until they are over the Drop Zone. As you move over the Drop Zone, the borders of the Drop Zone will be displayed. Release the mouse button when you see the borders of the Drop Zone (see Figure 15.8). A slideshow from the selected images will be created in the Drop Zone and will begin playing.

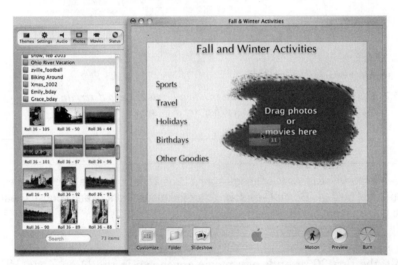

Figure 15.8 *When you drag images from the Photos pane onto a Drop Zone, a slideshow is created from those images and plays inside the Drop Zone.*

> **TIP**
>
> To import a slideshow into a Drop Zone, move the pointer inside the Drop Zone, hold the Control key down, click the mouse button, and choose Import from the pop-up menu. Use the Open sheet to select the images you want to use in the slideshow. Click Open, and a slideshow will be created from those images and will be added to the Drop Zone.

5. Move the pointer over the slideshow you placed in the Drop Zone. The pointer will become a hand.
6. Hold the mouse button down. The slideshow will be "grabbed."
7. Drag the slideshow until the portion of the images that you want to be displayed in the Drop Zone is shown.
8. Release the mouse button when the slideshow is displayed in the Drop Zone properly.

> **TIP**
>
> You can mix and match the contents of the Drop Zones on the same menu. For example, you might want to have a movie in one Drop Zone and a slideshow in another.

You can also add a single image to a Drop Zone; that image will be displayed inside the Drop Zone when that Drop Zone appears on the screen. To do so, use the previous steps, except that you select only the single image that you want to appear in the Drop Zone instead of a group of images.

Applying a Standard Theme to Every Menu on a DVD

If you want every menu on a DVD to have the same theme applied to it, use the following steps.

Apply the Same Theme to Every Menu on a DVD

1. Open the Themes pane in the Drawer.
2. Select the theme that you want to apply to every menu on the DVD. The theme will be applied to the current menu if it isn't already.
3. Choose Advanced, Apply Theme to Project. The theme you selected will be applied to every menu on the DVD.

Using Custom Themes to Design Menus

With iDVD's built-in themes, you can create very interesting DVDs by just using those themes that are included in iDVD "out of the box." However, you can have even more fun and build even more interesting DVDs by creating custom themes for a DVD. These themes can include just about any image, movie, or sound that you can create or find. And you can change the formatting of a menu to your heart's content.

Here are the elements of a theme that you can customize:

- ◆ Background image or movie and sound
- ◆ Title location and format
- ◆ Button style, location, title location, and title format

> **NOTE**
>
> Because buttons are a distinct and important part of a menu design, designing the buttons on a menu is covered in the section called "Designing Buttons" later in this chapter.

Since all menus on a DVD are initially formatted with one of iDVD's built-in themes, you start designing a custom theme by choosing the built-in theme on which you want to base a custom theme.

Sometimes, creating a custom theme is just a matter of tweaking one or two elements of a built-in theme, such as title format or button shape. In that case, choosing the built-in theme that you start with is important because you will retain most of that theme's elements. In other cases, you might want to change every aspect of a theme to really customize it, in which case, it doesn't make much difference which built-in theme you start with.

If you want to use images and movies in a menu's background or in its buttons, you probably won't want to base a custom theme on a theme that includes Drop Zones. Because Drop Zones are large, they will "drown out" the images and movies that play in the background or inside buttons. If you prefer to have just text buttons, then a theme that includes Drop Zones is a good choice.

Drop Zone themes are a good choice for main menus and other menus that have mostly folder buttons on them. By default, the buttons in Drop Zone themes use the Text style so that the button design does not interfere with the images and movies in the Drop Zones.

> **TIP**
>
> If you intend to change all or most of the elements of a theme, one of the plainer themes, such as one of the Brushed Metal themes, is a good choice because it gives you an empty canvas on which to work.

Applying a Background Image to a Menu

You can add a static image to a menu's background. This is a good option when you don't want the background to be obtrusive, but you do want to include something interesting for the other elements of the menu to appear over.

You can use just about any image as a background, including the following:

- Photos from your iPhoto Library
- Photos from other sources
- Images from iMovie projects
- Images you download from the Internet
- Images you create with a graphics application

> **NOTE**
>
> Many built-in themes use a static image as a background. Most of these are simple geometric shapes or gradients. These provide something interesting to look at, but don't distract the viewer from the buttons and other elements of a menu.

Adding images from any of these sources is similar.

Use an Image from Your iPhoto Photo Library as a Menu Background

1. Open the menu that you want to customize and open the Drawer.
2. Click on the Photos button.
3. Select the photo album containing the image you want to use as a background.
4. Use the scroll tools to move to the image you want to use.

5. Drag the image you want to use as a background from the Drawer onto the menu's background (see Figure 15.9). Release the mouse button when you are over the background. The image will be applied to the background (see Figure 15.10).

Figure 15.9 *When you drag an image from the Photos pane onto a menu, that image will fill the menu's background.*

Figure 15.10 *Here, you see the image that was moved onto the background.*

When you apply an image to the background, iDVD scales that image to fill the entire background. Depending on the image's resolution and size, you might end up with black bars on one side of the screen or another. If the scaling that iDVD does with the image results in an image you don't like, you will need to resize the image so it is 640x480 so that it will "fit" in the window without any scaling.

iDVD's image scaling also is applied to portrait images that you use as a background. These images will be "squished down" so the width of the image fills the screen. If this isn't the image you want, use an image editing application to composite the image on a graphic background that is 640x480.

You can also add an image to a menu's background by dragging it from a Finder window.

Add an Image from the Finder to a DVD Menu Background

1. Open the menu that you want to customize and open the Drawer.
2. Click on the Settings button. The Setting tools will appear.
3. Open a Finder window.
4. Move to the image that you want to use as the menu's background.
5. Drag the image from the Finder window onto the Image/Movie well (see Figure 15.11).

Figure 15.11 *When you drag an image file from the Finder onto the Image/Movie well, that image becomes the menu's background.*

> **TIP**
>
> You can also import an image as a background by choosing File, Import, Image and then opening the image you want to use.

6. Release the mouse button when the pointer is over the Image/Movie well. A thumbnail of the image will appear in the well, and the image will be applied to the menu's background (see Figure 15.12).

Figure 15.12 *This menu's background is an image that was dragged from the Finder onto the Image/Movie well, which shows a thumbnail of the image.*

> **NOTE**
>
> iDVD does the same scaling of images you add to menu background, regardless of how you add those images to an iDVD project.

When you apply a background image to a theme that includes one or more Drop Zones, the image of the theme is replaced by the new image you place there. However, the Drop Zones themselves still exist and will display any content you place in them. The background image you place on the menu might cover up the borders of the Drop Zones so it can be difficult to find them in order to place content into them. In that case, remove the background image. Then fill the Drop Zones with content. Then replace the background image again.

> **TIP**
>
> To remove a background image, drag its thumbnail out of the Image/Movie well. When you release the mouse button, the image's thumbnail will disappear in a puff of smoke, and the background will return to what it was under the theme that was previously applied to the menu.

Applying a Background Movie to a Menu

You can use a movie as a menu background. When the menu appears on the screen, up to 30 seconds of the movie will play and will continue to loop as long as the menu is displayed.

> **NOTE**
>
> If you apply a movie as a background to a theme that has one or more Drop Zones, the Drop Zones will still appear on the menu and will display the content you placed in them. However, the Drop Zones can be hard to see with a movie as the background. You should fill the Drop Zones before adding a movie so they are easier to work with.

You can use any QuickTime movie as a menu background; this includes movies you create with iMovie, those that you download from the Internet, and so on. You can add a movie to a background in a couple of ways, dragging a movie from the Finder onto the Image/Movie well or importing a movie.

> **NOTE**
>
> You might expect to be able to drag a movie from the Movies pane onto a background, but this creates a movie button instead. To use a movie as a background, you must drag it onto the Image/Movie will or import it.

You can drag a movie from a Finder window onto the Image/Movie well to use that movie as a menu background.

Use a Movie from the Finder as a Menu Background

1. Open the menu to which you want to apply a movie as a background.
2. Open the Drawer and click the Settings button. The Settings tools will appear.
3. Open a Finder window that contains the movie you want to use as a background.
4. Drag the movie from the Finder window onto the Image/Movie well (see Figure 15.13). Release the mouse button when the pointer is inside the well (the pointer will include a + sign to indicate you are inside the well). The movie will be applied to the background and will begin to play (see Figure 15.14). If the movie includes sound, you will hear the sound, too.

Figure 15.13 *You can drag a movie from a Finder window into the Image/Movie well to apply that movie to a menu's background.*

Figure 15.14 *The movie in the Image/Movie well plays when the menu to which it has been applied is on the screen.*

You can also import a movie as a background.

Import a Movie as a Menu Background

1. Open the menu to which you want to import a movie as a background.
2. Choose File, Import, Background Video. The Open sheet will appear.
3. Move and select the movie you want to use.
4. Click Open. The movie will be imported into the iDVD project and will be applied to the background of the current menu.

Here are a few movie-as-background points to ponder:

- To remove a movie from a menu's background, drag its thumbnail out of the Image/Movie well.
- Movies that you use as backgrounds always play in a loop that begins at the start of the movie.
- The loop lasts up to 30 seconds. You control the length of the loop using the Motion Duration slider (which is explained in a later section).

- A background movie always starts from the beginning and plays until it reaches the duration you set with the Motion Duration slider. If you want to show another part of the movie, use iMovie or QuickTime Pro to crop the movie to the part you want to use as a background and then use the cropped version as a background.
- While you can't apply a slideshow directly to a menu background, you can use iPhoto or iMovie to export a slideshow as a QuickTime movie and then apply that movie to a background.

> **TIP**
>
> As you change backgrounds, you might find that the text or buttons on the menu become hard to see. Because the background is the dominant aspect of a menu, you should carefully consider what you use. If you have lots of movie buttons that will show previews on a menu, you might not want to add another movie as a background if that will overwhelm the viewer. If you have only a few movie buttons, using a movie as a background can create some interesting effects. Also, because backgrounds have such a large impact on menus, you should design them first before you worry about the title formatting and button locations.

Applying Background Sound to a Menu

You can also add just about any sound as a background for a menu. When the menu appears on the screen, the background sound will play.

You can use several types of sound files as background sound for a menu, including the most common sound files types, such as AIFF, MP3, and WAV.

> **TIP**
>
> If you use a movie that includes sound as a background, that sound will be replaced when you add a background sound to the menu.

You can easily apply any music stored in your iTunes Library as background sound for a menu.

Use Music in Your iTunes Library for a Menu Background

1. Open the menu to which you want to apply a background sound.
2. Open the iDVD Drawer and click on the Audio button. The Audio tools will appear. In the upper pane, you will see your iTunes music collection.
3. Select the source, such as a playlist, that contains the sound you want to add to the menu. Its contents will be shown in the lower pane.
4. Drag the sound from the Drawer onto the menu background. Release the mouse button when the pointer is over the menu background; the pointer will include a + to show you that you are over the background (see Figure 15.15). The sound you dragged onto the menu will play (if motion effects are turned on).

Figure 15.15 *When you drag a song from the Audio pane onto a menu, that music will play when the menu appears on the screen.*

You can also apply a sound to a menu by dragging it from the Finder onto the Audio well.

Use an Audio File from the Finder as Background Sound

1. Open the menu to which you want to apply a background sound.
2. Open the iDVD Drawer and click on the Settings button. The Settings tools will appear.

3. Open a Finder window showing the audio file you want to use as a background sound.

4. Drag the file from the Finder window onto the Audio well on the Settings pane. Release the mouse button when the pointer is over the well (see Figure 15.16). The sound will be added to the menu's background. You will also see the audio file's icon in the well.

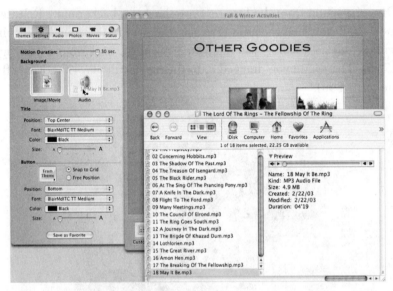

Figure 15.16 *When you place an audio file on the Audio well, it will be used as background sound for the current menu.*

And now, some background sound tidbits:

◆ To remove a background sound from a menu, drag its icon out of the Audio well. When you release the mouse button, the sound will be deleted from the menu.

◆ Just like movies, background sounds play in a loop that can last up to 30 seconds.

◆ Again just like movies, an audio loop always starts at the beginning of the file. If you want to use a different portion of a song, use an editing tool, such as iMovie or QuickTime Pro to edit the sound and then add the edited version to the menu.

- You can control the length of the loop using the Motion Duration slider.
- You can also import a sound by choosing File, Import, Audio. Then select the sound you want to use as the menu background and click Open. The audio file will be added to the menu and to the Audio well.
- The icon in the Audio well indicates the kind of file you are using. For example, MP3 files have different icons than do WAV or other audio file formats.
- You can mute the background sound by clicking the Speaker icon that appears in the Audio well. Click it again to hear the sound.

Setting a Menu's Motion Duration

All motion effects for a menu—including background movies, sound, and the contents of Drop Zones—play in loops that last up to 30 seconds. When the end of the loop is reached, the content starts over and repeats the loop as long as the menu is displayed. You can set the length of the loop.

Set the Length of the Motion Effects for a Menu

1. Open the menu for which you want to set the length of the motion effects loops.
2. Open the Drawer and click the Settings button.
3. Use the Motion Duration slider at the top of the pane to set the length of the loops from 0 to 30 seconds (see Figure 15.17).

> **NOTE**
>
> The Motion Duration slider controls the duration of all motion effects (movie and sound) that are part of the menu background. You can't set a different duration for a movie and a sound applied to the same menu.

Figure 15.17 *The Motion Duration Slider controls how long the motion effects loops play before starting over when a menu is displayed.*

Formatting Menu Titles

The built-in themes that you apply to a menu include formatting options for the menu's title, such as location, font, and so on. You can format menu titles to ensure that they are readable, that they enhance the background (or at least don't conflict with it!), and that they have the look you want to achieve. Format a menu's title with the following steps.

Format a Menu's Title

1. Open the menu for which you want to format the title.
2. Open the Drawer and click the Settings button. The Settings tools will appear.
3. Choose the position in which you want the title to be located on the Position pop-up menu in the Title section. No Title removes the title from the menu. Top Left places the menu at the top-left corner of the TV Safe Area while Top Center and Top Right places it at the top-center and top-right corner of the TV Safe Area, respectively. Custom enables you to drag the title to any location onscreen. For all but the Custom option, the title will move to the location you selected, and you can skip the following two steps. If you chose Custom, the title will become selected and will shift off to the right of the screen; you need to complete the next steps to position it on the menu.

4. Move the pointer over the title.
5. Drag the title to the location on the menu on which you want it to appear (see Figure 15.18).

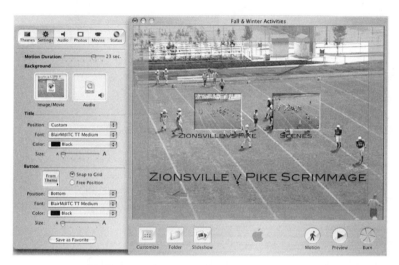

Figure 15.18 *You can drag a menu title to any location on the screen when you choose Custom on the Position pop-up menu in the Title section.*

6. Choose the font for the title on the Font pop-up menu in the Title section. The title will be reformatted with the font you selected (see Figure 15.19).

NOTE

Some font families include all uppercase letters, and many of iDVD's themes use these fonts by default. Note that text in all uppercase letters is harder to read than text with a mixed case.

7. Click on the Color pop-up menu in the Title section. The available colors will appear; the color currently applied to the title is marked with a check mark.
8. Click on the color you want to apply to the title. The color you selected will be applied to the title.

Figure 15.19 *Got Fonts? Then you can use them on your menu titles.*

> **TIP**
>
> When choosing a color for title text, you should almost always go for the most contrast with the background color over which the title appears. While there are many possible colors, you will likely find that White is the best choice for many backgrounds because it tends to look very good with almost any color and is almost always readable. If the background is very light, Black will sometimes work better. While you have lots of other options, you probably will end up with either White or Black.

9. Drag the Size slider in the Title section to set the relative size of the title. Move the slider to the right to make the text larger or to the left to make it smaller. The title will be resized according to the position of the slider (see Figure 15.20).

Figure 15.20 *The title is much more legible than it was.*

> **NOTE**
>
> You can only move the Size slider to the detent lines under the slider; in other words, you don't have infinite control over the size. You have only five size options, even though you use a slider control to select the size.

> **NOTE**
>
> If you based the menu on a theme that includes Drop Zones, you are limited to formatting the menu according to the Drop Zones. For example, you can't move a menu title above a Drop Zone if the Drop Zone appears at the top of the screen, and you will only be able to place buttons relative to the locations of the Drop Zones. When you use Drop Zones, the position menus become relative to the Drop Zone. By placing a menu title at the Top Center position, it might place the title in the middle of the screen if the Drop Zone appears at the top of the screen.

Designing Buttons

Buttons are the elements on a menu that enable users to select something to view. Remember that there are three types of buttons:

- ◆ **Folder**. Folder buttons represent menus. When the viewer clicks a folder button, the menu to which it points opens.

- **Slideshow.** When a viewer clicks on a slideshow button, the slideshow plays.
- **Movie.** I'll bet you can guess what movie buttons do.

Like menus, there are a number of ways in which you can design the buttons that appear on menus. You can name buttons and format them, such as choosing shapes, setting title formats, and so on. You can also add motion effects to buttons by setting button previews. You can also add static images to buttons.

> **TIP**
>
> The TV Safe Area becomes especially important as you start working with the titles and buttons on the menus of the DVD. Usually, if the background gets "clipped" somewhat it isn't all that big a deal. But when titles and buttons get cut off, that can be a real problem. Remember that the shortcut to show or hide the TV Safe Area is to press ⌘+T. Unless you are sure you won't be viewing the DVD on a TV, you should work within the TV Safe Area.

Naming Buttons

As you added buttons to a DVD project, you probably named them so you could keep them straight. If you didn't or if you need to change an existing button title, use the following steps to name a button.

Name a Button

1. Click the button. It will become highlighted, and you will see the slider above the button's icon.
2. Click on the existing button title. It will become highlighted to indicate you can edit it.
3. Type the new button name.
4. Press Return. The button will be renamed.

Designing Buttons by Applying Themes

When you apply a theme to a menu, that theme includes a set of button formatting options, such as button shape, location on the screen, title format and location, and so on. Each time you change the theme, the buttons change according to that theme.

> **NOTE**
>
> All formatting options, such as font and title location, apply to all the buttons on a menu. For example, you can't use a different font for buttons on the same menu.

Customizing the Buttons on a Menu

Fortunately, you can have lots of control over the buttons on a menu because you can customize them using tools that are similar to those you use to customize a menu. There are three basic attributes for all the buttons on a menu that you can customize:

- Shape
- Location
- Title format

You can choose the shape of the buttons on a menu by performing the following steps.

Choose the Shape of Buttons on a Menu

1. Open the menu whose buttons you want to design.
2. Open the Drawer and click the Settings button.
3. Click on the Button Shape pop-up menu in the Button section (see Figure 15.21). The button shape options will appear. By default, From Theme is selected. This takes the button shape from the theme that was most recently applied to the menu. The "T" changes the buttons to be text only, which shows only the button's title. The other buttons apply the shapes to the buttons on the menu.

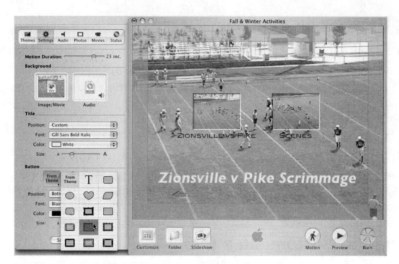

Figure 15.21 *The Button Shape pop-up menu enables you to choose the shape of the buttons on a menu.*

4. Click on the shape you want to apply to the buttons. That shape will be applied to the buttons on the menu.

There are two options for setting the location of the buttons on a menu. If you use the grid, iDVD will space the buttons evenly on the menu according to their number and the grid used by the theme that was previously applied to the menu. This often looks fine. You can also use the Free Position option to place the buttons in any location you choose.

Place the Buttons on a Menu

1. Open the menu whose buttons you want to design.
2. Open the Drawer and click the Settings button.
3. Click the "Snap to Grid" radio button. The buttons on the menu will be located according to the grid (see Figure 15.22). If this placement doesn't look good to you, use the following steps.
4. Click on the Free Position radio button.
5. Click on a button to select it.
6. Drag the button to the location on the menu where you want it placed.
7. Repeat Steps 5 and 6 for each button on the menu (see Figure 15.23).

Figure 15.22 *In this case, snapping the buttons to the grid resulted in the button titles colliding.*

Figure 15.23 *Ah, that's better.*

As you formatted a menu's title, you can also format the title of each button on a menu.

Format the Titles of Buttons on a Menu

1. Open the menu whose buttons you want to design.
2. Open the Drawer and click the Settings button.

3. Click on the Position pop-up menu in the Button section. You will see the position options. Top, Bottom, Left, or Right places the text at the respective side of the button. Center places the button title across the center of the button. No Text removes the button titles.

4. Choose the position of the button titles or choose No Text to remove the button titles. The button titles will be moved to the location you selected.

> **NOTE**
>
> The choice of button title location might cause you to have to readjust the location of one or more buttons so that the title remains in the TV Safe Area.

5. Click on the Font pop-up menu in the Button section. The fonts that are installed on your Mac will appear on the menu. The font currently being used will be marked with a check mark.

6. Click on the font you want to be used in the button titles. The button title text will be reformatted with your selection.

7. Click on the Color pop-up menu. The available text colors will appear. The color currently applied will be marked with a check mark.

8. Click on the color you want to be used for the button title text. The text will be reformatted with the color you selected.

> **TIP**
>
> The same guidelines apply to button titles as apply to menu titles. For example, you should generally choose a color that contrasts with the menu background colors.

9. Drag the Size slider in the Button section to set the relative size of the button title text. As with the Title Size slider, you have five detents that provide five size options for the text. The button title text will be resized according to your positioning of the slider (see Figure 15.24).

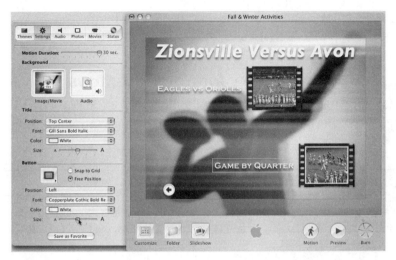

Figure 15.24 *Making your button text legible might require some experimentation if a menu has a complex background like this one does.*

> **NOTE**
>
> The return button is always formatted according to the theme most recently applied to the menu. That is one aspect of a menu that you can't change.

Setting Button Previews

Each button on a DVD is represented by an icon (except for those buttons that are set to be text-only, in which case only the button's title is shown on a menu). This icon can be an image, or it can contain motion effects.

> **NOTE**
>
> When you design a DVD, you can choose themes that have text-only buttons. In that case, setting a button's preview doesn't do a lot because that preview won't appear anyway. But you should set a preview for all of the buttons you add to a DVD so that if you do use a button design that shows it, you won't have to muck around with setting a preview at that time. And since setting a preview is so easy, there isn't really any compelling reason not to set one.

Setting a preview for a button depends on the kind of button you are working with.

Setting a Button Preview for Folder Buttons

The preview for a folder can be the generic folder icon, or you can set it to be an image from one of the buttons that is contained on the menu to which the button points.

> **NOTE**
>
> You can also apply an image or movie as a preview for a folder button as you will learn in the section called "Using an Image or Movie as a Preview for Any Button" later in this chapter.

Set a Folder Button's Preview

1. Select the folder button that you want to design. The button will be highlighted, and the Folder slider will appear at the top of the button.
2. Drag the Folder slider until the image you want to use in the button appears. The images you can choose are those shown in the buttons on the menu to which the folder button points. For example, if that menu contains a movie button, you can choose the movie button's preview image as the folder button preview.

Setting a Button Preview for Slideshow Buttons

The preview for a slideshow button can be the generic slideshow icon, or it can be any image from the slideshow itself.

> **NOTE**
>
> You can also apply an image or movie as a preview for a folder button as you will learn in the section called "Using an Image or Movie as a Preview for Any Button" later in this chapter.

Select an Image from a Slideshow for the Preview in the Slideshow Button

1. Select the slideshow button for which you want to set the preview. The button will become highlighted, and you will see the Slideshow slider at the top of the button.

> **TIP**
>
> If you use the TV Safe Area, the button and the slider must fit within the TV Safe Area in order to be able to use the slider. After you set the image for the button, you can move the button so that the slider is outside of the TV Safe Area. If you want to change the image again, you will either have to turn off the TV Safe Area or move the button so that its slider is contained within the TV Safe Area.

2. Drag the slider. As you drag, you will see each image in the slideshow within the button.
3. Stop dragging the slider when you reach the image you want to use as the button's preview (see Figure 15.25).

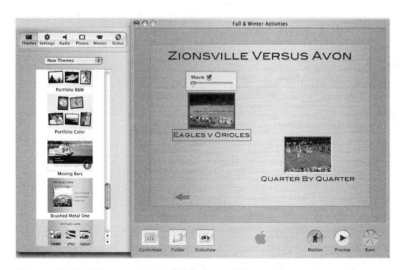

Figure 15.25 *You can use the Slideshow slider to select an image from a slideshow to use in the slideshow's button.*

Setting a Button Preview for Movie Buttons

You can set movie buttons so that the movie plays inside its button when the menu appears on the screen.

> **NOTE**
>
> You can also apply an image or movie as a preview for a folder button as you will learn in the section called "Using an Image or Movie as a Preview for Any Button" later in this chapter.

Set a Movie Button's Preview

1. Select the movie button for which you want to set the preview. The button will become highlighted, and you will see the Movie slider and check box at the top of the button.
2. If you want the movie to play inside the button, check the Movie check box (see Figure 15.26). If you don't check this check box, you can display a frame from the movie as the button's preview.

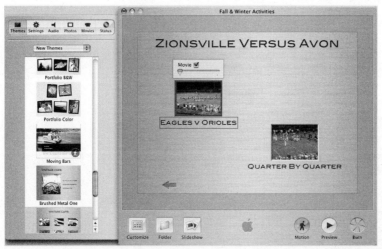

Figure 15.26 *With the Movie check box checked, a preview of a movie will play inside its button.*

Designing a DVD   Chapter 15   **447**

3. Drag the slider to set the starting location for the movie preview or to select the frame that you want to be displayed if you don't check the Movie check box.

Here are some additional points about movie buttons:

- Just like background movies, movie previews within movie buttons play in a loop that can last up to 30 seconds.
- The setting of the Motion Duration slider determines the actual amount of the loop that plays.
- Unlike background movies, you can set the starting point of the loop by using the Movie slider.

Using an Image or a Movie as a Preview for Any Button

You can apply an image or a movie to any button to display that movie or image within the button on which you apply it. You can do this in two ways: by using the iMedia Browser or dragging files from the Finder.

To use the Photos iMedia browser, do the following steps.

Use the iMedia Browser to Apply a Movie or Image to a Button

1. Open the menu containing the button for which you want to set a preview.
2. Open the Drawer.
3. Click the Photos button if you want to apply an image to the button or the Movies button if you want to place a movie in the button.
4. Select the source that contains the image or movie you want to apply to the button. The images or movies in that source will appear in the lower part of the pane.
5. Drag the image or movie from the iMedia Browser onto the button (see Figure 15.27).
6. Release the mouse button when you are over the button on which you want to place the image or movie. The image or movie will be applied to the button (see Figure 15.28).

Figure 15.27 *You can drag an image from the Photos pane onto a button to apply that image to the button.*

Figure 15.28 *The button on the right now has an image applied to it.*

> **NOTE**
>
> You can't adjust the starting point of a movie that you apply to a folder using either of these techniques. The first 30 seconds of the movie (or less if you have set the Motion Duration slider to a lower value) will loop inside the button. This is unlike a movie's button for which you can set the starting point of the preview using the slider that appears at the top of the button when you select it.

You can also place an image or movie from the Finder onto a button by using the following steps.

Add an Image or Movie from the Finder to a Button

1. Open the menu containing the button to which you want to apply an image or movie.
2. Open a Finder window showing the movie or image file that you want to apply to the button.
3. Drag the image or movie file from the Finder window onto the button. When you are over the button, it will have a blue border to show you that the image will be placed on the button when you release the mouse button. Release the mouse button. The image or movie will be pasted onto the button.

> **TIP**
>
> To return a button to a previous image, select it and use the slider to move to the image you want to use. When you drag the slider for a folder button all the way to the left, you will see the folder icon again. Move the slider to the right, and you will see the files you have added to the button, such as an image or movie.

Saving and Applying Custom Themes

If you think a custom theme is one that you will want to use again, you can save it as a Favorite, which means that it will be stored on the Themes list so that you can apply it to other menus by selecting it on the list.

Saving Custom Themes

To save a theme, use the following steps.

Save a Theme as a Favorite

1. Open the menu for which you have developed a custom theme that you want to save.
2. Open the Drawer and click the Settings button.
3. Click on Save as Favorite. The name favorite sheet will appear (see Figure 15.29).

Figure 15.29 *Saving your custom menus makes it simple to reuse them.*

4. Type a name for the theme you are saving.
5. Check the "Shared for all users" check box if you want the theme to be available to everyone who uses iDVD on your Mac or leave it unchecked if you want the theme to be available only when logged in under the current user account.

> **NOTE**
>
> If you don't check the Shared for all users check box, when people are logged into your Mac under another user account, the theme you save won't appear on the Themes list.

6. Check the "Replace existing" check box if you want your custom theme to replace the theme on which it was based or uncheck the check box if you want to add the custom theme to the list of themes instead of replacing a theme.

> **TIP**
>
> You shouldn't replace themes until you are really sure you won't ever want to use them again.

7. Click on OK. The custom theme will be saved as a favorite.

> **TIP**
>
> If you find yourself making the same change to a built-in theme each time you use it, such as a different font or button shape, save that modified theme as a favorite. Even if you usually make only one change to a theme each time you use it, saving it as a favorite can be a time-saver.

Applying Custom Themes to Other Menus

Applying themes you have saved to menus is done just like using one of the built-in themes (because in effect, you have made the custom theme into a built-on theme).

Apply a Favorite Theme to a Menu

1. Open the menu to which you want to apply a favorite theme.
2. Open the Drawer and click the Themes button.
3. Choose Favorites on the pop-up menu. You will see all of the custom themes you have saved (see Figure 15.30). These themes act just like the built-in themes that were installed with iDVD; you can click one of your Favorite themes to apply it to any menu in a DVD project.

Figure 15.30 *One custom theme has been saved as a favorite.*

> **NOTE**
>
> Favorite themes will also appear on the list of themes if you choose All on the pop-up menu.

4. Click the theme to apply it to the menu.

> **NOTE**
>
> You can apply a custom theme to every menu on the DVD by opening a menu to which that theme has been applied and choosing Advanced, Apply Theme to Project.

Removing a Custom Theme You Have Saved as a Favorite

If you want to remove a theme that you have saved as a favorite, do the following steps:

1. Quit iDVD.
2. Open a Finder window.

3. Move to the following folder: *Mac OS X*/Library/iDVD/Favorites, where *Mac OS X* is the name of your Mac OS X startup disk, if you checked the Shared for all users check box when you saved the theme. Move to the following folder: Home/Library/iDVD/Favorites if you did not check the Shared for all users check box when you saved the theme.

4. Select the favorite theme you want to delete.

5. Press ⌘+Delete. The theme will be moved to the Trash and will be deleted the next time you empty the Mac's Trash.

> **NOTE**
>
> When you delete a theme, it will no longer be available to you in iDVD so make sure you won't need it again before you delete it.

Chapter 16

Previewing, Fixing, and Burning a DVD

After you have built an iDVD project and designed all of its menus and buttons, you are almost done. I say almost because there are still a few important steps you need to take to bring the project to completion. Just like the last yards in a race, the final steps in the DVD-creation process are often the most important ones. Here are the general steps you need to take to complete an iDVD project:

1. Preview the DVD to make sure the content, organization, and appearance are what you want to record for all time.
2. Assess the status of the project to make sure there aren't any missing files.
3. Burn the DVD.

Previewing a DVD

In iDVD's Preview mode, you can view the DVD as it will be played in a DVD player (whether on a computer or on a TV). This is a critical step because it allows you to simulate how the actual DVD will perform before you burn it. While it might seem like a pain after all the other work you have done and it can be time consuming, previewing *all* of the DVD's contents before you burn it can save you hours of burn time and wasted DVD discs. There is nothing more frustrating than burning a DVD only to find a typo on the main menu. Previewing a disc carefully before you burn it will minimize the chances of making any mistakes you have made permanent.

Logging Problems

Before you jump into watching a disc, you should create a log so that you can record any problems you find during the preview. Rather than finding a problem, stopping the preview, fixing the problem, and then returning to the preview, you should record and describe any problems in your log as you preview the project. After you have found all of the problems on the DVD, you can go back and fix them at one time. This approach is much more efficient and will result in a better project than trying to fix each problem as you find it.

You can use a paper log to record problems, or you might keep a word processor open while you are previewing a disc so you can record problems electronically. Either way your goal should be to provide enough information for yourself that you can easily locate all the problems you find when it comes time to correct them.

Previewing an iDVD Project

If you have viewed a DVD before, using iDVD's Preview mode won't be a challenge because it works just like any other DVD player you have used. And if you haven't viewed a DVD before, not to worry, you still won't have any difficulty using the preview tools.

Preview an iDVD Project

1. Open the iDVD project.
2. Click on the Motion button to turn the motion effects on if they aren't on already.
3. Turn the TV Safe Area on if you intend to view the DVD on a TV.
4. Click on the Preview button. If the Drawer was open, it will close, and you will see the content area in the iDVD window. The iDVD Controller will also appear on the screen (see Figure 16.1).

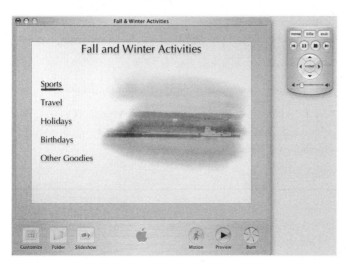

Figure 16.1 *In the Preview mode, you can view an iDVD project as it will be when you put it on a DVD.*

The controls on the Controller are shown in Figure 16.2 and are explained in Table 16.1.

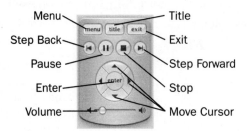

Figure 16.2 *Using the iDVD Controller is just like using the remote for a standard DVD player.*

Table 16.1 Controls on the iDVD Controller

Control	What It Does
Menu	Takes you back to the previous menu.
Title	Moves you to the main menu.
Exit	Stops the Preview mode and returns you to the Design mode.
Step Back	Moves a movie to the previous chapter.
Pause	Pauses the playback if the DVD is playing or plays if it is paused.
Stop	Stops the movie or slideshow when viewing one of those items or stops the preview and returns you to the Design mode when viewing a menu.
Step Forward	Moves to the next chapter in a movie.
Move Cursor	Moves the on-screen cursor in the direction of the arrow.
Enter	"Clicks" on the selected button. If the button represents a menu, that menu will open. If the button points to a movie or slideshow, the movie or slideshow will play.
Volume	Changes the volume.

> **TIP**
>
> You can also view the DVD in the Preview mode by using the mouse to point to and click on buttons. Even better, use the arrow keys on the keyboard to select buttons and then use the Return or Enter key to press them.

As you move the on-screen cursor to select buttons on a menu, they will be highlighted to show that they are selected. What this highlight looks like depends on the menu's design. For example, if the buttons are text only, the text of the selected button might be underlined, a square might appear next to the button, and so on. If the button includes a preview or an image, the button will be highlighted with a box whose color also depends on the menu's design.

Click on enter on the controller or press the Return key on the keyboard to press an on-screen button. The button will be pressed, and you will move to the menu the button represents; if the button is for a movie or a slideshow, the movie or slideshow will begin to play.

As you move through each menu and movie or slideshow on the DVD, record any problems you find in your problem log. Use the points in the next sections to guide your search for problems.

> **TIP**
>
> You can keep the problem log and the preview open at the same time. Start the preview. Then switch to your problem log and move its window so that you can view both it and the DVD preview. As the preview plays in the background, you can make notes in your log.

If you think this process is somewhat cumbersome and time-consuming, you're right. It is both. By the time you have reached this phase, you have probably seen all of the content more than once and are likely to be a bit tired of it. However, doing a thorough preview will pay off in a much better DVD (and fewer wasted discs!) than if you just assume everything is good.

> **NOTE**
>
> Your DVD plan is really helpful for making sure you "touch" every part of your DVD. Refer to your plan to make sure you open every menu and view all the movies and slideshows those movies contain.

Previewing Menus

As you preview menus, you should ask yourself the following questions (see Figure 16.3):

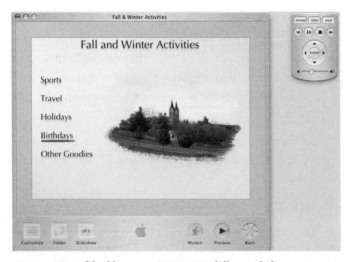

Figure 16.3 *Checking your menus carefully can help you prevent embarrassing mistakes, such as typos.*

- ◆ **Content.** Does the menu contain the content you intended (check your DVD plan)?
- ◆ **Background image or movie.** Is the menu background pleasing to look at? Does the background image or movie add to or distract from the menu's purpose, which is to provide the buttons leading to other menus or to content? Is the movie or image "right" for the contents of the menu?
- ◆ **Background sound.** If the menu includes sound in the background, does that sound complement the background's image or movie? Is the sound annoying when the menu appears on the screen for more than a few seconds? Does the sound complement or detract from the menu's overall look and feel?

- **Drop Zones.** If the menu includes Drop Zones, do the movies or images in the Drop Zones add to the menu's overall look and feel? Are the images and movies aligned with the menu's purpose?
- **Title and title format.** Does the menu's title make sense, given the contents of the menu? Is the text spelled correctly? Is the title legible? Does it contribute to or distract from the overall look and feel you are going for?
- **TV Safe Area.** If you intend for the DVD to be viewable on a TV, are all of the important elements, such as the titles and buttons, contained inside the TV Safe Area?
- **General layout of the menu.** Are the menu's buttons, title, and Drop Zones pleasing to look at and easy to understand?

> **NOTE**
> Unfortunately, iDVD does not include a spell checker. If you are spelling- or typing-challenged, make sure you carefully check the spelling of all the text on the DVD. Even better, have someone else take a look at the DVD for spelling errors because it is easy to become blind to one's own mistakes. There is nothing more frustrating than spending hours creating and burning a DVD only to see a glaring typo in a menu or button title when you view that DVD later.

Previewing Buttons

As you examine the buttons on a menu, ask yourself the following questions:

- **Location.** Are the buttons located on the screen in a pleasant and organized way? Does the location of the buttons contribute to or distract from the overall look and feel of the DVD and the menu on which they appear?
- **Shape.** Is the shape of the buttons on the menu pleasing, and do they seem appropriate for the content to which they point?
- **Button titles and title formatting.** Are the button titles spelled correctly, and do they clearly indicate the content to which the buttons point? Are the button titles located in a good position? Are the titles legible? Does the button title formatting add to or detract from the overall look and feel of the DVD and the menu on which it appears?

◆ **Preview.** If the button points to a movie, is a preview of the movie shown in the button? If so, does it start in the right place so that the appropriate part of the movie is shown in the button? If the button points to a slideshow, menu, or movie that doesn't use the movie as a preview, is the right image displayed in the button? Would the menu look better with text-only buttons?

Previewing Movies

While previewing a movie, consider the following questions (see Figure 16.4):

Figure 16.4 *When you preview a movie, it fills the iDVD window.*

◆ **Content.** Does the movie button point to the movie you planned? When you click on the movie button, does the right movie play? Does it look like it should look when it plays in the iDVD window?

◆ **Button preview.** Do you want to use part of the movie as the button preview? If so, is the starting point correct? If you want to use an image, is it appropriate for the movie?

Previewing Slideshows

When watching the slideshows on a DVD, keep the following questions in mind (see Figure 16.5):

Figure 16.5 *This image has not been sized according to the proportions that iDVD uses, so black bars appear at the top and bottom.*

- **Images.** Are the right images included in the slideshow? Are those images in the right order? Do any images need to be edited?
- **Soundtrack.** Does the soundtrack complement the slideshow's images?
- **Duration.** Is the slideshow's duration correct? If the slideshow has a soundtrack, is the duration set to be the length of the soundtrack? If so, is the length of the soundtrack appropriate for the number of images included in the slideshow (you don't want the images to be on the screen for too long or too short an amount of time). If there isn't a soundtrack, is the image duration appropriate for the type of images in the slideshow? Are the manual advance buttons displayed on-screen if desired?
- **High-resolution images.** If you want the images placed on the DVD-ROM part of the DVD, is the appropriate check box checked so this will be done?

Fixing Problems

As you preview a DVD, hopefully you won't find many problems (the more careful you were in the previous phases, the fewer problems you will find when you preview the results of your work). However, whether there are a few problems or lots of them, you need to fix them before you burn the DVD.

Fix Problems in an iDVD Project

1. Click the Preview button to return to the Design mode.
2. Click the Motion button to turn the motion effects off.
3. Click Customize to open the Drawer.
4. Refer to your problem log to find the location and description of the first problem.
5. Move to the menu where the first problem is located.
6. Use the appropriate tools to fix the problem. For example, if the problem is with a slideshow, use the slideshow tools to fix the problems with the show itself or use iPhoto to edit individual images. If the problem is with a movie, use iMovie to correct it and replace the current version with the revised one. If the problem is with a menu, use the Settings or Themes tools to correct it.

> **NOTE**
>
> To fix a movie, you have to delete the movie that is part of the project and add the revised movie to it. This means you have to reset the movie button previews, adjust button positions, work with the chapter selection menus, and so on. Hopefully, you are very careful when you edit movies so that you don't have to replace them after you have added them to a DVD because doing so is a pain.

7. Repeat Steps 4 though 6 until you have fixed all of the problems in the problem log.

> **TIP**
>
> Remember to save your project frequently!

> **NOTE**
>
> If you want to be very complete, you should repeat the preview process again. Sometimes, when you fix one thing, you mess something else up. If you don't preview again, that something else just might show up on the DVD.

Assessing a DVD Project's Status

Now that the content and design of the DVD are complete, you need to check that all of the files that are needed are included in the project, and you can also check on the encoding status of the movies that you have placed on the DVD.

Assessing a Project

To assess your project to see if it is ready to burn, use the following steps:

Assess an iDVD Project

1. Open the Drawer.
2. Click on Status. The Status tools will appear. At the top of the pane, you will see the current size of the project, both in time and in file size. You can place up to 90 minutes or 4.4GB of content on a DVD.

> **NOTE**
>
> If the length of your project is greater than 60 minutes, iDVD uses a lower-quality encoding scheme for your movies. Files that you add to the DVD-ROM part of the project add to the length of the project, and slideshow and movies you add mean more file space is required for the project. So you can lower the "length" of the project by removing files, such as images in the DVD-ROM part of the disc, from the project. If your project is close to the 60-minute limit, you might want to remove some files or content to get it down to 60 minutes so the better encoder is used. Generally, I haven't found this to be an issue as both encoders are really good. In fact, you might not even be able to tell the difference in image quality between the two.

3. Choose Encoder Status on the pop-up menu. You will see each movie that you have placed on the DVD (see Figure 16.6). For each movie, you will see the status of the encoding process. All movies must have the status of Done before you can burn a DVD. Fortunately, as you learned earlier in this book, iDVD handles all of the encoding for you in the background.

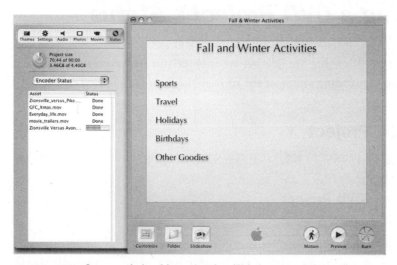

Figure 16.6 *One movie in this project is still being encoded.*

4. Choose DVD-ROM Contents on the pop-up menu. You will see the files and folders that are on the DVD-ROM portion of the DVD, such as the images in slideshows and other files you have added.

TIP

To delete files from the DVD-ROM part of the project, select them and press the Delete key. To delete original images from the project, you have to use the slideshow tools to uncheck the "Add original photos on DVD-ROM" check box.

5. Use the Expansion triangles to view the contents of folders.
6. Choose Project, Project Info. The Project Info window will appear (see Figure 16.7). At the top of the window, you will see the project's name.

In the lower part of the window, you will see every file that is used on the DVD. For each file listed, you will see its type and current status. If there is a check mark in the Status column, iDVD can find that file, and it is ready to be put on a DVD.

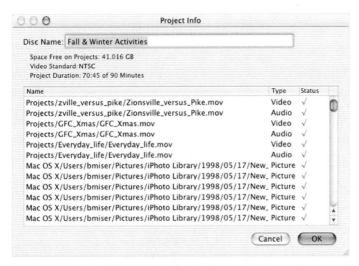

Figure 16.7 *Use the Project Info window to check out the status of the files used in an iDVD project.*

7. Use the scroll tools to review the list of files. If the status of a file is something other than the check mark, your project has a problem, most likely a file is missing (see the next section for help correcting this condition).

NOTE

In the Project Info window, you will see that iDVD maintains a path to each file in the project. If you move files from the locations shown on the file list, iDVD can lose track of the file and won't be able to write that file to the disc. When this is the case, an alert icon will appear in the Status column to show you that a file can't be found. You will also be warned if you attempt to burn the DVD. You should not move any files used in the DVD project until you have burned the DVD and are sure you have all the copies you need.

8. Click on OK. The Project Info window will close.

Finding Missing Files

One of the most likely causes of a failed burn attempt is that files included in the project are no longer available. This can happen for several reasons, but the most likely is that the files were moved from their location when you created the DVD project (this can easily happen when a long period of time passes between when you created a DVD project and when you attempted to burn it).

If you preview a project thoroughly and all the projects are displayed correctly, no files are missing. Likewise, you can use the Project Info window as you learned in the previous section.

Lastly, if you attempt to burn a DVD and iDVD can't find all of the files that are included in a project, you will be prompted with the Missing Files window.

> **NOTE**
>
> One insidious cause of the missing file problem can happen when you move files while the burn process is ongoing. In this case, iDVD loses its way to the file, but doesn't warn you that access to the file has been lost. Instead, the burn process gets stuck—it will appear to be making progress, but will eventually stop working and remain stuck with some amount of time to go (for example, it might stay in the "less than a minute to go" state for hours). When this happens, you have to abort the burn by clicking Cancel. If that doesn't work, you will have to force iDVD to quit. (If you force iDVD to quit, make sure you restart your Mac before working with the project again.) This is another reason I recommend that you don't use your Mac for any other purpose while you are burning a DVD. It is amazingly easy to move a file you have used in a DVD project without realizing it.

To find a missing file, use the following steps.

Find Files That Are Missing from an iDVD Project

1. Identify the missing files. You can do this through the Project Info window, or, if you are trying to burn an iDVD project from which files are missing, you will see the Missing Files prompt (see Figure 16.8).

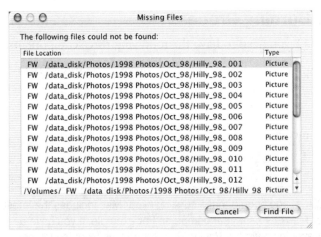

Figure 16.8 *This window lets you know that files are missing from a project.*

2. Use the scroll tools to review the list of missing files. You will see the location in which iDVD thinks the files are located in the window.

3. Click on the Find File button. The Open dialog box will appear.

4. Move to the first missing file's current location and select the missing file.

5. Click Open. iDVD will restore the path to the missing file. If other missing files are located in the same folder as the missing file you just found, iDVD will find them as well.

6. Repeat Steps 3 through 5 until you have found all the missing files.

Burning an iDVD Project on DVD

After you have built a DVD project, you can burn that project onto a DVD. The DVDs that you create can be played in computers that have DVD-ROM drives as well as in most standard DVD players that are used with TVs or home theater systems. In this chapter, you'll learn how to:

- ◆ Understand the burn process
- ◆ Maximize burn performance
- ◆ Burn a DVD

Understanding the Burning Process

In order to create a DVD, you need to have the following three components:

- ◆ Macintosh computer with a SuperDrive or other compatible DVD-R drive
- ◆ iDVD
- ◆ Blank DVD-R media

> **NOTE**
>
> Before you burn any DVDs, you should make sure that your Mac includes the latest SuperDrive updates for Mac OS X for your computer. For example, if you have a Power Mac and have never installed the Power Mac SuperDrive Update, you can damage your SuperDrive by attempting to burn a high-speed DVD-R or DVD-RW disc in it. Visit www.apple.com/hardware/superdrive/ to learn more about these important updates.

Since iDVD won't even run on systems that don't have a compatible DVD-R drive, you must have one to have made it this far in this book.

> **NOTE**
>
> While the DVDs you create by using iDVD are compatible with most standard DVD players, "most" does not mean "all." There are some DVD players that will not be able to play the DVDs you create. To get information about DVD players that are compatible with the DVDs you create, see www.apple.com/dvd/compatibility/.

You can obtain blank DVD-R media from many sources, but Apple only certifies the DVD-R media that it produces. You can obtain these discs from Apple retailers, such as www.smalldog.com. There are two types of DVD-R discs; the difference between these types is their rated recording speed. The slower rated discs are rated for 2x speed and cost about $3 per disc. The higher rated discs are rated for

4x recoding speed and cost about $4.60 per disc. After you burn the disc, there is no difference between the two types. The only difference is that the faster discs can support a higher recording rate, which means it takes less time to burn a disc. If your Mac has a 4x-capable drive, the faster burn process might be worth the additional cost of the discs.

> **NOTE**
>
> There are many other producers of blank DVD-R media, and many of these brands of discs are less expensive than the Apple brand. Be forewarned that you might not achieve as consistent results with non-Apple brands as you can with the Apple brand of DVD-R media.

Fortunately, iDVD manages all aspects of the burn process for you, and you don't need to understand the intricacies of the process to be able to create DVDs.

Maximizing Burn Performance

In order to maximize the performance of the burn process and achieve the best results, you should do the following steps.

> **TIP**
>
> If you have external FireWire or USB data devices (particularly hard disks) attached to your Mac, consider unmounting them and disconnecting them from your Mac prior to the burn process. Some FireWire devices can cause data bus activity that can slow the burn process. Of course, if files that are used in your DVD project are stored on the FireWire device, you won't be able to do this because that would mean that iDVD won't be able to find the files when they are needed (because the disk on which they are stored is no longer accessible).

Maximize DVD Burn Performance

1. Quit all open applications, except iDVD of course.

> **NOTE**
>
> Because Mac OS X features protected memory, you might wonder why I recommend that you shut down all applications except iDVD. It is true that Mac OS X provides each application with a protected memory space in which that application can work. The activity of other applications doesn't usually affect the memory space of other applications. However, all applications share the same data buses, drives, and other components. Open applications can write to and read from hard disks and other components, which reduces the bandwidth available for the burn process. If you have a high-end system, the steps in this section might not be necessary. But these steps will benefit the burn process on all systems and might be necessary to avoid problems on lower-end systems with less capability.

2. Choose Apple (the Apple menu), System Preferences. The System Preferences application will appear.
3. Click on the Energy Saver icon. The Energy Saver pane will appear.
4. Click on the Sleep tab (see Figure 16.9).

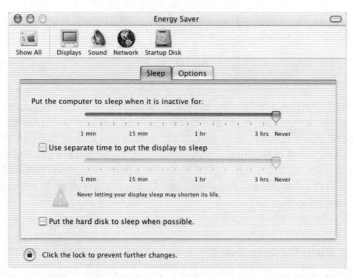

Figure 16.9 *You should disable sleep functions because they can interfere with the burn process.*

> **NOTE**
>
> Sometimes, your Mac's sleep mode can cause temporary system slowdowns and unnecessary loads on the system. You should disable all sleep modes on your Mac before burning a DVD and reenable them after you have successfully created the disc.

5. Drag the top slider to Never.
6. Uncheck the "Use separate time to put the display to sleep" check box.
7. Uncheck the "Put the hard disk to sleep when possible" check box.

> **NOTE**
>
> Turning off the display sleep function makes the displays connected to your Mac remain active all the time. This can shorten the life of flat panel displays. After you have burned a DVD, you should come back to the Energy Saver pane and reenable display sleep—and system sleep if you use it.

8. Click on the Show All button on the toolbar. All of the System Preference icons will appear again.
9. Click on the Screen Effects icon. The Screen Effects pane will appear.
10. Click on the Activation tab. The Activation tools will appear.
11. Drag the slider to Never. This prevents your screen saver from being displayed.

> **NOTE**
>
> Because the screen saver constantly displays graphics on your screen, it causes processor and disk activity that can slow down the burning process. You should disable the screen saver before you burn a DVD. After you have successfully burned a disc, you can reenable it.

12. Quit the System Preferences application.

Burning a DVD

After the extensive work you did to create a DVD project, actually burning the DVD will be somewhat anticlimactic. Because iDVD manages the burning process for you, there isn't much you need to do except start the process and wait for it to finish.

You should know that burning DVDs is still a somewhat persnickety process, and you shouldn't be surprised if you occasionally run into problems, such as the burn process never completing, the disc you create being defective, and so on. That is just part of the technology at this stage in its lifecycle. Fortunately, most of the burns you do will be successful, especially if you follow the advice in the previous section.

> **NOTE**
>
> Before you click the Burn button, make sure you have done everything you can to check the DVD project as explained in the earlier sections of this chapter. Since most of the discs you use can be written to only once, if the project contains mistakes when you burn it, you will waste a disc, a few bucks, and a bit of time.

Burn a DVD

1. Open the iDVD project.
2. Click the Motion button to turn motion effects on if they aren't on already. If you burn a disc with the motion effects off, those effects won't appear when the disc is played. If your menus use motion effects, make sure they are on before you burn.
3. Click on the Burn button. It will open, and you will see the "radioactive" version of the button.

> **NOTE**
>
> If you use your Mac during the burn process, you can slow the process down and increase the chances of an unsuccessful burn. You should leave iDVD active as the only running application during the entire burn process.

4. Click on the Burn button again. Your Mac will prompt you to insert a blank DVD-R disc into the drive (see Figure 16.10). If your Mac has a slide-out tray, the tray will open automatically.

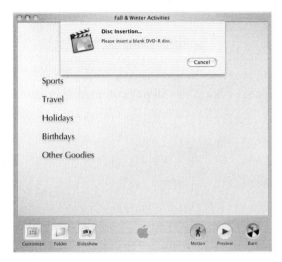

Figure 16.10 *Burn, baby, burn!*

5. Insert a blank disc into your Mac (and close the tray if necessary). iDVD will begin the burn process. At the top of the iDVD window, you will see a progress window that shows you what state the process is in and provides a rough estimate of the time it will take to complete the burn.

> **NOTE**
>
> The amount of time it will take to burn a DVD depends on many factors, including the amount of data in the project, the speed of your Mac and its DVD-R drive, the media you use, and whether all of the movies have been encoded previously. (If some files in the project have not finished the encoding process, that process will have to be completed before the burning process can start. This alone can easily double or triple the time it takes to burn a DVD.) While iDVD provides an estimate of the time until the burn process is complete, this is only an estimate. It is not unusual for this number to go up and down during the burn. The burning process can take from just a few minutes for a very fast Mac to burn a DVD that doesn't have much data on it to three or more hours for a relatively slow Mac to burn a DVD that is full to the brim.
>
> Also, don't be surprised if the image inside the iDVD window changes from the menu you were viewing when you started the burning process to a black screen with the iDVD logo. This happens occasionally as iDVD completes the burn and is not a sign that something has gone amiss.

6. Monitor the progress of the process (see Figure 16.11). You don't need to hover around your Mac; in fact, it is better if you leave your Mac alone during the process. You should just check every so often to make sure the process is still making progress. When the process has finished, the disc will be ejected from your Mac. You will be prompted to create another disc.

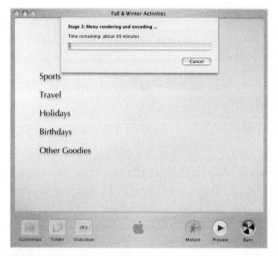

Figure 16.11 *Burning a DVD can take some time, but fortunately you don't need to hang around because iDVD takes care of it for you.*

> **TIP**
>
> The rate at which the Burn icon spins indicates how quickly and smoothly the process is moving along. If the icon spins fast, data is flowing smoothly, and the burn process is going well. The slower the icon spins, the slower data is flowing. If the icon stops entirely and remains stopped for an extended period of time, the process might have run into trouble. If that happens, just wait for iDVD to report an error. If you take action, you run the risk of aborting a burn when you might not have needed to.

7. Click on Done when you are done burning copies of the disc. You will return to the project window.
8. Save the project.
9. Quit iDVD. The DVD is ready for your viewing pleasure.

> **TIP**
>
> If you disabled energy saving and your screen saver, reenable them after the burn process is complete.

> **Recovering Disk Space**
>
> If you have limited disk space available, after you are *sure* that your DVD is right and that you have made all the copies you want, you can delete the iDVD project file. These files are large, so if you don't have the space to store them permanently, getting rid of them will free up disk space you need for your next projects. You can also delete the individual content files if you no longer want to store them. Ideally, you will have a tape backup system to which you can archive this data, but if not, you will have to decide which is more important—hard disk space or keeping all of the files. Try to save the content files, especially your iMovie projects, if you can because you can more easily re-create the DVD than you can re-create the individual content files.

PART V

iLife: The Only Way to Live

17 Adding Video and Sound from Movies or TV shows to iLife Projects

18 Creating Cool Soundtracks for iLife Projects

Chapter 17

Adding Video and Sound from Movies or TV Shows to iLife Projects

It's time for true confessions. I admit it—I am a television and movie junkie (of course, I'm only crazy about certain movies and television shows, but the few that I do like, I *really* like). Of course, being a techno geek, I am required by law to enjoy all the science fiction classics, such as *Star Trek*, *Star Wars*, *Babylon 5*, the *Terminator* series, and so on. But I like lots of other great movies and television shows as well, such as *Braveheart*, *Gladiator*, *Henry V*, and so on.

Because of this, it is great fun to capture great lines, sounds, images, or even entire scenes from favorite movies and television shows to use in iLife projects or to accent your Mac's desktop. If you enjoy any movies or television shows, I'll show you how to capture cool content from those sources. (If you don't like any movies or television shows, you might want to skip to the next chapter now.)

> **NOTE**
>
> Before you start capturing content from VHS or DVD sources, you need to make sure that you remain aware of copyright issues. All content on commercially produced VHS or DVD is copyrighted in one form or another. Almost all content that you record from television sources is also copyrighted. This means that you need to be very careful about extracting this content and using it in your own projects, which is the whole point of this chapter. As I mentioned earlier in this book, you are probably okay if you use this content *only* for your own amusement (this is usually referred to as "for your own use"). As soon as you start distributing such material, such as posting movies that include copyrighted material on the Web, you move onto dangerous ground from the legal perspective. Just respect material that other people have created as you would want your own work to be respected, and you should be fine. A good rule of thumb is that if you are going to distribute a project so that more than one or two people can access it, don't include any material in it that is copyrighted by someone else—unless you have written permission to do so.

Mining Sources of Content

There are lots of great sources of content out there. The sources that you'll learn about in this chapter are the following:

- **Television**. While most of television, whether broadcast, satellite, or cable, is a wasteland, there are a few gems that contain material you might want to include in your projects. With a VCR and a DV camera, you can capture television content easily.
- **Movies or television shows on VHS**. Most anything that is on a VHS tape can be brought into your projects. And since there are so many types of tapes out there, the VHS world can be your oyster.
- **Movies or television shows on DVD**. The DVD format has taken the world by storm—and with good reason. With its amazing quality and great special features, DVD is the media of choice for audio and video enthusiasts. Capturing content from DVD can be dicey, but the element of uncertainty makes it more appealing to try.
- **QuickTime movies from the Web**. Lots of great content is available on the Web in the QuickTime format. Some of my favorite QuickTime content comes from movie trailers that you can download and use in your projects. Of course, there are also lots of other kinds of QuickTime content available. The good news is that you can use it in the same way as the content I describe in this chapter.
- **Audio clips from the Web**. When it comes to using audio clips from movies and television in your projects, you'll find that someone, somewhere has probably already captured audio clips you might want to use and posted them on the Web. Obtaining these clips is just a matter of finding and downloading them.

Why a FireWire DV Camera Might Be the Only Digitizing System You'll Ever Need

In the olden, predigital days, capturing content from VCRs, camcorders, and other sources so that you could work with it on a computer was a real pain. Because this content was *analog*, it couldn't be used directly on a computer. It had to be *digitized* first. And to digitize content, you needed a *digitizer*. These devices, usually in the form of a PCI card, were expensive and quite difficult to work with. And the software you used to work with these devices was no walk in the park either. After lots of money and tons of time and effort, the results were usually marginal—at best. Unless you were a professional and had access to the best hardware and software, capturing content at a decent quality level was almost impossible.

And then came Digital Video (DV). Because DV cameras capture content in a digital form, there is no need to digitize that content. With FireWire, this content can be moved onto a computer very easily. Thus, the digital lifestyle came into its own.

A side benefit of DV cameras is that in addition to capturing content through their lenses, they can often record content from an external source. This is way cool because you can connect a DV camera to a VCR or DVD player and record content onto a DV tape. After you do so, you can move that content onto your Mac and work with it just like content you shoot with the DV camera. For most people, a DV camera will prevent you from ever having to fuss with a digitizer, and trust me, that is a good thing.

Capturing Content from VHS

There are two sources of content on VHS tape that you can capture and use in your projects. One source includes television shows or movies that you record yourself. The other source is commercially produced VHS content. The process that you use to capture material from either of these sources is very similar. The only difference is how the content gets onto a VHS tape in the first place.

NOTE

Some VHS content is copy-protected, and your DV camera won't be able to record it properly. When you attempt to record a copy-protected VHS tape, wavy lines and other artifacts will usually destroy the image, and the video will usually appear in black-and-white. The images from a copy-protected VHS tape will generally be unusable. In such cases, you will probably have to resort to a digitizing system in order to be able to capture that content on your Mac (digitizing systems are beyond the scope of this book). However, you can usually capture good quality audio from VHS tapes, even if they are copy-protected.

The following are the four general tasks you will do to capture content from a VHS source:

1. Obtain the VHS content that you want to use.
2. Connect the output of the VCR to the input of your DV camera.
3. Use the DV camera to record the segments containing the content that you want to use.
4. Import that content into iMovie.

Obtaining VHS Content

If you are going to use a commercially recorded VHS tape to capture content, you don't need to do anything to obtain the content—assuming that you have the tape that contains the material you want to use. If you are going to record the content yourself, record it as you would record anything else.

> **TIP**
>
> Using a VCR to record content is straightforward; however, one setting that you should check is the recording speed. Make sure that you choose the SP or standard option for recording. This option uses more videotape, but the quality of the recording will be better and thus the quality of the content you capture will also be better. (Most VCRs have at least two recording speed settings. The standard setting records less on a given tape length, while the extended play setting records more on a given tape length. However, the standard setting will provide a better quality playback, so you should use that when you are capturing material for your iLife projects.)

Connecting a DV Camera to a VCR

To capture content from the VCR onto your DV camera, connect the output of your VCR (that normally goes into a television or A/V receiver) to the input of your DV camera. Usually, you can use the same cable that you use to record from the DV camera to the VCR. On many DV cameras, you even connect this cable to the same port, regardless of whether you are recording on the camera or outputting what you have recorded to a VCR. This port is usually called the Audio/Video (A/V) port, Input/output port, or something similar. The cable you need should have been provided with the camera. When you have the camera connected, your configuration should look something like that in Figure 17.1.

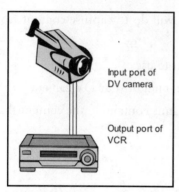

Figure 17.1 *If you connect the output of your VCR to the input of your DV camera, you can record content from a VHS tape onto a DV tape.*

Check the VCR's Connection to Your DV Camera

1. Power up the VCR and the DV camera.
2. Play the VHS tape. You should see its output in the Monitor screen on the DV camera. If you do, your capture system is ready to go. If not, check the connection to make sure that you are connected to the output port of the VCR. If the connection looks okay, make sure that your DV camera is capable of recording from an external source and that you have it set in the correct mode to do so (check the camera's user manual).

Recording VHS Content on a DV Camera

Recording VHS content on a DV camera is easy.

Record Content from a VCR on a DV Camera

1. Locate the content on the VHS tape that you want to capture.
2. Position the tape so that you are just before that content (allow some "wasted" space at the beginning of the capture).
3. Start recording on the DV camera.
4. Play the VHS tape until it finishes the segment you want to capture.
5. Stop the DV camera.
6. Repeat the previous steps until you have captured all of the content you want. You will have this content on a DV tape just as if you had recorded it using the camera's lens.

> **TIP**
>
> Some DV cameras have a *passthrough* feature. With this feature, the camera can output through the FireWire port whatever is coming into the camera through the A/V port. This means that you don't have to record the output from the VCR; you can simply pass it through the DV camera so that it goes directly into iMovie without having to record it to a DV tape. Of course, this requires that you have the camera connected to your Mac and a VCR at the same time.

Importing VHS Content into iMovie

After you have recorded content from VHS, you can import it into iMovie just like content you have captured using the camera's lens.

> **NOTE**
>
> For the detailed steps to import content from a DV camera into iMovie, see Chapter 9.

Import Captured Content into iMovie

1. Open iMovie and open or create the project in which you will use the content you have captured.
2. Import the content from the DV camera. When you are done, the clips will be just like those you captured with the camera itself. You can edit them, place them in movies, and so on.

If the VHS content is from a 16x9 or widescreen version, the clip you capture will have black bars at the top and bottom of the screen, just as it does when you play that content on a 4x3 television. There isn't anything you can do about that with iMovie.

> **NOTE**
>
> Some DV cameras enable you to capture content in the 16x9 format. If you are going to be mixing footage you shoot with content from a 16x9 or widescreen VHS, you should also capture content in the 16x9 format with your DV camera.

> ### Capturing Still Images from VHS Content
>
> You can also capture still images from VHS content. For example, you might want to use such images as desktop pictures, or you might want to print them. You can create an image from a clip you have captured by using the following steps.
>
> **Capture Still Images from VHS Content in iMovie**
>
> 1. Select the clip that contains the image you want to capture.
> 2. Move the Playhead so that the image you want appears in the Monitor.
> 3. Choose File, Save Frame As (or press ⌘+F).
> 4. In the Save Frame As Image dialog box, choose the format for the image on the Format pop-up menu; for most purposes, you should choose JPEG.
> 5. Choose a location in which to save the file, name it, and click Save.
> 6. Open the image in a viewing application or import it into the application in which you want to use it. For example, you can view the image in the Preview application, or you can import it into iPhoto.

> **NOTE**
>
> You can also capture audio clips from the VHS content you imported into iMovie—for example, to create an alert sound or sound effect. You'll learn how to do this in the next chapter.

Capturing Content from DVD

Because the DVD format offers so many benefits, all the best content comes on DVD these days. There are several ways to get DVD content onto your Mac. The easiest way is to record content from a DVD to a DV camera just like you do with VHS content. Unfortunately, because most DVDs are copy-protected, this method often does not work. The harder way is to rip a DVD. While this is much more work than recording, it almost always works.

Recording Content from DVD

For those DVDs that aren't copy-protected, you can use the same process to capture content as you do for VHS content. Simply connect the DV camera to a DVD player instead of a VCR. Otherwise, the steps are exactly the same.

If you try this with a DVD that is copy-protected, which most DVDs that contain recent movies are, the results will be terrible. The images will be distorted by wavy lines and will usually be in black-and-white. The video portion will be unusable. In such a case, you will need to use the ripping technique that is described in the next section.

> **TIP**
>
> If all you are interested in is the audio portion of a DVD's content, you might be able to record that successfully even from a copy-protected DVD. Even though the video track will be junk, the audio track often can be recorded just fine.

Ripping Content from DVD

There are applications that enable you to extract, more commonly called *ripping*, content from a DVD and create QuickTime versions of that content. After you have the DVD's content in QuickTime, you can use it in your digital lifestyle projects. This process works on just about any DVD.

To rip content from a DVD, you need a DVD ripping application. There are several available on the Internet, and most of them are freeware.

However, there are complex legal issues surrounding the software that enables you to rip DVD content, especially if you live in the United States. In fact, in the United States, distributing such software is currently illegal.

Because of this, I can't tell you about the details of this process. However, I can describe it generally since talking about it isn't illegal.

Basically, you use a DVD-extracting application to extract the video track and the audio track from the DVD. The tools that you use to do this are usually rough and sometimes don't work at all. And you need tons of disk space to be able to extract an entire DVD's worth of content—when it does work, the process takes a long time. If the process works, you end up with a file containing the video and another containing the audio.

You then use converters to decode these files into usable formats. For example, you convert the video file into QuickTime and the audio into AIFF or MP3. You can then import those files into an iMovie project to combine them. Save the project, and you have a DVD movie in the iMovie format. You can use this just like other iMovie movies, such as copying parts of it, exporting sounds from it, and so on.

If you want to explore how this process works in more detail, search the Web for information on DVD ripping and Macintosh. You will find information resources, and if you live in an area where the software isn't illegal, you can download a DVD extracting application. You'll also need to download decoding applications that you can use to translate files that you extract into usable formats.

Capturing Still Images from DVD

Because DVD content is encoded, you can't use the Mac's built-in screen capture feature to capture images from a DVD—if you try, all you will get is a black screen.

Even though ripping content from a DVD is problematic, you can capture images from a DVD fairly easily—if you have a Mac equipped with an NVidia graphics card. To determine if you have an NVidia graphics card, use the Apple System Profiler application or check the documentation that came with your Mac.

If you do have an NVidia graphics card, you can use Ambrosia Software's excellent screen capture utility Snapz Pro X to capture images when you play a DVD in OS X's DVD Player application. (In fact, all the screenshots in this book were captured with Snapz Pro X.) To download a copy of Snapz Pro, visit www.AmbrosiaSW.com, click the Utilities tab, and look for the Snapz Pro X section. Download and install the application on your Mac. (You can use the application on a trial basis for 30 days; after that you need to register it, which costs about $30 without QuickTime movie support.)

After you have installed and configured Snapz Pro, using it to capture a DVD image is simple.

Capture a Still Image from a DVD By Using Snapz Pro X

1. Insert the DVD containing the image that you want to capture and play it in the DVD Player application using the full-screen mode.

2. When you get to an image that you want to capture, pause the DVD using DVD Player's controls.

3. Hide DVD Player's Controller and Info window if they are visible.

4. Launch Snapz Pro X and activate it (by default, you press Cmd + Shift + 3 to do so, but you can set any hot keys that you want). The Snapz Pro X window will appear.

5. Click the Screen button.

6. In the resulting dialog, name the image you are capturing.

7. Press Return. The image will be captured and placed in your Pictures folder—unless you tell Snapz Pro X to store it elsewhere (see Figure 17.2). You can use this image in your digital lifestyle projects or anywhere else for that matter.

Figure 17.2 *Here, I captured an image from the excellent For All Mankind DVD.*

Downloading and Using QuickTime Movie Trailers from the Web

Most movie trailers are posted as QuickTime movies on the Web. If you like to play around with movie content, these trailers can be a rich source of content that is easy to mine.

> **NOTE**
>
> Depending on how the QuickTime content has been posted to the Web, you might need to upgrade to QuickTime Pro to be able to download that content and store it on your Mac as a QuickTime movie, which is necessary to get it into iMovie. If the trailer can be viewed online, this is the case. If the trailer is also provided as a .sit or .mov file, you can download it directly, and you will be able to add that content to an iMovie project.
>
> For information about upgrading to QuickTime Pro, see my book *Special Edition Using Mac OS X v10.2*.

One of the best sources of movie trailers in the QuickTime format is the Apple QuickTime Movie Trailer Web site located at www.apple.com/trailers/ (see Figure 17.3). Here, trailers from all the latest and greatest Hollywood productions are posted for your enjoyment.

Figure 17.3 *Apple's QuickTime Movie Trailers Web site offers a wealth of QuickTime content you can view, download, and use in your projects (if you have upgraded to QuickTime Pro).*

Adding Video and Sound from Movies or TV Shows Chapter 17   **493**

> **TIP**
>
> Another potential source of movie trailer clips is the Web site for the movie in which you are interested. Almost all movies have their own Web sites these days, and almost all of these sites have the movie's trailers available in a format that you can view or download.

Use a QuickTime Movie Trailer in an iMovie Project

1. Move to the trailer you want to view and download.
2. View the trailer.

> **TIP**
>
> If the trailer is provided as a .mov or .sit file, you don't need to view it. Just download it to your Mac. If it is a .sit file, unstuff it, and it will be a .mov file.

3. When the clip has finished playing, open the QuickTime Options pop-up menu and choose Save As QuickTime Movie (see Figure 17.4).

Figure 17.4 *"The Lord of the Rings" trailers are provided in both online and downloadable formats.*

> **NOTE**
>
> In Figure 17.4, you can see that the trailer is also provided in the .sit format. You can download a .sit file without upgrading to QuickTime Pro. After you uncompress the file, it will be a QuickTime movie file (the file extension will be .mov), and you can import it into iMovie as explained starting with Step 5.

4. In the resulting Save dialog box, choose a location in which to save the file and save it.
5. Open the iMovie project in which you want to use the trailer you downloaded.
6. Choose File, Import (or press ⌘+I). The Import sheet will appear.
7. Move to the file you downloaded, select it, and click Open. The file will be imported into the iMovie project. If the file is fairly large, this process can take a while; its progress is shown in the Import Files window. When the process is complete, the trailer will be placed on the Clips pane, and you can use it just like other clips located there (see Figure 17.5). For example, you can edit it, add it to a movie, extract its audio, and so on.

Figure 17.5 *I've added the trailer for "The Lord of the Rings: The Two Towers" to this iMovie project.*

Adding Video and Sound from Movies or TV Shows — Chapter 17 — 495

TIP

Adding a clip to iMovie makes it possible to extract sounds from that clip to use in projects as alert sounds and in other ways. If you want to capture movie lines or sounds, this can be a great way to do so since such lines are often part of the movie's trailer. This is explained in the next chapter.

Making a Resolution (Change That Is)

When capturing content from movies (whether on VHS or DVD), the format in which that movie was created becomes important. The standard format for analog television is 4x3 while movies are shot in 16x9 or widescreen format. If you mix the formats, in an iMovie project for example, the results might not be too pleasing as the application scales the content to match its current format.

And, if you import a trailer in the 16x9 format into iMovie, it might not look good because iMovie will scale it into the 4x3 format, resulting in the video looking "squished" from the sides.

You can use QuickTime Pro to resize content to better match the format of the project in which you are using it. Unfortunately, explaining how to do this is beyond what I have room to cover here. See my book *Special Edition Using Mac OS X v10.2* for detailed information about QuickTime Pro.

Downloading and Using Movie and TV Sound Clips from the Web

If you like to use movie and TV sounds in your projects, you can usually find the sounds you want to use on the Web as WAV or MP3 files. You can download these files and import them into iMovie, iTunes, or iDVD to use those sounds in your projects.

> **TIP**
>
> There are lots of great sites for sound files you can listen to and download. Use your favorite Web search tool to search for WAV files or start at one of my favorites, wave-central.com. This site has all kinds of sound clips, including movie and TV sounds, sound effects, and many more.

Download a WAV File and Add It to iTunes

1. Move to the Web site that contains the sound you want to use in your project (see Figure 17.6).

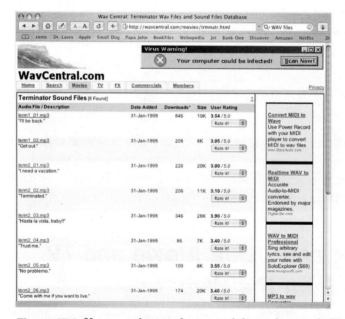

Figure 17.6 *You never know when you might need to use the Terminator saying, "I'll be back" in an iMovie project.*

2. Listen to the clip. Depending on how the file is provided, you might see the QuickTime player, or the file might play in some other way.

3. Download the file. Again, how you do this depends on how the file is provided on the Web site. If the file is in the MP3 format, you can download it using Safari's Save As command.

4. When you are "viewing" the audio clip, choose File, Save As (see Figure 17.7).

Adding Video and Sound from Movies or TV Shows Chapter 17 497

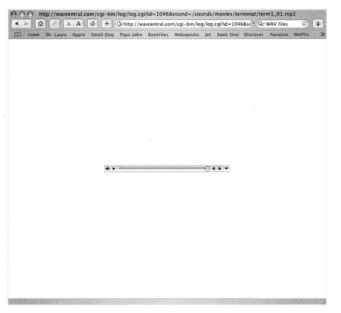

Figure 17.7 *This doesn't look like much, but it might just be the perfect sound for you.*

5. In the resulting save sheet, move to the location in which you want to save the file.
6. Name the file. In most cases, you will need to replace the default file name with one that includes the appropriate file name extension. For example, if the sound you are downloading is an MP3 file, add .mp3 to the end of the file name. If it is a WAV file, add .wav.
7. Click Save. The file will be saved in the location you chose.
8. Move to the file and double-click it. It will be imported into your iTunes Library, and you can use it just like any other sound you have added (see Figure 17.8).

Figure 17.8 *Now that "I'll be back" is part of my iTunes Library, I can use it in any of my iLife projects.*

> **TIP**
>
> If you don't want to add the sound to your iTunes Library, you can import it into an iMovie or iDVD project instead.

Using Captured Content in Your iLife Projects

After you have captured content from DVD or VHS sources, there are lots of ways to use that content. These include the following:

- ◆ Import content into iMovie and use it in your iMovie projects.
- ◆ Import content into iMovie and extract audio clips from it for sound effects or system alert sounds.
- ◆ Use images from your favorite movies as menu elements on a DVD that you create in iDVD.
- ◆ Add audio and video elements from your favorite movies and television shows to your desktop.

Chapter 18

Creating Cool Soundtracks for iLife Projects

Sound will be an important part of almost all of your iLife projects. From QuickTime movies to slideshows on DVD, what your audience hears is as important as what they see on the screen (and sometimes more important). You can use iTunes and iMovie to create sophisticated soundtracks for any of your digital lifestyle projects, including the following:

- iMovie and QuickTime movies
- iPhoto slideshows
- iDVD slideshows
- iDVD menus

The soundtracks that you develop for these projects can include music, of course, but you can also add sound effects, different layers of music, recorded sounds, and just about any other sound that you can hear.

The general steps to creating a soundtrack are the following:

1. Design the soundtrack that you need.
2. Use iTunes to produce the music and sound clips for the soundtrack.
3. Use iMovie to combine the iTunes music and sound with sound effects and other sounds that will be part of the soundtrack.
4. Prepare the soundtrack for use by exporting it in the appropriate format.
5. Add the soundtrack to the project.

You might impress yourself with the soundtracks you are able to create because the iLife tools are so powerful. If you do, you can even put your own soundtracks in iTunes and on CD so you can listen to them whenever you want to.

Designing a Soundtrack

Just like most iLife projects, the first step in creating a soundtrack is planning it. And the first step in the first step is selecting the project for which you are going to create a soundtrack.

After you have selected your project, figure out precisely how long you need your soundtrack to be. You might want the soundtrack to occupy the entire project's length, or you might want it to cover only a portion of it.

To keep your soundtrack project organized, create a folder in which to store the elements that you use in it. This will save time when you create the soundtrack because you won't have to hunt for the "pieces" you will use; they will all be located in one place.

Selecting the Music for a Soundtrack

If your soundtrack will include music, select the music that you want to include—this task requires some thought. The music you select should enhance your project. For example, if the project includes action (or if you want to make the project seem like it includes more action than it actually does), use music that has a driving beat, such as rock or jazz. If the project involves a special occasion, such as a holiday, you can go with the obvious and choose music that is associated with that holiday. Or you might go contrarian and choose something completely unrelated to the occasion. This can sometimes be very interesting. If the project is a slideshow of miscellaneous images, a mellow instrumental piece can be a good choice.

Many iLife projects involve trips or vacations in different parts of the world. Most areas of the world have specific types of music associated with them; the music associated with an area that you have visited can be a nice complement to a project that you create about that area. For example, when creating a project about a trip to the Smoky Mountains in Tennessee, using music associated with the people who first lived in that area might be a good choice, especially if you can find music that isn't widely heard in other areas. As you travel, keep your eyes (and ears) out for audio CDs offered in areas that you visit; these can provide unique music for your soundtracks that you might not be able to find elsewhere.

> **NOTE**
>
> When you select your music, make sure that you keep the means by which you will distribute your project in mind. If you are creating a project that you plan to distribute widely, you probably don't want to use music that is copyrighted. You need to use music that you have a license to distribute or license-free music instead. Later in this chapter, you'll learn about an application called SmartSound Sonicfire Pro that you can use to create a licensed music soundtrack for your digital lifestyle projects. In addition to providing tools you can use to really customize the music in your soundtracks, you will be able to distribute projects that include that music in any way you'd like.

Gather all the music that you will be using; if you are using multiple tracks, make a notation about where you want each track to start and stop in your project. This information will help you when it comes time to mix your soundtrack in iMovie.

Selecting Sound Effects for the Soundtrack

As you plan your soundtrack, identify sound effects that you might want to add. For example, if your project includes images of animals, you might want to add those animals' sounds to the soundtrack. If your project includes vehicles of some kind, sounds from such vehicles might make a nice addition.

If you read through earlier chapters in this book (and you did, didn't you?), you learned that almost any audio file can be imported into iTunes and iMovie so that you can use those sounds in your projects. These include the millions of WAV and MP3 files that are available on the Web.

Just like the music, sound effects should enhance what appears on the screen. Don't go crazy with sound effects; sound effects should be used sparingly because too many sound effects can overwhelm the rest of the project. While music playing throughout a project is usually just fine, you should include sound effects only at key points.

> **TIP**
>
> If you want to get the best results, create a script for your soundtrack that ties specific sounds to specific points in the project. Use this script to guide the creation of your soundtrack.

Using iTunes to Prepare Music and Sound Clips for the Soundtrack

After you have selected your music, use iTunes to prepare the music for your projects. To do this, encode the music in the format you need for your projects. For most projects, you should encode the music in the MP3 format.

If the music you are using is already in your iTunes Music Library, you don't need to encode it because it is already encoded. If the music isn't part of your iTunes Library, you need to add the music to your Library to encode it (see Chapter 2 for the steps to do this).

While you mostly use iTunes for music, you can actually store any sound in your iTunes Library. For example, if there is a WAV file that you use frequently in your projects, add that file to your iTunes Library so that it is available when you create projects. Basically, if you can hear it, you can add it to iTunes and so can access it from within the other applications. An example of this is provided in the section "Downloading and Using Movie and TV Sound Clips from the Web" in Chapter 17.

> **NOTE**
>
> If a sound effect isn't one you want to use frequently, you can import it into iMovie to use it in a soundtrack without adding it to your iTunes Library.

Because the iLife applications are integrated with one another, as you have seen in earlier chapters in this book, you can access your iTunes Library from within the application you use to create a project, such as iMovie or iDVD.

Make the process of finding all the music and sounds for a soundtrack even easier by creating a playlist in iTunes and adding the music and sounds you will use in a soundtrack to that playlist (see Figure 18.1). Then, when you need a sound or song, you can select that playlist to locate the sound you need quickly.

Figure 18.1 *This playlist called "DVD Project Sound" contains music and sound loops I have planned for a DVD I want to create.*

Using iMovie to Create the Soundtrack

After you have created a plan for your soundtrack, it's time to use iMovie to build the soundtrack from the elements that you have selected.

Creating the iMovie Soundtrack Project

First, create the iMovie project for your soundtrack.

Create an iMovie Soundtrack Project

1. Launch iMovie.
2. Choose File, New Project.
3. Name the project, choose a location in which to save it, and click Create.

If you are creating a soundtrack for something other than a QuickTime movie, you can create it without any video.

If you are creating a soundtrack for a QuickTime movie in one form or another, import the movie into iMovie and add it to the movie by placing it on the Clip

Creating Cool Soundtracks for iLife Projects   Chapter 18 | **505**

Viewer or Timeline Viewer. You can use the QuickTime movie to time the soundtrack you are creating, even if you don't end up using the video track that you import (see the following sidebar for an example of when you might want to do this).

Going Pro with Slideshows

When you create slideshows in iDVD or iMovie, you might notice that the resolution of the images appear to be less than they are in iPhoto. In fact, the images might appear to be quite fuzzy in the other applications. They look this way because these applications reduce the resolution of the images to be that used for TV displays, which is 640x480. This resolution is actually quite low when compared to the images that most digital cameras create, which are typically 2 or 3 mega-pixels. This is fine if you are viewing the slideshow on a TV because the lower resolution is the most those devices can handle anyway. However, if you want to view a slideshow in high resolution on a computer, you can do so. Here's how:

Note: You must upgrade to QuickTime Pro to be able to remove or add soundtracks from QuickTime movies in QuickTime Player. See my book *Special Edition Using Mac OS X v10.2* for detailed information about QuickTime Pro.

1. In iPhoto, create a photo album containing the images you want to be included in the slideshow.

2. Export that photo album as a QuickTime movie. When you do so, choose the resolution at which the images were captured (use the iPhoto information area to determine this).

3. Import the movie you created into iMovie.

4. Use the techniques you are learning in this chapter to create a soundtrack for the slideshow.

5. Export the soundtrack from iMovie.

6. Import the soundtrack into the slideshow QuickTime movie using QuickTime Player.

7. Save the slideshow. You can view the slideshow using QuickTime Player on a computer, and the images will be in the higher resolution.

> **TIP**
>
> You could add the QuickTime version of the slideshow to the DVD-ROM portion of a DVD to make it available from a DVD. (If you add the high resolution version to an iDVD project, it will be converted to the lower resolution.)

Creating the Music Track

Use iMovie tools to create the music track for the sound track. You learned the details of how to do this in Chapter 11, but here is a summary just to refresh your memory.

Build the Music Track for a Soundtrack

1. Open the Timeline Viewer.
2. Click the Audio button to open the Audio palette.
3. Choose the source of the music on the pop-up menu. If you created a playlist containing the music you will use in the soundtrack, choose that playlist.
4. Add the music to the Audio 2 track in the order in which you want the music to play (see Figure 18.2).
5. Use the crop and fade tools to make the music match the duration of the project for which you are creating the soundtrack.

Creating Cool Soundtracks for iLife Projects

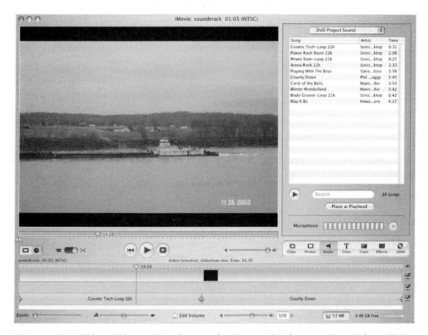

Figure 18.2 *Here, I have placed a couple of songs in the soundtrack for a high resolution slideshow project.*

Adding Sound Effects

Now add the sound effects to the soundtrack. There are three ways to do this, which are the following:

- **Add sound effects from your iTunes Library**. If the sound effects you want to use are stored in your iTunes Library, you can add those effects just like you add music that is stored there.

- **Use iMovie's built-in sound effects**. In Chapter 11, you learned how to use iMovie's sound effects to add interesting audio elements to a soundtrack.

- **Import sound effects**. You can import just about any sound file, such as .wav, .mp3, or .aiff, into iMovie to use that sound in a soundtrack. The steps to do so are explained in the section called "Adding Your Own Sound Effects" in Chapter 11.

Adding Recorded Sounds

Use iMovie's recording tools to record narration or other sound effects if those are called for in your soundtrack's script. (See Chapter 11 to learn how to record sound in iMovie.)

Mixing the Soundtrack

After you have placed all the sounds in the soundtrack, it is time to mix the soundtrack. Using the sound editing skills that you learned in Chapter 11, do the following tasks:

- ◆ Crop sounds that are too long.
- ◆ Move sounds on the Timeline Viewer to change the time at which they play.
- ◆ Change the relative volume level of the various sound clips at appropriate points in the project.
- ◆ Fade sounds in or out.

If you have imported a video track to use to time the sound effects, you can use that track to ensure that sounds play at the right time and that the soundtrack is the right total length for your project.

If you aren't using a video track as a timing tool, you will have to keep a close eye on the timecode information for your movie. You can select a sound clip and view its information at the top of the Timeline Viewer to see when that sound starts and stops. You can also use the movie's timecode information to monitor the total length of your soundtrack.

Continue mixing your soundtrack until it matches the plan you have for your project.

Exporting the Soundtrack as an AIFF File

After you have developed a soundtrack in iMovie, you need to prepare it for the project in which you will be using it. You do this by exporting the movie as an AIFF file.

Export a Soundtrack as an AIFF File

1. Choose File, Export (or press Shift+⌘+E).
2. In the Export Movie dialog box, choose To QuickTime.
3. On the Formats pop-up menu, choose Expert Settings.
4. Click Export. You will see the Save exported file as dialog box.
5. On the Export pop-up menu, choose Sound to AIFF (see Figure 18.3).

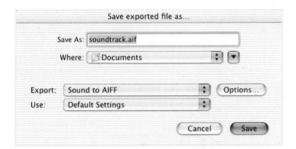

Figure 18.3 *When you choose the Sound to AIFF option, only the audio portion of a movie is exported.*

6. If you want to configure the settings that are used to export the file, open the Use pop-up menu and choose the settings you want to use or click the Options button to configure the file you export.
7. Name the file and choose the location in which you want to save it.
8. Click the Save button. The movie will be exported and saved in the location you selected.

Now you have an AIFF version of your soundtrack (see Figure 18.4). If the project for which you have created the soundtrack can work with AIFF files (which means any iMovie, iDVD, iTunes, or iPhoto project), you are done and are ready to add the soundtrack to that project.

> **TIP**
>
> If the project you are creating can't import an AIFF file, you can always import the AIFF file into iTunes and use that application to convert it into another format, such as WAV or MP3.

Figure 18.4 *The soundtrack.aif file is ready to be used in any iLife project.*

> ### Back to the Pro Slideshow Example
>
> If you are creating a high resolution version of a slideshow, you can add the AIFF soundtrack you just created to the QuickTime movie version of the slideshow that you exported from iPhoto. This creates a slideshow with a soundtrack worthy of the high resolutions images it contains.

Creating Your Own Soundtrack CDs

Some great audio CDs have been produced from the soundtracks of equally great movies. In fact, some movie soundtracks are masterworks of music in their own right. Just as the iLife tools enable you to create your own movie masterpieces, you can also put your own movie soundtracks on an audio CD.

> **NOTE**
>
> Want some examples of great music that also happens to be an important part of a great movie? Here are some of my personal favorites: *Star Wars*, *Gladiator*, *Braveheart*, *Glory*, and *The Lord of the Rings: The Fellowship of the Ring*.

Creating your own soundtrack audio CD requires the following general steps:

1. Use iMovie to create the soundtrack. You learned how to do this earlier in this chapter.
2. Export the soundtrack as an AIFF file. If you have read to this point in this chapter, you know how to do this too.
3. Import the soundtrack into iTunes and burn the audio CD. See Chapter 2 for the steps to add an AIFF file to your iTunes Library and Chapter 3 for the steps to put music on a CD.

> **TIP**
>
> Know a child who has a music recital? Use a camcorder to record the recital. Then create an iMovie project to capture the recital in all its glory. Export the music as an AIFF and burn it on a CD. Whammo, the child's first music CD!

Creating Soundtracks Like a Pro

You can build very complex and complete soundtracks using the iLife applications, particularly iMovie. However, matching a soundtrack to a project's content and length can require a substantial amount of time and effort on your part. That is where Sonic Desktop's SmartSound Sonicfire Pro comes in.

This amazing application helps you create very high quality soundtracks for any QuickTime project. Because it is not part of the digital lifestyle applications and costs additional money, I didn't include a chapter on it in this book. However, this is one of the few third-party applications that warrant some coverage in this book, even though it doesn't come from Apple.

SmartSound Sonicfire Pro actually automates the process of creating a soundtrack for a QuickTime movie project. The application's many cool features include the following:

- The Maestro feature helps you select and orchestrate music for a soundtrack.
- The music collection CDs available for the application include many types of royalty-free music (meaning that you can use the projects in which the music is included in any way you'd like).

- The application automatically adjusts music tracks to fit the segments of the QuickTime movie that you select. Instead of just chopping the music off or even fading it out, Sonicfire Pro actually changes the music to fit the length of the segment as if the music were designed for that segment (which it actually has been).

- The application's editing tools enable you to fine-tune various aspects of the music track, such as the volume levels of specific tracks as they play. For example, you can lower the volume level of a music track when narration is happening, no matter where in the track that occurs.

- Sonicfire enables you to save the soundtrack with the movie, or you can export it separately, for example, to import it into iMovie or QuickTime Player Pro.

It is stunning how fast you can create professional sounding soundtracks. Not many applications impress me the way this one has. It is truly amazing.

Unfortunately, I don't have room in this book to give this application the coverage it deserves. However, to demonstrate how easy it is to use, the following steps show you the basics of creating a soundtrack in SmartSound Sonicfire Pro.

Create a Professional Sounding Soundtrack in Sonicfire Pro

1. Create the project for which you want to create a soundtrack and save that project as a QuickTime movie or as a DV file.
2. Launch Sonicfire Pro.
3. Choose File, Choose Video.
4. In the resulting dialog box, move to the project for which you want to create a soundtrack, select it, and click Open. The movie will open in the application's movie window.
5. Choose Timeline, Maestro. The Maestro tool will appear (see Figure 18.5).
6. Choose the style of music you want by checking one of the radio buttons and then clicking Next. You will see the options available for that music style along with a description of the music and where you might want to use it.
7. Choose the option you want by checking its radio button and clicking Next. You will see the sources you have for that music style and option.

Creating Cool Soundtracks for iLife Projects — Chapter 18 — 513

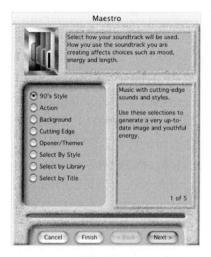

Figure 18.5 *The Maestro tool guides you through the creation of a soundtrack.*

8. Choose the source by clicking its radio button and then clicking Next.
9. Choose the length for the soundtrack and then click Next. If the music isn't already installed on your hard drive, you will be prompted to insert one of the SmartSound music collection CDs. The music will be imported, and you will see a dialog box that presents several variations of music from which you can choose (see Figure 18.6).

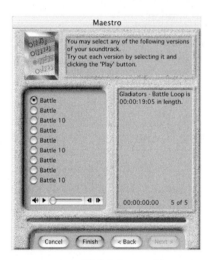

Figure 18.6 *This Maestro has composed several musical options for you to choose from.*

10. Select the variation you want to preview and click the Play button. The music will play along with the movie in the application's movie window, so you can see how well the music matches the project.
11. Continue previewing options until you find the one that is best.
12. Click Finish. The application will create the soundtrack for you and match it to the movie's length. You can then either save the music with the movie or export the soundtrack as a QuickTime movie.

This brief example just scratches the surface of what Sonicfire can do. For example, you can easily create segments of a soundtrack and include different music in each segment. As with an entire movie, the application automatically fits the music to the segment.

> **NOTE**
>
> You can also import your own music to use in Sonicfire, although the results you get aren't quite as spectacular as they are when you use music from the SmartSound collection.
>
> The only downside to the application is that it costs about $299 for the application and a couple of music CDs. Additional CDs are about $49 or $99, depending on the quality that you select. However, if you want to create amazing soundtracks that sound as if they came from a professional studio, the results you get will be more than worth the investment you have to make to get the application.
>
> For more information about this great tool, visit www.smartsound.com/sonicfire/index.html. In addition to lots of detailed information about the application, you can download a demo or order a copy.

Hasta la Vista, Baby

If you've hung with me throughout this book, you are now ready to be the undisputed master of your digital domain. Equipped with a Mac, the iLife suite, and your personal creativity, you can create as well as consume digital media. From mastering your music to capturing images to creating movies to making your own DVDs, you have seen how the iLife is the creative life. There are no limits to your digital world! So explore, create, achieve—it's all out there for you. Go forth and do!

Index

A

AAC encoding, 28
AAC (Advanced Audio Coding) file format, 6–7
    Apple Music Store, 57
    iPod, 96
action buttons (iTunes), 11
Add Folder (Shift+⌘+N) keyboard shortcut, 373, 375
Add Slideshow (⌘+L) keyboard shortcut, 377
Add To Library dialog box, 54
Add To Library (⌘+O) keyboard shortcut, 54
Adjust Colors effect, 222
Adobe Acrobat, 186
Advanced, Apply Theme to Project command, 421
Advanced, Extract Audio command, 308
Advanced, Lock Audio Clip at Playhead command, 325
Advanced, Open Stream command, 50
Advanced, Paste Over at Playhead command, 298
Advanced, Restore Clip command, 292
Advanced, Reverse Clip Direction command, 295
Advanced, Show TV Safe Area command, 412
Advanced, Unlock Audio Clip command, 326
.aif file extension, 7
AIFF (Audio Interchange File Format), 7, 341, 508–509
AIFF encoding, 28
Albums folder, 125
Apple, System Preferences command, 472
Apple Music Store, 5, 32–34
    1-Click method, 58, 61
    AAC format, 57
    accessing, 15
    account creation, 59–60
    Add button, 62
    adding music to iTunes Library, 56–62
    Apple ID and password, 59, 60
    authorizing and deauthorizing Macintoshes, 57
    burning CDs limits, 57
    Buy Now button, 61
    configuring preferences, 58
    Contents pane, 60–61
    downloading music limitations, 57, 62
    music previews, 34
    playing downloaded music, 34
    Purchased Music playlist, 62
    purchasing music, 33–34
    searching for and previewing music, 60–61
    Shopping Cart method, 33–34, 58, 62
    Sign In account dialog box, 59
    signing in, 59–60
Apple online store account creation, 178, 187
Apple Pro Keyboard, 14
Apple QuickTime Movie Trailer Web site, 492
Apple SuperDrive, 346
Apple System Profiler, 490
Apple Web site, 98, 121
applications, setting for emailing images, 175
Audio CD mode, 9
audio CDs, 15
    adding
        to Library, 52–53
        music to movies from, 317–318
    amount of silence between songs, 29–30
    automatically
        importing songs from, 52
        playing, 46
    burning, 29–30, 84–90
    controlling actions of, 22
    double-clicking tracks, 47
    encoding songs from, 52
    identifying, 23, 52
    importing songs automatically from, 46
    information about, 8
    jumping to tracks, 47
    listening to, 44–48
    looking up information about, 45
    maximum storage capacity, 87
    relative volume levels, 46
    reordering track playing, 47
    selecting to burn, 29–30
    skipping tracks, 47
audio clips, 295
    adjusting relative volume levels, 323
    extracting, 308–309
audio devices, recording sound from, 318

Index

audio files
    adding from Finder to iDVD slideshow, 389
    as background sound, 431–433
    slideshows, 354
    as sound effects, 313–314
audio formats, 5–7
Audio palette (iMovie), 216–217, 506
    Edit Volume check box, 323
    iMovie Sound Effects option, 310
    iTunes Library option, 315
    playlists, 315
    Record button, 319
    recording tool, 318–319
    Skywalker Sound Effects, 310
    Source pop-up menu, 310, 315, 317
    Standard Sound Effects, 310
audio tracks and sound effects, 312
audiometer, 46
avi format, 341

B

background images
    menus, 423–427
    removing, 427
background movies for menus, 427–430
background sound for menus, 430–433
basic video track, 243
black-and-white images, 163
Book mode, 111–113
Brightness & Contrast effect, 291–292
Browse (⌘+B) keyboard shortcut, 63
Browse pane (iTunes), 15, 63, 65, 95
Brushed Metal Two theme, 371–372
built-in sound effects, 310–313
built-in themes
    basing custom themes on, 422–427
    designing menus, 415–417
Burn Disc dialog box, 195–196
Burn mode, 354
burning
    audio CDs, 29–30
    DVDs, 349, 355
    iDVD projects on DVD, 469–477
    maximizing process, 471–473
    processes, 470–471
    shutting down extraneous applications, 471–472
    time required for, 476
burning CDs, 84–90
    choosing burn format, 87

data transfer rate, 90
images to, 109, 195–196
playlists for, 87–88
selecting type of CDs, 29–30
speed, 29
button previews, 443
    folder buttons, 444
    images or movies as, 447–449
    movie buttons, 446–447
    slideshow buttons, 444–445
buttons
    applying themes, 439
    button previews, 443–449
    customizing, 439–442
    designing, 437–449
    formatting titles, 441–442
    highlighting, 459
    location, 461
    naming, 438
    placing, 440
    previewing, 461–462
    shapes, 439–440, 461
    titles, 461

C

Camera mode, 207–208, 212–213
captions, 217, 277–278
capturing content
    from DVDs, 488–491
    from videotape, 484–488
Catalog theme, 180
CD Audio file format, 5
CD burner, 85–86
.cdda file extension, 5
CD-R discs, 88
CD-RW discs, 88
CDs
    putting images on, 195–196
    ripping, 50
    selecting type of, 29–30
Centered Multiple style, 220
Centered Title style, 275
Chapter Marker Import prompt, 397
check mark keyword, 131
Classic, large images theme, 180
Clip Info window, 254, 297
Clip Viewer (iMovie), 207, 225, 260
    Clip Speed slider, 296

Photos button, 263
rendering title clip, 276–277
clips
    adding captions, 277–278
    arranging in movies, 268
    audio, 295
    boundaries of, 262
    brightness and contrast, 291–292
    changing playing direction, 295–296
    changing speed, 293–295
    copying frames, 258
    cropping, 259
    deleting, 253, 262
    editing, 250–259
    End Crop Marker, 256–257
    extracting native sound, 308–309
    finding, 214
    holding area for, 214
    iMovie-compatible DV camcorder, 245–247
    importing, 212–213
    making look old, 289–290
    naming, 246
    opening credits over, 274
    pasting over, 298
    placing between clips, 261
    playing, 262
    previewing, 251–252
    removing frames from, 256–258
    renaming, 254
    rendering, 289–290
    restoring without special effects, 292
    selecting, 251
    shooting for movies, 241–242
    splitting, 255
    stocking Shelf with, 244–250
    transitions, 220–221
    undoing actions to, 257
    unselecting, 261
    viewing and changing information, 253–254
Clips pane (iMovie), 214
    renaming clips, 254
    still image clip, 297
    stocking with images and clips, 244–250
    viewing imported images, 249
color
    captions, 278
    opening credits, 274
    titles, 435–436
commands
    iDVD, 361–362
    iMovie, 233–237
    iPhoto, 116–117
    iTunes, 13, 37–41
comments, finding images by, 140
CompactFlash media, 91
Complete Idiot's Guide to iMovie 2, The, 240
Content window, 354
Contents pane (iDVD), 347–348, 352
Contents pane (iPhoto), 103–104, 183
    arranging images on-screen, 135
    configuring in Organize mode, 134–135
    film roll information, 135
    grouping images on-screen, 135
    image titles, 135
    keywords, 135
    Page Design pop-up menu, 181
    Page Numbers check box, 180
    resizing images on-screen, 105
    Retouch button, 162
    Show Guides check box, 180
    Theme pop-up menu, 180
    Thumbnail Size slider, 135, 156
    viewing
        images for photo book, 180
        sources differently, 136
    zooming images, 156–157
Contents pane (iTunes), 16–18
    browsing iPod, 95
    Equalizer column, 20
    font size, 22
    listing audio CD contents, 45
    memory status of MP3 player, 92
    reordering columns, 17, 47
    resizing columns, 17
    selecting columns displayed, 18
    sorting, 16–17
    viewing
        Browse pane selections, 64
        playlist contents, 74
        source contents, 14
copying frames, 258
copyrights, 482
Create New Project dialog box, 243
Create Still Frame (Shift+⌘+S) keyboard shortcut, 296
credits, 218
Crop (⌘+K) keyboard shortcut, 259
cropping
    clips, 259
    images, 110, 154–155, 158–159

sound, 321–322
sound effects, 312
Cross Dissolve transition, 220
custom themes, 449
    applying to menus, 451–452
    Drop Zones, 422
    menus, 421–427
    naming, 450
    removing saved as Favorite, 452–453
    saving, 450–451
Customize (Shift+⌘+B) keyboard shortcut, 378
Customize Panel, 349–350
Customize sheet (iPhoto), 152
customizing buttons, 439–442
Cut (⌘+X) keyboard shortcut, 257

D

data CDs, burning, 30
default keywords, 129–130
Design mode, 351–353
desktop
    adding images, 192–193
    applying images to, 109
digital cameras
    automatically starting iPhoto, 121
    communicating information to iPhoto, 138
    compatibility with iPhoto, 121
    downloading images to iPhoto, 121–122
    erasing images after importing, 107–108
    importing images from, 106–107, 120–122
digital effects and music, 24
digital video (DV) cameras
    16x9 format, 487
    connecting to VCR, 485–486
    passthrough feature, 487
    recording
        iMovie project on, 331–332
        to VHS tape, 333
        videotape content to, 486
digitizers, 483–484
Dir.data file, 125
Disk Gauge (iMovie), 229–230, 247
disk space, monitoring available, 229–230
Dock, controlling iTunes from, 48
downloading
    buffer size, 35
    images from digital camera to iPhoto, 121–122
Drop Zones
    adding

content, 417–421
    movies, 417–419
    slideshows, 419–421
custom themes, 422
filling, 427
formatting menu titles, 437
images, 421
importing
    movies, 418
    slideshows, 420
menus, 461
removing movies, slideshows, or images, 419
themes, 416
Duplicate (⌘+D) keyboard shortcut, 150
duplicating images, 150
DVD Controller, 384
DVD players, 470
DVD ripping applications, 489
DVD-R discs, 346, 470–471
DVD-R (DVD Recordable) drives, 346
DVDs
    adding
        content, 351–353
        iMovie movies to, 393–401
        movies with iMedia Browser, 396–398
        other files to DVD-ROM portion, 405–406
        QuickTime movies, 401–403
    burning, 30, 349, 355
    burning iDVD projects, 469–477
    button previews, 443–449
    buttons for menus, 367
    capturing content from, 488–491
    controls for playing, 354
    copyrights, 368–369
    custom themes, 421–427
    custom themes to menus on, 452
    description of buttons, 367
    designing, 408–412
        buttons, 437–449
        menus, 413–437
    exporting movies to, 333–336
    file location, 367
    fixing problems, 464
    high-resolution iDVD slideshow images on, 391–392
    images, 366
    importing movies, 399
    length of content, 356
    licenses for copyrighted material, 369
    main menu, 364
    menus, 349
        creation, 371–376

    limitations, 365
    names, 367
motion effects, 349, 410–411
movies, 366
MPEG-2 format, 355
music, 366, 367
naming menus, 372
nested menu structure, 364–365
organizing content by menu, 366–368
outlining content, 366–368
planning, 364–376
previewing, 349, 354, 456–465
putting images on, 194–195
putting movies on, 224–225
QuickTime movies, 366
recording content from, 489
removing movies, 403
ripping content from, 489–490
royalty-free content, 369
slideshows, 349, 376–392
sound, 367
space limitations, 365
standard theme for all menus, 421
still images, 490–491
TV Safe Area, 411–412, 438, 457
type of content, 366

E

Edit, Clear command, 258
Edit, Create Still Frame command, 296
Edit, Crop command, 259, 321
Edit, Cut command, 257
Edit, Delete command, 384, 403
Edit, Keywords command, 130, 132, 133, 139, 140
Edit, Rotate, Clockwise command, 149
Edit, Rotate Counter Clockwise command, 149
Edit, Select All command, 74, 142
Edit, Select None command, 74, 261
Edit, Split Video Clip command, 255
Edit, Undo command, 257
Edit, Undo Convert to B & W command, 163
Edit, Undo Crop Photo command, 159
Edit, Undo Enhance Photo command, 160
Edit, Undo Reduce Red-Eye command, 161
Edit, Undo Retouch command, 163
Edit, View Options command, 18
Edit List command, 20
Edit mode, 109–111, 252
    importing images, 249

    Monitor (iMovie), 209–212
Edit window, 152–154, 156–158
editing
    clips, 250–259
    in Edit window, 152–154
    images, 109–111, 150–157
    within iPhoto window, 150
    movies, 209–212
    with other applications, 166
    selecting parts of images, 154–156
    sound, 320–326
    zooming images, 156–157
Effects palette (iMovie), 222–223, 289, 291–292
emailing
    images, 109, 175–176
    setting application for, 175
emptying iMovie Trash, 230
encoders, selecting, 25
encoding, 25–26
    AAC encoding, 28
    AIFF and WAV encoding, 28
    canceling process, 53
    listening to music while, 53
    movies, 403–404
    music, 50
    songs from audio CDs, 52
    varying quality level, 27
End Crop Marker, 256–257
Equalizer, 19–20
Equalizer (⌘+2) keyboard shortcut, 19
Equalizer window, 19
Export Movie dialog box, 509
Export Movie (Shift+⌘+E) keyboard shortcut, 331, 338, 340, 509
Export Photos dialog box, 197–201
Export Photos (Shift+⌘+E) keyboard shortcut, 197, 200
Export sheet (iPhoto), 199, 201
exporting
    frames from movie as image file, 298
    images from slideshows, 174–175
    iPhoto images, 197–202
    photos, 197–202
    soundtracks as AIFF file, 508–509
exporting movies
    chapter markers, 334
    to DVD, 333–336
    Expert Settings format, 339–342
    to QuickTime, 336–342
    standard format, 337–339
    to videotape, 330–333

external FireWire or USB devices, 471
Extract Audio (⌘+J) keyboard shortcut, 308
extracting native sound, 308–309

F

Fade Out transition, 281–283
Fade to transition, 220
fading
   native sound, 304–307
   sound, 322
Favorites and custom themes, 451–453
File, Add to Library command, 54
File, Duplicate command, 150
File, Empty Trash command, 230
File, Export command, 197, 200, 338, 340, 509
File, Export Movie command, 331
File, Get Info command, 20, 68, 69
File, Import, Audio command, 389, 433
File, Import, Background Video command, 429
File, Import, Image command, 381, 426
File, Import, Video command, 399, 402
File, Import command, 123, 247, 248, 313, 494
File, New Album command, 142
File, New Playlist command, 73
File, New Playlist From Selection command, 74
File, New Project command, 369, 504
File, New Smart Playlist command, 77
File, Open Recent command, 242
File, Print command, 185
File, Remove from Album command, 144
File, Revert to Original command, 166
File, Save As command, 496
File, Save Frame As command, 298, 489
File, Show Current Song command, 47
File, Show Info command, 254
File, Show Photo Info command, 137
File, Show Song File command, 53
Film Roll (Shift+⌘+F) keyboard shortcut, 135
film rolls, 135–137
Finder
   adding
      audio files to iDVD slideshow, 389
      image or movie to button, 449
   audio files as background sound, 431–433
   images and iDVD slideshows, 380–382
   images for DVD menu background, 425–427
   importing images for iDVD slideshows, 381–382
   movies as menu background, 428

finding
   images with film rolls, 137
   missing files, 468–469
   MP3 files, 8
   Photo Library images, 138–141
FireWire DV cameras, 483–484
folder buttons, 437, 444
Folder slider, 444
folders (iDVD), 365
fonts, 22
frames
   copying, 258
   exporting from movie as image file, 298
   removing from clips, 256–258
freeze frame, 296–297
From Black transition, 220
Full Page style, 169

G

genres, 70
Get Info command, 68, 69
Get Info (⌘+I) keyboard shortcut, 20, 68, 69
graphic equalizer, 19–20
Greeting Card style, 169–170
grouping images, 135

H

hardware (iDVD), 346
HDTV (High-Definition Television), 360
HomePage Web site, 188–190

I

iDVD, 346
   adding content to
      Drop Zones, 417–421
      DVDs, 351–353
   background
      images for menus, 422–427
      movies for menus, 427–430
      sound for menus, 430–433
   Burn mode, 354
   burning DVDs, 474–476
   button previews, 443–449
   chapter selection menu, 224
   commands, 361–362
   configuring slideshow, 195

Index **521**

Content window, 354
Contents pane, 352
controls, 348–349
custom themes, 421–427, 449–453
Design mode, 351–353
designing
   buttons, 437–449
   DVDs, 408–412
   menus, 413–437
encoding movies, 403–404
fixing DVD problems, 464
folders, 365
formatting menu titles, 434–437
hardware, 346
HDTV (High-Definition Television), 360
iLife projects, 361
importing images, 426
keyboard shortcuts, 361–362
logging problems, 456–457
menu controls, 354
modes, 351–355
Motion button, 370
MPEG-2 format, 403–404
playback controls, 354
preferences, 356–360
Preview mode, 354, 457–459
previewing DVDs, 456–465
remote control, 354
removing movies from DVDs, 403
Save button, 370
scaling images to fit background, 425
sending images to, 109
Slideshow mode, 353–354
standard them for all menus, 421
themes, 408–409
iDVD, Preferences command, 394
iDVD Controller, 457–458
iDVD Drawer, 349–350
   All option, 415
   Audio button, 350, 387, 431
   Button Shape pop-up menu, 439
   Color pop-up menu, 435, 442
   Customize button, 378
   DVD-ROM Contents option, 466
   Encoder Status option, 466
   Favorites option, 416
   Favorites pop-up menu, 451
   Font pop-up menu, 435, 442
   Free Position option, 440
   Motion Duration slider, 433
   Movies button, 350, 396, 402, 417
   Movies folder, 396
   New Themes option, 416
   No Text option, 442
   No Title option, 414
   Old Themes option, 416
   Photos button, 350, 378, 420, 422, 447
   Position pop-up menu, 414, 434, 442
   Replace existing check box, 451
   Save as Favorite button, 450
   Settings button, 350, 414, 425, 428, 431, 433, 434, 439–431, 450
   Shared for all users check box, 450
   Size slider, 436–437, 442
   Snap to Grid radio button, 440
   Status button, 350, 392, 404–405, 465
   Themes button, 350, 371, 415, 451
iDVD palette (iMovie), 224–225
   Add Chapter button, 334
   Create iDVD Project button, 400
iDVD Preferences dialog box, 356–360, 394–395
iDVD projects
   adding
      movies to, 336
      other files to DVD-ROM portion, 405–406
   applying themes to menus, 371–372
   assessing, 465–467
   burning on DVD, 469–477
   creation from iMovie, 225
   creation of, 194, 355–356, 369–370
   deleting files, 466, 477
   finding missing files, 468–469
   length, 465
   listing files in, 467
   location to save, 370
   menu creation, 371–376
   motion effects and menus, 370
   MPEG-2 format, 355
   naming, 370
   naming menu buttons, 373
   previewing, 457–459
   removing buttons from menus, 375
   saving, 372
   status, 465–469
   submenus, 372–375
   titles, 351
iDVD slideshows, 353–354, 376
   adding
      button to menu, 377
      images, 378–382
      music to well, 389

changing appearance, 382
determining order of images, 382–383
duration, 385–386
Finder images, 380–382
high-resolution images on DVDs, 391–392
image resolution, 376
importing Finder images, 381–382
iTunes music, 387–3389
naming buttons, 390
previewing, 384–385
removing
    images, 384
    soundtracks, 389
setting playback, 385–386
soundtracks, 387–389
titles, 382
iDVD window, 346–350
    background images for menus, 352
    Burn button, 474
    button titles, 352
    buttons, 352
    content area, 457
    Contents pane, 347
    controls, 348–349
    cursor controls, 354
    Drop Zone, 352
    menu titles, 352
    menus, 352–353
    Motion button, 474
    project title, 351
    TV Safe Area, 411–412
iLife projects
    audio clips from Web, 483
    audio formats, 5–7
    captured content usage, 497
    capturing content from
        DVDs, 488–491
        videotape, 484–488
    iDVD, 361
    iMovie and, 233
    iPhoto, 115–116
    iTunes, 36–37
    movies or TV shows on videotape or DVD, 483
    QuickTime movie trailers, 491–495
    QuickTime movies from Web, 483
    sound clips from Web, 495–497
    soundtrack CDs, 510–514
    soundtracks, 500–514
    sources of content, 483
    television, 483

images
    See also photos
    640x480 format, 250
    accessing from iPhoto Library, 215–216
    adding to
        desktop, 192–19
        movies, 263–267
        photo albums, 142
    applying to desktop, 109
    associating keywords with, 129–131
    background for menus, 422–427
    black-and-white, 163
    brightness and contrast, 110, 164
    burning to CD, 109
    as button previews, 447–449
    cleaning up areas, 110
    comments, 126, 127–129
    constraining, 110, 154–156, 158
    converting to black-and-white, 110
    cropping, 110, 154–155, 158–159
    dates, 126, 128
    default iPhoto title, 128
    detailed information for, 137–138
    determining order in iDVD slideshows, 382–383
    downloading from digital camera to iPhoto, 121–122
    Drop Zones, 421
    duplicating, 150
    duration, 265–266
    DVDs, 366
    editing, 109–111, 150–157
    emailing, 109, 175–176
    enhancing, 110, 159–160
    exporting from iPhoto, 197–202
    film roll, 126
    from Finder, 380–382, 425–427
    finding
        with film rolls, 137
        in Photo Library, 138–141
    grouping, 135
    iDVD slideshows, 378–382
    importing, 248–250, 426
        from other sources, 123–124
        into Photo Library, 120–124
    Ken Burns effect, 265
    keywords, 126–127
    labeling, 122, 124, 126–134
    Landscape orientation, 148
    moving between, 111
    ordering prints, 109, 177–179
    organizing, 108–109, 144–145

Index

photo albums, 103–104
Portrait orientation, 148
printing, 109, 168–171
publishing to .Mac tools Web site, 109
putting on CD, 195–196
putting on DVD, 194–195
reconfiguring for movies, 268
red-eye, 110, 160–161
removing
   from iDVD slideshows, 384
   keyword, 133–134
   from Photo Library, 125
repeating in photo albums, 144
resizing, 113, 135
retouching, 162–163
reverting to original, 111, 165–166
rotating, 111, 148–149
as screen saver, 192–193
selecting, 111, 128, 132, 154–156
sending to iDVD, 109
slideshows, 171–175, 354
stocking Shelf with, 244–250
storing, 125–126
technical information, 127, 137
titles, 126, 127–129
zooming, 156–157, 265–266
iMedia Browser
  adding
    iMovie projects, 394–395
    movies to DVD, 396–398
    QuickTime movies to DVDs, 402
  applying movie or image to button, 447, 449
  listing movies in, 417–418
iMovie, 206
  accessing images in iPhoto Library, 215–216
  adding
    movies to DVDs, 393–401
    QuickTime movies to DVD, 401–403
  Audio palette, 216–217
  building basic video track, 259–268
  built-in sound effects, 310–313
  Camera mode, 207–208
  chapter selection menu, 224
  Clip Viewer, 225
  Clips pane, 214
  commands, 233–237
  deleting clips, 253
  Disk Gauge, 229–230
  Edit mode, 207–208, 252
  editing clips, 250–259
  Effects palette, 222–223
  emptying Trash, 253
  enhancing movies, 293–298
  exporting movies to videotape, 330–333
  iDVD button, 400
  iDVD palette, 224–225
  iLife projects, 233
  Import button, 246
  Import (Camera) mode, 245
  importing videotape content into, 487
  keyboard shortcuts, 233–237
  modes, 207–208
  moving on-screen, 211–212
  naming clips, 246
  New Project button, 242
  Open Project button, 242
  opening credits, 273–277
  organizing movies, 243
  Photos palette, 215–216
  Playhead, 211
  preferences, 230–233
  Quit button, 242
  Shelf, 214
  soundtrack creation, 504–508
  special effects, 286–293
  splitting clips, 255
  stocking Shelf with clips and images, 244–250
  Timeline Viewer, 2260229
  titles, 270–280
  Titles palette, 217–220
  Tools palette, 214
  transitions, 280–286
  Transitions palette, 220–221
  Trash, 230
  undoing actions, 230
  viewing and changing clip information, 253–254
iMovie: Export dialog box, 331–332, 338, 340
iMovie, Preferences command, 230
iMovie file, 243
iMovie projects
  basic video track, 244
  creation of, 242–243
  music track, 506
  opening, 242
  QuickTime movie trailer, 493–494
  recording on DV cameras, 331–332
  soundtracks, 504–508
  storing, 243
iMovie window, 207

Index

iMovie-compatible DV camcorder, 245–247
Import Files progress window, 248
Import (⌘+I) keyboard shortcut, 494
Import (Shift+⌘+I) keyboard shortcut, 123
Import mode, 106–107
Import (Camera) mode, 245
Import Movie (Shift+⌘+I) keyboard shortcut, 247
Import Photos dialog box, 123
Import sheet, 247, 248, 313, 399
importing
   clips, 212–213
   digital camera images, 120–122
   images, 426
      from Finder in iDVD slideshow, 381–382
      from other sources, 123–124
      into Photo Library, 120–124
   iMovie-compatible DV camcorder clips, 245–247
   music and sound into file formats, 24–28
   photos, 106–107
   QuickTime movies, 247–248, 402–403
   slideshows to Drop Zones, 420
   sound, 433
   still images, 248–250
   videotape content into iMovie, 487
importing movies
   Drop Zones, 418
   to DVD, 399
   as menu background, 429–430
Information window (iTunes), 11
   all information available in, 13
   Artwork tab, 68
   encoding progress bar, 53
   Info tab, 68
   information about songs, 46
   labeling downloaded music, 54
   modes and, 12
   Next Song button, 68
   Options tab, 68
   Prev Song button, 68
   Summary pane, 67
   Summary tab, 68
instant replay, 296
Internet
   connections and Apple Music Store, 33
   downloading audio to iTunes Library, 54–55
   downloading *versus* listening to MP3 files, 55–56
   identifying audio CDS, 23
   information about audio CDs, 8
   playing MP3 files on, 8

QuickTime movie trailers, 491–495
   sound clips, 495–497
Internet radio, 15, 49–50
iPhoto
   adding images to iDVD slideshow, 378–380
   albums, 103–104
   Book mode, 111–113
   Book mode button, 180
   building photo albums, 141–145
   Burn button, 195
   commands, 116–117
   Contents pane, 103, 104
   controls, 104–105
   detailed photo information, 137–138
   downloading images from digital camera, 121–122
   Edit button, 109, 156
   Edit mode, 109–111
   editing images, 150–157
   emailing images, 175–176
   Enhance button, 160
   exporting images, 197–202
   HomePage Web site, 188–190
   iLife projects, 115–116
   Import button, 106, 121
   Import mode, 106–107
   Information button, 104
   keyboard shortcuts, 116–117
   labeling images, 126–134
   mode buttons, 105
   modes, 106–113
   New Photo Album button, 104, 142
   Number of images text box, 105
   Order Prints button, 177
   ordering prints, 177–179
   Organize mode, 108–109, 121, 127
   photo books, 179–188
   Play Slideshow button, 104
   preferences, 113–115
   Preview button, 184
   Print button, 169
   printing images, 168–171
   putting images on CD or DVD, 194–196
   Rotate button, 104, 149
   rotating images, 148–149
   Sample Music, 172
   slideshows, 171–175
   Source pane, 103–104
   storing images, 125–126
   Thumbnail Size slider, 105
   Tool pane, 103

Index

tools, 106–113
user-defined keywords, 129–131
iPhoto, Preferences command, 113
iPhoto Library
    accessing images from iMovie, 215–216
    background images for menus, 423–425
iPhoto Library folder, 125
iPhoto palette (iMovie), 264–266
iPhoto Preferences dialog box, 113–115
    changing direction of rotation, 149
    Mail pop-up menu, 175
    Opens in other radio button, 166
iPhoto window, editing within, 150, 153–154
iPod, 5, 57, 93–98
iPod Preferences dialog box, 96–98
iTunes, 4
    action buttons, 11
    Audio CD mode, 9
    audiometer, 46
    automatic lookup, 23
    automatically launching, 45
    Browse button, 63
    Browse pane, 15
    Burn CD button, 88
    burning audio CDs, 84–90
    commands, 13, 37–41
    Contents pane, 16–18
    controlling from Dock, 48
    controls, 10–14
    Create playlist button, 11
    downloading wave files, 496–497
    Eject button, 12
    Equalizer button, 12, 19
    graphic equalizer, 19–20
    iLife projects, 36–37
    Import button, 52
    information about audio CDs, 8
    Information window, 11–13
    iPod Preferences button, 96
    keyboard shortcuts, 13, 37–41
    Library, 50–72
    Library mode, 9
    listening to
        audio CDs, 44–48
        Internet radio, 49–50
    Mode Change button, 12
    modes, 9–10
    moving music to MP3 player, 91–93
    music for iDVD slideshows, 387–3389
    New Playlist button, 73, 77
    playback controls, 11
    playing MP3 files on Internet, 8
    Playlists mode, 10
    Portable Music Player mode, 10
    preferences, 21–36
    preparing music and sound for soundtracks, 503
    Radio mode, 9
    Repeat button, 11
    resize handle, 12
    Search box, 11
    Search tool, 65–66
    selecting source, 14–15
    Setup Assistant, 8
    Shuffle button, 11
    Source pane, 14–15
    Visualizer button, 12
iTunes, Preferences command, 22
iTunes Music folder, 34–36
iTunes Preferences dialog box
    1-Click method, 58
    Advanced pane, 34–36, 54
    Audio CD format, 87
    Burning button, 85, 87
    Burning pane, 29–30
    Burning Preferences pane, 85–87
    Buy and download using 1-Click radio button, 33
    Buy radio buttons, 33–34
    Buy using a Shopping Cart radio button, 33
    On CD Insert pop-up menu, 22
    Connect to Internet when needed check box, 23
    Copy files to iTunes Music folder, 54
    Copy files to iTunes Music folder when adding to library check box, 36
    Create files names with track numbers check box, 27
    Crossfade playback slider, 23–24
    Data CD radio button, 87
    Disk Format radio buttons, 29–30
    Display pop-up menus, 22
    DVD radio button, 87
    Effects pane, 23–24
    Gap Between Songs pop-up menu, 29
    General pane, 22–23, 55
    Import Using pop-up menu, 25, 27
    Importing button, 26
    Importing pane, 24–28
    Internet section, 23
    iTunes Music folder location, 34–35

Keep iTunes Music Folder organized check box, 36
Load complete preview before playing check box, 34
Look for shared music check box, 30, 81
MC3 CD radio button, 87
MP3 Encoder option, 27
Play songs after downloading check box, 34
Play songs while importing check box, 27
Preferred Speed pop-up menu, 29
Require Password check box, 32, 81
selecting encoder, 25
Set button, 55
Setting pop-up menu, 27
Share entire library radio button, 81
Share my music check box, 32
Share my music radio button, 32, 81
Shared Name field, 81
Shared name field, 32
Sharing pane, 30–32, 81
Shopping Cart method, 58
Show Genre When Browsing check box, 22, 64
Show iTunes Music Store check box, 32
Shuffle by radio buttons, 36
Sound Check check box, 24, 30
Sound Enhancer slider, 24
Store pane, 32–34, 58
Streaming Buffer Size pop-up menu, 35
Use Sound Check check box, 87
iTunes Preferences (⌘+,) keyboard shortcut, 22
iTunes window, 8, 47–48

K

kbps (KiloBits Per Second), 25
Ken Burns effect, 263, 265
keyboard shortcuts
    iDVD, 361–362
    iMovie, 233–237
    iPhoto, 116–117
    iTunes, 13, 37–41
keywords, 126–127
    adding year to, 130
    assigning to Photo Library images, 132–133
    associating with images, 129–131
    default, 129–130
    deleting, 131
    displaying, 132
    finding images by, 138–140
    modifying, 131
    removing, 133–134
    user-defined, 129–131

Keywords (⌘+K) keyboard shortcut, 130, 132, 133, 139, 140
Keywords/Search dialog box, 130–131, 132–134, 139–140

L

labeling images, 126–134
Last Import 9 (iPhoto), 104
Library (iTunes), 15, 50–51
    adding
        audio CDs, 52–53
        Genre column, 22
        music from Apple Music Store, 56–62
        music to iMovie movies, 315–316
    automatically importing audio CD songs, 52
    browsing and listening to music, 63–65
    browsing contents of, 15
    classifying and configuring music, 67–72
    downloading
        audio from Internet, 54–55
        songs to MP3 player, 92
    finding location of encoded files, 53
    losing track of song, 76
    music
        as background sound for menus, 430–431
        during slideshows, 172
    preloaded music, 54
    preparing music and sound for soundtracks, 503
    rating songs, 71
    removing songs from, 67
    searching, 65–66, 387
    sharing, 35
    standard organization scheme, 36
    synchronizing with iPod, 97
Library mode, 9
Library.cache file, 125
Library.data file, 125
local networks and sharing music, 15, 30–32
Lock Audio Clip at Playhead (⌘+L) keyboard shortcut, 325

M

.m4p file extension, 6
.Mac Web site, 109, 176, 188–192
Macintosh
    active at all times, 473
    adding purchased music to, 62
    authorizing and deauthorizing, 62

Index

installing iTunes Library on, 63
Sleep mode, 473
Mail (Apple), 175–176
Mail Photo dialog box, 175–176
Make Preset command, 20
markers, 307
Media folder, 243
memory
   iPod, 93
   MP3 players, 91
menus
   applying custom themes to, 451–452
   background images, 422–427, 460
   background movies, 427–430, 460
   background sound, 430–433, 460
   built-in themes for designing, 415–417
   content, 460
   custom themes, 421–427
   customizing buttons, 439–442
   default title, 413
   designing, 413–437
   designing buttons, 437–449
   Drop Zones, 461
   formatting titles, 434–437, 441–442
   general layout, 461
   importing movies as background, 429–430
   motion effects duration, 433
   naming, 413–414
   placing buttons, 440
   previewing, 460–461
   removing background sound, 432
   return button, 443
   standard theme for all, 421
   titles, 461
   TV Safe Area, 461
   without titles, 414–415
Missing Files prompt, 468
Mobile Music Player, 15
Monitor (iMovie), 207, 210
   Camera Connected message, 245
   Camera mode, 212–213
   Edit mode, 209–212
   End Crop Marker, 256–257
   Start Crop Marker, 256–257
motion effects, 410–411
   duration for menus, 433
   themes, 416–417
Motion Effects (⌘+J) keyboard shortcut, 411
.mov files, 493–494
movie buttons, 438, 446–447

Movie slider, 446
movies
   adding
      audio CD music, 317–318
      captions to clips, 277–278
      to Drop Zones, 417–419
      to DVDs, 393–401
      with iMedia Browser, 396–398
      titles or opening credits, 276
   AIFF format, 341
   arranging clips, 268
   avi format, 341
   background for menus, 427–430
   basic video track, 243
   building, 225
   as button previews, 447–449
   button previews, 462
   captions, 217
   changing
      clip speed, 293–295
      direction clips play, 295–296
      relative volume of native sound, 302–304
      titles in, 279–280
      transitions in, 284–286
   chapter markers, 334
   clips to include in, 241
   content, 462
   credits, 218
   cropping clips, 259
   deleting clips, 262
   details of, 226–229
   DVDs, 224–225, 366
   editing, 209–212
   encoding, 403–404
   enhancing, 293–298
   exporting to videotape, 330–333
   Fade Out transition, 281–283
   fading native sound, 304–307
   final edit, 330
   freeze frame, 296–297
   full-screen mode, 262
   general content, 241
   importing
      to Drop Zones, 418
      to DVDs, 399
      as menu background, 429–430
   instant replay, 296
   iPhoto images, 263–267
   logging video contents, 241
   monitoring available disk space, 229–230

MPEG-4 format, 341–342
music, 314–318
native sound, 301–309
opening credits, 273–277
organizing, 243
pasting over clips, 298
planning, 240–244
playing, 262
previewing, 462
Push transition, 283–284
QuickTime format, 341
QuickTime margins, 270
recording sound, 318–319
removing from DVDs, 403
scripted, 241
Sepia Tone effect, 289–290
shooting clips, 241–242
sound, 216–217, 300, 320–326
sound effects, 310–314
special effects, 222–223, 286–293
spontaneous, 241
still image clips, 296–297
text, 217–220
timeline, 226–229
titles, 218, 270–280
tools for building, 214
total playing time, 262
tracks, 226
transitions, 220–221, 280–286
video tracks, 300
viewing raw video, 241
Movies folder, 396
MP3 Encoder dialog box, 27
MP3 encoding, 25–27
.mp3 file extension, 6
MP3 file format, 5–6, 7, 87
MP3 files, 6
    downloading to iTunes Library, 54–55
    downloading *versus* listening to on Internet, 55–56
    finding, 8
    kbps (KiloBits Per Second), 25
    playing on Internet, 8
    storing music or sound as, 25–26
MP3 players, 5, 6, 91–98
MP3.com Web site, 54
MPEG (Motion Picture Experts Group), 5
MPEG-2 format, 355, 403–404
MPEG-4 format, 341–342
MPEG-4 Settings dialog box, 342

MPEG-4 specification, 6
music, 4, 300
    adding
        from audio CD, 317–318
        from iTunes Library to movies, 315–316
    as background sound for menus, 430–433
    browsing, 63–65
    choosing for sharing, 32
    classifying and configuring, 67–72
    copyrights, 316
    digital effects, 24
    DVDs, 366–367
    encoding, 50
    importing into file formats, 24–28
    from iTunes for iDVD slideshows, 387–389
    labeling downloaded, 54
    listening to, 63–65
    listening to while encoding, 53
    movies, 314–318
    moving to iPod, 95
    as MP3 files, 25–26
    MP3 players, 90–93
    organizing files, 54
    permanently association with slideshows, 173
    playing at same volume level, 24
    purchasing from Apple Music Store, 33–34
    randomly playing, 36
    searching for, 65–66
    selecting for soundtracks, 501–502
    sharing on local networks, 15, 30–32, 80
    slideshows, 172–173
    songs stored on Internet, 55–56
Music Store. *See* Apple Music Store
Music Store source, 59
music track and iMovie projects, 506
Music Video style, 274
muting native sound, 301–302

N

narration, 300
native sound, 300, 301–309
networks, sharing music, 80–81
New Album dialog box, 142
New Album (⌘+N) keyboard shortcut, 142
New Playlist From Selection (Shift+⌘+N) keyboard
    shortcut, 74
New Playlist (⌘+N) keyboard shortcut, 73
New Smart Playlist (Option+⌘+N) keyboard shortcut, 77
NVidia graphics card, 490

O

Open dialog box, 394
Open sheet, 381, 402, 418
Open Stream dialog box, 50
opening credits, 273–277
Order Book dialog box, 188
Order Prints dialog box, 177–179, 187
ordering
    photo books, 186–188
    prints, 171, 177–179
Organize mode, 108–109, 121, 127, 134–135, 181
Outdoor Cheer sound effect, 313

P

passwords and sharing music, 32, 81
Paste command, 296
Paste Over at Playhead (Shift+⌘+V) keyboard shortcut, 298
pasting over clips, 298
PDF files, 183, 186
photo albums, 103–104
    adding images, 142
    building, 141–145
    changes to images, 144
    creation of, 142
    dragging images to create, 144
    images for photo book, 180
    listing in iDVD Drawer, 420
    naming, 142
    ordering images, 180
    organizing, 108–109, 135, 144–145
    removing photos, 144
    repeating images, 144
    viewing contents, 104
photo books, 111–113, 179
    adding text to pages, 183
    changes to, 183
    cost, 188
    cover, 180
    creation of, 180–183
    designing pages, 181
    editing text, 181
    jumping directly to pages, 185
    locking pages, 183
    numbering pages, 187
    optimum number of pages, 183
    ordering, 109, 186–188
    orientation of images, 182
    page design for cover, 180–181
    page numbers, 180
    PDF version of, 183, 186
    previewing, 184–185
    printing, 185–186
    recording images on pages, 181–182
    shipping, 188
    spell-checking text, 183
    themes, 180
    turning information on and off, 180
    viewing images, 180
Photo Info (⌘+I) keyboard shortcut, 137
Photo Info window, 137
Photo Library (iPhoto), 103–104
    assigning keywords to images, 132–133
    dragging images to create photo album, 144
    finding images, 138–141
    importing images, 106–107, 120–124
    organizing images, 108–109
    placing images in Photo Library, 144
    Progress bar, 121
    removing images from, 125
photos
    See also images
    exporting as separate files, 197–199
    importing, 106–107
Photos palette (iMovie), 215–216, 263
Playhead, 211, 252
playlists, 72
    adding more songs, 76
    Audio palette, 315
    burning audio CDs, 87–88
    creation of, 73–76
    deleting, 76
    dragging and dropping songs onto, 74
    editing names, 76
    information about, 74–75
    Internet radio, 50
    listening to, 75
    modifying, 76
    naming, 74
    reordering songs, 74
    selecting, 15
    selecting and deselecting songs for, 74
    silent time between songs, 23–24
    smart. *See* smart playlists
    viewing contents, 74
Playlists mode, 10
Portable Music Player mode, 10

preferences
    iDVD, 356–360
    iMovie, 230–233
    iPhoto, 113–115
    iTunes, 21–36
presets, associating with song, 20
Preview mode, 186, 354, 457–459
Preview window, 184–185
previewing
    buttons, 461–462
    clips, 251–252
    DVDs, 349, 354, 456–465
    iDVD slideshows, 384–385
    menus, 460–461
    movies, 462
    pages in photo books, 113
    photo books, 184–185
    printing, 170
    slideshows, 463
    songs, 173
    special effects, 290
    titles, 273
Print dialog box, 169–170, 185–186
Print (⌘+P) keyboard shortcut, 185
printers, 169–170, 186
printing
    images, 109, 168–171
    photo books, 185–186
prints, ordering, 171, 177–179
Project, Add Folder command, 373, 375
Project, Add Slideshow command, 377
Project, Project Info command, 466
Project Info dialog box, 466–467
Publish HomePage dialog box, 189–190
Purchased Music source, 80
Push transition, 283–284

Q

QuickTime format, 341
QuickTime margins, 270
QuickTime movie trailers, 491–495
QuickTime movies
    adding to DVD, 401–403
    appropriately sized, 339
    DVDs, 366
    exporting
        movies to, 336–342
        photos as, 202
    file size, 337

    importing, 247–248
    importing to DVD, 402–403
    as menu background, 427
    video tracks, 259–262
QuickTime Pro, 492, 505

R

Radio mode, 9
randomly playing music, 36
Recently Played playlist, 76
recorded sounds, 300
recording
    from DV camera to VHS tape, 333
    sound, 318–319
red-eye, 110, 160–161
rendering, 222, 268
    clips, 289–290
    special effects, 292
    title clip, 276–277
    transitions, 282–283
resizing
    Edit window, 158
    images, 113
    iTunes window, 47–48
    Source pane (iTunes), 17
    thumbnails, 135
retouching images, 162–163
return button, 443
Reverse Clip Direction (⌘+R) keyboard shortcut, 295
Revert confirmation dialog box, 166
ripping CDs, 50
Rotate Clockwise (Shift+⌘+R) keyboard shortcut, 149
Rotate Counter Clockwise (⌘+R) keyboard shortcut, 149
rotating images, 111, 148–149

S

Save exported file as dialog box, 340, 509
Save Frame As dialog box, 488
Save Frame As (⌘+F) keyboard shortcut, 298, 489
Save (⌘+S) keyboard shortcut, 372
Save sheet, 369
Save to File dialog box, 186
Screen Effects dialog box, 193
Screen Effects pane (iPhoto), 193
screen savers from iPhoto images, 192–193
scripted movies, 241
scroll tools for slideshows, 354
Scroll with Pause style, 274–275

Index

Scrolling Block style, 220
searching for music, 65–66
Select All (⌘+A) keyboard shortcut, 74, 132, 142
Select None (Shift+⌘+A) keyboard shortcut, 74, 261
selection box, 155
Sepia Tone effect, 222, 289–290
Settings dialog box, 92
sharing music, 30–32, 80
Shelf, 214
    adding images to video tracks, 263
    QuickTime movies, 247–248
    still images, 248–250
    stocking with images and clips, 244–250
Show Current Song (⌘+L) keyboard shortcut, 47
Show Info (⌘+I) keyboard shortcut, 254
Show Song File (⌘+R) keyboard shortcut, 53
.sit files, 493–494
Skywalker Sound Effects, 310
slider buttons, 438
slides and .Mac tools Web site, 109
slideshow buttons, 444–445
Slideshow mode, 353–354
Slideshow Settings dialog box, 171–173
Slideshow slider, 445
slideshows
    adding to Drop Zone, 419–421
    audio files, 354
    configuring, 171–173, 354
    configuring with iDVD, 195
    duration, 463
    DVDs, 349, 376–392
    exporting images from, 174–175
    high-resolution, 463
    HomePage Web site, 190
    images, 354, 463
    importing to Drop Zones, 420
    .Mac Web site, 191–192
    music during, 172–173
    number of seconds on-screen, 171
    pausing, 173=174
    permanently associating music with, 173
    previewing, 463
    putting on DVD, 194–195
    random order slides, 171
    repeating, 172
    resolution, 505
    scroll tools, 354
    soundtrack, 463
    temporary, 174
    viewing, 171–173, 174

Small Dog Web site, 84
Smart Playlist window, 77–79
smart playlists, 15, 76–80
SmartSound Sonicfire Pro, 502, 511–514
Snapz Pro X, 490–491
Song Information window (iTunes), 20, 69–72
songs
    applying equalizer preset, 72
    associating preset with, 20
    associating with genre, 70
    changing relative volume, 72
    configuring options, 71–72
    dragging and dropping onto playlist, 74
    editing information, 69–70
    information about, 46, 50
    playing at selected point in, 72
    previewing, 173
    rating, 71–72
    viewing information, 68–69
sorting Contents pane (iTunes), 16–17
sound, 300
    changing location on soundtracks, 321
    cropping, 321–322
    DVDs, 367
    editing, 320–326
    Fade Out or Fade In transitions, 304
    fading, 322
    importing, 24–28, 433
    locking in place, 325–326
    movies, 216–217
    MP3 files, 25–26
    music, 314–318
    native sound, 301–309
    recording, 318–319
    sound effects, 310–314
sound clips
    renaming, 327
    from Web, 495–497
sound effects, 300, 310–314, 502, 507
soundtrack CDs, 510–514
soundtracks
    adding sound effects, 507
    changing location of sound, 321
    designing, 501–502
    exporting as AIFF file, 508–509
    iDVD slideshows, 387–389
    iLife projects, 500–514
    iMovie creation of, 504–508
    iTunes for preparing music and sound, 503
    mixing, 508

recorded sounds, 508
removing, 389
selecting music for, 501–502
sound effects, 502
Source pane (iPhoto), 103–104
   accessing images from, 196
   Comments box, 128
   Desktop button, 193
   Information button, 128
   Last Import album, 121
   Last Import photo album, 127
Source pane (iTunes), 14–15
   Apple Music Store, 57
   blank playlist, 73
   font size, 22
   importing songs from, 52
   MP3 player, 91–92
   Music Store source, 32, 59
   playlists, 75
   predefined smart playlists, 76
   Purchased Music playlist, 57
   resizing, 17
   selecting audio CD, 45
   shared music, 30
sources, 18
Special Edition Using Mac OS X v10.2, 86, 492, 505
special effects
   brightness and contrast, 291–292
   changing, 292
   making clips look old, 289–290
   movies, 222–223, 286–293
   multiple, 293
   previewing, 290
   rendering, 292
   restoring clips without, 292
   transitioning in and out, 289, 291
Split Video Clip (⌘+T) keyboard shortcut, 255
splitting clips, 255
spontaneous movies, 241
Standard Sound Effects, 310
Start Crop Marker, 256–257
still image clips, 297
Story Book theme, 112, 180
Straight Cut transition, 220
Stripe Subtitle style, 278
SuperDrive, 470
System Preferences application, 193
System Preferences dialog box, 472–473

T

text and movies, 217–220
themes
   background image or movies, 409
   background sound, 409
   built-in and designing menus, 415–417
   button location, 409
   button style, 409
   button title format, 409
   button title location, 409
   buttons, 439
   custom, 421–427, 449–453
   Drop Zones, 409–410, 416
   DVDs, 408–409
   motion effects, 416–417
   photo books, 112–113, 180
   replacing, 451
   standard for all DVD menus, 421
   title format, 409
   title location, 409
thumbnails, resizing, 135
Timeline Viewer (iMovie), 207, 226–229, 293
   Clip Speed slider, 293
   Edit Volume check box, 304
   Mute check box, 301–302
   Native track, 303
   Relative Volume slider, 303, 306–307
   viewing clips with speed changed, 294
   Volume Level bar, 304–306
   Zoom pop-up menu, 305
   Zoom slider, 293
title clip, rendering, 276–277
titles, 218
   adding to movies, 276
   changing already placed in movies, 279–280
   color, 435–436
   finding images by, 140
   formatting for
      buttons, 441–442
      menus, 434–437
   iDVD projects, 351
   iDVD slideshows, 382
   movies, 270–280
   previewing, 273
   properties of text, 271
   QuickTime margins, 270
   rendering, 222
   still image clips, 297
   text styles, 270

Index

Titles (Shift+⌘+T) keyboard shortcut, 135
Titles palette (iMovie), 217–220, 270–275, 278
Tool pane (iPhoto), 103, 107–113, 154, 207
    Announce Slideshow button, 192
    Email button, 175
    HomePage button, 189
    iDVD button, 194
    .Mac Slides button, 191
    No Camera is selected message, 121
    Play Sideshow button, 174
    Slideshow button, 171
Tools palette (iMovie), 214
transitions, 220–221, 280–286
    rendering, 222
    still image clips, 297
Transitions palette (iMovie), 220–221, 281–284
Trash (iMovie), 230, 253
troubleshooting hardware, 86
TV Safe Area, 411–412, 438, 457
    button previews, 445
    menus, 461

U

Undo (⌘+Z) keyboard shortcut, 257
Unlock Audio Clip (⌘+L) keyboard shortcut, 326
USB or FireWire CD-RW drives, 84

V

VCR, connecting to DV camera, 485–486
video clips, 259–262
video tracks, 300
    adding Shelf images, 263
    building, 259–268
    iPhoto images, 263–267
    native sound, 301–309
    QuickTime movies, 259–262
    video clips, 259–262
videotape, 484–488
View, Arrange Photos command, 135, 144
View, Film Rolls command, 135
View, Keywords command, 132, 135
View, Titles command, 135
View options dialog box, 18, 20
View Options (⌘+J) keyboard shortcut, 18
Viewing/Hiding Keywords (Shift+⌘+K) keyboard shortcut, 135

W

WAV (Windows Waveform) audio format, 7
WAV encoding, 28
.wav file extension, 7
wavecentral.com Web site, 496
Web sites, 199–202
Window, Equalizer command, 19

Y

Year Book theme, 112, 180

Z

zooming images, 156–157

"Yes, we have that too."

At Small Dog Electronics you will find Apple computers plus a whole lot more! We carry everything you need for work and play, including: scanners, printers, hard drives, hubs, memory, upgrades, games and more!

We also carry a full line of Apple Factory Refurbished equipment. Each factory refurbished product is made "like new" at Apple and comes with a 1 year warranty.

Visit us on the web or in our showroom!

1673 Main Street • Waitsfield • Vermont

E-Mail: sales@smalldog.com